RECREATIONAL SPORT

Program Design, Delivery, and Management

Library of Congress Cataloging-in-Publication Data

Barcelona, Robert J., 1970-
Recreational sport : program design, delivery, and management / Robert J. Barcelona, PhD, University of New Hampshire, Mary Sara Wells, PhD, University of Utah, Skye Arthur-Banning, PhD, Clemson University.
pages cm
Includes bibliographical references and index.
1. Recreation--Management. 2. Recreation--Planning. 3. Strategic planning. I. Title.
GV181.5.B37 2015
790.06'9--dc23
2015009208

ISBN: 978-1-4504-2239-0 (print)

The web addresses cited in this text were current as of June 2015, unless otherwise noted.

Acquisitions Editor: Gayle Kassing, PhD; **Developmental Editor:** Melissa Feld; **Managing Editor:** Anne E. Mrozek; **Copyeditor:** Alisha Jeddeloh; **Indexer:** Dan Connolly; **Permissions Manager:** Dalene Reeder; **Graphic Designer:** Julie L. Denzer; **Cover Designer:** Keith Blomberg; **Photographs (cover):** © Human Kinetics; **Photographs (interior):** iStockphoto/Bob Ingelhart (chapter 1 opener); Monkey Business/fotolia.com (chapter 2 opener); photo courtesy of the Keene NH Department of Parks and Recreation (chapter 4 opener); © Bob Brookover (chapter 6 opener); zonch/fotolia.com (chapter 9 opener); Galina Barskaya/fotolia.com (chapter 10 opener); © Mary Sara Wells (chapter 11 opener); Andres Rodriguez/fotolia.com (chapter 13 opener). All other photos © Human Kinetics, unless otherwise noted; **Photo Asset Manager:** Laura Fitch; **Photo Production Manager:** Jason Allen; **Art Manager:** Kelly Hendren; **Associate Art Manager:** Alan L. Wilborn; **Illustrations:** © Human Kinetics, unless otherwise noted; **Printer:** Sheridan Books

Printed in the United States of America 10 9 8 7 6 5 4 3 2 1

The paper in this book is certified under a sustainable forestry program.

Human Kinetics
Website: www.HumanKinetics.com

United States: Human Kinetics
P.O. Box 5076
Champaign, IL 61825-5076
800-747-4457
e-mail: humank@hkusa.com

Canada: Human Kinetics
475 Devonshire Road Unit 100
Windsor, ON N8Y 2L5
800-465-7301 (in Canada only)
e-mail: info@hkcanada.com

Europe: Human Kinetics
107 Bradford Road
Stanningley
Leeds LS28 6AT, United Kingdom
+44 (0) 113 255 5665
e-mail: hk@hkeurope.com

Australia: Human Kinetics
57A Price Avenue
Lower Mitcham, South Australia 5062
08 8372 0999
e-mail: info@hkaustralia.com

New Zealand: Human Kinetics
P.O. Box 80
Mitcham Shopping Centre, South Australia 5062
0800 222 062
e-mail: info@hknewzealand.com

E5629

RECREATIONAL SPORT

Program Design, Delivery, and Management

Robert J. Barcelona, PhD
University of New Hampshire

Mary Sara Wells, PhD
University of Utah

Skye Arthur-Banning, PhD
Clemson University

HUMAN KINETICS

CONTENTS

Preface ix
Acknowledgments xiii

PART I THEORY, PHILOSOPHY, AND FOUNDATIONS OF RECREATIONAL SPORT

1 **INTRODUCTION TO RECREATIONAL SPORT** **3**

Leisure 5
Sport 10
The Recreational Sport Profession 13
Conclusion 15
Learning Aids 15

2 **PHYSICAL ACTIVITY AND RECREATIONAL SPORT** **17**

Understanding Physical Activity and Inactivity 19
Benefits of Physical Activity 21
Promoting Physically Active Recreational Sport 22
Conclusion 28
Learning Aids 28

3 **DIVERSITY AND DEVELOPMENT IN RECREATIONAL SPORT** **31**

Sport for All 33
Legislation Guiding Professionals 33
Age 35
Demographics 38
Constraints on Participation 42
Programming Considerations 43
Conclusion 46
Learning Aids 47

PART II COMPETENCIES OF RECREATIONAL SPORT PROFESSIONALS

4 **RECREATIONAL SPORT PROGRAM PLANNING 51**

Programming Philosophies 53
Programming Components 56
Conclusion 69
Learning Aids 70

5 **STRUCTURED TOURNAMENT SCHEDULING 71**

Big Picture of Tournament Design 73
Round-Robin Tournaments 80
Elimination Tournaments 85
Challenge or Extended Tournaments 89
Conclusion 92
Learning Aids 93

6 **FACILITY PLANNING AND DESIGN 95**

Developing and Refining Strategic and Master Plans 99
Benchmarking and Space Standards 102
Program Statements 103
Design and Construction Process 104
Facility Considerations 107
Conclusion 112
Learning Aids 112

7 **FINANCING AND MARKETING RECREATIONAL SPORT 115**

Expenditures 116
Major Sources of Revenue in Recreational Sport 118
Marketing Techniques and Considerations 121
Customer Service 124
Conclusion 126
Learning Aids 126

8 RISK MANAGEMENT 129

Liability and Risk 130
Liability Concerns 133
Creating a Plan to Manage Risk 139
Conclusion 145
Learning Aids 146

9 HUMAN RESOURCES IN RECREATIONAL SPORT 149

Recreational Sport Personnel 151
Human Resources Processes 156
Conclusion 168
Learning Aids 169

10 TECHNOLOGY IN RECREATIONAL SPORT 171

Understanding the Scope of Technology 173
Computing Technology and Recreational Sport 176
Conclusion 184
Learning Aids 185

PART III RECREATIONAL SPORT SETTINGS AND CONTEXTS

11 RECREATIONAL SPORT IN THE COMMUNITY 189

Community Benefits of Recreational Sport 190
Community Recreational Sport Management in Typical Communities 191
Community Recreational Sport in Nontypical Communities 195
Community Recreational Sport for People With Disabilities 198
Conclusion 199
Learning Aids 199

12 RECREATIONAL YOUTH SPORT 201

Recreational Youth Sport Experience 203
Needs of Young Athletes 205
Changing the Current Culture of Recreational Youth Sport 211
Conclusion 213
Learning Aids 213

13 **CAMPUS RECREATIONAL SPORT** **215**

Foundations of Campus Recreation 217
Campus Recreation Facilities and Programs 226
Professional Development in Campus Recreation 231
Conclusion 234
Learning Aids 234

14 **INTERNATIONAL INFLUENCE ON RECREATIONAL SPORT** **237**

Sport as a Unifying Body 239
International Sport Organizations 241
International Sport Models 241
Sport and the Olympics 246
Jobs and Career Opportunities 247
Conclusion 248
Learning Aids 249

15 **CAREERS IN RECREATIONAL SPORT** **251**

The Recreational Sport Field 253
Professional and Career Development in Recreational Sport 255
Conclusion 262
Learning Aids 263

Glossary 265
References 271
Index 281
About the Authors 289

PREFACE

Recreational sport programs have experienced tremendous growth over the last couple of decades with sport participation far surpassing all other types of recreational activities. The recreational aspect of sport in American culture is well established and is a recognized contributor to human enjoyment and vitality. With this growth and interest have come increased opportunities for employment in recreational sport settings, with positions ranging from the face-to-face leadership roles of part-time personnel to top administrative positions.

Sport in North American society has undergone tremendous change over the past several decades. These changes have had a significant impact on the way sport and leisure services are delivered. On the one hand, sport has become more entertainment and spectator oriented with attendance records being broken at numerous athletic sporting events. On the other hand, sport has also become more participant oriented, involving people from all walks of life who possess varying degrees of physical ability and interest in sport. With such a wide spectrum of sport participation by such large numbers of people, the impact of recreational sport on society has grown significantly.

Because of the tremendous role that sport plays in our society and the demand for increased opportunities to participate in a myriad of recreational sport activities, there is a need for broad-based recreational sport programming that reflects these needs and interests. In turn, this requires people who possess programming and management skills in recreational sport. *Recreational Sport: Program Design, Delivery, and Management* explores recreational sport as a component of community leisure services. It provides a wide-ranging discussion of recreational sport as both a context for human development and a professional career option.

The settings, or locations where one might find recreational sport personnel, are varied. The municipal setting consists of city and community park and recreation programs that provide sport experiences for various age groups residing in that particular location. Businesses implement recreational sport as a benefit to their employees, oftentimes providing on-site programs and facilities. Nonprofit organizations provide another setting for recreational sport, with organizations such as YMCAs, YWCAs, and Boys and Girls Clubs offering recreational sport opportunities to their constituents. Recreational sport programs in these organizations are provided not only for fun but also to help develop character, fitness, and positive life skills. Military installations, correctional facilities, and educational institutions also serve as settings for recreational sport, providing a wide variety of activities for their clientele. Private clubs provide recreational sport opportunities to their members, and vacation resorts, such as hotels, motels, and cruise ships, offer a wide variety of activities and special events for their guests.

ORGANIZATION

Throughout the text, practical material and advice are provided for current and future recreational sport professionals. The book aims to simplify the complicated process of designing and delivering recreational sport programs in various recreation and leisure settings. The information it presents is based on years of practical experience in recreational sport organizations by the three primary authors and also reflects research studies that they and others have conducted on recreational sport. Case studies of real-world recreational sport issues and best practices, as well as examples of theory to practice, are interwoven throughout the book. This integration of theory and practice are the cornerstones of the book.

The book is divided into three parts. Part I is composed of three chapters that discuss the philosophical and foundational concepts that define the field of recreational sport, as well as the benefits that recreational sport provides for individuals and communities.

Chapter 1. Chapter 1 discusses the definitions and key theoretical perspectives related to leisure, recreation, and sport and helps the reader understand what constitutes a recreational sport activity. The differentiation between participation- and performance-based sport experiences and how such differences influence the design, delivery, and management of these unique sport formats are examined. Throughout the chapter, competencies of recreational sport professionals are introduced with a specific focus on program design and participant development.

Chapter 2. The relationship between obesity (and its related diseases) and a lack of physical activity is closely linked and well documented. Chapter 2 discusses the need to promote physical activity and healthy lifestyles in a community and explores how recreational sport programs can help improve community health awareness in both the short and long term.

Chapter 3. One of the hallmarks of recreational sport management is the concept of sport for all. Chapter 3 highlights this concept by discussing sport participation trends, preferences, and issues based on various dimensions of diversity, including age, race, sex, and ability. The chapter highlights research on constraints to participation in recreational sport, and it includes evidence-based considerations for programming strategies that take into account the diversity of recreational sport participation.

Part II is comprised of seven chapters. These chapters focus on the core competencies that prospective managers need in order to effectively deliver recreational sport programs and events and to lead successful organizations.

Chapter 4. Planning, conducting, and evaluating programs is the central function of the recreational sport profession. Chapter 4 focuses on the fundamental aspects of programming including understanding the philosophical foundation of the sport organization, assessing the needs of the target population, developing program outcomes, and designing, implementing, and evaluating recreational sport programs.

Chapter 5. Tournament scheduling depends on a number of factors, such as the objectives of the tournament; characteristics of the participants; specific program or sport rules and regulations; facility, equipment, and personnel needs and limitations; and actual number of entries. Chapter 5 discusses these factors and presents a variety of tournament designs.

Chapter 6. In recreational sport, facilities are everything. Facility planning and design are integral parts of the recreational sport program. Chapter 6 presents a systemized approach to recreational sport facility planning and discusses the daily facility operations that greatly enhance the success of facility management.

Chapter 7. In the increasingly resource-restricted environments where recreational sport professionals often work, knowledge of sound finance, budgeting, and marketing strategies is key to the successful delivery of recreational sport programs. Chapter 7 introduces both finance and marketing, including the major sources of revenue in recreational sport, the key expenditures associated with programs, budget types and strategies, marketing strategies, and the importance of customer service for the fiscal health of the recreational sport organization.

Chapter 8. Over the last three decades, the recreational sport profession has witnessed a society that has become increasingly litigious. This chapter provides an overview of risk management issues frequently encountered by professionals responsible for providing recreational sport programs. The final outcome of the chapter is a checklist to guide the reader in developing a new risk management plan or assessing an existing plan that can help control and diminish the risks that confront today's recreational sport professionals.

Chapter 9. The human resources of any organization represent one of its largest investments, underscoring the importance of the manager's role in leading the staff. Chapter 9 outlines the steps involved in successfully managing the human resources (both paid and volunteer) of a recreational sport organization. The goal of this chapter is to assist the reader in becoming more knowledgeable about trends in and issues of managing the organization's most valuable resource—its employees and volunteers.

Chapter 10. The use of technology in recreational sport design and delivery continues to increase, mirroring similar trends in society at large. Chapter 10 provides an overview of technology used in recreational sport organizations, and it discusses how to incorporate mobile communication technology and social networking tools into recreational sport programming.

Finally, part III comprises the final five chapters. These chapters provide insight into the settings and contexts where recreational sport takes place. They also discuss the key ideas, issues, and career opportunities that each setting holds.

Chapter 11. Chapter 11 provides an overview of recreational sport organizations in the community. It also discusses recreational sport programming in nontraditional settings (e.g., military MWR programs, campus recreation, senior communities) and for people with disabilities.

Chapter 12. Chapter 12 addresses a variety of challenges in recreational youth sport. This includes an overview of the various settings where recreational youth sport occurs, the personnel necessary to operate successful programs, parent roles and behaviors in youth sport, and parent and coach training. In addition, it discusses the needs of young athletes and how to meet them.

Chapter 13. Chapter 13 provides an overview of the diverse recreational sport opportunities found on college and university campuses. The history of campus recreational sport is presented as well as a discussion of the unique programming areas that are offered in comprehensive campus recreation programs. The chapter focuses on the outcomes of campus recreational experiences, such as student learning and development, and it discusses career opportunities and professional development in this field.

Chapter 14. Recreational sport delivery in the United States is different than in other areas of the world—even in Canada. Chapter 16 provides an international perspective of recreational sport delivery, including the international sport-for-all concept and governmental policy related to recreational sport programming and opportunities. Job and career opportunities in the international arena are also discussed.

Chapter 15. The recreational sport profession is growing in popularity both in terms of employment potential and in the proliferation of academic programs in higher education. Chapter 15 discusses the process of securing a job in a recreational sport setting by providing practical tools and advice for future professionals. The chapter provides information on academic preparation, real-world practical experience, and professional associations.

FEATURES

Recreational Sport: Program Design, Delivery, and Management prepares students and practitioners alike for the many challenges they will face as recreational sport professionals. Throughout the text, the authors provide a comprehensive, up-to-date understanding of program design and delivery from a recreational sport perspective. Each chapter includes the following:

- Learning outcomes that emphasize key takeaways and knowledge areas from the text
- Case studies that provide real-world scenarios and context for the chapter learning material
- Research to Reality segments that highlight research in recreational sport and provide students and practitioners with takeaways from key studies
- Chapter content that weaves together key learning concepts, practical examples and management implications, career advice, and research studies that directly relate to the field of recreational sport
- Learning activities and assignments that help students apply chapter content
- Instructor ancillaries, including an extensive instructor guide, a test package, and PowerPoint presentations available online at www.HumanKinetics.com/RecreationalSport

ACKNOWLEDGMENTS

Writing a textbook is a huge undertaking. Believe it or not, it is even more challenging when the book's content is as close to the author's heart as Recreational Sport is to mine. First, I would like to be sure to thank all of our employers, including the University of New Hampshire, Clemson University, and the University of Utah for giving us the support and space to write over the past several years. In particular, I would like to thank the all of the students who have taken my RMP 560 (Recreational Sport Management) course over the years at UNH. They helped me to form and hone the content, sequencing, and many of the examples that are used throughout the book.

I would also like to thank the Human Kinetics staff for their efforts on this book. I have done several projects with Human Kinetics and they are always great to work with and very understanding and helpful. In particular, I'd like to thank Gayle Kassing, Melissa Feld, and Anne Mrozek for their help and patience with us as we worked on various pieces of this manuscript. I would also like to thank all of those Human Kinetics staff who helped to put the book together behind the scenes. Their effort is what makes a book.

I also want to thank my colleagues in recreational sports throughout the country. In particular, I want to thank my mentor, Dr. Craig Ross, Professor Emeritus at Indiana University. More than anyone, Craig gave me my academic start in recreational sports, and I owe him a tremendous amount of gratitude as a mentor, colleague, and friend. I also want to thank Dr. Sarah Young, Associate Professor at Indiana University. Sarah was my first supervisor when I was a graduate assistant in campus recreation at Indiana University, and has become a valued colleague, writing partner, and friend over the past 20 years. Finally, I would like to thank Bill Kingery, the long-time (and now retired) Director of Campus Recreation at the University of Mississippi. Bill gave me my start in the field of recreational sports as an undergraduate student at Ole Miss, and hired me as a professional years later.

I would also like to acknowledge the role that my friends and colleagues in the field have played for me over the years. I have a tremendous amount of respect for the practitioners on the ground who are working day-to-day managing and leading recreational sport organizations, programs, and staff. My work over the years has been dedicated to supporting the work they do. I couldn't do what I love without partners in the field. In particular, I would like to thank the professionals in the New Hampshire Recreation and Parks Association (NHRPA) and the South Carolina Recreation and Parks Association (SCRPA) for their help and support over the years. I would also like to thank those agencies and organizations that contributed photos to the book. These include Greenville County (SC) Parks, Recreation, and Tourism; the City of Rock Hill (SC) Department of Parks, Recreation, and Tourism; the Keene (NH) Parks, Recreation, and Cemeteries Department; the Gilford (NH) Department of Parks and Recreation; the Moultonborough (NH) Recreation Department; and the UNH Department of Campus Recreation.

Last but not least, I would like to continue to thank my family for all of their help and support during the textbook writing and editing process. To Heather, Madeline, Nathan, Emily, Dominic, and Lucy – thank you!

-Robert J. Barcelona

First and foremost, I want to thank my wife, family and friends for giving me the time, energy, support and wisdom to get me through this process. Your knowledge, experiences, and information provided invaluable insight into the content of the book.

Thanks to the many students, faculty, staff, mentors, and professionals in the field who have long been supporters of our programs. This book is a culmination of the many hours of programs, tournaments, classes, and activities that each one of you have worked on or been involved with and will help shape how future professionals grow and build upon what each of you has accomplished. Our field is strong and growing as a result of your efforts.

Finally, to Mckinley and Brooklyn, for letting me share in each little piece and part of your growth and development into beautiful girls. You grow up so fast and yet will always be daddy's little girls.

-Skye Arthur-Banning

First, I would like to thank my co-authors in this project. Bob, thank you for providing me with this opportunity to begin with and for your advice and mentorship along the way. Skye, thank you for, as always, your friendship, being a sounding board and support, and for being a great colleague in the process. Next, thank you to the editorial team at Human Kinetics including Melissa Feld and Gayle Kassing. This project would have been impossible without each of you keeping us on task, your detailed knowledge of the system and what readers are looking for, and in some cases, your extreme patience with the authors. To my friends and colleagues at the University of Utah and throughout the country, thank you for all you have done for me. Whether it was reading drafts, listening to me brainstorm, or simply being there when I was stressed, your support means the world to me and I hope that I am as good to you as you are to me. Most importantly, I have a large and wonderful family without whom I would accomplish nothing. Some of this family I was born into and some of it I picked up along the way, but all of you mean the world to me and I am incredibly grateful that you let me sacrifice some of my time with you to accomplish this.

-Mary Sara Wells

THEORY, PHILOSOPHY, AND FOUNDATIONS OF RECREATIONAL SPORT

chapter 1

INTRODUCTION TO RECREATIONAL SPORT

LEARNING OUTCOMES

By the end of this chapter, readers will be able to

- define *leisure, recreation, sport,* and *recreational sport;*
- differentiate between participation- and performance-focused sport experiences and how such differences influence program design, delivery, and management; and
- define *philosophy* and articulate a personal and professional philosophy of recreational sport.

Case Study

KICKBALL OR SOFTBALL IN ROCKVILLE?

Each year, the sport program staff of the Rockville Park and Recreation Department go over participation numbers for the past 12 months. Detailed record keeping allows them to track participation in a variety of adult and youth sport activities over time. One year, the staff noticed that participation in adult softball leagues declined by 16 percent. To determine whether this was a onetime dip or indicative of a larger trend, the staff looked at participation trends over the past 10 years and noticed that slow-pitch numbers were down by 23 percent over that time.

To understand the reason behind these trends, the staff did some digging. What they found among the long-time participants who no longer played was that the leagues were no longer focused on recreation, fun, and healthy competition; instead, they were dominated by tournament-type players interested in high levels of competition. Even traditionally recreation-focused softball divisions sponsored by the city recreation department, such as the church league and coed leagues, were experiencing this same trend.

The upside to all of this was that the quality of the league was increasing and the city's reputation as a softball mecca was growing. This reputation helped Rockville attract several major state and national softball tournaments over the past year, which increased interest among local, regional, and national sponsors and gave the recreation department quite a bit of positive press in the local media. However, complaints from city residents focused on the perception that Rockville was more interested in using its facilities to host out-of-town teams for tournaments where only a relative handful of Rockville teams got to play instead of providing recreational-level softball programs that met the needs of Rockville residents.

Curiously, one of the things that the staff noticed was that while participation in adult softball leagues was declining, participation in their new adult coed kickball league was growing. Participation increased 67 percent between the first and second year of the program and increased 33 percent between the second and third year. One of the things that participants liked about the kickball program was that it offered the chance to compete with family and friends in a fun atmosphere and didn't require expensive equipment or high-level athletic skills. The kickball league also demanded a lot less time—participants could just show up to play games without spending a lot of time practicing beforehand, and families could participate in the same activity together. The coed kickball league now has a waiting list.

If you are like most students, you are taking this class and reading this textbook because you love sport. You probably grew up playing youth sports in your local community, moved on to playing sports in school, and perhaps now you are active in sports in college. Maybe you or a few of your peers are varsity athletes. Regardless, you are likely to be competing on the intramural fields, playing pickup ball in the gym, throwing a Frisbee around the college quad, swimming laps in the pool, or working out in the campus fitness center. You are a recreational sport participant, and although you may not realize it, it is the job of recreational sport professionals to make sure that people like you have the opportunity to participate in the activities you love.

Recreational sport professionals work in a career that focuses on providing sport and physical activity opportunities to the widest range of participants. They wear many hats and have multiple job responsibilities, but their primary objective is providing opportunities for active participation. Whereas other jobs within the broader sport management profession might focus on marketing elite teams or staging spectator-focused sport events, recreational sport professionals focus on getting people actively involved in sport and fitness activities in their leisure time. Sample responsibilities of recreational sport professionals include the following:

- Planning, developing, and managing indoor and outdoor sport and fitness facilities that provide adequate spaces to play
- Designing and delivering sport programs that meet the needs of a wide variety of participants, regardless of skill level or ability
- Developing policies, procedures, rules, and governance structures to ensure program safety, integrity, and fair play
- Marketing and promoting recreational sport programs and activities to participants and sponsors
- Purchasing, ordering, and inventorying sport and fitness supplies and equipment
- Training sport personnel, including officials, coaches, event staff, and volunteers
- Scheduling tournaments and facilities
- Planning sport programs so that they are age and developmentally appropriate and so that they maximize desirable short- and long-term outcomes for participants
- Evaluating program effectiveness and using data to inform decision making

Although this list is not exhaustive, it provides a snapshot of the kinds of knowledge, skills, and abilities needed by a person who is interested in a recreational sport career.

This chapter is designed to get you started on the journey of developing the competencies needed to be an effective recreational sport professional by helping you understand what recreational sport is, helping you understand its philosophical foundations, and giving you an overall awareness of the profession. The rest of the chapters in the textbook focus on the philosophies, definitions, and specific knowledge areas that underlie recreational sport and help you become aware of the settings and contexts where recreational sport takes place. If you love sport and believe that participating in these activities can be a powerful tool in enhancing quality of life, then keep reading. You just might find your future profession in the pages of this book.

The sport program staff of the Rockville Park and Recreation Department faced a dilemma. On the one hand, participation numbers in their competitive softball program were declining because participants who were interested in playing primarily for fun and socialization believed that the leagues had become too competitive. On the other hand, competitive tournament-level softball players helped to increase the overall quality of Rockville's programs, and the city gained a reputation as a softball travel destination for out-of-town softball players and their families. The organization's mission and service mandate undoubtedly played a role in trying to resolve the dilemma. However, it was also important for the staff to understand the underlying reasons behind participation in Rockville's sport programs. Being well grounded in the definitions of *leisure*, *recreation*, and *sport* could help staff understand some of these key reasons.

LEISURE

Recreational sport can be thought of as leisure. When people think of leisure, many imagine relaxing activities such as watching television or taking a nap. They might have trouble thinking of leisure as a competitive activity or an activity that requires physical exertion. At its core, **leisure** consists of nonwork activities that are freely chosen and done primarily for intrinsic reasons. However, leisure motivations are diverse, and what one person might consider to be leisure, another might consider to be work. It is useful, then, to think about leisure and its relationship to recreational sport from three perspectives (Henderson, 2010):

1. Leisure as time
2. Leisure as activity
3. Leisure as a state of mind

As you read about the three perspectives, consider how recreational sport professionals might need to take into account elements of each in order to satisfy the diverse needs of a wide range of participants.

Leisure as Time

Recreational sport takes place in a person's leisure time, and it must be available in ways that are as convenient as possible given the finite amount of discretionary time that most people have. **Discretionary time** refers to time that is free from obligation (Russell, 2005). Recreational sport professionals need to be aware of the demands that are placed on people's time when planning and scheduling recreational sport activities. It is not a surprise that most Americans, for example, spend more time working and taking care of family and household responsibilities than participating in discretionary activities (U.S. Bureau of Labor Statistics, 2012a). In fact, some research has shown that the lack of time due to work or family obligations is one of the top constraints on leisure participation (Young, Ross, & Barcelona, 2003). Leisure constraints are those factors that limit the formation of leisure preferences or inhibit or prohibit participation and enjoyment in leisure (Jackson, 2000). Certainly, people's perceptions of the time that they have available are a constraint on participation in leisure activities such as recreational sport.

Although it would be nice, recreational sport professionals cannot magically create more time. Thus, it is important to be creative in designing and delivering recreational sport activities so that a lack of time is not seen as a significant constraint to participation.

Consider the Rockville case study at the beginning of the chapter. Participants appreciated the coed kickball league because it did not place time burdens on them. They could show up and play games with their family members and friends without the preparation and specialized equipment that other recreational sport programs required. Other ways to take the time issue into account might include allowing participants to choose the days and times of their games and practices, instituting flexible registration methods, taking family structure into account when forming teams (e.g., allowing siblings to participate on the same team when age and developmentally appropriate), and generally reducing or eliminating the many hurdles that get in the way of participating in one's sport of choice. What are some other ways that recreational sport professionals might enable people to negotiate the lack of leisure time they have available to participate in activities?

Leisure as Activity

Leisure activities are often defined by their structure and form. Leisure can be thought of purely as discretionary time, but we can also think about it as the kinds of activities that we engage in during our free time. Leisure that is thought of as a freely chosen, organized, nonwork activity pursued for personal and social benefits (Kelly & Freysinger, 2001) is referred to as **recreation**. We can use the elements of this definition to understand the concept of recreation more deeply. As you think about each of these elements, consider how they might be related to the effective delivery of recreational sport activities.

Form and Structure

Recreational activities have some sort of form and structure and are oriented toward a specific outcome or set of benefits. They take some level of planning, they have some sort of formal or informal organizational system, they take place at a particular time and location, they use specialized equipment, and they have a beginning and an end. These characteristics are fundamental to our understanding of recreational sport programming because recreational sport professionals are responsible for handling the various details associated with each of them. However, for definitional purposes, it is important to understand that not all recreational activities are sports. Drama, music, art, cooking, and the like could be considered recreational activities, but most of us would not consider them to be sports. We will discuss what makes something a sport later in the chapter. However, part of what makes these activities recreational is the freedom of choice that participants exercise. Good recreational sport professionals ensure that participants have a wide variety of activities to choose from. Consider again the case study. Although some Rockville residents were unhappy or not particularly interested in softball, they had an alternative activity choice—the sport of kickball.

A full-service recreational sport program would ideally offer the widest range of activities possible. Sport offerings could encompass team activities such as softball, soccer, basketball, flag football, ice hockey, volleyball, and lacrosse. They could include individual or dual sports such as tennis, racquetball, badminton, table tennis, or squash. A wide array of sport choices could also include meet sports or special events such as 5K and 10K

Providing opportunities to play sport at different competition levels helps to maximize choice for recreational sport participants.

road races, criterium cycling events, and swim meets. The activities that are offered will obviously be based on factors such as the mission of the organization, the needs of the participants, and the resources that are available. However, most participants will not be interested in any one particular recreational activity, and providing a range of activities maximizes choice and helps to ensure that the leisure needs of participants will be met.

Styles of Recreation Participation

As we saw, some of the Rockville residents preferred to play a more laidback sport like kickball, and some preferred to play competitive, tournament-level softball. The park and recreation department was able to meet the diverse needs of participants by offering a choice of recreational sport activities. Looking more deeply at the case, however, reveals that the park and recreation department at one time attempted to satisfy additional needs within the community. For example, the department offered softball leagues that were both competitive and recreational. They offered leagues based on the gender of participants, including a coed league. To make it easier to form teams, they offered leagues based on intact social groups, such as a church league. At least on paper, the city was trying to accommodate different **participation styles**, or the various ways that people prefer to participate in recreational sport. Some typical ways to address diverse participation styles include offering activities to accommodate differences in skill, ability, gender, competitiveness, age, geographic location, and scheduling preference.

How many other ways can you think of to accommodate various styles of participation? Consider the sport of basketball. How many ways could basketball be offered to maximize participant choice? Here are some ideas:

- Offer classes to teach the basics of playing basketball.
- Provide facility space for residents to shoot in or play pickup basketball.
- Run an organized 5-on-5 or 3-on-3 basketball tournament for citizens in the community.
- Host out-of-town teams to compete in a state, regional, or national championship series.

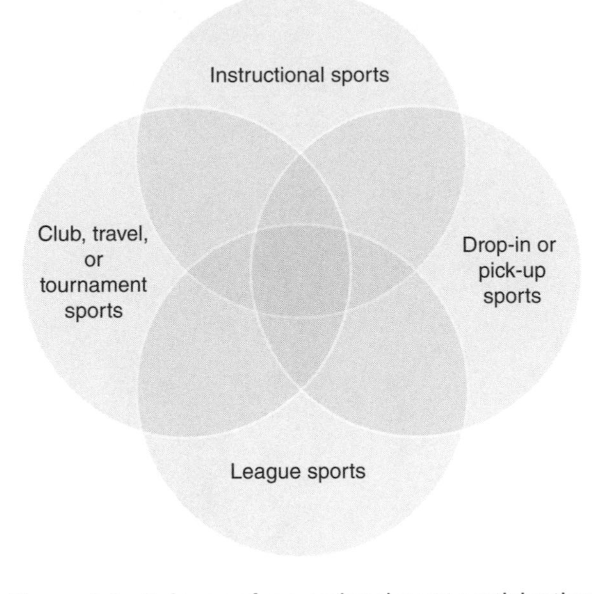

Figure 1.1 Spheres of recreational sport participation.

Figure 1.1 shows each of the spheres of recreational sport participation. People might choose to play basketball in one, two, or more of these participation styles. Even within these spheres, creative recreational sport professionals can try to tap varying levels of need. For example, you might modify the rules of the 5-on-5 basketball tournament to prohibit fast breaking so the team with the ball can only cross midcourt after the last defender does.

Benefits

Participation in well-planned, intentionally designed activities has the potential to improve people physically, cognitively, emotionally, socially, and spiritually. At the same time, meaningful and positive recreation can provide numerous societal benefits, including contributing to the economy of a community, improving community health, decreasing juvenile crime rates, and building social capital. Leisure pursuits primarily involve **intrinsic motivation**—that is, they are done primarily for their own sake. Recreational activities, on the other hand, also involve **extrinsic motivation**—that is, they are oriented toward some desired individual or societal end. For example, a person may love to swim, but she might also need the physical and emotional benefits that swimming provides, so she regularly participates in a variety of swimming activities at the local aquatic center. The swimmer's motivations are both intrinsic (she loves to swim) and extrinsic (she want to stay in shape and feel good). At the same time, the park and recreation department in the swimmer's hometown knows that if it invests in a first-rate aquatic facility, it may have the chance to host state, regional, or national swim meets that bring in hundreds of out-of-town swimmers and spectators who will spend money in the local economy. Recreational sport professionals need to be aware of the individual and social benefits that can accrue through sport participation and design programs to maximize these benefits.

Recreational Sport Delivery System

Recreational sport is offered to the public through a wide variety of agencies and organizations. Generally, the major management sectors that compose the broader economy can be categorized as public, not-for-profit, and commercial. These organizations offer not only opportunities to participate in recreational sport but also employment opportunities for recreational sport professionals.

- The **public sector** refers to government-sponsored sport and recreation services. The breadth and scope of public-sector recreational sport differs depending on the country. In the United States and Canada, the public sector generally comprises government-supported recreational sport organizations and initiatives operating at the local, state or provincial, and federal levels. Local-level recreational sport organizations could include municipal and county park and recreation agencies, military recreation programs, state or provincial games, correctional institutions, PK-12 school-based intramural sport and clubs, and university recreational sport departments.
- The **not-for-profit sector** includes those sport and recreation organizations that operate in the public interest but do so outside the direct control of the government. These include private community organizations such as the YMCA or Boys and Girls Clubs; local community sport organizations; state or provincial games; national governing bodies of sport and national sport federations; sport advocacy organizations; faith-based youth sport programs such as the Catholic Youth Organization (CYO), Jewish Community

Centers, or Upward Sports; and national or international youth sport organizations.

- The **commercial sector** includes recreational sport organizations that exist to make a profit for their owners or shareholders. Examples include resorts, cruise lines, racket sport and fitness clubs, martial arts studios, merchandise and equipment sales, and sport management and marketing firms.

Table 1.1 shows the three major sport management sectors along with examples of agencies and organizations (Barcelona, 2010).

Although the three management sectors can be thought of as separate entities, the boundaries between organizations are often quite permeable and provide opportunities for a wide range of collaborations and partnerships. For example, municipal park and recreation departments often work closely with voluntary sport organizations to deliver youth sport activities in their communities. The park and recreation agency may provide and maintain athletic facilities, offer programming support, and train coaches, while the voluntary sport organization handles the day-to-day aspects of running the league, such as recruiting volunteers, scheduling games and practices, seeking sponsorships, selling concessions, and managing game-day events (Barcelona & Young, 2010). For large tournaments and meets, the park and recreation agency may also work with the chamber of commerce to write bids to host state and national events and to strategize ways to maximize economic impact.

Understanding the concept of leisure in terms of recreational activity is important for recreational sport professionals. It helps us to understand what recreational sport activities should look like (form and structure), why it is important to maximize choices to meet participants' needs (styles of participation), how to intentionally design activities so they maximize desired individual and societal outcomes (benefits), and how best to provide activities for participants (delivery system). However, recreational sport professionals still need a third definition to better understand the psychological construction of the leisure experience for participants—leisure as a state of mind.

TABLE 1.1 Recreational Sport Sectors and Selected Organizations and Agencies

Public sector	Not-for-profit sector	Commercial sector
Definition: Government-sponsored recreational sport services, primarily at the federal, state or provincial, and local levels	*Definition:* Sport and recreation organizations that operate in the public interest but do so outside the direct control of government	*Definition:* Recreational sport organizations that exist to make a profit for their owners or shareholders
Municipal park and recreation agencies	Private, not-for-profit organizations (e.g., YMCA, Boys and Girls Clubs)	Resorts
Armed forces (morale, welfare, and recreation)	Local voluntary youth sport organizations	Cruise ships
State and provincial games	State and provincial games	Racket sports and fitness clubs
Correctional institutions	National governing bodies and national sport federations	Martial arts studios
PK-12 school-based intramural sport and clubs	Sport advocacy organizations (e.g., National Alliance for Youth Sports, Up2Us)	Merchandise and equipment sales
Campus recreational sport	Faith-based sport programs (e.g., CYO, Upward Sports)	Sport management and marketing firms
	National and international youth sport organizations (e.g., Little League baseball, Pop Warner football)	

Sagamore Publishing LLC. www.sagamorepub.com. Reprinted from R.J. Barcelona, 2010, Sport management. In *Introduction to recreation, parks, and tourism careers*, edited by C. Stevens, J. Murphy, E. Sheffield, and L. Allen (Urbana, IL: Sagamore Publishing).

Leisure as a State of Mind

Leisure as discretionary time or as a particular set of activities is an easy concept to grasp. However, it has also been defined as a **state of mind**, or as "an attitude, a psychological construction, or a state of being related to personal experiences" (Henderson, 2010, p. 6). This is a much more difficult concept, because it requires us to think more deeply about what leisure means rather than how much of it we have or what it looks like.

The state-of-mind definition suggests that at the heart of any true leisure activity lie two important notions. The first is the notion of freedom. Obligatory activities such as work, school, homework, and child care often lack the element of free choice. They must be done in order to live or to fulfill our social responsibilities. The purest leisure activities, however, are always freely chosen. *Freedom* can refer to the activities that one chooses to participate in or the styles of participation that one chooses. The second notion is the idea that the purest leisure activities are pursued primarily for their own sake—in other words, they are intrinsically motivated. Though any number of benefits may accrue from participation in leisure activities, these activities are done primarily because they are enjoyable and fun. Anything that detracts from these two key notions—freedom and intrinsic reward—makes an activity less like leisure and more like work or other obligations.

You may be tempted to ask why the state-of-mind definition of leisure is important for recreational sport professionals. Again, consider the Rockville case study. The complaints from many citizens stemmed from the fact that the city's softball leagues were no longer intrinsically rewarding. The leagues became focused less on enjoyment and more on extrinsic benefits—maximizing economic impact, focusing on elite competition, soliciting corporate sponsorship, and garnering media attention. The kickball league, however, was growing in popularity precisely because it appealed to the intrinsic desires of many Rockville residents for a fun recreational experience. Do not misunderstand—healthy competition, economic impact, and media and corporate attention are all worthy benefits of the recreational sport experience. However, because recreational sport activities are leisure activities and they exist primarily for the enjoyment of participants, these external benefits should never be the primary focus of recreational sport organizations.

SPORT

Have you ever debated with your friends about what makes something a **sport**? Would all of your friends agree that football, soccer, basketball, ice hockey, and lacrosse are sports? How about gymnastics, ballroom dancing, auto racing, bass fishing, skydiving, or synchronized swimming? Is cheerleading a sport? What about chess, billiards, darts, or poker? Years of teaching recreational sport courses to undergraduates have yielded some great debates on these questions, with most students starting out making emotional arguments based on subjective opinions. However, these are more than just academic arguments or discussions among friends. Understanding what makes an activity a sport is important because the very definition of sport can become the basis for the kinds of activities that a recreational sport program offers.

Definitions of Sport

To make good decisions, a recreational sport professional needs more than just subjective opinions on what makes something a sport. There are two definitions that are helpful for understanding what makes something a sport. Both definitions are widely used in the sport literature, have overlapping attributes, and contribute something unique to our understanding of sport:

- Sport is "institutionalized physical competition occurring in formally organized or corporate structures" (Nixon, 2008, p. 8).
- Sports are "institutionalized competitive activities that involve physical exertion or the use of relatively complex physical skills by individuals whose participation is motivated by a combination of personal enjoyment and external rewards" (Coakley, 2004, p. 19).

We can glean a number of key attributes of sport based on these definitions. First, sport is *institutionalized*, *organized*, and has a *gamelike structure*. In other words, sport has rules and regulations, involves strategies, requires special facilities and equipment, and takes place at a certain time and place. There is a bureaucratic mechanism or governance system in place to make policy and enforce the rules. Corporate organizations such as school or college athletic departments, park and recreation agencies, and

Does billiards exhibit the characteristics and qualities of sport? Under what conditions?

community athletic boards exist to provide sport opportunities for their constituents.

Second, sport involves *physical activity*. In other words, the definition of *sport* connotes action or some level of physical exertion. The level of physical exertion necessary for something to be considered a sport is debatable. Almost all leisure pursuits require at least some movement; playing cards or chess, for example, requires a person to move to play the game. To engage in sport, however, participants must use physical skills. The skill involved in the physical movement of chess pieces or cards is incidental to the game; the real skill required to play is primarily mental (Nixon, 2008). However, sport activities may also involve physical exertion or at least require complex physical skills. This could include the physical stamina needed to compete in a triathlon or the complex physical skills needed to play golf (Coakley, 2004). Both of these definitions leave room for interpretation and argument. However, both suggest that to be considered a sport, an endeavor must require both physical action and skill.

Third, sport is a *competitive activity*. Shooting baskets by oneself for no purpose other than to shoot baskets is fundamentally different from playing in a single-elimination 3-on-3 basketball tournament such as Hoop It Up. The first is an individual leisure activity, whereas the second is a competitive recreational sport. Competition can be direct, such as when two individuals or teams test and compare their skills against one another. In a **direct competition**, one wins and another loses. This is called a *zero-sum game*. However, there can also be **indirect competition**, where individuals or groups compare their skills with their own past performance, focusing on skill improvement or mastery. Sport psychologists call this a **mastery orientation** or task orientation, where the focus is on building competence in sport by improving or mastering sport-related skills. Research shows that these types of sport environments tend to be associated with higher levels of enjoyment (Daniels, 2007).

There is a debate among scholars and practitioners about whether competition is good or bad in sport. Although there are good arguments on both sides, competition is embedded in both of these definitions of sport. As with most human endeavors, competition can be framed positively or negatively. For example, competition can take place within the context of task- or mastery-oriented environments where the focus is on building competence or in situations where opponents are taught to value one another and the competitive process (Doty, 2006). Similarly,

Practicing foul shooting by competing against one's personal best is an example of indirect competition.

cooperation is a necessary component of sport. After all, without agreement among competitors on the rules to play by, the location and time for games, the authority of the officials, and the eligibility of participants, there can be no game in the first place. Sport, therefore, is both competitive and cooperative.

Finally, participation in sport is motivated by both *personal enjoyment* and *external rewards*. All forms of sport encompass both, but the primary focus of recreational sport as a leisure activity is on personal enjoyment and fun, although external benefits may also be associated with the activity, such as improved fitness or external recognition. The sport development pyramid in figure 1.2 shows various levels of sport experiences and the mix of intrinsic and extrinsic motivators that athletes may experience as they progress through the model. For example, participants might choose to learn a martial art because they think it would be fun, so they take part in *foundational* classes and instruction where the focus is on learning and enjoyment. As they develop competence, they may choose to broaden their *participation* to include more in-depth practice sessions and local sparring tournaments. As they progress,

These three-on-three basketball teams are engaging in direct competition because they are competing against one another.

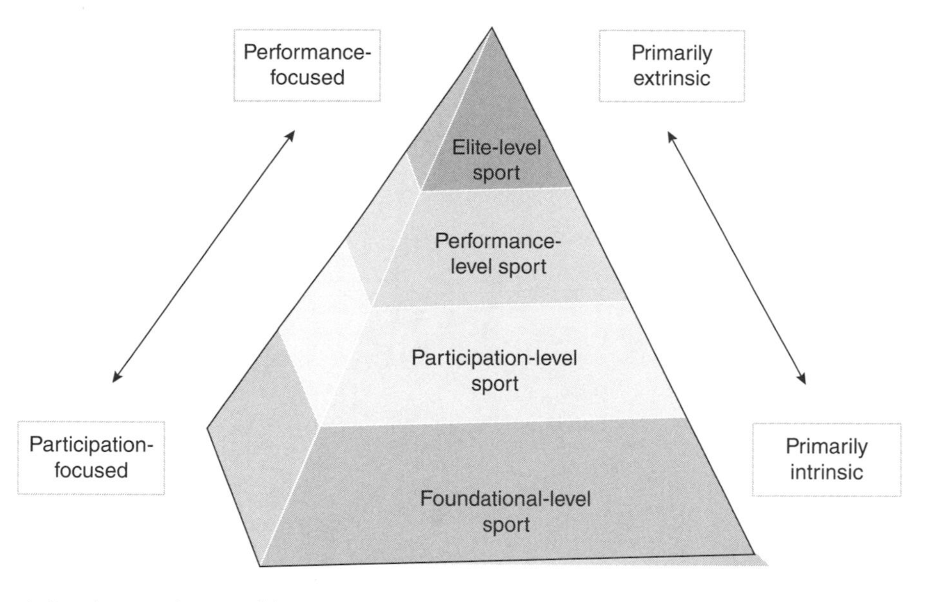

Figure 1.2 Sport development pyramid.

they may compete in regional or national tournaments where the focus is more on *performance*, and finally, if they are good enough, they may be chosen to train with an *elite* national team that competes in world championship events where the standard is excellence.

Recreational Sport

Recreational sport activities are both leisure activities and sports. However, not all sports are leisure activities. It would be hard to say that a professional basketball player is engaging in leisure activity when her team takes the court or that a college football player is freely choosing to run stadium bleachers as part of the team's spring practices. Recreational sport, on the other hand, shares characteristics of both sport and leisure activities—it encompasses the physical and active involvement of participants who freely choose to participate in a sporting event. Participants play the game, run the race, or swim in the meet.

THE RECREATIONAL SPORT PROFESSION

The broader sport industry represents a continuum of sport opportunities, programs, services, and venues ranging from primarily participation focused on one end to primarily performance focused on the other (Coakley, 2004). Figure 1.2 depicts this relationship in connection with the sport development pyramid. **Sport management** can be defined as the professional career of planning, organizing, leading, and controlling sport events, programs, personnel, and facilities (Barcelona, 2010). Members of the **recreational sport profession** are sport managers who focus on designing and managing sport programs for the primary purpose of encouraging active participation. Sport management and marketing professionals in other areas of the sport industry focus on managing and marketing sport opportunities for elite athletes or staging events for spectators.

There is certainly some crossover between the two sides of the continuum. Recreational sport professionals may offer programs for elite athletes, such as travel-oriented youth sport clubs, and they may run events that attract spectators, such as road races or national championships. However, the general objective and philosophical orientation of recreational sport is to promote active participation in sport opportunities to the widest possible audience.

Personal and Professional Philosophy

Think back to the opening case study and the earlier discussion about the benefits of sport participation. The **empirical** evidence—that is, the factual evidence about things that can be

© Bob Barcelona

These 5K road racers are actively participating in the sport experience.

measured—showed that participation in softball was declining while participation in kickball was increasing. How empirical evidence is filtered, interpreted, and acted upon, however, is based on a philosophical perspective. Philosophical questions revolve around the pursuit of truth (Lumpkin & Cuneen, 2001). A **philosophy** encompasses a system of knowledge and beliefs about things—their characteristics, value, relative goodness, and beauty. Philosophical thinking is not a passive, academic exercise disconnected from action or practice; instead, it is the platform for action. When you have developed a sound personal and professional philosophy, it is much easier to solve problems, make decisions, and take action.

It is probably safe to assume that you have already started to develop a philosophy of sport as you have gained knowledge and experience. If this is something that you have not thought about, consider the following questions:

- Why do you participate in sport?
- What do you like about sport? What do you dislike about it?
- What do you believe to be true about sport? What do you value most about sport?
- How have you come to know these things about sport? How certain are you in your beliefs?
- How consistent are you in putting your values of sport into practice?

As a future recreational sport professional, it is important to start thinking about your answers to these questions as you develop your personal philosophy of sport. Remember that your personal philosophies often have an impact on others because philosophies are a foundation for action and decision making (Grecic & Collins, 2013).

Toward a Philosophy of Recreational Sport

The idea of **sport for all** holds that sport is a human right and should be available to everyone regardless of age, race, sex, economic status, disability, or any other potential barrier (International Olympic Committee [IOC], 2012). Think about it—if sport can yield positive benefits for individuals and society, then it stands to reason that these opportunities should be made available to the widest possible audience. This provides a challenge for recreational sport professionals to ensure that they are upholding this standard. Some questions to consider within the sport-for-all framework include the following:

- Are programs accessible to as many people as possible?
- Do existing policies promote or inhibit access to recreational sport programs?
- Are facilities readily available in all neighborhoods and accessible to all participants?
- Are there structural barriers such as money, lack of transportation, lack of child care, inability to speak a certain language, or other factors that limit participation?

It is true that organizations have their own service mandates, and not every organization is designed to meet the unique needs of all people. For example, for-profit recreational sport organizations (and even many nonprofits) primarily serve the needs of paying members. However, recreational sport professionals in these settings can still employ a sport-for-all philosophy by ensuring that programs and facilities are widely accessible to members and that they do their best to promote active participation in sport opportunities. For example, reputable commercial organizations actively comply with public accommodation laws so that patrons with physical disabilities are able to access facilities and be fully included in recreational sport programs. In addition, many private organizations offer scholarships or other forms of financial assistance to people who are not able to afford their services.

CONCLUSION

Recreational sport activities are leisure activities. People freely choose to participate in them, primarily for enjoyment. The grounding philosophy of recreational sport programs is sport for all—the idea that opportunities to participate in sport are a human right and should be available to everyone regardless of age, race, sex, economic status, or ability. To that end, recreational sport professionals are responsible for designing and delivering recreational sport activities for a diverse group of participants with a wide range of interests and abilities. They need to know the needs and interests of their participants and intentionally design recreational sport activities to meet those needs. The following chapters will begin to provide the framework for the practice and profession of recreational sport.

RESEARCH TO REALITY

Forsyth, C.J. (2005). Discerning the symbiotic relationship between sport, leisure, and recreation: A note on the sportization of pastimes. *Sociological Spectrum*, *25*, 127-131.

In this article, Forsyth argues that although many want to conceptually separate leisure, recreation, and sport, the three constructs are part of the same sociological phenomenon. Drawing from the tenets of exchange theory (Crone, 1999), Forsyth suggests that the relationship between leisure, recreation, and sport can be examined from the perspective of three key variables: the amount of emphasis placed on winning, the amount of emphasis placed on extrinsic rather than intrinsic rewards, and the level of bureaucratization required to deliver and control the activity.

From this perspective, a process of *sportization* occurs whereby activities that start out as purely leisure pursuits tend to become sports as a greater emphasis is placed on winning and extrinsic rewards (e.g., recognition, money). This process results in the need for greater external control through bureaucratic organizational structures that take control of the activity out of the hands of the participant. Forsyth points to fishing, rock climbing, skateboarding, and snowboarding as leisure activities that have undergone the sportization process as they have developed competitions, tournaments, and championships and have garnered significant media attention.

Consider Forsyth's argument. As activities become sportified (i.e., where there is an increasing emphasis on winning, extrinsic rewards, and bureaucratic governance), how is the nature of the sport experience changed? Consider potential effects such as access to participation opportunities, the athlete's control over the participation experience, freedom of choice, and the outcomes of participation such as fun and enjoyment. What parallels can you draw between Forsyth's perspective and the Rockville case study that opened the chapter, the definitions of leisure and sport that we outlined earlier, and the sport-for-all philosophy that underlies recreational sport? Consider what implications, if any, the sportization process has for recreational sport professionals.

REFLECTION QUESTIONS

1. Is all recreation considered to be leisure? Is all leisure considered to be recreation? Defend your answer.
2. Think about the following list of activities: football, soccer, basketball, ice hockey, lacrosse, gymnastics, ballroom dancing, auto racing, bass fishing, skydiving, synchronized swimming, chess, billiards, darts, and poker. Which of these activities do you consider to be sports? What makes them sports? Use the definitions in the text to help.
3. If you were planning a recreational sport calendar, what types of activities would you include to maximize participant choice? How might you offer those activities to take into account diverse styles of participation?

LEARNING ACTIVITIES

1. According to the principles set forth by the United Nations (UN) Inter-Agency Task Force on Sport for Development and Peace, "Sport is far more than a luxury or a form of entertainment. Access to and participation in sport is a human right and essential for individuals of all ages to lead healthy and fulfilling lives." In broadening this concept, Kofi Annan, former secretary-general of the UN, stated in 2002 that "sport can play a role in improving the lives of individuals . . . [and] I might add . . . whole communities" (United Nations Interagency Task Force on Sport for Development and Peace, 2002). Think about what you believe the philosophy and value of recreational sport should be, and in the process, defend these statements. Explain why opportunities for recreational sport participation are important for individuals and the community, describe what areas are most important to consider in the management and programming of such opportunities, and discuss what factors go into making a quality, comprehensive recreational sport program.
2. Revisit the opening case study. If you were the director of the Rockville Park and Recreation Department, how would you respond to some of the participation trends in the recreational sport leagues? If residents complained to you that there was too much attention on competitive tournaments and not enough on local recreation opportunities, what would you do? Do some research and see what other park and recreation departments have done to encourage a healthy balance between these two types of recreational sport events. The Parks, Recreation, and Tourism department of Rock Hill, South Carolina, is a good place to start (www.cityofrockhill.com/departments/parks-recreation-tourism/more/parks-recreation-tourism).

chapter 2

PHYSICAL ACTIVITY AND RECREATIONAL SPORT

LEARNING OUTCOMES

By the end of the chapter, readers will be able to

- explain the recommended types and levels of physical activity,
- describe the benefits of increasing physical activity through sport participation,
- explain why people of all ages and abilities should engage in physically active recreational sport to the extent possible, and
- develop a plan for how recreational sport professionals can increase the physical activity of participants in their programs.

Case Study

YOU'RE NEVER TOO OLD TO GET PHYSICALLY ACTIVE

Win and Betsy are a married couple in their early 70s. Win had his second heart attack about 5 years ago, and as part of his rehab he and Betsy decided to enroll in a walking program at their local YMCA. After a few months of participating, they realized that not only were they able to walk more and faster, but they received several other benefits that they had not counted on. Win's cardiologist told him that his risk of a heart attack had gone down, and Betsy had lowered her blood pressure, which had always been a health concern for her. In addition, they found that the early morning walks were becoming a highlight of their days. Waking up to go walking had once been a chore, but now it was something they looked forward to as they got to know the people with whom they were walking. They even began to meet up with their walking friends outside of the YMCA for golf, theater, and other activities. In short, while they improved their health, they also increased their social network.

One of Win and Betsy's friends from church, Elaine, is in her upper 60s and has recently had heart problems along with a knee-replacement surgery. Despite Win and Betsy's frequent urging, she has continually declined to join them in the walking program at the YMCA. Elaine grew up at a time when physical activity and sport were not popular activities for girls and she never learned to enjoy them. She has decided that it is too late to start at her age, and she is also convinced that it would not be good for her knees or her heart to suddenly begin something strenuous. Unfortunately, this fear severely limits her both physically and socially. She has become more socially isolated partially due to her fear of doing too much, and while Win and Betsy's health seems to be maintained, Elaine's continues to decline. This is just the beginning of an unhealthy cycle for Elaine: Her health decreases, which causes her to limit her physical activity, which causes her health to further decrease.

Everyone should be somewhat careful with physical activity, especially if engaging in it for the first time or the first time in a while, but fears of physical activity are often unwarranted. Most people, like Elaine, can further harm themselves in many ways by not maintaining a physically active lifestyle throughout their lives. In addition, although no amount of physical activity can make you live forever, the life you do lead can be vastly improved through participation in physical activity, much as it was for Win and Betsy.

Physical inactivity is considered to be one of the most crucial public health problems of today (Blair, 2009; WHO, 2010). The World Health Organization (WHO) has even stated that it is the fourth leading risk factor for mortality worldwide. The prevalence of overweight and obesity in the United States alone has doubled in the past 25 years, with approximately two-thirds of adults overweight and almost one-third obese. More than 25 million children and adolescents in the United States are also overweight or obese. Physical inactivity is also a concern in the United States and the rest of the world due to its potential financial impact. Physical inactivity and obesity may result in health costs in excess of $100 billion in the United States alone each year (Hammond & Levine, 2012; Myers, 2008).

Physical activity and **physically active recreational sport** can play an important role in this global health crisis by lowering morbidity and mortality rates from several chronic diseases (Mountjoy, 2011). This chapter discusses the need to promote physical activity and active, healthy lifestyles and explores how recreational sport programs can have a tremendous impact on improving health awareness in both the short and long term.

UNDERSTANDING PHYSICAL ACTIVITY AND INACTIVITY

Clearly, physical activity and inactivity are crucial issues in the world today. However, less clarity exists when discussing what these topics mean and how they relate to recreational sport. Therefore, the first step in decreasing the prevalence of physical inactivity through sport is to understand the basic aspects of the issue. To begin, it is important to know how physical activity is classified and what the recommendations of physical activity are for various age groups.

Classifications of Physical Activity

According to WHO (2010), *physical activity* can be defined as any bodily movement produced by skeletal muscles that requires energy expenditure. This can include many unstructured activities, such young children playing, as well as more formal and organized activities, such as playing a hockey game. Types of physical activity can be further broken down into two main categories: moderate and vigorous. **Moderate physical activity** requires a medium amount of effort and typically accelerates the heart rate a noticeable amount. Examples would be brisk walking, playing games with children, and gardening. **Vigorous physical activity** typically requires a larger amount of effort than moderate physical activity and leads to a substantial increase in heart rate. Activities that generally require vigorous intensity are running, cycling, swimming, and aerobics. Recommendations for physical activity are typically given in terms of moderate to vigorous physical activity (MVPA), but research suggests that vigorous activity provides greater health benefits than moderate activity. Therefore, physically active recreational sport programs should ensure that they promote not only moderate activities but vigorous activities as well (Riddoch & O'Donovan, 2006).

Physical Activity Recommendations and Rates

In 2010, WHO came out with a list of global recommendations for physical activity by age group. These recommendations are based on extensive scientific research and are helpful for professionals involved in recreational sport (see table 2.1).

Children

Children between the ages of 5 and 17 should engage in at least 60 minutes of MVPA daily. This should include aerobic, muscle-strengthening, and bone-density-building activities (WHO, 2010). This does not mean signing a 6-year-old up for a weightlifting program, however. The vast majority of a young child's physical activity should come from play. These activities may include active games with family members, physical education classes in school, and youth sport activities. Unfortunately, only approximately 42 percent of children aged 6 to 11 and 8 percent of adolescents aged 12 to 18 meet these recommendations (Troiano et al., 2008). In fact, some studies suggest that the average child is sedentary for six to eight hours each day, and this time increases with age and among minorities and children with a low socioeconomic status (Pate, Mitchell, Byun, & Dowda, 2011).

TABLE 2.1 WHO (2010) Recommended Physical Activity by Age Group

Age group	Recommended physical activity
5-17	60 minutes MVPA daily (including aerobic, muscle-strengthening, and bone-density-building activities)
18-64	150 minutes moderate or 75 minutes vigorous activity weekly (increments of at least 10 minutes in addition to muscle-strengthening activities twice a week)
65+	150 minutes or 75 minutes of vigorous activity weekly as able (increments of at least 10 minutes in addition to balance and muscle-strengthening activities)

© Mary Sara Wells

Children prepare for their 60 minutes of MVPA.

Well-designed youth sport programs are critical for children to meet the physical activity recommendations. Studies have shown that about 23 percent of weekly MVPA is met through youth sport participation. However, even within sport there are concerns about activity levels because more than half the time in a typical youth sport practice or game is spent in either sedentary or light activity (Wickel & Eisenmann, 2007).

Adults

Adults between the ages of 18 and 64 should engage in at least 150 minutes of moderate activity or 75 minutes of vigorous activity each week for at least 10 minutes at a time, with more activity leading to greater health benefits (WHO, 2010). This could include activities such as commuting by bicycle, engaging in a recreational soccer league, or playing basketball in the driveway. Muscle-strengthening activities should also be conducted at least 2 days a week.

Older Adults

Similar to the recommendations for those who are younger, adults over the age of 65 should engage in at least 150 minutes of moderate physical activity or 75 minutes of vigorous activity during the week. Furthermore, this activity should be done in increments of at least 10 minutes. Additional health benefits can be achieved with more engagement, but this is not always possible due to health conditions; if this is the case, older adults should be as active as their abilities allow (WHO, 2010). In addition, these adults should pay attention to improving their balance to help prevent falls and doing muscle-strengthening activities to help reduce the deterioration of muscle mass.

Physical activity is particularly a concern for older people because it tends to decrease with age (Baker, Fraser-Thomas, Dionigi, & Horton, 2010). However, physical activity can help seniors better negotiate the aging process and maintain their independence for longer, make life more enjoyable and social, and minimize general health declines associated with aging. A common misperception exists among older adults that physical activity and physically active recreational sport are too risky, but for most the benefits outweigh the risks. Masters sport programs and Senior Games are excellent examples of what can be accomplished at older ages (Baker et al.).

BENEFITS OF PHYSICAL ACTIVITY

Engagement in physical activity and physically active recreational sport is crucial for a plethora of reasons. The most obvious benefits of physical activity are related to physical health, but several other benefits can also result, including improved psychosocial health and cognitive functioning.

Physical Benefits

Physical activity and physically active recreational sport play a vital role in maintaining physical health (Bergeron, 2007; Mountjoy, 2011; Taliaferro, Rienzo, & Donovan, 2010). In general, there is a direct relationship between physical health and activity level, meaning that the more people increase their physical activity, the more their health improves as a result (Mountjoy, 2011; Warburton, Nicol, & Bredin, 2006). Some of the greatest health improvements come from the switch from inactivity to low-moderate levels of activity (Warburton et al., 2006).

The physical health improvements from physical activity cover a vast number of areas such as chronic health issues, the cardiovascular system, and the musculoskeletal system, as will be discussed in the following sections. In addition to these areas, other benefits from physical activity include an improved immune system, a higher metabolic rate, and lower cholesterol and triglyceride levels (Bergeron, 2007; Miles, 2007). Perhaps even more important, physical activity has been repeatedly linked to a better quality of life (Bailey, 2006; deMontes, Arruza, Arribas, Irazusta, & Telletxea, 2011). This means that people who are active are likely to live both longer and better lives.

Chronic Health Issues

Recent research into physical activity has shown that a number of chronic health conditions, such as type 2 diabetes and cancer, are related to a person's activity level. This does not mean that by doing more physical activity a person can completely eliminate the risk of these conditions; it simply means they are less likely to occur.

One of the most common health conditions related to physical activity is type 2 diabetes. Whereas type 1 diabetes is typically a genetic condition related to the inability to produce the insulin necessary to properly use the energy from food, in type 2 diabetes, the person still produces insulin, but it may not be enough. This is one of the reasons type 2 diabetes is associated with obesity. As people increase in size, the amount of insulin they produce is no longer sufficient. Physical activity can improve this problem in two ways. First, increased physical activity often leads to weight loss, thereby reducing the amount of insulin necessary for healthy functioning. Second, physical activity increases insulin sensitivity, making the insulin that is produced more effective (Miles, 2007; Warburton et al., 2006).

In addition to type 2 diabetes, physical activity is also related to the lowered risk of several types of cancer. The two most common relationships that exist are with colon and breast cancer, which also happen to be two of the most common types of cancer (Miles, 2007; Warburton et al., 2006). Other evidence suggests that physical activity has a direct impact on the prevention of lung, prostate, and endometrial cancers (Miles, 2007).

Cardiovascular System

Another way activity can improve health is through its effects on the cardiovascular system. Physical inactivity has been clearly linked with heart disease (Bailey, 2006), and not surprisingly, the reverse is also true—physical activity tends to lead to lower rates of cardiovascular disease and in some cases has even been shown to improve cardiovascular functioning (Miles, 2007; Sagiv, 2011; Taylor et al., 2004). When done at safe levels, physical activity provides healthy exercise for the heart muscle and can improve aerobic capacity. Improvements can be magnified even further due to additional benefits such as lower cholesterol and triglyceride levels and less risk of high blood pressure, all of which have a relationship with heart disease.

Musculoskeletal System

Physical activity has also been shown to improve physical health through its impact on the musculoskeletal system. People who are physically active are likely to have better bone health, particularly when they engage in high-impact activities such as running, tennis, and soccer (Bergeron, 2007; Miles, 2007). Each time a person's foot strikes the ground, the impact leads to strengthening of the bones, so activities that involve an element of running or walking are especially beneficial. Although bone health is essential for all age groups in order to minimize the risk of fractures, it is an even greater concern for older adults. As people age, they have a higher risk of osteoporosis, and bone-strengthening activity can help minimize this risk along with the risk of any debilitating fractures that can reduce independence (Taylor et al., 2004).

Psychosocial Benefits

Though not as well documented as the effects of physical activity on physical health, the benefits to psychosocial health are also crucial to overall well-being (Bailey, 2006). The most research in this area has been done regarding anxiety and depression. Although more research still needs to be completed (Berk, 2007; Saxena, Van Ommeren, Tang, & Armstrong, 2005), numerous studies have suggested that a relationship exists between physical activity and depression symptoms (Da Silva et al., 2012) and that physically active people tend to report fewer depression and anxiety symptoms (Bailey, 2006; Berk, 2007; Saxena et al., 2005). Many of these studies have not been designed to show a direct causal link between the two, but studies on interventions for depression have shown that physical activity is an important component of a treatment plan to lessen the likelihood of relapsing (Berk, 2007; Donaghy, 2007; Saxena et al., 2005).

Other areas of psychosocial health have also been correlated with participation in physical activity or physically active recreational sport. Among these are increased self-esteem (Bailey, 2006), emotional well-being (Saxena et al., 2005), and social functioning in older adults (Taylor et al., 2004).

Cognitive Benefits

Improved cognitive abilities are benefits that are less commonly associated with physical activity but are just as real and just as important. Evidence suggests that physical activity has a positive impact on cognitive functioning across age groups. Children who are physically active are likely to have higher rates of academic achievement as demonstrated by math, IQ, and reading scores (Fedeway & Ahn, 2011; Ratey & Hagerman, 2008). This may be caused by the increased blood flow to the brain that occurs in physical activity, leading to enhanced mood and mental alertness (Bailey, 2006).

An additional cognitive benefit from physical activity occurs with age. As people grow older, they are more likely to develop diseases such as dementia or Alzheimer's. These diseases can rob people of their cognitive functioning and memories, which can be devastating. Physical activity, however, has been shown to prevent and delay these symptoms, again possibly as the result of increased cerebral blood flow (Smith, Nielson, Woodard, Seidenberg, & Rao, 2013; Taylor et al., 2004).

PROMOTING PHYSICALLY ACTIVE RECREATIONAL SPORT

One of the responsibilities of recreational sport professionals is to promote physical activity and its benefits whenever it is relevant to the sport and population that they are working with. To do this well, we must first understand why people choose to be inactive and why they are motivated to be active. This will then provide a background for ways that sport programs can help encourage increased physical activity among participants.

Reasons People Are Inactive

If recreational sport professionals are to promote engagement in physically active recreational sport, their programs need to meet participants' needs. The first step in creating physically active recreational sport programs is to understand the reasons why people decide to be inactive. It would seem that people who know about the benefits of physical activity would find it necessary to engage in recreational sport on a regular basis. However, despite the importance of physical activity, not enough people are engaging in it (Baker et al., 2010; Davey, Fitzpatrick, Garland, & Kilgour, 2009). Some studies have suggested that around half of all people who start an exercise program quit within the first six months (White, Randsell, Vener, & Flohr, 2005). Several reasons exist for these low activity levels, including a lack of enjoyment, a lack of support, inaccessible programs and facilities, and being in a stage of life that makes activity difficult.

Lack of Enjoyment

One of the major contributing factors to whether or not people engage in physically active recreational sport is their enjoyment of it (Brockman, Jago, & Fox, 2011; Davey et al., 2009; Ketteridge & Boshoff, 2008; Kilpatrick, Hebert, & Bartholomew, 2005; White et al., 2005). To put it simply, people like to have fun. This means that the more fun or rewarding an activity is, the more people will continue to do it after initially trying it. Therefore, people who enjoy being physically active are more likely to become lifelong participants and to receive the many benefits that result from participation (Smith, 1999; Yungblut, Schinke, & McGannon, 2012).

The level of enjoyment experienced in physical activity can be related to several factors. In particular, physically active recreational sport programs that involve high levels of friendship and promote a sense of physical self-worth are likely to lead to increased overall enjoyment (Smith, 1999).

Peer involvement plays a big role in the level of enjoyment in physical activity. Research suggests that a lack of people with whom to engage in physically active recreational sport is one of the highest rated barriers to participation (Casper, Bocarro, Kanters, & Floyd, 2011). Meanwhile, those who do have friends who engage in physical activity are more likely to maintain their own participation and to enjoy it. This is especially true for adolescents (Ketteridge & Boshoff, 2008; Yungblut et al., 2012) and for women (White et al., 2005).

Also related to enjoyment is the idea of competence in physical activity. People tend to enjoy activities more when they feel capable of doing them; conversely, they are less likely to engage in physical activity when they feel they lack the ability to perform the activity. Those who feel they do not have the required skills are less likely to begin a physical activity program (Biddle, Wang, Chatzisarantis, & Spray, 2003; Fairclough, Ridgers, & Welk, 2012). Interestingly, though, once people have begun a physical activity program, their confidence tends to increase, suggesting that overcoming that first obstacle of competence can have great implications for long-term participation (White et al., 2005).

The good news is that enjoyment level is not set at the initial experience; it can change with experience. If that experience is a positive one, it may lead to overall increased physical activity (Dunton, Schneider, & Cooper, 2007). However, this also means that negative experiences can lead to decreased physical activity levels. For this

Having fun is one of the keys to keeping people physically active.

reason, it is crucial for recreational sport professionals to design programs that consistently maximize enjoyment to the extent possible.

Lack of Support

The support of others is another critical factor in promoting involvement in physically active recreational sport because people who feel a lack of support are less likely to engage in these activities. Support can take several forms, including role modeling, time, and money.

Role modeling is particularly relevant to children and adolescents, who tend to follow patterns of physical activity set by their parents. Adult role models, and parents in particular, can influence whether children become physically active. Children who see their parents participate in physically active recreational sport are more likely to become physically active for the long term (Yang, Telama, & Laakso, 2006); in fact, adolescents are four times as likely to be active if they see their parents being physically active (Sanz-Arazuri, Ponce-de-Leon-Elizondo, & Valdemoros-San-Emeterio, 2012). Unfortunately, most parents do not realize the extent of their influence (Sanz-Arazuri et al.). For this reason, youth sport professionals should encourage the parents of their athletes to be physically active.

Children with parents who support physical activity in addition to merely serving as models are more likely to be active (Edwardson & Gorely, 2010; Fairclough et al., 2012; Woods, Graber, & Duan, 2012). This support can take many forms. Financial support from parents is often necessary because recreational sport programs are becoming increasingly expensive. Money is needed not just for registration but also for traveling expenses, equipment, uniforms, and miscellaneous expenses.

Finally, support for physically active recreational sport is also demonstrated through time spent in the child's activity. To begin with, parents are generally the ones who introduce children to the activity either at home or by registering them with a program (Castelli & Erwin, 2007). Parents then frequently serve as transportation to and from practices and events, cheerleaders during performances, and sometimes as coaches or officials. The time parents spend performing these functions demonstrates to their children that they think highly of the activity, which typically leads their children to value it as well.

The issue of support for physical activity can be partially related to cultural expectations (Lata, 2010; Seefeldt, Malina, & Clark, 2002), particularly in terms of gender (Yan & McCullagh, 2004). For several cultures, there is a cultural expectation that females should not be physically active. Physical activity can be seen as a male role and, therefore, women who participate are being too masculine and may be seen as neglecting other duties such as maintaining the home or raising children. This can severely affect a woman's motivation to participate in physical activity, and the cultural pressure can outweigh the potential benefits of participation (Yan & McCullagh, 2004).

Inaccessibility

People might also be inactive as the result of inaccessible programs, equipment, or facilities. This is a growing concern particularly as is applies to socioeconomic status (Lata, 2010; Telama, Laakso, Nupponen, Rimpela, & Pere, 2009), which may unfairly affect minorities (Seefeldt et al., 2002). Inaccessibility issues may include safety concerns and a lack of affordable, close facilities (Fairclough et al., 2012; Seefeldt et al., 2002). In order to engage in recreational sport, participants need to have the means to do so. They need to have the infrastructure available and the financial resources to take advantage of it (Pano & Markola, 2012). Furthermore, the quality of a facility also matters (Casper et al., 2011). Participants are less likely to be physically active when the facilities appear to be unattractive or unsafe.

Stage of Life

The stage of a person's life can influence whether or not she engages in physical activity (Engberg et al., 2012; Hirvensalo & Lintunen, 2011; White et al., 2005). For example, between the ages of 15 and 29 there tends to be a decrease in overall physical activity. This decline occurs partially because of changes that occur when going from high school to college and then from going to college to becoming a working adult, getting married, and having children (Hamilton, Cox, & White, 2012; Zick, Smith, Brown, Fan, & Kowaleski-Jones, 2007).

These shifts in physical activity are typically the result of two things: time availability and sport opportunity. In terms of time, as we progress through life we tend to have less time available for personal pursuits. The more responsibility a person has in a job, a spouse, and children, the less time is available for physical fitness. Although it is still crucial to engage in some level of physical

Engaging in lifetime recreational sports helps people remain physically active as they age.

activity, it becomes increasingly more difficult (Zick et al., 2007).

In terms of opportunity, team sport, which is a source of much physical activity for young people, becomes less common in college, although some students engage in intramurals or recreational leagues, and it is even less common once people graduate. In order to remain physically active, it is often necessary to change to sports that are more lifelong pursuits, partly because it becomes difficult to find time to play on teams. In particular, individual sports such as running, swimming, skiing, and kayaking tend to be more popular for maintaining physical activity as a person gets older (Zick et al., 2007).

Motivation for Physical Activity

Although there are many reasons why people are inactive, there are also some motivating factors that help lead to a physically active lifestyle. For the most part, research suggests that there is little difference in motives for physical activity between men and women (Reed & Cox, 2007), although there are some. For example, girls are typically more motivated than boys to use physical activity as a means of controlling weight (Butt, Weinberg, Breckon, & Claytor, 2011; Kilpatrick et al., 2005; Pano & Markola, 2012), and men may be more motivated than women by performance and exertion (Butt et al., 2011; Kilpatrick et al., 2005). For both genders, however, a number of motivating factors are similar. These include peer relationships, fun, and improved physical performance (Pano & Markola, 2012; Smith, 1999). By addressing these factors and more, administrators should be able to help promote physically active recreational sport participation.

How to Create Physically Active Recreational Sport Programs

A clear understanding of why people do and do not engage in physical activity can assist recreational professionals as they attempt to create programs that promote physically active lifestyles. In spite of a seemingly obvious connection between physical activity and sport, there is no automatic relationship between the two. They can be related, but only when recreational sport professionals ensure that this happens through quality programming (Bailey, 2006). Some studies have even shown that athletes are inactive for up to half the time they are involved in either a sport practice or competition (Wickel & Eisenmann, 2007). This means that attention should be paid to ensure that programs are being offered in a way that yields physical activity benefits. Currently, this is a focus of several national efforts within the United States, including NFL Play 60 (www.nfl.com/play60) and First Lady Michelle Obama's Let's Move campaign (www.letsmove.gov), both of which are designed to promote physical activity among young people. Although recreational sport professionals have a limited impact on the physical activity in which people engage, there are certain ways they can try to promote physical activity among their participants. By addressing aspects of education, the physical setting, rules, and the focus of their programs, administrators can improve their ability to reach and promote physical activity to all.

Providing Education and Training

One of the primary methods for increasing participation in physical activity and physically active recreational sport is through education and training. Training young children to engage in physically active recreational sport has a significant influence on their activity levels as adults. Children who begin youth sport and continue participation through adolescence are much more likely to be active as adults (Bergeron, 2007; deMontes et al., 2011; Dodge & Lambert, 2008; Hallal, Victora, Azevedo, & Wells, 2006; Hirvensalo & Lintunen, 2011; Kjonniksen, Anderssen, & Wold, 2009; Miles, 2007). This might partially be a result of the fact that these adults have experienced sport as part of their lives at an early age and are unlikely to deviate from that norm. On the other hand, young adults who were not exposed to physically active recreational sport as children tend to have a much more challenging time overcoming this obstacle to physical activity (Hirvensalo & Lintunen, 2011). This could be in connection to a lack of confidence in what they can do and therefore a fear of trying something new (Bocarro, Kanters, & Casper, 2006). Thus, it is important for administrators to promote recreational sport to young people to encourage lifelong activity.

A great example of this takes place in Utah, where ski resorts have a vested interest in recruiting participants. They offer a program where every fifth grader in the region receives a free day pass to each of the major resorts. Although the initial cost of such a program is expensive,

Bananastock

Learning skills while young increases the likelihood of practicing them when older.

the investment pays off through its recruitment of future skiers. The students in the state learn the skills necessary to engage in skiing at a time of their lives when it is easy to do so. When they are older, they have no need to be hesitant about trying something new, because they already have the basic skills and have developed a love of the activity.

In addition to the influence of youth sport participation on adult physical activity, there is another area where education can come into play. Research has shown that a lack of education is a major barrier to physical activity participation (Lata, 2010). Oftentimes, people fail to see the necessity of a physically active lifestyle and therefore do not feel the pressure to ensure it happens. Because so many people are unaware of the full extent of the benefits that they can receive from physical activity, they need education and training (Nowak, 2010). For example, recreational sport professionals working in youth sport could provide parents with informational sessions and handouts on the benefits of physical activity. This information should not only include the many health benefits to sport participants but should also detail facts such as the link between parent and youth participation so that parents can understand that signing their children up for a program is not enough. Instead, to more fully encourage a healthy lifestyle for their children, parents should engage in physical activity themselves as a crucial form of modeling behavior.

Changing the Physical Setting

Another factor that recreational sport professionals can control is the environment in which sport takes place. Some research even suggests that the environment is one of the most of important factors in promoting physical activity among the general population (Hills, King, & Armstrong, 2007).

To begin with, facilities need to be accessible. Whether it is a park, a recreational center, or a bike path, people are more likely to engage in physical activity if the environment is easy to get to. For example, research suggests that the close proximity of green space or a cul-de-sac is likely to lead to an increase in physically active play in young children (Brockman et al., 2011), and results from other studies have shown that physical activity is heightened when children live within 5 miles (8 km) of their school (Cohen et al., 2006). For professionals hoping to encourage physical activity, this means providing facilities close to where the target markets are. It will be easier to secure participants if they do not have to travel far to get there. And it would be even better if they could get there by a form of physical activity (e.g., walking, riding a bike).

The appeal of a facility also matters. This means that the environment should be safe and should appear clean and well maintained. Finally, the environment itself should be designed for physical activity. Clear paths and sidewalks with appropriate signage will encourage people to be more physically active in their general access to facilities as well as in their participation once they arrive (Mutrie & Parnell, 2011). By addressing these issues, administrators can create positive places for physical activity, thereby increasing the overall number of participants (Edwards, Kanters, & Bocarro, 2011).

Changing the Rules

Recreational sport professionals might also look at adapting rules in order to heighten physical activity within sport. Small changes in this area can have a big impact. For example, in tennis it would be easy to use the lines for a doubles court in practice for singles tennis. This would increase the amount of running a player would need to do in rallies. In team sport, team sizes could be reduced to force participants to be more active (Bergeron, 2007). If team size needs to remain the same, using additional balls or pucks makes it more challenging for participants because they essentially have to keep up with multiple games at once.

Changing the Focus to Lifetime Health

Finally, to improve participation in physically active recreational sport, it might be beneficial for recreational sport professionals to think beyond the typical sport offerings. Although variety is becoming more common, there is still a tendency for professionals to focus on more traditional sports such as football, baseball, and soccer. Although these sports present excellent opportunities to learn, develop skills, and enjoy being physically active, they are also somewhat limiting. It is difficult to engage in such activities after young adulthood for the mere fact that team sport requires the participation of larger groups. This means coordinating many people at a time when physical activity in general has decreased, partially as a result of less free time.

Consequently, in order to encourage long-term physical activity, it is crucial for professionals to keep in mind nontraditional activities that may be more conducive to lifelong participation (Mutrie & Parnell, 2011). Sports such as skateboarding, dance, kayaking, and skiing all have potential for lifetime involvement and should therefore be encouraged in addition to team sports.

CONCLUSION

This chapter has presented a firm foundation for recreational sport professionals to help address the obesity crisis through their programs. Professionals should have a clear understanding of what physical activity is and how much is recommended for their participants. Furthermore, professionals can use the information about the benefits of physical activity for physical, psychosocial, and cognitive health to educate participants in order to motivate them to participate in physically active recreational sport. Finally, professionals can use the suggestions presented in this chapter to develop more physically active programs through education and training and by changing the physical setting, rules, and focus. All of this should benefit both the organization and its programs and, more importantly, help create healthier people and communities.

RESEARCH TO REALITY

DeBate, R.D., Gabriel, K.P., Zwald, M., Huberty, J., & Zhang, Y. (2009). Changes in psychosocial factors and physical activity frequency among third- to eighth-grade girls who participated in a developmentally focused youth sport program: A preliminary study. *Journal of School Health*, *79*, 474-484.

DeBate and her colleagues were concerned about the decline in physical activity among adolescent girls and wanted to assess the benefits of a developmentally focused youth sport program aimed at increasing life skills concurrently with physical skills (in this case, running). Girls on the Run and Girls on Track work with girls between the ages of 8 and 13 and deliver life-skills training while helping them prepare to run a 5K during a 12-week program. Topics include self-worth, teamwork and cooperation, and community development. Researchers in this study had participants complete a questionnaire at the beginning and end of the program to determine if participants were able to increase their self-esteem, body-size satisfaction, physical activity values, physical activity attitudes, physical activity motivation, and physical activity frequency.

Results from the study showed that participation in Girls on the Run and Girls on Track led to improved self-esteem, body-size satisfaction, and physical activity frequency. This means that programs intentionally designed to increase physical activity among girls can successfully address some of the issues involved with declines in physical activity as girls age, leading to the potential for healthier girls in the long run.

REFLECTION QUESTIONS

1. As a college student, how often do you engage in physically active recreational sport? How has this participation changed in the past 10 years? What changes do you notice in yourself at these varying levels (e.g., moderate, vigorous) of physical activity?
2. Looking back at your experiences in youth sport, how physically active were you in practices? In games? How do you think your coaches could have adapted the experiences to increase your physical activity level?
3. As the administrator of a community recreation center, you decide to approach a local senior community about creating a partnership to increase physical activity among its members. In terms of the effects of physical activity, how would you persuade the leaders of this facility that this partnership would benefit its members? How would this argument differ if you were trying to create a partnership with a local school district to develop its youth sport programs?

LEARNING ACTIVITIES

1. Think about a sport you would like to work with as an administrator. Design a week's worth of activities for beginners that aim to meet the recommended rates of physical activity for this age group. Keep in mind that beginners could be of any age, so designate a specific age range for participants before creating these activities.
2. Interview someone at least 20 years older than you about the changes in physical activity levels and sport participation he or she has experienced over their lives. When did these changes take place, what caused them to occur, and how did it affect the interviewee physically, psychologically, and cognitively? Is there anything she would do differently related to physical activity and sport participation?

chapter 3

DIVERSITY AND DEVELOPMENT IN RECREATIONAL SPORT

LEARNING OUTCOMES

By the end of this chapter, readers will be able to

- identify broad categories of diversity,
- understand how various populations require specific considerations in sport management programming,
- identify constraints on sport participation for a diverse population, and
- provide examples of how to modify programs to accommodate a diverse population.

Case Study

RELIGIOUS DIVERSITY AND RECREATIONAL SPORT

Jose is a Mexican American living just outside a large city in the Mountain West with his wife and four children. They participate in the local Mexican community, and they have a large group of extended family members around the area. Jose and his children are very involved in soccer both as spectators and as participants.

Due to the predominant religion in the area, it has been a common cultural understanding that recreational sport programmers do not program leagues on Sunday so that families can attend church services and honor the Sabbath. The problem lies in the differences between this culture and the culture to which Jose belongs. Jose and his family enjoy spending time in the local city parks and playing games on Sunday, including soccer. However, there are no leagues that play on Sunday. Jose feels that his opportunity to participate in a recreational soccer league on the day he and his family want to be active is hampered due to cultural differences.

To solve the problem, Jose starts his own league; fields are lying dormant on Sundays anyway and there are others in the area who share Jose's desire to participate in a league on Sunday despite the predominant religious programming influences. The league immediately has upward of 40 teams sign up, with most participants coming from the Latino communities in the region. The league grows and even becomes a weekly celebration of Latino cuisine as families set up food stands to share with one another. The league continues to grow and the community support extends to smaller cities in the area to allow for various league exchanges in matches and tournaments.

In this example, people who belong to the dominant religion in the area have perhaps inadvertently created opportunity based on their own schedules without consideration for those around them simply because of the differences in belief and culture. Although it is important to hold onto the traditions and values of a religion, there still needs to be a clear understanding that not everyone shares those same beliefs and that perhaps there is a need in the community beyond the predominant religion that could be met differently. Recreational sport professionals need to be aware of their own personal biases or cultural beliefs and look to accommodate the desires of the diverse population they are charged to serve.

As the global population continues to grow toward an estimated 8.9 billion by 2050 (UN, 2004), the demand for recreational sport continues to grow with it. However, recreational sport activities are no longer simply for the social elite. They have become an avenue for people from a range of social classes, ethnicities, cultures, and backgrounds to participate together, thanks to recreational sport professionals who provide such opportunities. In many countries, sport is seen as a way to get out of poverty, to reduce crime rates, or to earn college scholarships (Smith & Waddington, 2004), even though the ratio of academic scholarships to athletic ones in the United States is approximately 10:1 (Arthur-Banning & Wells, 2010). Events such as the Olympics provide exciting opportunities for athletes and spectators from countries around the world to come together in a form of social unity through sport.

On a smaller scale, recreational sport programs in a number of states and provinces use sport as a medium for social change and acceptance. However, if recreational sport professionals do not understand how populations interact or engage with one another, then sporting events will not have the impact they could. For this reason, a discussion about **diversity** and development in recreational sport is important.

SPORT FOR ALL

Sport for all has taken on a larger meaning in the world; for instance, the UN operates with a sport-for-development framework, and the International Olympic Committee (IOC) hosts a regular sport-for-all conference to discuss the many benefits that sport can provide. The types of sporting activities people engage in within their own communities might have less global impact, yet they are largely recreational and should be available to everyone.

As a unified movement, the term *sport for all* was initially proposed by the Council of Europe in 1966. Its aim was to use sport to help develop a society that is more integrated. The Council recognized, even in 1966, that sport had the ability to be a unifying force that could transcend race, social class, ability, and religion. Rather than seeing sport as an entity in itself, the Council saw sport as a medium through which lessons could be learned, skills taught, and differences understood. As we will see in chapter 4, this is only the case if sport programs are designed intentionally with specific outcomes in mind. However, if this is done well, there certainly is potential for sport to have an immense impact on personal, community, and national development.

LEGISLATION GUIDING PROFESSIONALS

In addition to the sport-for-all movement, a body of legislation has been introduced to make sport inclusive and help a common activity with common rules and goals to influence people in a positive way. By learning about such legislation, recreational sport professionals can better understand how to shape the sport environment to benefit the most people. Following are examples of legislation in the United States, but many countries around the globe have implemented similar policies regarding diversity and the rights of all people. This is simply a brief overview; you should seek additional information so as to better understand how each piece of legislation might affect your facility or program. The United States Access Board has a more comprehensive list of documents to reference for creating a more inclusive sporting environment (www.access-board.gov/guidelines-and-standards).

Title VI of the Civil Rights Act of 1964

This act states that no program or activity that receives federal financial assistance can discriminate against people on the basis of them being different in any way. The act specifically mentions race, color, national origin, age, and disability. It goes on to identify examples of **discrimination** such as denial of services or benefits, services that are offered in a different manner for certain groups, and aspects of segregation or inclusion that are not appropriate (www.doi.gov/diversity/civil_rights.html).

Americans With Disabilities Act of 1990

According to the ADA website, "The Americans with Disabilities Act (ADA) gives civil rights protections to individuals with disabilities similar to those provided to individuals on the basis of race, color, sex, national origin, age, and religion. It guarantees equal opportunity for individuals with disabilities in public accommodations, employment, transportation, State and local government services, and telecommunications" (www.ada.gov/q&aeng02.htm#29). This act has been used by multiple agencies both in education as well as in recreation to provide access to services for people with disabilities. The act was updated in 2015 and includes provisions to help eliminate discrimination against people with disabilities.

If you are running a public recreation agency or are using public facilities, you need to be aware of how accessible your programs are and seek to accommodate people with disabilities. Although many programs around the country do this well, there are still misconceptions about the skills and abilities of people with disabilities. Hopefully, events like the Paralympics and organizations like Disabled Sports USA are having a positive influence on the opportunities for and perceptions of people with disabilities in the sport world.

Title IX of the Education Amendments of 1972

Title IX is an educational amendment that addresses discrimination on the basis of sex. It stipulates that people should not be excluded from participation in any program or activity that is

The Americans with Disabilities Act ensures that persons with disabilities are able to access recreation and leisure facilities, programs, and services.

receiving federal financial assistance or be denied benefits in such programs because of their sex (www.dol.gov/oasam/regs/statutes/titleix.htm).

With respect to sport, Title IX stipulates that men and women be provided the same opportunities to participate. This is not to suggest that identical sports need to be offered but rather that opportunities should not be denied based on sex alone. The National Collegiate Athletic Association (NCAA) has even more specific requirements for scholarships and benefits that assist in opportunity equality at the university and college level (www.ncaa.org).

Individuals With Disabilities Education Improvement Act of 2004

The Individuals with Disabilities Education Act (IDEA) was enacted by Congress in 1975 and has since been updated numerous times, including as the Individuals with Disabilities Education Improvement Act of 2004 (IDEIA). This legislation ensures that children who have diagnosed disabilities receive a free and appropriate public education. From a recreational sport perspective, it is important to understand that the most beneficial environment for a person with a disability is one that is least restrictive for all participants involved (Ohtake, 2004). There are times when a fully inclusive program is appropriate, and there are also times when a completely separate sporting event, such as a local Paralympic event, is appropriate to best accommodate the disabilities involved. In addition, this act may be applicable to agencies that have partnered with educational institutions or if participants with disabilities are enrolled in sport camps or summer activities. You can read more about the legislation to see the current additions and how IDEIA might help your participants with disabilities at The Center for Parent Information and Resources (http://www.parentcenterhub.org/topics/disability/).

Legislation provides the foundation for offering opportunities to a variety of populations; however, it is also necessary to understand how populations differ. Age, disability, race, religion, sex, and social class all require specific considerations and accommodations, and they all experience constraints on participation differently. Therefore, each is briefly discussed in the following sections. When programming, make every effort to consider each constraint for each group to provide the most positive environment possible.

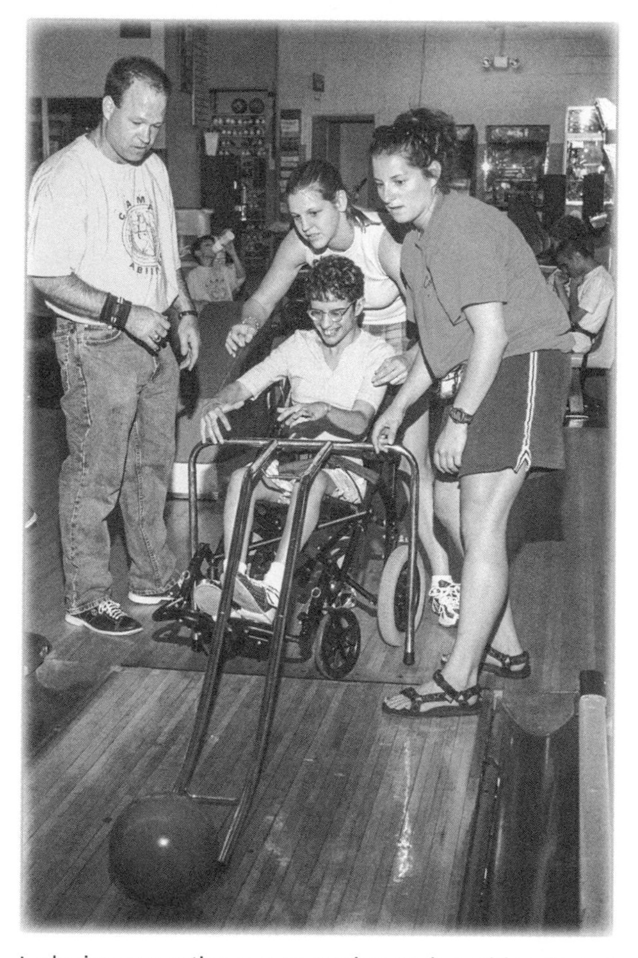

Inclusive recreation programming such as this adapted bowling program enables youth with disabilities to fully access and participate in recreational sport activities with their peers.

AGE

Recreational sport should involve participants of all ages, and a recreational sport professional with a solid understanding of the preferences and developmental milestones of people at each stage can provide a better program with increased participant satisfaction. Erik Erikson (1968) was a German psychologist who came up with a theory of how humans develop. He used eight stages of psychosocial development as a framework for understanding developmental milestones (figure 3.1). Infancy (0-18 months), early childhood (18 months-3 years), preschool (3-5 years), school age (6-12 years), and adolescence (12-18 years) all occur up to age 18 and thus fall under the youth development framework that many recreational sport programs promote. Young adulthood (18-35 years), middle adulthood (35-60 years), and late adulthood (60 years to death) are included in university recreational activities and in the adult and family programs that recreational sport professionals typically organize.

The following breakdown is based on Erikson's eight stages of development and should help recreational sport professionals understand how programs fit into the developmentally appropriate stages of activity. Although age ranges are provided, people may move through these stages at slightly different times. However, this should still be a helpful guide for programming for various age ranges (Erikson, 1968).

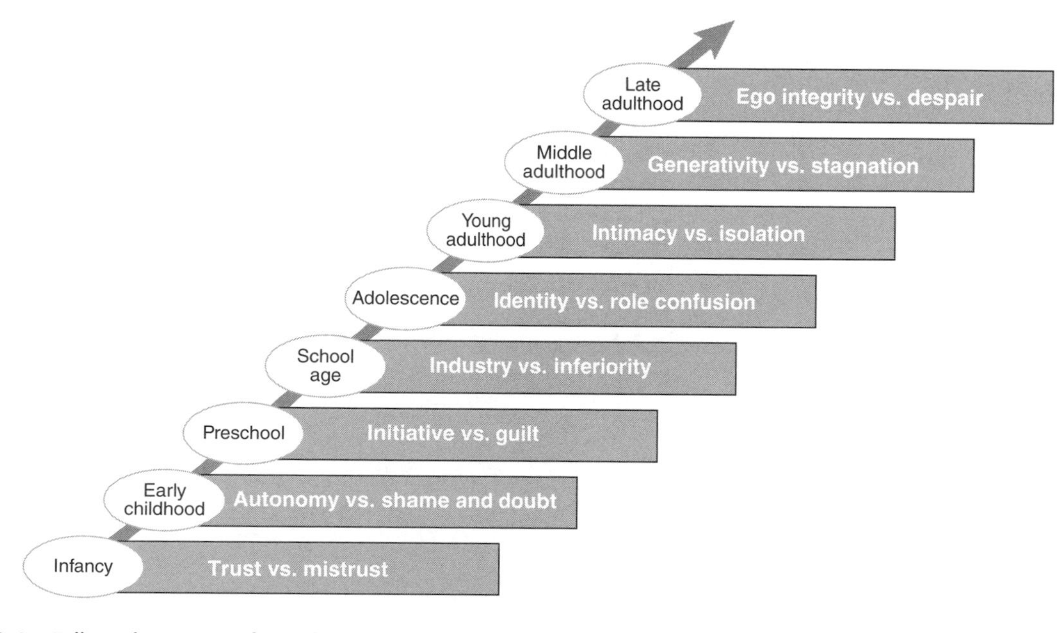

Figure 3.1 Erikson's stages of psychosocial development.

Infancy (0-18 Months)

A newborn most certainly is not going to be involved in recreational sporting events, although there has been a growing demand for parent–infant programs. Infants tend to use oral sensory processing, meaning they like to put everything in their mouths to explore. They are attached to their mothers in particular, seeking close contact, love, and affection from the mother figure in this stage. This is why programs such as mommy–infant yoga or swim time have become so popular. These activities allow children to experience a close sense of contact with their moms and begin to develop trust while moving and engaging the senses in an intimate way.

Early Childhood (18 Months-3 Years)

Children at this stage seek to establish control over events as they figure them out and explore the world around them. They are learning gross and fine motor skills through skill exploration and seeking opportunities to build self-esteem. However, if they are shamed or if they experience continued bouts of failure, they are significantly less likely to continue trying new activities. Finally, the most important relationships in the child's life are still with parents or immediate caregivers. Recreational sport programs for early childhood can be designed with exploration and opportunities for success in mind. Exploratory programs, such as offering basic gymnastics equipment with mats where the children are encouraged to play with the equipment at low levels, will encourage their sense of investigation and ensure that their opportunity for success is high while removing the elements of failure and shame. Another example would be a gymnasium program with objects such as balls and beanbags in many sizes, shapes, and textures. This activity would allow for motor development to progress as children begin to mimic sport-specific skills and techniques while still including the opportunity for parental play and interaction in a nonthreatening way in an area that is safe and secure.

Preschool (3-5 Years)

As children continue to develop, they seek to mimic those around them and their play becomes much more purposeful and structured. Children at this age are capable of imagination and make-believe, and they often re-create the experiences they witness among adults, especially family members. This stage of development is highlighted by children taking initiative in their activities—"No, let me do it"—coupled with beginning to understand guilt. Children who experience success through their own ventures are likely to continue to explore, while those who fail will slow their development and take less initiative. It is important to provide lots of tools, balls, and equipment for children at this age and then let them simply explore the items. In most cases, there is no need for structured rules or games except as the children dictate when trying to mimic what they've witnessed in games. For example, at this stage, there is little value in telling a child to put down a soccer ball if he picks it up with his hands. Allow him to explore the ball in any way he chooses; you can introduce the rules of the game at a later stage when they are more relevant. Family games are still most important in this stage, and including family members in the activities will allow for greater levels of exploration and comfort.

School Age (6-12 Years)

In this stage, children make efforts to learn new skills and accomplish new tasks provided to them. This is the age when most children begin to learn sport-specific activities in a structured environment, including the rules. In addition, children are beginning to understand the roles that people play within the sport environment, such as coach, player, parent, team captain, skilled player versus unskilled player, and so on. Home is no longer the only source of socialization and companionship as school and sport begin to play a bigger role in shaping the world around them. More so at this stage than any other previously, children understand the role of success and how it leads to a greater sense of competence and self-esteem. Failure, especially among 10- to 12-year-olds, leads to feelings of inferiority and withdrawal from activities that cause failure. Sport in this phase must be developmental and exploratory with lots of opportunity for success at all levels of play. Task-oriented activities with realistic goals serve the children much better and encourage future exploration and successes.

As a result of the influence that parents and coaches have at this age, including on socialization, adult behavior and examples are crucial and as such need to be considered in league planning and rule setting. In addition to the daily socialization at school and at home, each sport and league has specific socializing agents and environments that stay with children throughout their playing careers. It is extremely important to model and encourage rules, respect, and ethical behavior in this stage.

Adolescence (12-18 Years)

In this stage, teens develop a sense of self and identity. In earlier stages, the largest developmental milestones tend to get accomplished based on what parents, teachers, and coaches provide for the child. According to Erikson (1968), in this phase and beyond, development is largely based on the decisions teenagers make for themselves. Life is getting complex for the adolescent, with relationships outside of family becoming increasingly important along with work exploration, school expectations, and socialization opportunities that are independent of the family. Adolescents are seeking to determine who they are and how they fit within the larger society. In this stage, failure often leads to insecurity and role confusion unless it is dealt with in a positive way and lessons are learned from it.

From a sport perspective, this is the age when the most opportunities tend to be available. With local leagues, school teams, and traveling opportunities, participation rates tend to be high. Social identity can be closely tied to participation in sport, and success in sport can lead to many opportunities. Unfortunately, this is also the stage that provides the greatest chance of dropping out of sport due to negative experiences or lack of opportunity. A growing trend in recreational leagues is to offer fewer opportunities when a particular sport is being played in the high school season, which means that anyone who does not make the high school team actually has fewer opportunities to participate, leading to even higher dropout rates and identity formation that does not involve recreational sport.

Young Adulthood (18-35 Years)

In this stage, people tend to put significant effort into relationship formation in seeking a partner. They are also focused on their career placement and advancement, which tends to present a significant shift in their leisure and sport opportunities. Moving away from the parents and seeking to establish their own family with children also tends to reduce sport opportunities, and leisure time shifts from participating in sport to being spectators at their children's sporting events. Success in developing these newly formed intimate relationships further strengthens the bonds, whereas continued failure in relationship development often leads to social isolation and separation.

By this age, participants who were successful in sport in their younger years have developed sport identities and are seeking continued opportunities to express these identities in familiar ways, such as being involved in the local adult sport league. In some instances, people who were unsuccessful in sport in the adolescent years are willing to return to recreational sport for relationship development and opportunity when programming encourages socialization rather than strictly emphasizing winning. For the early young adult, programs could encourage team formation such as running a group marathon so individuals within the team can continue to build significant relationships. Programs should also recognize the need to foster the significant relationships through coed leagues or opportunities that include participants' children, such as daddy–daughter playtime or mommy-and-me swim times. In addition, participation times should be considered for families and activities, such as a 3K family walking event on the weekend or adult leagues that take place after work or during lunch.

Middle Adulthood (35-60 Years)

People in this stage are well established in their relationships as well as their jobs and want to continue to work toward making both family and work successful. They are also beginning to consider new opportunities such as volunteering or creating something that will outlast them, such as legacy development. This legacy could be in the form of physical structures or buildings but more likely is displayed through program contributions and planning, such as sitting on the local sport board or coaching a team so as to have an impact on the next generation. Success tends to lead to feelings of accomplishment, while failure or even the status quo leads to feelings of a life unfulfilled.

At this stage, participation in organized team sport continues to decline; however, participation in individual sport can remain constant or even increase. Thus, activities such as running, swimming, skiing, and bowling that allow for informal sport opportunities tend to be most prominent. A midlife crisis might also lead to exploration of new sport activities and outdoor pursuits such as fishing or canoeing (Harder, 2002).

Late Adulthood (60-Death)

For most adults, this stage is a time for reflection on their place in the world as well as their accomplishments. They are typically experiencing retirement from work, and the emergence of grandchildren may bring a new sense of legacy development and the passing on of life lessons and wisdom to those around them. Interestingly, adult participation in recreational sport in this stage is growing rapidly. With a greater emphasis being placed on healthy lifestyles and active participation, recreational sport programs are expanding their opportunities for the older adult. Sport programs should focus on social opportunities; for instance, bowling, golf, and curling provide not only physical activity but also a social component with other participants. In the later stages of late adulthood, recognizing the need for transportation will become important. Additionally, older adults may be experiencing the loss of a spouse or friends, and the companionship that sport programs can provide is a valuable opportunity to get people out of their homes and active.

Figure 3.2 illustrates participation rates by age group in the United States. It is clear that school age and adolescence are the two groups that participate in recreational sport most often.

DEMOGRAPHICS

The following sections describe a host of demographic considerations that a recreational sport professional should consider when it comes to programming. Each population group is briefly described and then an example of how a professional might accommodate the specific population is provided.

Disability

The ADA defines a person with a disability as follows: "An individual with a disability is a person

Recreational sport programming for senior adults should take into account the physical and psychosocial needs of this age group. Activities like disc golf enable seniors to stay active while providing needed social opportunities.

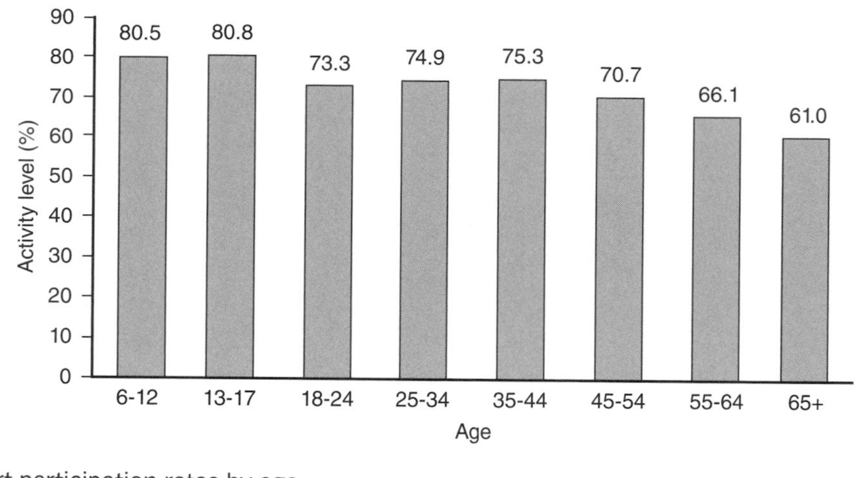

Figure 3.2 Sport participation rates by age.

From Sports and Fitness Industry Association, 2013, *Sports, fitness and leisure activities topline participation report.*

who: (1) has a physical or mental impairment that substantially limits one or more major life activities; OR (2) has a record of such an impairment; OR (3) is regarded as having such an impairment" (ADA.gov). As such, the term *disability* has the potential to encompass a rather large group of people, such as those with mental illness, cerebral palsy, or traumatic brain injury. This definition also includes people whom most would recognize as having a disability, such as a person who has had a limb amputated or uses a wheelchair. Regardless of the disability, recreational sport programmers must be prepared to offer the most appropriate level of accommodation possible to ensure the success of all participants involved in the program. Perhaps the most important factor to address when including people with disabilities in a program is that not everyone is the same. Each person with or without disabilities requires slightly different services and modifications in order to be successful. A good manager is able to recognize this and make the necessary changes to a program. If you have this attitude toward program modification, then it does not matter whether someone with a disability is in your program because each modification to your program will encourage success.

Having an understanding of the most common forms of disability gives recreational sport professionals the greatest likelihood of making successful modifications. The most common categories of disability tend to be physical impairments, cognitive impairments, hearing and visual impairments, learning disabilities, speech and language impairments, traumatic brain injuries, and autism. This is certainly not an exhaustive list of disabilities but rather a list of general categories of disabilities that recreational sport professionals are likely to encounter. In addition, not every disability occurs in isolation and certainly a person can have multiple disabilities, each of which may manifest differently from person to person or even within the same person from day to day. The important part of working with people with disabilities is to recognize that each person is unique and modifications should be as well.

There is clear evidence that people with disabilities tend to be much less active in sport and recreation compared with people without disabilities (www.collegesportsscholarships.com/disabled-children-sports.htm, n.d.) For example, 53 percent of people with disabilities in Australia were active in sport-related activities compared with 68 percent of people without disabilities. Within the United States, estimates place participation by young people with disabilities in sport at about 56 percent compared with almost 90 percent participation by young people without disabilities (Centers for Disease Control and Prevention [CDC], 2014).

More and more recreational sport agencies around the United States have been providing adaptive sport opportunities such as wheelchair basketball or visually impaired soccer. Clearly they are meeting a need within their communities, and once word spreads about such programs, they tend to be well attended and successful.

Race

Race is a socially defined phenomenon that categorizes a group of people who have similarities

© Skye Arthur-Banning

Many athletes with disabilities like this hand-cyclist compete at the highest levels of their sport. Providing and promoting disabled sport opportunities can increase health, encourage social interaction, and break down stereotypes.

that are largely based on biological traits such as eye shape, body type, skin color, and so on. For example, the U.S. Census in 2010 listed several categories of race: white, black, American Indian and Alaskan Native, Asian, Native Hawaiian or other Pacific Islander, Hispanic or Latino origin, those reporting more than one race, and other race not listed.

It is difficult to get a sense of how to modify and adapt programs for various races. Each state and even community has a socially constructed view of which races should be involved in which sports and activities. In the United States, it is clear that blacks make up a significant proportion of the basketball population while whites make up a great percentage of hockey participants. The way to encourage diversity in recreational sport is by reaching out to nontraditional participants.

Religion

Religious demographics worldwide have changed little over the last 10 years, but within the United States they have evolved much more as a result of immigration. Due to this melting pot of people moving to communities (see figure 3.3), it is important to understand the variety of religions that exist and the vast array of beliefs and behaviors associated with each religion.

Only some religions use Sunday as a special day of rest, while others believe that Saturday should be held sacred. Nonetheless, the most important thing from a recreational sport perspective is to gain an understanding of the community or region you are working in and seek to accommodate as many potential participants as possible. In the case study at the beginning of the chapter, the program was not working to accommodate a larger population because it didn't offer activities on Sunday. A greater understanding of the participants within the community and seeking to work with all of the groups would be a more beneficial model to follow.

Similarly, rules and regulations such as permitted clothing or jewelry need to be considered as they relate to religion. Certainly safety concerns should be the most important factor in any sport; however, programmers often hide under the umbrella of safety when they are afraid to tackle the religious differences being presented. For example, FIFA, the international governing body of soccer, recently clarified that turbans,

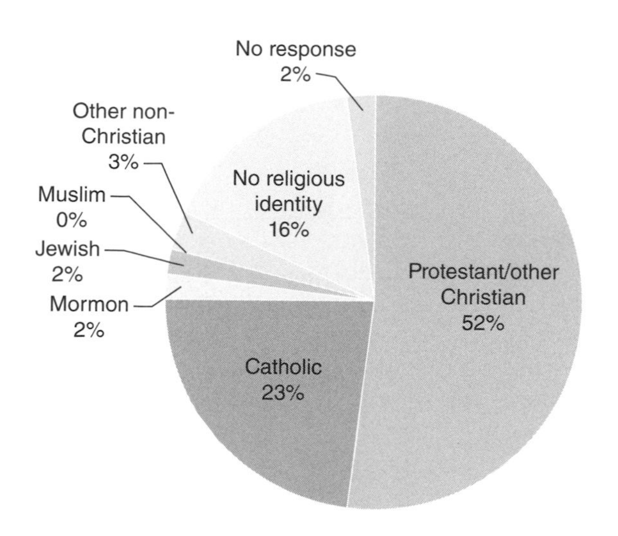

Figure 3.3 The great melting pot of religions in the United States.

a common headdress for males in the Sikh and Muslim communities, and hijabs, commonly worn by Muslim women, are both acceptable parts of the uniform in a soccer match (FIFA, 2013). Obviously FIFA has recognized the need to address religious differences so that all participants can be equally involved in the sport a safe way. Typically the international federation, in this case FIFA, makes a decision, and then it is up to community organizations and agencies to figure out how to best implement the decision within their own programs.

Sex

Sex typically refers to the physical characteristics normally associated with men and women, such as their reproductive organs or physical features. The difficulty in sport is that a variety of **stereotypes** tend get reinforced in a negative way through programming and advertising. For example, figure skating tends to be viewed as a female activity, and therefore many programs focus their marketing efforts on the female population even though many males might be interested if it were not for the stereotypes associated with the sport. Similarly, an activity such as rugby is typically male dominated, and yet there is a growing population of female rugby players who could help build a rugby program at a local sport venue. As these two examples show, recreational sport managers need to be aware of the social parameters placed upon a sport and recruit nontraditional participants to their programs.

Social Class

In Western society, *social class* typically refers to a group of people with similar economic circumstances; however, it could also be related to their social status or the circle of acquaintances they are most closely associated with. Though many sports require little to no financial resources other than inexpensive equipment such as a soccer ball, in order to excel in most sports in North America, participants need significant financial resources and support. For example, a soccer ball can be purchased at a local sport store for somewhere around $20 and a group of adolescents could play in a local park for virtually no cost. For a participant to play in a highly skilled league that travels and participates in various tournaments, however, costs may approach $8,000 to $10,000 per year. This is a figure that clearly is not for the average sport participant, but college coaches and recruiting groups attend these elite tournaments. Thus, athletes often must make such a financial commitment if they want to be recruited.

In addition to the increasing costs of organized sport, opportunities for local recreational sport diminish as children age. This creates a barrier to participation, which then leads to an increased dropout rate at the age when adolescents are most in need of organized sport opportunities (Blodgett et al., 2008). Recreational sport programmers need to remember to provide recreational sport opportunities that meet the needs of people of all social statuses within their communities.

Interestingly, sport participation by sex tends to change with social class (Hasbrook, 1986; Women's Sports Foundation, 2008). For young males, there appears to be little distinction in participation rates by social class in that young males in upper, middle, and lower social classes participate at approximately the same rates. However, females in lower social classes tend to participate in sport less. Essentially, boys tend to participate in sport, organized or not, regardless of income level, and girls participate in sport at decreasing levels as social status decreases.

Finally, although sport has a way of defining social class, it also has a way of leveling differences in class discrepancies if programmed correctly. A sport such as soccer requires relatively little equipment beyond the ball, so by simply providing opportunity to all social classes, a program can involve participants from a multitude of economic backgrounds. Keep in mind that accessories such as sport-specific shoes and clothing can still distinguish one social class from another, and a program seeking true invisibility in social class needs to consider how to address such inequities.

CONSTRAINTS ON PARTICIPATION

Each community has its own unique makeup of diverse people with their own needs and desires. Each participant in a community will encounter a variety of constraints that can make participation difficult or even prevent it altogether. As such, it is important for recreational sport professionals to understand the types of constraints people experience so that they can help participants negotiate through them.

A **constraint** is "any factor which limits an individual's frequency, intensity, duration, or quality of participation in recreation activities" (Ellis & Rademacher, 1986, p. 18). Although many of these constraints are imposed by society or self-imposed by the participant, many are also reinforced by recreational sport professionals through their programming, marketing, language, or actions. Several types of constraints should be considered, including attitudinal, consumptive, communication, economic, temporal, health, experience, social and cultural, leisure values and skills, and environmental.

- **Attitudinal.** These constraints are related to the mind and attitude of the individual. They are often associated with constraints that relate to cultural or social norms. For example, many Middle Eastern cultures believe that women should not participate in sporting events because of religious beliefs or because of the attitude that women should be the primary care providers and therefore should not be wasting time with sport. Most Western nations do not share this view of sport participation; however, it can still be a constraint on people from these cultures even when they are living in Western countries.
- **Consumptive.** A consumptive constraint typically occurs when a person is unable to find a healthy balance between leisure and work. On one end of the spectrum are people who are so busy with their work schedule that they have little time for leisure, and on the other end are people who are so involved in their leisure that they ignore their work obligations or fail to see the true value of leisure.
- **Communication.** In the case of communication constraints, people lack the necessary knowledge to make informed decisions about leisure. This could manifest in multiple ways, from information being written in a language that is not understood to information being presented in a format that is not easily available, such as exclusively online registration when some participants may not have access to the Internet. In the case of someone with a disability, it could be information presented in a format that is not accessible. Finally, some people might be overwhelmed by all of the information and might not be able to process all the choices available. For example, this could occur when a flier is too cluttered or when an overload of information is presented upon completion of an instructional class.
- **Economic.** The ability to pay for sport and leisure services has a strong influence on the activities that participants choose. Sports such as downhill skiing or hockey have always been relatively expensive. Sports such as soccer or basketball were once thought of as affordable sports for all; however, at the highest levels of competition this has dramatically changed with traveling teams, equipment, and training requirements as well as coaches' salaries, facility rentals, and referee costs. In some cases, participants can't afford the program.
- **Temporal.** This constraint is based not only on participants' actual available free time but also their perception of free time that they can use for sport and leisure. Some people seem to be able to make time for sporting events either as participants or as spectators, while others seem to never have enough time, pushing sporting activities to the bottom of the agenda. This could simply be an issue of poor time management, or it could be caused by reduced time to participate in sport due to the demands of family, school, work, and other community activities.
- **Health.** Mental and physical abilities can have a large impact on the ability to engage in sport and recreation. They might have an impact on mobility in an activity, the ability to comprehend the rules or safety measures of a sporting

event, or the ability to derive enjoyment from a sporting activity because of negative experiences caused by poor health. For example, a person who has become more obese as a result of an injury may not be able to perform at the same level as before the injury.

- **Experience.** This constraint is related to the experiences a person has had or witnessed. If people have had a negative experience in a sport setting, their desire to participate is significantly reduced. However, the experience constraint could also be related to the lack of experience or opportunity someone has had in a particular activity. For example, up until recently, the lower classes were discouraged from or could not afford playing on golf courses. Although this social norm has virtually been eliminated through programs such as The First Tee and an increase in community golf courses, novice players may still feel intimidated to play at a club where they might be compared with people who have much more experience or where they fear they will be mocked for not being as skilled.

- **Social and cultural.** This is perhaps the most frequent constraint to recreational sport participation because the social norms or culture of an agency, activity, or sport are difficult to change without methodical, intentional planning. For example, historically, American football has had social norms for what position players typically play, such as having a white quarterback and a black running back and although there are many excellent players who have overcome this social constraint, the predominant norms continue to exist in many parts of the game. The same can be said for participation in hockey, basketball, or tennis, and it is only through continued examples of players who break down the social norms of participation that those norms begin to change. Jackie Robinson in baseball and Tiger Woods in golf are excellent examples of how one person at higher levels of play can help young people overcome social and cultural constraints by being role models for young people to follow.

- **Leisure value and skills.** People who lack the skills necessary for success or perceive they lack the skills may restrict their involvement in a sporting activity. Similarly, people who lack confidence in their ability as a result of failed experiences in the past are also likely to limit their involvement in a sporting activity, especially at the more advanced levels. If someone perceives that she does not possess the skills necessary to perform a sport in a successful way, she is much more likely to withdraw from the activity to avoid making a fool of herself.

- **Environmental.** A lack of sport facilities, areas, structures, fields, or other resources in communities might restrict involvement in an activity. It would obviously be difficult to participate in an ice-hockey game if the nearest skating rink were two hours away. Even if a facility or field is near, if it is not easily accessible because it is fenced in or because the terrain is difficult for people who are less mobile, it is an environmental constraint. Finally, a facility that has the wheelchair ramp at the back door or in an area separate from the main entrance sends the message that the environment is less accepting of people with disabilities.

Each of these constraints can stand alone as a barrier to involvement in a sport program, but more often than not there are multiple constraints that act in unison to prevent or reduce participation. It should be the goal of recreational sport managers to recognize the possible constraints on their programs and to make every possible effort to accommodate and modify programs in order to encourage participation and assist people in their ability to negotiate constraints.

PROGRAMMING CONSIDERATIONS

When addressing diversity in recreational sport, there are several factors to consider in order to most efficiently meet the needs of the community or organization. Understanding your population and social environment; understanding who you are marketing to; having appropriate mentors, role models, and coaches; being intentional in programming; making changes in space, rules, time considerations, and equipment; and including quality program animation all lead to more successful program modifications and ultimately a more enjoyable program for all.

Population

Now that you have gone through the chapter and identified various population types by age, social class, and so on, it should be clear that understanding the population you are working with has a profound impact on the types of programs and modifications that are needed. What one person may need to be successful in a sport may actually constrain another. The key to a successful program for all is listening to the needs of each person and making the necessary modifications. A needs assessment might be the most efficient way of determining the population and needs within the program.

In all situations, providing a least restrictive environment is likely going to be the most successful angle to take on a program. A least restrictive environment is one that uses modifications to provide the greatest success for all participants. For example, if a person in a wheelchair shows up to a youth tennis program, certainly modifications can be made to ensure success for that person, such as simply allowing the ball to bounce twice for that participant. This might also be a good modification for many of the beginning tennis players to ensure their success in the sport. In this case, a two-bounce rule would not restrict participation for anyone and would encourage success. However, should that same participant in a wheelchair arrive at a tennis program for advanced tennis players, a two-bounce rule might restrict the other players' success in the sport, so only making that modification for that particular person would set up a least restrictive environment for the whole group.

Going back to the case study at the beginning of the chapter, understanding that there is more than one religious group in the community would allow recreational sport programmers to make unique modifications or programming considerations to encourage the greatest degree of participation. For example, they might offer both a Saturday and a Sunday league.

Social Environment

Just as the environment is a socially constructed phenomenon, so is the acceptance of multiple groups of people within an activity. An organization needs to make a conscious effort to create an environment where acceptance of multiple groups is expected and encouraged (Nathan, Kemp, Bunde-Birouste, MacKenzie, Evers, & Tun, 2013). In addition, there must be an acceptance of differences, and administrators should encourage people from a particular group to go outside their comfort zone and try a sport that may not fit their traditional model of participation.

Marketing

Program marketing sends a significant message to potential participants. For example, if a black child sees all white children on the pictures of a marketing flier for a baseball league, there is little incentive for that child to make a social connection to the advertisement. However, if there are examples of children that he can easily relate to in terms of race, it may be much easier for him to consider participating in the activity. Similarly, providing programs that are inclusive of people with disabilities can be a great opportunity, but unless a program intentionally promotes the inclusiveness of the activity, such as through marketing pictures, participants may not consider the program as an option.

Mentors and Role Models

One of the keys to a diverse program is having a mentor or series of mentors to look up to as a goal of achievement. This might well be you as the programmer or someone in your agency acting as a face for the program, but it might also be external role models who provide exposure to the sport and someone to look up to. For example, when the Williams sisters began winning multiple tennis tournaments on the international level, it provided young black women with a picture of the possibility that they, too, could participate in tennis. More recently, Jeremy Lin, one of the first prominent Asian Americans to be successful in the NBA, has opened the door for a new group of players at the youth levels. As a recreational sport manager, highlighting these examples and perhaps finding local examples within the community to be involved in a program would provide children with someone they can relate to. Similarly, bringing a local Paralympian to the program for a day or promoting The First Tee as a way for inner-city kids to participate in a traditionally upper-class sporting activity could encourage a more diverse group of participants.

Coaching

Ideally, each sport organization has the ability to hire a diverse group of coaches for its leagues; however, this is not always the case. It might take going to a local community center or church to recruit a coach willing to serve as a role model to the kids in that particular sport. Similarly,

Volunteer coaches have the potential to be powerful role models for youth, and are often strong ambassadors in promoting their sport.

there may be someone who played hockey at a high level in the area who could act almost as a spokesperson in the community to attract more youth to a hockey program.

Intentionality

The intentionality of programming ultimately determines success more than anything else. If your program is being run simply because it was run last year or because it is done this way at the professional level, you almost certainly are setting it up for failure. A good recreational sport program is designed with intent and goals in mind before the teams even start to practice. Simply rolling the ball out does not mean the intended program outcomes will just happen. Each and every aspect of the program must be considered, from registration to pregame meetings to officials' involvement in the league to how parents are situated within the environment to postgame activities.

Environment

Modifying the environment can have a profound impact on the program and its outcomes. For example, sports such as soccer and tennis have significantly reduced the playing surface for young participants to allow them to have more opportunities to play the ball and reduce the amount of open space. This encourages the young athletes to play the ball more frequently and allows for increased skill development in close quarters. Similarly, a person with autism is likely going to be much more successful when excessive noise is kept to a minimum, so activities such as golf or tennis might be good environments for participation.

Rules

Sometimes people do not feel they are playing a sport if they are not using all of the equipment they see on TV. Parents are skeptical when modifications are put in place, and young athletes want to pretend they are doing what the professionals are doing. However, this is a harmful attitude, especially for young participants. Pitching counts are put in place to encourage the healthy development of a young baseball player's arm, for example, but if a 12-year-old is playing on several teams, injuries still are likely to occur unless a parent or guardian keeps track of the pitches with each team.

Recreational sport programmers should not worry that rule modifications harm the purity of the game as long as the changes help participants achieve the mission and goals of the league. Pressure may come from the sport purists; however, programmers have to believe in the value of their mission and goals and stick with the rule modifications as designed.

Time

Most leagues are good about recognizing that time can be modified to fit the programming structure of the organization or to accommodate more games in a tournament. In recreational sport, most participants want to experience the game environment, socialize with friends, and engage in a competitive activity. They often are not as interested in a full 90 minutes of soccer or five sets of tennis. Equally good experiences can be had in a 70-minute soccer match or in three sets of tennis, which require less time to complete. Obviously, the younger the age, the less amount of time a sporting activity should be simply because the participants' attention span and cardiorespiratory ability are more limited. On the other hand, people with disabilities may need more time to complete a task or practice a skill, so modifications can also be made to increase time.

Equipment

With the continued advancement of equipment and modification, sport is becoming more and more possible for all. Amy Purdy, a double amputee and Paralympic snowboarder, is a prime example of how equipment and modern science can provide opportunity to a diverse population of people. Many more examples are evident in recreation programs around the United States, such as ramps and bumpers for bowling or the entire sport of tee ball, which is based on modifying equipment to encourage success.

Animation

Animation refers to events or actions that bring an otherwise average activity to life. With respect to diversity and inclusion, animation provides energy and excitement as almost a value-added component to the sporting event. The most important aspect of animation as it relates to diversity is to recognize that various races and cultures might celebrate or animate differently, and accommodations should be made for each unique animation component as long as it is consistent in meeting the overall goals of the program. For instance, local Latino leagues often do a great job of animating their recreational sporting events by providing music, food, and flags from the various countries of the participants and having team jerseys in the colors of the countries' flags. See chapter 4 for a more in-depth discussion on animation.

CONCLUSION

Sport has the ability to bridge gaps in language, culture, religion, and understanding. However, none of these gaps can be bridged if diversity in programs is not encouraged. More importantly, if modifications are not made to ensure the success of each participant, programs will be one-dimensional and will not be representative of the entire population that a recreational sport manager is charged with serving. Recognizing that various ages, races, abilities, social classes, and sexes may need something slightly different in your program is an important component of recreation sport management. The ability to modify activities and programs to accommodate this diversity will ensure sport for all in its truest sense, where no one is excluded and opportunities exist for every member in the community.

RESEARCH TO REALITY

Allen, J.T., Drane, D.D., Byon, K.K., & Mohn, R.S. (2010). Sport as a vehicle for socialization and maintenance of cultural identity: International students attending American universities. *Sports Management Review, 13,* 421-434.

Allen and his coauthors sought to determine if sport provided for cultural identity, increased socialization, and increased ability to adapt in multicultural environments. This is becoming increasingly important as immigrants move into communities and change the demographics. Community centers and sport leagues are increasingly pressured to design new programs and integrate all cultures. The research determined that sport certainly has the ability to assist immigrants in adapting to the multicultural environments that surround them, largely through participation in sports that they were familiar with in their country of origin. For example, participants from Latin America and Europe played soccer most frequently, while participants from Asian countries enjoyed sports such as badminton. Interestingly, males saw sport as a better mechanism to acculturate to the new environment than females did.

This research provides recreational sport administrators with a very real example of the importance of their facilities and programs for all members of the community. It is the commonality of sport that makes the international student or new immigrant feel more comfortable and welcome in the community. It is equally necessary to recognize the sex and country-of-origin differences in sport selection, identification, and importance, and recreational sport professionals should seek to understand and accommodate the differences within the facilities or programs that they are running.

REFLECTION QUESTIONS

1. What populations are most prominent in your community, and how do you get information to them? Perhaps more importantly, what populations attend your facility or enroll in your programs, and what populations are being neglected? How do you then work to involve all populations?
2. What parts of a program do you modify to best accommodate people of all abilities and skills? How might those modifications assist in including people with disabilities while also benefiting people without disabilities?
3. If school groups from around the county visit your facility on a regular basis to use your pool for high school swim meets, what modifications and parts of legislation do you need to be most concerned with?

LEARNING ACTIVITIES

1. Your facility is hosting a high school track meet that more than 500 kids will participate in. You learn from one of the school organizers that the meet also hosts a wheelchair 400-meter event. What constraints do you need to consider before the day of the event?
2. Your facility hosts a weekly curling event for seniors and has been approached by a group of teens wanting to learn the sport. How do you work to integrate the two populations of participants into one cohesive program?

COMPETENCIES OF RECREATIONAL SPORT PROFESSIONALS

chapter 4

RECREATIONAL SPORT PROGRAM PLANNING

LEARNING OUTCOMES

By the end of this chapter, readers will be able to

- explain the steps necessary for successful recreational sport programming,
- identify how events can fit within the scope of programs,
- recognize the components that can enhance a program or event, and
- explain the importance of evaluation in a program.

Case Study

RECREATIONAL SPORT PROGRAMMING ON A SHOESTRING

McKinley has just graduated with a degree in park and recreation management and has recently accepted a position at a local park and recreation agency as a recreation programmer. The agency is fairly new, and the expanding community is looking for it to spearhead various programs that will bring the community together. McKinley is a new member of the community herself, and although she has a little knowledge of the population, facilities, and programs, she has virtually no knowledge of the wants and needs of the community. The expectation is that she organize, plan, and provide a series of sport programs and events to bring the community closer together.

Because this is a new position in a new facility, there is no manual of what has been done in the past; however, McKinley was involved in many sport leagues growing up, and she always knew there was something more to making programs successful than simply throwing a ball out for kids to play with. Making the challenge even more difficult, her supervisor has given her a small budget and has requested that she make the program as self-sustaining as possible.

The difficulty is that in most cases, the modern vision of recreation programming is not simply organizing leagues and tournaments but also coordinating with various community agencies. McKinley spends the first two weeks simply taking inventory of all the possible partnerships that might be available to her, including the obvious agencies, such as the other recreation or sport agencies in the area, the local gym and pools, and the various referee and community sport groups that are user groups of the previous facilities or that wish to expand. These connections are easy and make sense. However, McKinley finds that the less obvious connections within the community that might assist with programming are more difficult to connect with initially.

She approaches the local hospital system to discuss sponsorship possibilities as well as opportunities for health days or expanding the reach of the hospital to a more community-based model of rehabilitation. The hospital suggests she start an Alcoholics Anonymous group a few times a week in the facilities' meeting rooms to fill a major gap in the health of the community.

The local convention and visitor's bureau sees the potential for bigger tournaments and events hosted by the city with the new facility, and getting the additional out-of-town visitors for five or six events a year would generate large amounts of revenue for the city and the facility. Many of the local restaurants and hotels are certainly interested in this as well and are happy to provide their low periods for McKinley to consider when scheduling and seeking to attract out-of-town visitors. Many of the hotels even offer part of their marketing budget to assist in the tournament organization.

McKinley finishes by approaching the various education partners in the area. The obvious connection with children in programming is there, but several teachers also talk to her about offering more adult programs and programs for children with disabilities, a need that has grown as more families have moved into the growing community. Finally, McKinley contacts a few professors at the local universities to talk about possible internships, volunteers, and student service learning opportunities as well as the potential for evaluation and research. McKinley knows that she has the population and the professors have the knowledge of research, so bringing those two assets together could be a great connection. She also knows that as she expands programs and opportunities, grant writing will become even more critical, and having a university partnership to assist in the process will be mutually beneficial.

All in all, what started out as an exciting new job within a growing community has exploded into not just recreation programming but also community involvement, partnerships, and fund-raising in the interest of providing the most accessible, affordable, and exciting programs in the area.

The scenario in the opening case study is one that young graduates face on a regular basis. They move to a new community where the energy and excitement of a new job in a new building with new coworkers is exciting, and then the reality of the job hits them. McKinley needs to plan and implement a series of programs that are designed to keep hundreds of people active and engaged within the community, all in an innovative and cost-effective way. This is a daunting task to say the least, so searching out the best resources and people to assist her is of the utmost importance.

Planning, conducting, and evaluating programs is the most important function of the recreational sport profession. This chapter focuses on the fundamental aspects of programming, including assessing the needs of the target population and understanding the philosophical foundation of the sport organization. Based on the results of these initial steps, program outcomes are defined and programs are designed. Implementing and conducting the program involves actual delivery as well as management of the operational details. Most programmers would agree that this step is the most time consuming of the programming cycle. Evaluating the program throughout or at its completion assists the recreational sport professional in determining the future of the program in terms of continuing to offer it, modifying particular aspects, or terminating it.

PROGRAMMING PHILOSOPHIES

Before beginning to plan a program, it is important to have a solid understanding of why the program exists. Organizations should have defined how they are going to operate within the community, what role they are choosing to play within the community, and how that role is designed to improve the lives of people within the community. Particularly in recreational sport programs, organizations are likely to highlight their emphasis on participation, healthy competition, and enjoyment.

Similarly, the community will have an idea of the philosophy of the recreational sport program. It may be to provide adequate facilities, to facilitate affordable programs, or to provide a safe environment for children to participate in. The problem is that sometimes the philosophy of the agency is not consistent with the philosophy of the residents that it is serving.

Why People Choose a Program

With the multitude of programs available in every state and town, understanding why a participant might choose one program over another is important. For example, when it comes to selecting a hockey program, the facilities, the instructor's ability, the customer service, the coach's approach to the sport, the winning percentage, and the cost can all play a role in swaying one participant from program A to program B. Perhaps most important, though, are the mission and philosophy of a program and how those foundational components of a program are expressed in the overall planning of the activities.

More specifically, in the recreational sport setting, there is a move for programs to attempt to distinguish themselves as either recreational or competitive. The benefit is that participants can then make an informed decision about the nature and level of competition they desire in a program as well as the costs and amount of travel and time they want to invest in the activity. The drawback to this type of philosophical approach and subsequent programming is the misperception that *competitive* means less sportsmanship and youth development and *recreational* means less skill development and less talented participants.

A recreational sport program can have a philosophy that is extremely competitive and also focuses on skill development and high-level talent. It might simply involve less travel, have shorter seasons, or be more game oriented so participants only have to devote two or three days a week to the sport. Similarly, an elite program can focus on training at a high level but also on youth development, ethical behavior in the activity, respect for opponents, physical fitness, and lifelong fitness behaviors.

This is one example of how a program philosophy (elite or recreational) might attract or detract from a participant's desire to be involved. Clearly, it is critical for recreational sport professionals to clearly define the philosophy of a program. A program that clearly defines what it philosophically represents is much more likely to be successful because it is going to attract participants who more closely align with the philosophy of the organization to begin with.

Program Design

There are three types of program designs that might attract or push participants away from a particular sport program. In the first design, often referred to as the **blended program**, a variety of offerings are presented within a specific sport league. For example, in a basketball program there might be pickup times, recreational and elite leagues, coaching and training sessions, and various tournament offerings within each of the leagues or even a small-sided tournament such as 3 on 3. The major benefit of the blended design structure is that it offers a variety of programs for a large population in an effort to meet the needs of constituents. However, a negative of the blended program tends to be quality. If an agency is running a variety of programs over the course of a season, it becomes difficult and potentially expensive to run each program well.

The second design type is often referred to as the **targeted program**, in which a facility focuses on a limited type or number of programs. For example, a facility may choose to run an elite basketball league with a few traveling teams for each age group and then offer pickup basketball. With fewer demands being placed on the facilities, coaches, and financial resources, it is much easier to focus on the one or two types of programs being run and to do them well. Because few programs are being organized, the staffing and financial resources could be closely targeted and the few leagues would be run well. However, the drawback is that the narrow offering of programs targets only one type of participant, therefore limiting the number of customers served.

A third type of program is a **tiered program**, where people can join a variety of activities at multiple levels of participation with the intent of progressing from one level to the next. In the base or introductory level, participants get a sense of the activity, rules, equipment, and so on for a short amount of time without having to commit to an entire season or spend a lot of money. Programs might provide rental equipment or instructional classes to allow participants an opportunity to experiment with the activity. The most important aspect of a tiered program is that participants can see a clear progression through the programs from one tier to the next, allowing them to make progressive decisions about their commitment to the programs.

For example, a learn-to-skate program might be offered once a week for five weeks with skate rentals provided. In the midlevel program, various

This learn-to-skate program is an example of a tiered program, where people can progress through various stages based on their skill and competence.

After progressing through an instructional skate program, participants might join a city-wide hockey league.

Michael Chamberlin/fotolia.com

A top-tier program might involve participants in a competitive travel ice hockey program. This is an example of a progression for someone whose hockey skills increased through participating in a variety of lower-tiered recreational sport programs.

recreational or drop-in opportunities might be scheduled to allow participants to progress up the tier of involvement and activity. Activities at this level might include an introductory program for hockey or figure skating. Participants who took the learn-to-skate program and are looking for ways to get more involved in skating can therefore progress up the tier of participation from less investment to progressively greater investment. The top tier would then be the leagues or competition in hockey or figure skating, and even within this tier there could be multileveled participation. One could enter the top tier in a recreational hockey league, a local city league, or a traveling league, which require increasing amounts of commitment, time, costs, and resources.

PROGRAMMING COMPONENTS

Having determined the philosophy and design of the program, a recreational sport professional can begin to consider the components of the program itself. The following seven steps are designed to build on one another to foster a sense of cohesion and unity within a program while directly representing the overall philosophy of the organization.

Step 1: Needs Assessment

Many professionals new to the field might ask, "Why should we conduct a needs assessment? The game of basketball has not changed over the years, so why would we need to make any changes to our leagues or programs?" The simple answer is that the population in the area and the expectations of the participants may have changed, the equipment almost certainly has changed, and the way parents, players, and administrators interact has changed as well. The most important reason to do a needs assessment is that things change, as they should. This is how a program of any kind continues to improve. An agency must not believe that because programs have been run a certain way for 10 years, it must mean that is the best way to run them; this mentality simply supports a stagnant environment. Constant changes, even small ones, can continue to improve the programs and events that you organize and draw new participants to your facility.

An effective needs assessment typically consists of six steps.

- Write the objectives. Solid assessment objectives will keep it on track and prevent extraneous information from creeping into the analysis.
- Determine the populations you wish to address.
- Select the tools to use. Often a needs assessment is a combination of collecting historical documents (previous program registration numbers, for example); communicating with important stakeholders through interviews, focus groups, and questionnaires; and gathering information on current situational variables such as budgets, staffing charts, and community supports and their roles.
- Collect the data. Organized collection methods and the time frame in which the data need to be collected are important to keep the results current and accurate.
- Analyze the data. This involves comprehensive analysis of the collected material. Multiple people within the agency often help with this step so that multiple aspects are covered.
- Create an action plan. An assessment is useless unless it is followed by action. The most frustrating component for stakeholders is being asked for their input in an assessment but not seeing any results. Even if nothing is going to be changed, it is helpful to explain the reasons why.

What to Assess

Typically there are four or five components to consider when conducting a needs assessment. These vary based on the goals and mission of the program; however, each factor should be considered to some degree in the assessment. The five most common components of the needs assessment are the social, economic, cultural, political, and targeted factors.

1. Social factors might seek to answer how easily people are making connections in the recreational sport program, how supportive the community is of the program, or to what degree the program promotes social connections beyond the walls of the facility.
2. Economic factors could address the simple costs of the program, how those costs are excluding participants or social groups, or the economic impact of events.
3. Cultural factors might look at when the program is being run, for example, and whether offering a program on Sunday morning or Wednesday evening excludes people who might be interested in a specific program or sporting event.
4. Political factors might seek to determine the effectiveness of the board of directors or how participants are assigned to teams. Recreational sport programmers who have been involved in a draft of sorts for determining participants in a community sport league know just how political the process can become.

5. Finally, a targeted assessment might address a specific component of the needs assessment, such as the need for officiating changes or a partnership that has been proposed. This component could include almost anything that the organization wants answered through the assessment that does not fit in any of the general factors.

Whom to Assess

When doing a needs assessment, there are several populations to consider. Certainly the populations you intend to serve need to be consulted with respect to their expectations, their interests, and their level of commitment; however, there are many other factors to consider as well. It would be helpful to determine why some participants might not be interested, so getting a sense of the needs of the uninterested population could be helpful if program growth is a goal. Staff members are often a neglected population who should be consulted in a complete needs assessment. They likely have the best sense of the equipment, program history, staffing needs, level of interest, benefits or pitfalls of the program, and so on.

Other stakeholders in the program should also be involved in the assessment. For instance, the board of directors or sponsors could take part in the process to help determine needs as well as the ability to fulfill those needs from within the program.

Assessment Approach

How the agency chooses to approach the needs assessment could have an impact on the types of answers that are recorded. Similarly, understanding the approach of stakeholders provides context for the responses to the assessment. For example, an agency that needs to determine what makes its programs more competitive to its customers might want to do a comparative needs assessment, whereas an agency that needs to determine how its programs fit with professional standards of practice would require the professional approach. The three most common approaches to a needs assessment are the comparative needs approach, the professional needs approach, and the participant needs approach (Mull, Bayless, & Jamieson, 2005).

Comparative Needs Approach

In the recreational sport field, most participants and certainly the parents of young participants have been involved in or have seen a sport in some form or fashion before. This previous experience then provides for a comparison of programs. For example, a parent who was involved in a baseball league himself and now is enrolling his child in a league would expect things to be as good as or better than his experience some 25 or 30 years ago. Clearly, this challenge is a difficult one because recreational sport has come a long way in 25 years.

When it comes to recreational sport programming, the idea that the grass is always greener on the other side, or in this case at another facility, is a common perception that must be addressed. In doing so, it is crucial to refer to the mission and philosophy of the organization and be able to articulate what strengths the program brings to the community. This also allows recreational sport programmers to understand the types of improvements that community members are looking for in a program while analyzing whether the organization can offer such a program. There are times when a referral to another organization that offers other opportunities is what is best for both participant and program.

Professional Needs Approach

A professional need, sometimes referred to as a *standards need*, is one in which a professional organization has a professional standard in place in order to provide certification, issue insurance, meet building codes, or determine the level of training that has taken place. Much in the same way a university requires students to obtain a certain number of credit hours or internship experiences in order to receive a degree, recreational sport agencies provide standards that must be met in order the maintain certification or accreditation. One such example might be the Professional Golfers' Association (PGA) of America, which has a professional standard that its golf pros need to meet in order to become Class A members. This professional standard is in place to ensure that a member representing the organization has an established level of knowledge and skills. Similarly, other organizations have standards that provide guidance about given criteria, such as the number of tennis courts per specific area or density of population. This encourages a healthy level of facility development and avoids overexpansion that would reduce the sustainability and capacity of each facility.

In recreational sport management, there are numerous coaching organizations that provide a professional standard to certify their coaches. An agency might suggest that its coaches achieve a certain level of professional certification in order to be able to coach. This tells participants that the coaches must have a specific level of training. Thus, a professional need can be either facility based, as in the case of the tennis courts, or program based, as in the coaching and golfing examples.

Participant Needs Approach

A participant need is one where participants believe they need a tool or resource from a program in order to be successful within it. So, instead of comparing two agencies or comparing a program against a professional standard, this approach looks directly to the participants for information regarding their direct and indirect needs within a program. Equipment and space could be assessed, as well as motivation, staffing, and scheduling as they relate to the participant experience.

An effective needs assessment should address the following:

- Impact—What impact does your program have within your facility, community, or state?
- Awareness—Who knows about your program and how did they find out? For those who know about it, what do they know? Do they know just the good aspects of your program or just the bad parts of it? Where are they getting their information?
- Credibility—Does the community believe in your program? Are you a leading organization in the community or one that drags the community down?
- Demand—Do you meet the needs of the community in not only programming but also location, staffing, and so on?
- Outlook—The assessment should provide information about the existing program that can be compared against program outcomes.

Step 2: Determining Goals and Objectives

Now that you've conducted a needs assessment of participants, staff, and stakeholders, you're ready to determine the goals and objectives of the program. This is often the most overlooked step because it is assumed that things like leadership and cooperation simply happen as a result of being involved in recreational sport. In reality such characteristics need to be planned for and specific goals and objectives must be aligned with various activities in order for the positive benefits to occur. However, writing good goals and objectives with the understanding of how they fit within your program's philosophy and mission is often a challenge.

Program or Participant Centered

The discussion that surrounds programming for outcomes often involves the top-down versus bottom-up model of development. Let's say an agency organized a baseball league under the assumption that the outcomes resulted from the kids participating in it. This would be considered a top-down or program-centered approach because the league was established as the priority and the outcomes appear to be secondary. More ideally, a bottom-up or participant-centered approach would be used so that the outcomes are the priority and the activity is the result. For example, if the needs assessment determines that the community needs a recreational sport for youth in the spring season that encourages socialization and participation, then a baseball league certainly could provide those outcomes with proper planning. The key difference is that in the top-down approach, the activity is placed first with the outcomes being secondary, whereas in the bottom-up approach, the outcomes are the foundation the activity is built upon, making it more outcome focused.

Similarly, most people believe that team sport is inherently social when in fact an ultracompetitive league can be alienating for those who are less skilled or less willing to be social, especially in the technological era that young people are growing up in today. However, if a get-together is planned after each match where all teams that played in the time slot are invited to a small social with refreshments, or if a team goes out together for pizza after a tournament, that league or team is much more likely to accomplish a more social agenda because that outcome is planned for.

A goal is important because it is the target that a programmer aims at in order to reach the desired outcome of the program. Another great way of looking at it is that the goal is the finish line of a race. Oftentimes in a longer race, a runner cannot see the finish line (goal), so instead she needs to find several more detailed ways to get to the end (objectives). An objective is a specific set of instructions or criteria that are measurable and behaviors that are easily observable. For example, our runner might say that she is going to run an eight-minute mile in the race to get to the finish line. This is a specific, measurable, and observable behavior that will help her accomplish her goal. Obviously, a runner can have more than one objective to help her accomplish her goal. A second objective might be that she is going to pick up at least one glass of liquid at each water station throughout the course of the race.

There are at least three types of objectives that can assist recreational sport programmers in accomplishing their goals.

1. *Behavioral objectives* are aimed at changing or guiding a specific behavior as well as the subsequent products of the behavior.
2. *Community-level objectives* are aimed at changing a group's behavior to achieve a desired outcome. In a team sport, for example, each person on the team might have a series of objectives to accomplish, but also it would be important to have team (community) objectives to accomplish the main goals of the program.
3. *Process objectives* are the system or series of actions that need to be taken to work toward the accomplishment of the goal. In other words, they outline how someone might go about accomplishing other objectives or goals.

Writing Good Objectives

For an organization to continually progress and move forward to keep up with market trends, a population's needs, ever-changing financial situations, program trends, and improvements in sport equipment, rules, and training, it must write good goals and attainable objectives. The most effective objectives are **SMART objectives** (figure 4.1).

- **S**pecific: The objective is designed to quantify the number or performance of a specific behavior (e.g., the floor will be swept on a daily basis). It is clear how often the behavior is to be performed.
- **M**easurable: Information about the objective can be written down, recorded, or tallied. This makes it much easier to determine the accomplishment of the objective.
- **A**chievable: At some point in the near future, there is a possibility of accomplishing the objective. An objective must be achievable both from a personal standpoint as well as from an organizational standpoint. Often an objective is determined but the organization has no staff or resources available in support of the objective.
- **R**elevant: The objective must work as a stepping stone toward meeting the desired goal or it will simply be an erroneous step leading to nowhere in accomplishing the goal.
- **T**imed: The objective must have some sort of time frame so that it provides direction to the person or groups of people given the task of accomplishing the objective. This also means that at some point it can be

Figure 4.1 SMART goals and objectives.

determined if the objective has been met or not. This component would be especially important, for example, for determining personnel productivity over a given period of time (Creating objectives, n.d.).

Step 3: Activity Analysis

Having established the foundation of your program coupled with setting its goals and objectives, it is time to begin planning the actual program. This is one instance where significant planning and organization at the front end of the program will help prevent trouble during the activity and at the back end of the program. Certainly things can go wrong in any program; however, proper planning should reduce the incidence of problems.

An activity analysis helps everyone involved in the activity to understand the larger picture of the entire program or event. It is specific to the activity or program down to the minute details of where to store the balls and how to mark the field properly.

A comprehensive activity analysis identifies the necessary components of the sport program and then outlines the important components needed to successfully run the program. Because the analysis is designed to be as comprehensive as possible, it is beneficial to consider multiple aspects of the program in detail. Following are examples of categories that you might consider including in your activity analysis.

Environment

Perhaps the most central yet underanalyzed component of successful sport programs is the environment. Much like a teacher, if a recreational sport professional is able to control the environment of the activity, it is much less likely that the activity will get out of hand. The environment is the combination of the physical facility, the people, and the social expectations of the program. A recreational sport programmer must ask himself what facilities exist, whether the amenities of the facility (e.g., washrooms, water availability, proximity to medical services) adequately support the program, and how the facility is prepared. For example, are the fields lined, are the lanes ready for the pool, and are there enough mats for the aerobics room? From a more social perspective, it is important to understand how many and what types of visitors (e.g., youth, older adults, participants, spectators, vendors) are expected to visit the facility. Similarly, what culture exists at the facility and at this event? A facility is simply a physical space; the culture that an organization establishes is what makes it an environment. Culture can be demonstrated through signs depicting appropriate or inappropriate behavior, announcements that encourage the desired environment, rules and regulations, trainings, staffing (is there a single staff member at the door or are staff members constantly roaming and engaging with participants), the shape and lighting of the space, and so on.

Personnel

Understanding what personnel will be required and what skills they need to have is important in the success of the program. Similarly, whether they are paid staff or volunteers helps you understand the level of buy-in and commitment that the staff might bring to the table. Certainly, determining the scope of duties for each staff member might help in deciding the number of people that will be needed to perform the tasks efficiently and how many of those people need to be managers, workers, or volunteers. Keep in mind that a larger staff will require a more efficient method of communication, although it also allows for a more diverse set of skills that may be needed to deal with unexpected circumstances. Finally, it is important that all levels of personnel, from volunteers up to the highest level of management, understand the philosophy, vision, goals, and objectives so they know how to best carry out each one.

Supplies and Equipment

Even though supplies and equipment may seem to be the most important aspect of planning, recreation professionals often forget to check the safety or maintenance of the equipment to determine their effective use. For example, it is not enough to have enough soccer balls for a practice; they must also be safe to play with and properly inflated. Additionally, participants want the most up-to-date gadgets and will change programs or facilities to get them. This doesn't necessarily mean a facility needs to spend millions of dollars every year on new equipment. It simply means that thinking about upgrading parts of the equipment or sharing equipment with other facilities in the area might provide a positive benefit for all involved. Keep in mind that equipment requires control as well, and staff are needed to monitor the use of the equipment, clean it, move it, and inspect it on a regular basis.

Communication

A program or event will not be successful without a solid understanding of how the event is going to be promoted and how the event is portrayed within the community. In addition, just as in a good marketing campaign, you need to know who your target audience is and whether you are using the right avenues of communication to reach them.

During an event, communication needs to be clear. Even if staff members are not exactly sure what is to happen at a particular moment, if they understand the goal of the program then they can rely on their own expertise to continue making decisions. Programs must also communicate information to participants in order to better facilitate organizational structures that have been put in place. For example, if participants do not know where to sign up for the event upon arrival, they immediately sense a lack of organization before anything has even begun. Often there is a need to communicate various rules or responsibilities to participants at events, and how this information is communicated speaks volumes. Finally, communicating with staff is equally important as communicating with participants.

Financial Concerns

An activity analysis needs to address financial concerns such as the cost of the program and where the expenses will come from; however, there are other financial considerations that need to be assessed as well. For instance, it is important to determine who is responsible for collecting funds and in what mode the funds can be collected, such as cash, check, or credit card. If there are program expenses, who is responsible for distributing the funds and in what time frame? In addition, sponsors are becoming a larger part of any community event, particularly given the recent cuts to many recreation programs. Thus, organizations need to understand the difference between a cash sponsorship, where a sponsor might simply write a check in exchange for its name being displayed, and an in-kind donation sponsorship, where a company might provide 50 golf balls as prizes at a tournament in exchange for its product being put on display. Organizations are also relying more on alternative revenue streams such as concessions and appearance fees.

In addition to program financials, there is a growing demand on agencies to determine what economic impact a program will have on local communities and how it will support the local tax base in order to justify using public funds. Agencies need to demonstrate to residents that the program or event is a worthwhile endeavor for the community.

Modifications and Problem Solving

Perhaps the most overlooked aspect of event sport and event planning is that things will go wrong no matter how organized the event might be, and staff must be prepared to solve problems and make adjustments. The goal of good planning is to minimize the things that go wrong, and having the right staff and policies in place to allow for quick and easy decisions will make the process much more effective. Staff must feel that they are empowered to make quick decisions on their own rather than having to constantly seek management approval, which slows the process to a crawl and thus angers participants. This means that all staff must understand the goals of the program so that they can best work within the framework provided to solve the problem quickly and efficiently. Moreover, sport programmers must have a plan in place for accommodating people with disabilities and have an understanding of what modifications can be made to activities that retain their integrity for all while also providing the least restrictive environment.

Step 4: Program Animation

Animation is the act of taking an ordinary activity or event and bringing it to life with field design, energy from the announcer, music, history, characters such as mascots, intensity, or visuals. In essence, it is making an ordinary activity an experience for participants. For example, in theory, an NCAA football game could be played by any two teams on any regulation field in any local park with a few officials and coaches. According to the rules, the game could be played and would stand as official. However, NCAA football is a multibillion-dollar industry, and this is largely due to the animation of its events. There is nothing in the NCAA rule book to suggest that fans must be present at a football game, balloons must be released, tailgating must take place, a band must

© Skye Arthur-Banning

It is important to modify an instructional tennis program based on the age and ability levels of participants to ensure the program's success while at the same time maintaining the program's integrity.

be present, or music must be played over a speaker system, and yet all these things happen on any given Saturday in the fall on university campuses all across the United States. All of these aspects are part of the animation that makes the game a bigger event than it really is.

On a much smaller scale, recreational sport can be animated equally as well and with as effective results. Main categories in which animation could take place include the facility, the equipment, and the props.

Facility

The facility is perhaps the most obvious place for animation. Playing an important football game in the local park is not likely to be as exciting and animated as playing in the high school stadium. Holding the 12-year-old youth league championships on the big local football field simply adds something to the game. Although playing on Lambeau Field will never be an option for most, recreational sport professionals can still use the high school field for the championship game. This allows more spectators to attend, providing a sense of the importance of the event and allowing the animated energy of the spectators to be translated to the players. Another example might be using the squash court with the glass backing rather than the solid wall.

The game remains the same, but the environment has completely changed and the heightened awareness of where the game is brings a sense of magnitude and excitement to the game. Animation doesn't just have to be in the championship game, either. In a regular season game, players notice when the field has been mowed in a neat design or the baseball field has been repainted in new colors. It gives the participants a sense that they matter and that the activity is worth being involved in.

Equipment

Changing the equipment within the game brings a feeling of something new. Participants can sense that the game has become more exciting and animated. For example, in sporting events all across the United States in the month of October, you might notice everything seems to be pink—pink shoe laces, pink soccer balls, pink jerseys, and even pink baseball bats. This is all part of a well-planned campaign for breast cancer awareness. All of these changes to pink equipment do little to enhance the actual game, and yet when the pink is introduced, the important meaning is evident and the game appears to be more animated as a result. Even something as small as providing pink tape for the players to use can add animation.

Props

Props and design can add animation to an event in a number of ways. This is perhaps the most common form of animation. If you think of the Disney theme parks as the ultimate in event animation, it becomes obvious how a simple ride can become a bigger experience with props, historical memorabilia, signs and design, music, costumes, gift shops, and even food supporting the theme. Most programs do not have those sorts of resources, but they can still animate their programs with props. For example, signs and sponsorships are almost always up around local soccer and baseball fields. Teams often bring their own music to warm up to before the game, and even something as simple as having multiple uniforms has become common, allowing players to remove their warm-up jerseys to reveal their game uniforms.

All of these are great examples of how animation can play out. They are all things that transform a simple game into an incredible event.

Step 5: Implementation

The preparation for the program is almost over. As a programmer, you have completed a needs assessment; made every effort to set realistic goals and objectives based on the mission of the organization; put the planning process into place, taking special care to try to think through all of the components that will be needed for a successful event; and thought about how to animate the event. Now it is time to put the wheels in motion. Having made all of these decisions and put so much thought into this event, you need an organized plan to direct your staff, volunteers, and sponsors toward the end of the race. In much the same way you would use a road map to get from the planning point of a trip to the final destination, a sport programmer needs a map to get to the end of the event.

The business community uses a multitude of tools on a regular basis to help lay out the road map to successful endeavors. Here are but a few examples of how recreational sport agencies can map out their program plan.

The Gantt chart, developed by Henry Gantt in the early 1900s (www.gantt.com), is one tool for event management. It is a bar chart of sorts that allows the programmer to incorporate the timeline, task list, people responsible for each series of tasks, degree of completion, and overlap between a series of planning initiatives (figure 4.2).

The benefit of the Gantt chart is that it is a great visual representation of all the tasks that need to be accomplished for a given event, and

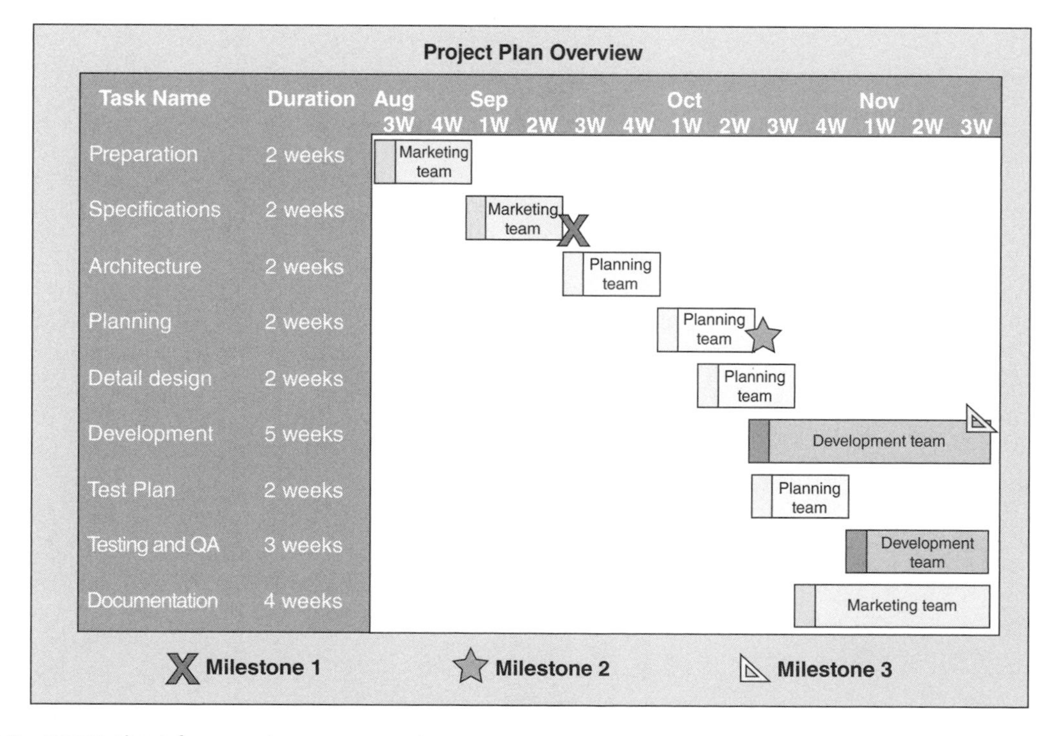

Figure 4.2 Gantt chart for event management.

it identifies the time frame and who is to accomplish each task. It is a motivating visual tool to help the programmer realize the progress that is being made on the overall event. Much like the donation boards or fund-raising thermometer that we all have seen charting the progress of an organization's fund-raising goals, the Gantt chart can visually display the progress of the planning toward completion.

However, with a large event, this visual representation obviously needs to be large, which can make it cumbersome to follow. In addition, the tasks appear to require equal amounts of energy or planning when often this is not the case. Agencies could use a color scheme or something of that nature to represent the magnitude of each task; for instance, event managers could see that a red bar line requires significant amounts of work to complete the task and a green bar line requires few skills to complete.

A PERT (program evaluation and review technique) chart is another tool similar to the Gantt chart, although it is more of a flowchart that visually represents the task and provides estimations of time to task completion in optimal conditions as well as less than desirable conditions (figure 4.3). The benefit of a PERT chart is that it virtually forces task completion before moving on to the next task because it is a more linear flowchart. This could also be a drawback of a PERT chart because in many cases multiple key tasks in an event could be performed simultaneously. A PERT chart is often used in conjunction with the critical path method (CPM) in that multiple flowcharts are included in the timeline, allowing tasks to take place in any given time frame. Similarly, the true PERT chart requires statistical estimations of optimistic time (O), pessimistic time (P), and most likely time (M), which might deter some programmers from using it.

A final benefit of using either of these tools is that they can become the first point of program evaluation. This is because they are a record of the process, the task accomplishments, the time it took to accomplish each task, and the people involved in completing the task.

Step 6: Troubleshooting

Regardless of how much preparation, planning, and organization you put into an event or program, there are going to be things that do not go as you had hoped. This is where troubleshooting comes in. Multiple components of good customer service go into dealing with difficult situations in an efficient and timely manner. Unfortunately, participants may not recognize the many hours of planning that went into a quality event, but they will remember the one instance when something went wrong and how it was handled. Staff who are trained to troubleshoot should be knowledgeable, quick thinking, empowered to make their own decisions, innovative, and calm.

- **Knowledgeable.** Staff who are trained to deal with problems as they arise must have knowledge of the organization and the event or activity. A staff member who is familiar with the event, all the tasks involved in presenting the event, who was responsible for each task, and what each component of the event should look

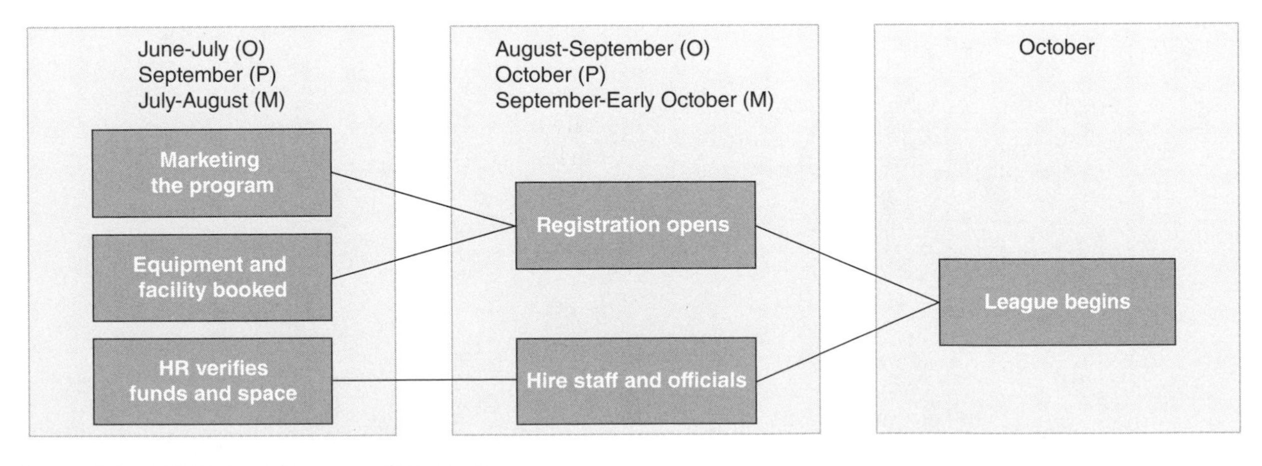

Figure 4.3 PERT chart for a sporting event.

like will be the most effective at correcting any problems. Proper staff training and communication between departments and task groups can enhance the knowledge base of the entire staff and enable them to deal with problems effectively.

- **Quick thinking.** Staff members need to be able to think quickly on their feet. A staff member who is able to recognize a problem before any participants realize something is wrong is an invaluable member of the team. Again, knowledge of how the event is supposed to look coupled with an experienced programmer who understands the demands of the event will help in dealing with the problems that come up. For example, something as simple as a referee getting hurt just before one of the games requires the tournament to be flexible in scheduling or have a backup plan for another referee to shift from one field to another.
- **Empowered to make decisions.** Perhaps one of the most important characteristics of staff members who can troubleshoot effectively is that they are empowered to make the tough decisions on their own or with little assistance. This is a critical step in the process because decisions that must be passed up the chain of command for approval obviously will be much slower in getting resolved, which not only frustrates participants but makes the staff on the ground appear insufficient and incompetent. Management can provide preapproved options for staff in the event that things go wrong and provide the necessary tools for staff on the ground to deal with difficulties that come up.
- **Innovative.** Innovative staff who can think outside the box are much better able to deal with situations as they arise. The traditionalist programmer might have difficulty seeing how one problem can be solved through creative thinking. For example, a person who uses a wheelchair has arrived at the bowling alley to participate in a few games, but the facility only has one ramp and it is already in use. The traditionalist programmer might feel she was prepared with the ramp and yet two ramps are now needed. Now she needs to think outside the box. What else could be used as a ramp? Often, there are pool tables in the bowling alley, and two pool cues affixed to each other could make a great ramp for the second participant bowling in a wheelchair. While the cues might not be ideal, it could be the difference between this individual being able to participate or not. A different alternative could be something as simple as making an effort to move the two bowlers' lanes closer together so that they can share the ramp. Both of the solutions work, but they require quick, innovative thinking.
- **Calm.** Finally, remaining calm could be a staff member's best asset in dealing with unforeseen problems. Participants are often upset or disappointed when something goes wrong, and a calming personality may be all that is needed to deal with the issue. Much the same way that a good referee can bring calm to a heated situation in a sporting event, a relaxed staff member who has been given the tools to deal with difficult situations can easily diffuse a heated situation and help participants become satisfied with the outcome.

Step 7: Evaluation

The final step of the programming process is the evaluation of the event, which is designed to get a clear sense of how well everything went. It is important to consider evaluating your event from multiple angles or with multiple considerations in mind, such as the program, staff, flow of the events, and various processes throughout the event such as registration or transitions. This is perhaps the step in the programming process that is done least well. Participants have high expectations for quality programs, and when one league or activity is over, the next is just around the corner, making it difficult to invest time and effort into evaluation of the previous program. Even more troubling is that there are times when programmers are afraid of the evaluation results or that they may somehow show deficiencies in people. However, a quality evaluation is designed to help determine the perceived value of an activity and how such value can be enhanced in the future with proper modification or repetition.

Although this is the last step in the programming process, it does not necessarily mean that it only occurs at the end of the event. As discussed earlier, a needs assessment is an initial form of evaluation for determining need and how the league or event is going to take place. Similarly, an evaluation can guide the changes or additions you need to make for the next time, much as a needs assessment might do.

Types of Evaluation

There are multiple times when an evaluation can occur throughout the course of the event, and when it is performed often determines the type of evaluation it is. Formative evaluations tend to occur as the league or event is forming. You can use several tools to gather information; however, the more common tools tend to be the Gantt or PERT charts. In many cases formative evaluations occur in the planning phase of the process through discussions and meetings as the event comes together.

Formative evaluations are also done during the event. This allows programmers to make changes to an event while it is actually occurring instead of waiting until the completion to make changes for the next time. An example of this would be determining levels of enjoyment in a youth sport league on a weekly basis and posting the results each week. Each week provides a snapshot of the season and changes can be made during the season if participants are not enjoying themselves. If youth participants in a basketball league did not enjoy a particular week, it would be important to determine why. It might simply be looking at the scores of the basketball games for that week and seeing that each game was a blowout. If this happens early in a season, it may still be possible to make slight adjustments to members of teams in order to balance the teams to allow for a more enjoyable overall experience.

Summative evaluations are done at the end of the program or event as a summary of the actions that took place. They often seek to answer questions about the effectiveness of a program in meeting its stated goals and objectives or the satisfaction of a particular aspect of the program. Similarly, the process could be evaluated through the completion of the Gantt chart and the entire staff could assess how to most efficiently plan the event in the future.

Perhaps the most important component of any evaluation is doing something with the resulting information. If a program is simply evaluated and no changes or actions result from the evaluation, then the entire process becomes a waste of time. Staff, participants, stakeholders, sponsors, and facility operators should either be able to see that the evaluation they participated in resulted in some sort of change to the program or be given an explanation as to why changes are not being made. This empowers each of these groups and reminds them that their opinions are valued and are being heard. For example, if the participants of the local swim club provide feedback that the pool needs to be deeper, that is valuable feedback but the change may be cost prohibitive. Participants then need to be told that although their opinion was heard in the evaluation, the change simply cannot happen at the facility due to cost.

Participants in an Evaluation

There are three main groups of people who should be involved in the evaluation process. The most obvious is the participants in the program. Ultimately, their input and approval of the program is most important to sustain the program in the long run. The staff or members of the organization should also be involved in the evaluation process because they are the ones who can speak to the process of the event organization, facility use, cost and budget structures, and so on. Staff buy-in and input are essential for continued organizational support for the program. Finally, outside stakeholders such as sponsors, facility owners, community members, city council members, and board members should be involved in the process so that you may fully understand how the program fits in the big picture of the organization and the community.

Tools for Evaluation

There are many methods for evaluating programs, and each one has its place in the sport setting. Questionnaires, observations, checklists, mind maps, program data, and interviews and focus groups, as well as being creative and coming up with your own tools, can all assist in getting a sense of the success of the program.

- **Questionnaires.** Questionnaires tend to be the most frequently used tools used for evaluation and typically are administered in a written format at the end of a program. They are effective at capturing a large amount of data in a short time if they are administered well to a representative sample of the population. Four types of questions are often asked in a questionnaire. *Participant demographics questions* ask about age, income, years in the program, and so on. This information often provides a foundation that the other information can be compared with. Categorical questions are typically yes-or-no questions or ask which program participants are involved in (e.g., learn to swim, diving and technique, competition team). The third typical question format is often referred to as a *Likert scale* and involves a range from 1 to 5, for example, as a measure of opposite ends of a spectrum (figure 4.4). For instance, a

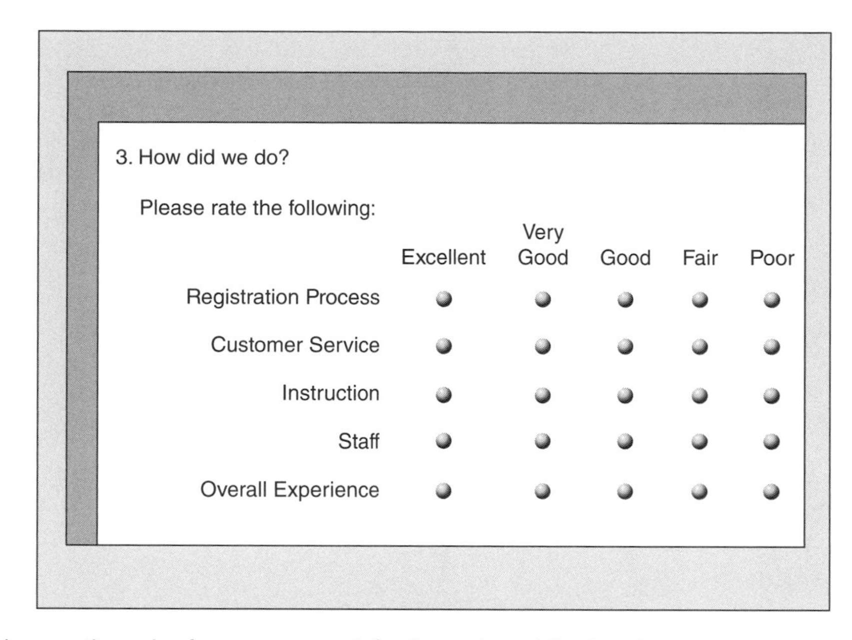

Figure 4.4 Simple questionnaire for program satisfaction using a Likert scale.

program might ask, "How satisfied were you with the registration process?", where 1 is very dissatisfied, 2 is dissatisfied, 3 is neutral, 4 is satisfied, and 5 is very satisfied. Participants then simply need to circle the answer that best represents their level of satisfaction with registration. Finally, there are *open-ended questions* where the person filling out the questionnaire can write her own answer to the question.

- **Observations.** Observations can be an efficient method for data collection and evaluation if they are done intentionally and planned well. An observation involves having a staff member or someone hired to do an evaluation to look for something specific within the program. Typically a trained observer has a data collection form that lists a set of behaviors relevant to the activity. The observer then takes notes or tallies the frequency or duration of the observed behavior over a given period of time. For example, when facilities are seeking to determine specific area use such as the swimming pool, they might have a staff member do an observation every 15 minutes in that particular area and count the number of people using it. This would help determine the hours to be open or the number of lifeguards needed on duty at various times throughout the day.
- **Checklists.** Checklists are often done to evaluate equipment or safety protocol to ensure that certain criteria are being met. For example, when hosting a waterskiing event, you may need to be sure all of the proper equipment is on board the boat before beginning the competition (see figure 4.5).
- **Mind maps.** A mind map is a tool that can be used as a visual evaluation to make connections or links to a particular entity. For example, an organization might map out where its members are commuting from to get an idea of the radius of transportation. After increasing marketing outside of the radius, the organization may complete the mind map again the following year. An overlay of year 1 to year 2 would give a nice visual representation of the effectiveness of the marketing program and increases in the commutes of participants in year 2.
- **Program data.** Most agencies already document certain events within their programs as a function of other aspects of their programs. Score sheets, for example, are common tools for keeping track of statistics in a basketball game and are turned into the league director on a weekly basis. The league director could then look at the number of technical fouls from week to week or even game to game to determine the rate of technical fouls and which teams might be more prone to receiving them and then seek ways to change the undesired behavior for those

Figure 4.5 Sample Checklist

Utah Boating Laws and Rules

This list shows the required safety equipment that must be on board your boat. This is a general list; in some cases there are more specific requirements. Please read our brochure, *Highlights from Utah's Boating Laws and Rules*, for more specifics about laws and rules. Because the equipment requirements vary depending on the size of the boat, you may need additional types, sizes, and quantities of specific pieces of safety equipment. Please also take a look at the second list of recommended optional equipment at the bottom of the page. (*PFD* means personal flotation device, and *PWC* means personal watercraft.)

Required Boating Safety Equipment

Checklist item	Under 16 ft (5 m) long	16 ft (5 m) to less than 26 ft (8 m)	26 ft (8 m) and longer
Display of registration decals	Yes (a)	Yes (a)	Yes (a)
Registration card on board	Yes (a)	Yes (a)	Yes (a)
Display of bow numbers	Yes (b)	Yes (b)	Yes (b)
Fire extinguisher	Yes (c)	Yes (c)	Yes (c)(d)(e)
Spare propulsion	Yes	Yes for vessels under 21 ft (6 m); recommended for others	Recommended
Bailing device	Yes	Yes	Yes
Sound-producing device	Strongly recommended	Yes	Yes (f)
One life jacket for each person on board (kids under 13 wearing)	Yes	Yes	Yes
Type IV throwable floatation device (PFD)	Strongly recommended	Yes	Yes
Proper navigation lights	Yes	Yes	Yes
Meets noise/muffler requirements	Yes	Yes	Yes
Adequate ventilation	Yes	Yes	Yes
Approved flame arrestor	Yes (g)	Yes (g)	Yes (g)
Capacity plate displayed	Yes (h)	Yes for vessels under 20 ft (6 m) (h); manufacturer's option for 20+ ft	Manufacturer's option
Hull identification number (HIN)	Yes	Yes	Yes
Proof of liability insurance	Yes for PWCs and motorboats with 50 hp or greater engines	Yes for motorboats with 50 hp or greater engines	Yes for motorboats with 50 hp or greater engines

(a) Required for all registered vessels. Registration is required for all motorized and sailing vessels.

(b) Required for all registered vessels except U.S. Coast Guard documented vessels.

(c) Not required for outboard motorboats of open construction; however, they are recommended for all motorboats.

(d) Vessels 26 ft to 40 ft (8-12 m) must carry two B-I or one B-II fire extinguisher(s).

(e) Vessels 40 ft (12 m) and longer must carry three B-I or one B-I and one B-II fire extinguisher(s).

(f) Vessels 40 ft (12 m) and longer must carry a bell in addition to a horn or whistle.

(g) Required for inboard gasoline engines equipped with a carburetor.

(h) Vessels exempt from this requirement include sailboats, canoes, kayaks, inflatable vessels, and vessels manufactured prior to 1973.

particular teams. Similarly, as part of the risk management plan, a swimming pool should keep track of all the incidents that occur around the pool deck. Those incidents could be evaluated to determine whether particular areas of the pool are more prone to accidents, and those areas could be monitored more closely or changed to make them safer.

- **Interviews and focus groups.** Similar to the questionnaire, an interview is simply a way of asking someone specific questions as a more personalized form of evaluation. A focus group is a group interview where several people are asked various questions about a particular topic. Focus groups are most effective when performed at the end of the session or program, although for season-long events, for example, formative interviews or focus groups could still allow for changes in the current season.

- **Creative tools.** The previous methods of evaluation and data collection are all fairly common, and as a result participants might get tired of filling out questionnaires or staff members might get tired of using checklists. When this is the case, more creative evaluation tools can be designed, provided that they meet the needs of the organization and assist in measuring the effectiveness of the goals and objectives. One such example is the fun-o-meter that an agency used to determine the amount of fun participants were having in the program (figure 4.6). The fun-o-meter was a five-tiered bird feeder that had a Likert scale of 1 to 5 on it. It was placed immediately outside the gym of a sport program, and upon completion of each game, participants were given a marble to drop in the box of the birdfeeder that corresponded with the amount of fun they had in the game that day, with 1 equaling no fun at all and 5 equaling the most fun they've had in a game. This evaluation tool was simple, easy to understand even for younger children, and fairly accurate, assisting the programmers in determining if they were meeting their goal of ensuring participant enjoyment in the program.

Figure 4.6 A fun-o-meter that an agency used to determine the amount of fun participants were having in a program.

CONCLUSION

This chapter provides the framework for programming recreational sport experiences from beginning to end. From the needs assessment to the activity to the summative evaluation, it is clearly important to understand each step in the process. Should one step be left out or misunderstood, a program will likely be less enjoyable for the participants and more difficult for the recreation sport professional to administer. In addition, throughout the process, it is important to recognize that participants and communities are unique, and techniques that might have worked in a community on the East Coast may not work for a community on the West Coast. This is why the assessment components at each step of the programming process are vital.

RESEARCH TO REALITY

Fraser-Thomas, J.L., Cote, J., & Deakin, J. (2005). Youth sport programs: An avenue to foster positive youth development. *Physical Education and Sport Pedagogy*, *10*(1), 19-40.

Fraser-Thomas and her colleagues were interested in using youth sport programs as a medium for positive youth development. They sought to create a model for youth development that would highlight the role of policy makers and sport programs in incorporating participants from all races, socioeconomic status, cultures, and genders. It was understood that although sport had the potential to be beneficial, planning for intentional youth development outcomes was ultimately more important than promoting skill development in the programming model so that programming would develop good people who could contribute to society. The authors emphasized the importance of recognizing the various stages of social, physical, and intellectual development when programming for successful outcomes. In essence, the intent of this article was to clearly show that a program with systematic and intentional outcomes in mind from the beginning can lead to a more positive program and youth development outcomes for all, whereas programs with undeveloped or misaligned outcomes can actually be detrimental to participants.

REFLECTION QUESTIONS

1. What are the steps to programming a successful recreational sporting event? Why is each step important, and what might be the result of skipping one of the steps?
2. Large sporting events such as the Super Bowl are wonderful examples of how animation makes a sporting event an experience for millions around the globe. What elements of the Super Bowl could be modified and applied to a recreational sport program to make it an experience?
3. How would you evaluate a recreational sport program before, during, and after the program? What information might be gained from each phase of the evaluation process?

LEARNING ACTIVITIES

1. Pick two outcomes that the community you grew up in might be interested in promoting at its local recreation facility. Using the seven steps outlined in the chapter, design a sport program around those outcomes.
2. Do an online search for youth sport programs. Look through their activities and see if you can determine the program philosophy and outcomes. If you are unable to determine the program philosophy or desired outcomes, think through how you might better represent that program to make its philosophy, goals, objectives, and outcomes clear.

chapter 5

STRUCTURED TOURNAMENT SCHEDULING

LEARNING OUTCOMES

By the end of this chapter, readers will be able to

- describe the features that make a successful recreational sport tournament,
- explain the importance of sport facilities in the tournament scheduling process,
- compare the advantages and disadvantages of the three major tournament categories (round-robin, elimination, and challenge) and know the programming contexts appropriate for each, and
- accurately schedule various types of round-robin, elimination, and challenge tournaments.

Case Study

WE CAN'T PLAY ON FRIDAY

Robert M. Beren Academy had perhaps its best boys' high school basketball season ever. The school had just won 24 games and narrowly lost 46–42 to Abilene Christian in the Texas Association of Private and Parochial Schools (TAPPS) state championship game.

However, just a few days earlier, it looked like the championship game would never be played. Beren Academy, an Orthodox Jewish day school, has a school policy against playing games between sundown on Friday through sundown on Saturday in observance of the Jewish Sabbath. Beren's semifinal game was originally scheduled for 9:00 on Friday night, and the TAPPS executive board denied the school's request to reschedule the game. TAPPS, a state athletics association with voluntary membership, has a bylaw that requires teams to notify the association if they cannot participate in all play-off games upon qualifying for the play-offs. At that point, teams must remove themselves from the play-offs. Beren Academy apparently did not do this, and they played—and won—their play-off games, leading to the scheduling conflict.

According to TAPPS, if schedules are changed for some schools, it causes difficulties and is potentially unfair for other schools. Edd Burleson, the director of the association, stated, "If the schools are just going to arrange their own schedule, why do we even set up a tournament? Over a period of time, our state tournament, which is a highlight of our association, deteriorates to nothing. That's the whole point of having an organization" (Pilon, 2012, B12). When Beren was accepted into the association, it was informed that the inability to play games on Fridays and Saturdays could be problematic and that no future scheduling accommodation would be made (TAPPS, 2012). However, in this case, the Covenant School, Beren's opponent in the state semifinal game, was "open to rescheduling" if TAPPS were to allow it (Pilon, 2012, p. B16).

The Beren Academy coaches, players, and administration never intended to violate their religious principles and were prepared to forfeit their semifinal game. However, national media coverage of the incident, attention from Houston's mayor and a former NBA basketball coach, and—perhaps most importantly—a lawsuit filed by Beren students and parents in the U.S. district court in Dallas put pressure on TAPPS to change the schedule. The semifinal game, which Beren won, was played at 2:00 on Friday afternoon (before sundown) and the championship game, which Beren lost, was moved to 8:00 on Saturday evening (Associated Press, 2012).

When the season ended, there was discussion about whether or not TAPPS should consider changing its bylaws, which, it should be noted, prohibit any games from being played on Sundays (the Christian Sabbath). TAPPS board members suggested that they would "wait until the dust settles" (Pilon, 2012, p. B9) before considering any bylaw changes.

If healthy competition is embedded in the definition of recreational sport, then tournaments provide the structure for the competitive process. Tournaments facilitate individual and team participation, promote cooperation between competitors, provide a just and fair framework for competition, and lay out a pathway toward determining a true champion. All tournaments do each of these things; however, certain tournament formats place more or less emphasis on participation, cooperation, competition, and determining a true champion. Round-robin, single- and double-elimination, and various types of challenge tournaments all have their advantages and disadvantages, and it is the task of recreational sport professionals to choose the best tournament format for their participants.

During the tournament design process, recreational sport professionals need to know the overall philosophy and objectives of their tournament; the characteristics of their participants; the demands placed on participants by the specific sport; sport-specific rules and regulations; facility, equipment, and personnel needs and limitations; and the demand for and limits on tournament entries. Tournament design is as much an art as it is a science. Though it is important to know the mechanics of scheduling games, meets, and matches, it is also important to understand participant needs and other human dimensions. The Beren Academy case presented in the opening of the chapter demonstrates the level of thought and diligence required of tournament administrators during the tournament design and scheduling process. This chapter will help you understand both the art and science of tournament design and will help you avoid the pitfalls associated with poorly structured sport tournaments.

BIG PICTURE OF TOURNAMENT DESIGN

The events that unfolded in the Beren Academy case presented a dilemma for TAPPS. On the one hand, if they rescheduled the match, they would facilitate cooperation and participation between the two teams that won their games and deserved to play in the semifinals of the tournament. On the other hand, rescheduling would create administrative and logistical challenges. Consider all that needs to happen to stage a tournament game. First, you need an available facility. You also need to coordinate the schedules of the various tournament personnel—referees, athletic trainers, scorekeepers, ticket takers, concession workers, and in some cases media. Rescheduling could also create an unfair advantage or at least change the conditions under which the tournament would be played. Consider the difference in atmosphere for a tournament semifinal game played at 9:00 on a Friday night compared with one played at 2:00 in the afternoon. This could potentially neutralize a home-court advantage that may have been earned or could limit the impact of a team's fans. Finally, rescheduling games in one instance opens the door to rescheduling in other instances. New administrative structures would need to be created to determine when rescheduling is allowed and when it is not, possibly creating even more logistical upheaval and conflict.

You might be tempted to think that these are only considerations for high-level athletic tournaments. However, because recreational sport tournaments focus on broad participation, they often comprise 50, 75, or 100 (or more) teams. The logistical challenges in staging and scheduling these events can be just as complicated as in high-level tournaments, if not more so. It is fair to say that tournament administration is serious business and an important job-related competency for recreational sport professionals.

Tournament Design Goals

Successful tournaments often attract large numbers of entries, including a high percentage of repeat participants. It is not uncommon for individuals and teams to participate continually in their favorite tournament events. Organizations that successfully stage tournaments are often at an advantage in the bid process for hosting future tournaments. Hosting events that attract out-of-town entries can garner positive attention for the sponsoring organization and often leads to a sizable economic impact for the host community.

Sport tournaments have three major philosophical goals—to facilitate sport participation, to promote cooperation, and to provide a framework for just and fair competition—and recreational sport programmers must make a multitude of decisions to satisfy each goal. The success or failure of a tournament is based on the degree to which the recreational sport programmer meets these goals.

Individual and Team Participation

Any organizational effort is about the simplification of complex phenomena. To **facilitate** something means to make it easier. It is the tournament administrator's job to help participants be able to play the sport of their choice and to make the process of playing as straightforward as possible. Even the smallest local tournament with just a few teams requires adequate planning and foresight, and a large-scale tournament that attracts

Successful tournaments are well-organized with little or no chaos, like this high-level table tennis tournament.

a large number of teams and spectators requires sophisticated coordination and decision making.

Tournament participants need to know several details about the tournament ahead of time so they can plan and make arrangements. At a minimum, participants need to know details such as who is eligible to play, when and where games will take place, what it costs to participate, how many days the tournament may take to complete, what equipment is required (including what they need to bring and what will be provided), and where they will be able to arrange for overnight stays. Tournament administrators must also make myriad other decisions to facilitate successful events, as we will discuss throughout the chapter. Ultimately, the success of a tournament is determined by how well organized it is. Successful tournaments are ones that have no chaos. They make it as easy as possible for participants to show up and play.

Cooperation Between Competitors

A good tournament design provides clear boundaries and expectations for competitors. Organization is enhanced when these boundaries and expectations are clearly defined and communicated. When individuals and teams register for a tournament event, they agree to abide by the frameworks set up by the tournament administrators. There is no need for participants to negotiate where games will be played, what rules will be used, or who will have the authority to interpret and enforce the rules. A strong tournament design removes ambiguities that can lead to conflict between competitors.

Just as a house needs scaffolding to strengthen it while it is being constructed, cooperation is strengthened when the interactions between participants have appropriate scaffolding via a framework or structure for participation. This includes the following:

- Developing a clear and common set of tournament policies, procedures, and rules
- Providing a contest schedule or system that facilitates self-scheduling, as is the case with many challenge tournament formats
- Facilitating opportunities to interact outside of the competitive structure, such as by holding preevent captains' meetings to discuss tournament policies, providing common areas where teams can interact in

between contests, and providing a posttournament awards and recognition event, such as a banquet or ceremony

Cooperation is often overlooked in the process of designing sport events. However, when recreational sport programmers intentionally take it into consideration, it can help to alleviate many of the problems that can be associated with the sport experience.

Fair Framework for Competition

Notions of fairness and justice are embedded in the fabric of recreational sport competition. The competitive process is about testing oneself or one's team against some objective standard and seeing how one fares. In direct competitive experiences, this objective standard is usually the performance of an opponent. The role of the recreational sport tournament is to provide a structure that allows for true performance comparison.

Ideally, true comparison should be based exclusively on assessing the talents and skills of the competitors against one another. However, sometimes other factors enter the competitive process that can have an effect on the outcome. The most obvious of these are poor calls by officials, mistakes by timers or scorekeepers, and problems with facilities or equipment. In many cases, poor tournament designs or scheduling can also affect the outcome of a contest. Some notable examples include scheduling a team to play back-to-back games when the opponent is well rested, having a team play late at night and then first thing the next morning, and scheduling teams to play on long travel days.

Another example is when recreational sport programmers do not consider the differences among competitors' skill levels when scheduling contests. One way to avoid this is by allowing participants to self-select tournament divisions based on skill level. For example, highly skilled participants might choose a competitive division whereas less skilled participants or beginners in a sport might choose a recreational division. This system can include a variety of participation categories based on the characteristics of the teams in the tournament. One could organize the tournament based on the participants' skill level, their age, or the size of the schools or communities that they represent. The point is to make the competitive process as fair as possible. Instant scheduling is one way to help take some of these decisions out of the hands of the recreational sport programmer. In **instant scheduling**, individuals or teams schedule themselves in the tournament divisions that are most appealing to them during the registration process well in advance of the tournament.

Another method of creating a fair and just competitive process is tournament seeding. **Seeding** is the process of ranking teams based on their ability and scheduling so as to provide the highest chance of the best teams facing off in the later stages of the tournament. The idea of seeding is to avoid having all of the best teams in one round-robin league or having the best two teams compete against one another in an early round of an elimination tournament. If the higher-seeded teams all take care of business and win their games, the best teams will be facing off against one another as the tournament progresses. This might not seem fair to less skilled teams, but it can make for a more just tournament because the best teams are rewarded for past performance. Consider the example of a team that goes through its regular season undefeated. Would it be fair or just if that team were to face another undefeated team in its first single-elimination play-off game while a team with multiple losses received a bye to the second round?

We will talk about the best methods to handle these cases during the discussion on tournament scheduling later in this chapter. Of course, in some cases these decisions cannot be avoided. For example, if the tournament is facing tight time frames and limited facility availability, teams may be forced to play back-to-back games. In other cases, the objectives of the tournament might lend themselves to just one competitive division, putting all eligible teams in the same tournament. In still other cases, it may be impossible to seed teams because the tournament administrator may not have objective knowledge of the teams' past performance. However, wherever possible, recreational sport programmers should take fairness into account as they schedule contests in order to mitigate external factors that could influence the competitive process.

Tournament Design Considerations

Earlier it was mentioned that recreational sport programmers must make many important decisions in order to meet the three major goals of sport tournaments. They must take into account a large number of variables when putting together a tournament design. These variables cluster around six main areas:

1. Tournament philosophy and objectives
2. Participant characteristics
3. Demands placed on participants
4. Facility, equipment, and personnel needs and limitations
5. Demand for and limits on tournament entries
6. Sport-specific rules and regulations

Each of these is discussed next. As you read, think about how you might incorporate these variables into your tournament design decisions.

Tournament Philosophy and Objectives

Sport tournaments come in all shapes and sizes. The backyard badminton tournament played at a family reunion has a completely different set of objectives from the TAPPS postseason basketball tournament. This may be an extreme distinction, but there is quite a bit of diversity in tournament philosophy and objectives even within the overall domain of recreational sport. The first place to start when thinking about tournament design is the main objective of the tournament. Why does the tournament exist in the first place? What is its main point? What is it trying to achieve? Answers to those questions will help lead you to an appropriate tournament format.

Think about the intramural flag football program at your university. The philosophy of intramural sport at most colleges and universities is sport for everyone—or at least providing sport opportunities so the largest number of people can participate. If the objective of the intramural flag football tournament is to maximize participation over a period of time, then using an exclusive elimination format such as a single- or double-elimination design where there is a strong possibility of going one and done (or even two and done) would be inappropriate. Using a round-robin format, discussed later, would be a more appropriate choice. However, if the objective is to determine an all-campus champion, then an elimination design offered after the round-robin regular season makes sense.

Consider other scenarios. Suppose you and your university are in charge of running a regional flag football tournament with the objective of sending the best men's, women's, and corecreational teams to the NIRSA Flag Football National Championships. Because it is a regional tournament, some teams may need to travel and pay a considerable amount of money to get to your campus. To minimize costs, these tournaments are usually played over the course of three days. The objective of the tournament is to determine a set of champions, lending itself to an elimination design. However, the costs to participate are high, so any tournament design that sends a team home after playing just one game would not be well received. In this case, a series of small three-team round-robin tournaments followed by a single-elimination tournament might be the best design. These are just a few examples that demonstrate how the objectives of a tournament lend themselves to a particular tournament format. Thus, the purpose and objectives are the best place to begin thinking about good tournament design.

Participant Characteristics

The characteristics of participants are generally closely aligned with the philosophy and objectives of the tournament and have an impact on the choice of tournament format. Think about a town's postseason 10- to 12-year-old baseball tournament. The objective of the tournament might be to give kids an opportunity to play more baseball after the regular season is complete and to provide an opportunity for the best team to compete in the state tournament. In addition to knowing the tournament objectives, it is also important to take into account the characteristics of the participants. Kids in this age group are still developing physically. Overuse injuries are becoming more prevalent in youth sport and are a growing concern for recreational sport professionals. The kids may have just finished a regular season where they played 20 or more games. In this case, the objective of the tournament (to determine a champion) combined with the need to protect developing athletes might lend itself to a tournament design where teams play a minimal number of games, such as a single-elimination format.

In addition to physical development, recreational sport programmers should take into account other participant characteristics. For example, some people may be interested in playing for fun without having to worry about whether their team wins or loses in order to keep playing. In this case, using large round-robin leagues that

Andersen Ross/Digital Vision/Getty Images

It is important for recreational sport professionals to know the characteristics of their participants, particularly when trying to match tournament design formats with participant needs.

lend themselves to a large number of games or offering double or triple round-robins where teams play each other multiple times makes the most sense. In another case, participants might not want to be locked into particular dates and times to play games and would rather have a more flexible playing schedule. For individual sports that are not personnel dependent and where facilities are readily available (e.g., tennis, racquetball, badminton), challenge formats that allow participants to mutually schedule games at their convenience make a lot of sense. Knowing the participants, their motivations, and their needs is an important variable for recreational sport programmers to consider.

Demands Placed on Participants

Risk management should be at the forefront of a tournament administrator's concerns when considering the demands that various sports place on participants. Sports such as rugby or tackle football place a heavy physical demand on participants' bodies, whereas sports such as badminton or horseshoes are not nearly as physically intense. Considering the physical demands of sport activities is important because one of the decisions that tournament administrators need to make is how frequently individuals or teams will be scheduled to play their games or contests. Think about soccer, a physically demanding game. Soccer teams are often asked to play multiple games per day in order to complete a tournament in a reasonable time frame. What is the ideal time between games to keep players well rested and safe? Would you allow soccer teams to play more than one game per day? If so, how many games could a team realistically play in a day without physically compromising participants or radically changing the integrity of the game? These are questions that you must consider in the tournament scheduling process.

In addition to safety concerns, certain sport events may place other demands on participants. Consider the example of teams that have to travel long distances to participate in a tournament, or think about the concerns of student-athletes who must balance their sport schedules with school and academic work. Similarly, adult participants need to balance their tournament experience with full-time jobs and family responsibilities. All of these demands are key factors that recreational sport programmers must consider as they put together a tournament schedule.

Facility, Equipment, and Personnel Needs and Limitations

In tournament design and scheduling, facilities are everything. The availability of playing facilities generally dictates the number of entries that a tournament can accommodate, the number of games that each team will play, and the tournament format itself. For example, where there is limited facility availability, recreational sport programmers are forced to use tournament formats that require fewer games to complete, such as small round-robins (i.e., round-robins with three or four teams) or single-elimination tournaments.

Limits on facility availability also require recreational sport programmers to limit the number of entries that can be registered. In a simple example, consider a facility reservation that allows games to be played at 12:00 p.m. and 1:00 p.m. on Monday, Tuesday, and Wednesday. In this case, six total games can be played over three days. A recreational sport programmer has a number of choices. She could choose a single-elimination tournament and allow seven teams to register, guaranteeing that each team will play one game. She could choose a three-team round-robin in a two-league format and allow six teams to enter, guaranteeing each team will play two games. Or she could choose a four-team round-robin format with one league and limit entries to just four teams but guarantee each team will play three games. Her decision will largely depend on the factors that we have been discussing, including the philosophy and objectives of the tournament, the characteristics of the participants, and the sport demands placed on participants, as well as other considerations that we will discuss later, including participant demand for the tournament and sport-specific rules and regulations. Later in the chapter, we will discuss the mechanics of scheduling round-robin and single-elimination tournaments and the methods that tournament administrators use to determine the number of games available and the maximum number of teams they can accommodate given their facility availability.

In addition to facilities, recreational sport programmers need to think about their personnel and equipment needs. Some sports are personnel dependent, such as 5-on-5 basketball, which generally requires at least two game officials as well as an official scorekeeper and timekeeper. Other sports, such as ultimate Frisbee, are typically unofficiated and can be scheduled with a minimum number of personnel. Consider the example of 5-on-5 basketball, which requires at least two officials per game. If you only have four qualified basketball officials, it will limit the number of games that you can schedule at any given time regardless of the available facility space. In this case, personnel availability limits the number of entries that you can accommodate in your tournament. Other scenarios, such as sports that require specialized and potentially limited equipment (e.g., regulation soccer goals, natural grass or synthetic turf, football goalposts) could also limit the number of games that can be played and thus the number of teams that can be accommodated in the tournament design.

Demand for and Limits on Tournament Entries

Another factor to take into account when considering tournament designs is participant demand. As you will see later in the chapter, it is always necessary to secure a facility reservation before you begin taking tournament entries. There have been notable examples where inexperienced and overeager recreational sport programmers registered more teams than they could accommodate given their facility availability. This placed them in the unenviable position of having to call team captains or players and tell them that they could not participate.

The demand for a particular tournament must be taken into account along with the other relevant considerations we have been discussing. For example, in the postseason play-off tournament discussed in the opening case, there was a natural limit on the number of tournament entries because of TAPPS policies on postseason eligibility. The objective of the tournament was to determine a state champion, and the participants were all highly skilled high school basketball players who had qualified for postseason play after a successful regular season. Similarly, even though the demand to participate in the NIRSA Flag Football National Championships might be high, participation is limited to the winners of the various regional tournaments that take place around the United States.

However, recreational sport programmers need to consider participant demand in recreational sport tournaments where access is more open. In this case, the tournament administrator needs to weigh the importance of serving a large number of entries with the importance of giving each team a large number of games to play. This decision between maximizing tournament entries and maximizing the number of games played per team is a critical one when there is a finite number of games to play based on the available facility reservation. Later in the chapter, we will discuss how this decision-making process applies to both round-robin and elimination tournament formats.

Sport-Specific Rules and Regulations

Recreational sport programmers also need to consider the sport-specific rules and regulations that govern particular sports. In many cases, these rules and regulations will have an impact on the tournament scheduling process. Most recreational sport tournaments focus on maximizing participation, either through accommodating the most entries or guaranteeing entries a maximum number of games. This need to maximize participation typically places a premium on scheduling as many games in a day as possible. The length of time that it takes to complete one game and start the next is vital in both maximizing the number of games that can be played in a day and keeping the tournament running efficiently and on time.

Think about this example: A high school basketball tournament is required by the National Federation of State High School Associations (NFHS) to play four quarters of 8 minutes each, with a stopped clock on dead balls. Intermissions between quarters are generally 1 minute and intermissions between halves are 10 minutes. In addition, teams are typically granted three 60-second time-outs and two 30-second time-outs per game (NFHS, 2012). Considering this, recreational sport programmers would most likely need to allow at least two hours to finish one game and start the next. However, if the timing rules could be modified, limiting game time to two 18-minute running-clock halves with the clock only stopping on dead balls in the final 2 minutes, having a 5-minute halftime, and limiting teams to only two 30-second time-outs per half, the recreational sport programmer could realistically schedule games every hour. This would double the number of games that could be played per day over the original NFHS format.

In some cases, recreational sport programmers have little or no flexibility to modify the rules under which games can be played. This is typically the case in tournament events that are governed by state, regional, or national governing or regulatory bodies for a particular sport, where the desire of the sanctioning organization is to create a consistent standard for competition across multiple tournament sites. Events that are not sanctioned by a governing or regulatory body may allow more flexibility in modifying rules to fit the needs and objectives of the local situation. Recreational sport programmers need to know the specific rules and regulations that they must operate under and which ones have the potential to affect tournament format and scheduling.

Today, there are software programs and online services that can handle most of the mechanics of tournament scheduling. For example, more than 600 colleges and universities use IMLeagues (www.imleagues.com), a free Web-based league scheduling program, for team registration, player tracking, and league scheduling (IMLeagues, 2013). Tournament scheduling technology can provide master game schedules as well as schedules for individual leagues and teams. A quick Web search will bring up hundreds of tournament scheduling websites with advice on how to draw elimination brackets and determine round-robin matchups, rendering the tournament scheduling process fairly easy.

However, good tournament design is both an art and a science. Good tournament design is multifaceted and complex, requiring recreational sport programmers to exercise sound judgment when taking into account many variables. A tremendous amount of work must be done and many decisions must be made before you can even think of registering entries and scheduling the tournament. These decisions cannot be made by computer programs or Web applications; they require the expertise of recreational sport programmers. In the sections that follow, you will learn about tournament design formats, their advantages and disadvantages, and how you can use them to deliver the best tournament experience for participants.

ROUND-ROBIN TOURNAMENTS

Round-robin formats are popular with both participants and recreational sport programmers. In a basic round-robin design, each entry plays all other entries in the assigned league or pool at least once. Wins and losses do not affect future participation as long as there are still games left on the schedule. In other words, entries continue to play until all scheduled games are completed. This makes round-robin tournaments easy to organize and administer because participant matchups can be scheduled completely in advance. Round-robin tournaments tend to emphasize participation because even the smallest round-robin league (three entries) still guarantees that an entry will play two games. Round-robin tournaments are also advantageous because they allow recreational sport programmers to easily rank teams based on their win–loss performance during league play.

Although round-robin tournaments are popular with participants and have multiple advantages, they do have their drawbacks. Disadvantages of round-robin tournaments include the following:

- Time and facility intensive
- Difficult to maintain participant interest
- Unable to determine a true champion
- Need to deal with tiebreakers

Round-robin tournaments tend to be time and facility intensive because they guarantee that league entries will all play one another at least once. Round-robin leagues with six or more entries require entries to play a large number of games. This is an advantage if the objective of the tournament is to maximize participation for tournament entries. However, more games mean the need for more facilities, equipment, and personnel.

Additionally, sometimes in large round-robin leagues, teams lose interest over the course of a long season. For example, a team that loses most of its games and is guaranteed to not make a postseason tournament may not have an incentive to show up for meaningless late-season matchups.

Another disadvantage of round-robin tournaments is their inability to determine a true champion when there is more than one league. Think about a women's basketball tournament that is organized with five round-robin leagues. After league play is completed, there are five first-place teams decided by the teams' win–loss records in league play. Round-robin play does not determine a true champion; a postseason elimination format is required to achieve that objective. One way to think of this is to consider the number of people who advocated for a true play-off system for the Bowl Championship Series (BCS) in college football because of the confusion that existed about who the best team was at the end of the regular season.

Finally, sometimes round robin leagues themselves end in ties with two or more teams holding the same record after all games are played. In that case, some policy mechanism must be in place to determine the league champion. The solutions may be different depending on whether there is a two-way or three-way tie. In the case of a two-way tie for first place, one need only to look at the head-to-head matchup in the regular season. In this case, the team with the best head-to-head record would be the champion. In the event that there is still a tie, the two teams could play an additional game to determine the league championship, assuming time and facility space is not an issue. In the case of a three-way tie or in the case of a two-way tie when there is no time to play an extra game, total points scored, point differential, or fewest points allowed could all be used as possible tie-breakers.

The next section will help you to understand the mechanics behind scheduling a round-robin tournament. When tournament administrators get to this point, they have already thought through many of the complex decisions that we discussed earlier. It is important not to make these decisions before the tournament scheduling process is complete. Remember, tournament design is about more than just creating league and facility schedules. A well-conceptualized tournament requires both art and science, and a tournament administrator cannot sacrifice one for the other.

Round-Robin Terminology

Round-robin tournament scheduling can be confusing because of the inconsistent terminology that is often used in connection with the mechanics of the scheduling process. Recreational sport organizations may use their own labels, but for the sake of consistency in this chapter, please refer to the following:

- **Round-robin tournament.** This refers to the overall sporting event. For example, an intramural sport director might offer a campus-wide flag football tournament for 100 teams. The word *tournament* refers to the entire event.
- **Round-robin division.** This refers to the various participation categories that a tournament administrator might offer to help manage competition. Earlier we talked about taking into account participant or team skill level, age, and gender. In the case of the intramural flag football tournament, the intramural director might organize the tournament by divisions based on the gender and skill level of participants.
- **Round-robin leagues.** These are the smallest groups to which entries are assigned. In some recreational sport organizations, leagues are referred to as *pools* or *groups*. Imagine that the 100 flag football team entries are placed into 20 leagues. This would be a round-robin tournament with five team leagues. Each league would then be nested within a division based on the gender and skill of the teams.

See figure 5.1 for a visual breakdown of the teams and leagues within this flag football tournament.

Round-Robin Formulas

Figuring out the league size (e.g., four-team leagues, five-team leagues) is a critical decision. The size of the round-robin league will determine a number of key factors related to tournament design, including the number of games each team will be scheduled to play, the number of games it will take to complete each round-robin league, and ultimately the number of games it will take to complete an entire round-robin tournament. Determining the appropriate league size is based on two main factors: how many total games are available to play given a set facility reservation and how many games each team is guaranteed to play. After considering these two factors, the tournament administrator must then determine two additional key factors: how many games it will take to complete the entire round-robin tournament and how many total entries can be accommodated. We can use several simple mathematical formulas to figure out each of these.

Total Number of Games Available

One of the first things the recreational sport programmer needs to do is reserve an appropriate playing facility for the round-robin tournament. In tournament design, facilities are everything. The total number of games available to play based on the facility reservation is the first necessary piece of information. To figure the total number of games available, multiply the following: the number of weeks the facility is reserved times the number of days that games will be played per week times the number of playing areas (e.g., fields, courts, diamonds) times the number of game slots per playing area.

To see this in practice, imagine that you are offering a round-robin doubles tennis tournament. You have reserved four tennis courts on Monday through Friday from 4:00 to 7:00 p.m. for a week. You have decided to modify the tennis rules so that matches will consist of one set. The winner

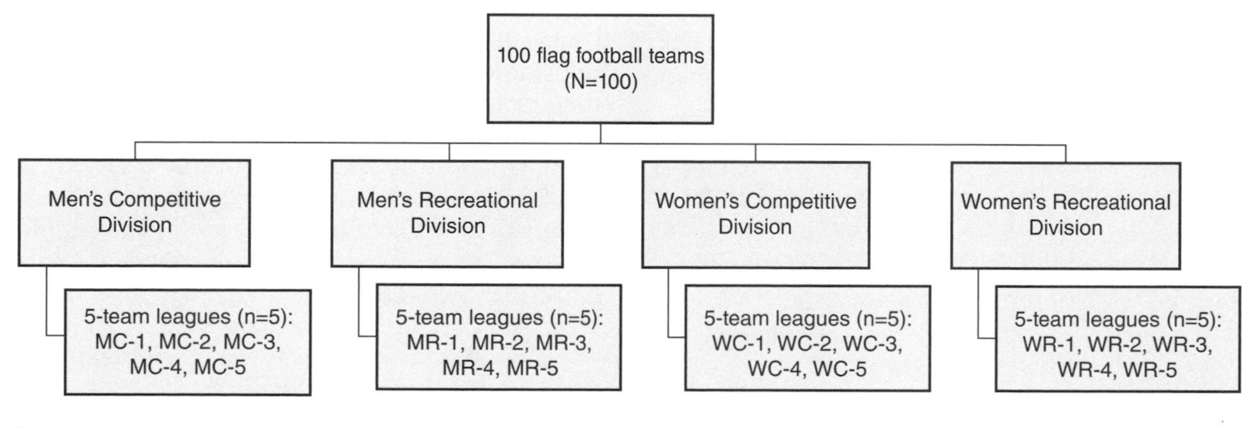

Figure 5.1 Teams and leagues in a flag football tournament.

of the set wins the match, and you feel confident that participants should be able to complete a set in approximately 45 minutes. Allowing time for injuries, check-in, and other possible delays, you decide to schedule matches every hour, so you will be offering three matches per tennis court from 4:00 to 7:00 p.m. Using the formula to determine the maximum number of matches available for this tennis tournament would give you the following:

1 week × 5 days × 4 tennis courts × 3 matches per court = 60 total tennis matches.

In this case, the facility schedule allows you to play 60 total tennis matches. You cannot play more, so decisions regarding the number of doubles tennis teams that you register and the size of your round-robin leagues depend on this number.

Games Each Team Is Guaranteed to Play

There are many reasons why a recreational sport programmer might want to guarantee participants a certain number of games in a round-robin tournament. To figure out how many games an entry will play in a round-robin tournament, use the following formula:

$n - 1$ = total number of games each entry will play.

In this case, *n* is the number of entries in each round-robin league. Let's revisit the tennis tournament discussed earlier. Imagine that, because of the tournament objectives, each doubles team was guaranteed to play at least four games. Using the formula, the appropriate league size to guarantee teams at least four games is five. In this tennis tournament, doubles teams would be placed in five-team leagues and would play each team in their league once.

Number of Games to Complete Each Round-Robin League

In round-robin tournaments, every entry plays every other entry in its own league once. To figure out how many games it will take for each entry to play every other entry in the league one time, use the following formula:

$n(n - 1) / 2$ = total number of games to complete the round-robin league.

Again, *n* refers to the league size. In the case of our doubles tennis tournament, *n* is 5, because the previous step determined that the most appropriate league size is five when guaranteeing teams 4 games. According to the formula, it would take 10 games for each team to play all of the other teams in the league one time.

Total Entries to Accommodate

To determine how many entries can be accommodated, you must go back to the first step. In the doubles tennis example, the facility reservation dictated that a total of 60 tennis matches could be scheduled, assuming every available day, court, and time were used throughout the tournament. Assume that the goal of the tournament is to maximize participation and that demand for the tournament is strong. Now, go back to the last step. Recall that it takes 10 games to play all of the games in a five-team round-robin league. How many doubles tennis leagues can this tournament accommodate?

60 total games available / 10 games to play 1 league of 5 teams = 6 leagues of 5 teams each.

6 leagues of 5 teams = 30 total teams.

Depending on the interest levels and backgrounds of participants, a recreational sport programmer might then create divisions based on gender. For example, the six leagues could be broken down into two men's, two women's, and two mixed doubles divisions. This would provide an opportunity for 10 men's teams, 10 women's teams, and 10 mixed doubles teams to register for the tournament.

Determining Round-Robin Matchups

At this point, the recreational sport programmer has made many of the tough decisions. In some recreational sport organizations, the programmer may have the luxury of entering all of the information thus far into a tournament-scheduling software program. These programs can produce team, league, and master tournament schedules quickly and efficiently. Many recreational sport organizations do not have access to this technology, however, and need to schedule tournaments by hand. Although hand scheduling can take longer, it is often the best way to customize tournament schedules based on the unique contexts of specific round-robin tournaments.

The first step in scheduling round-robin matchups is to *determine how many rounds* are going to be played in the tournament. A **round** is a completed set of games where every team in a league is scheduled to play (or has a bye) in one game. A **bye** is a round where one team is not scheduled to play and occurs in leagues with an odd number of teams (e.g., 3, 5, 7). When all of the rounds are complete, every team will have played every other team one time.

To determine how many rounds will be played in a round-robin tournament, use the following formulas. Remember, *n* refers to the number of teams in a league.

For odd-numbered leagues (e.g., 3, 5, 7), n = number of rounds.

For even-numbered leagues (e.g., 4, 6, 8), $n - 1$ = number of rounds.

In the case of a league with five teams (an odd number), it would take five rounds to complete the league schedule. In the case of a league with eight teams (an even number), it would take seven rounds to complete the league schedule.

The second step in determining matchups is to figure out *how many contests will be played in each round*. You can use the following formulas to figure this out:

For odd-numbered leagues (e.g., 3, 5, 7), $(n - 1) / 2$ = number of contests per round.

For even-numbered leagues (e.g., 4, 6, 8), $n / 2$ = number of contests per round.

In the doubles tennis tournament, which is scheduled in five-team leagues, there would be five total rounds ($n = 5$) and two games played in each round [$(5 - 1) / 2 = 2$]. Remember, however, that in an odd-numbered league, a bye will also be scheduled in each round. In the case of a league with eight teams, there would be a total of seven rounds ($n = 7$) and four games played in each round ($8 / 2 = 4$). Because there is an even number of teams in the league, there is no bye game—every team plays in every round.

The final step is to *determine the actual matchups in each round*. Although it might seem easy, this step is more complicated than it looks. Many novice recreational sport programmers have tried to do this and ended up with a schedule that did not make sense. If you do the following steps, you will guarantee that by the end of your schedule, every team will have played every other team, and in the case of odd-numbered leagues, every team will have taken its turn as the bye. Start by creating a grid such as in tables 5.1 and 5.2. Put the number of rounds across the top row and the number of games in the first column.

As with the first two steps, the process is slightly different for odd- and even-numbered leagues. In an odd-numbered league, each team receives a bye in each round, so the bye should be included in the grid. Even though the bye is not a game, it is still accounted for because this makes the scheduling process easier. In the case of the five-team league, there are five rounds across the top row and a bye and two games in the first column. To schedule matchups, begin in the first round. Place a *B* in the upper left-hand corner, followed by a sequence of numbers starting with 1 for each contest in the round. When you hit the last game listed, come back up the column,

TABLE 5.1 Five-Team (Odd-Numbered) League Matchups

	Round 1	Round 2	Round 3	Round 4	Round 5
Bye	B–5	B–4	B–3	B–2	B–1
Game 1	1 vs. 4	5 vs. 3	4 vs. 2	3 vs. 1	2 vs. 5
Game 2	2 vs. 3	1 vs. 2	5 vs. 1	4 vs. 5	3 vs. 4

TABLE 5.2 Four-Team (Even-Numbered) League Matchups

	Round 1	Round 2	Round 3
Game 1	1 vs. 4	1 vs. 3	1 vs. 2
Game 2	2 vs. 3	4 vs. 2	3 vs. 4

going from the bottom to the top. To schedule subsequent rounds, again begin with a *B* in the upper left-hand corner. Refer back to the previous round. Rotate the numbers counterclockwise around the *B*, beginning with the bye team. The *B* always stays in the same place. See table 5.1 on the previous page for an example of this rotation system.

The same principle is used in leagues with an even number of teams, except that there is no bye. Start with the number of rounds across the top row and the number of games in the first column. In the first round, start with a 1 in the upper left-hand corner and follow with a sequence of numbers until you hit the last game listed, coming back up the column. In the second round, use the same rotation method as before. Refer back to the first-round games and rotate the numbers around the 1. The 1 should always stay in the upper left-hand corner. Do this for all subsequent rounds until the grid is complete. See table 5.2 on the previous page for an example of the rotation system for a league with an even number of teams.

Scheduling the Tournament

After you determine the contest matchups, it's time to create a master schedule for the tournament. Although the objectives of every tournament and the demands of every sport are different, there are several rules of thumb to consider in order to be fair to participants. When possible, try to adhere to the following four steps:

1. Try to keep participants' match or game times consistent throughout the tournament.
2. Try not to schedule participants to play more than one match on a given day.
3. If participants have to play more than once per day, try not to schedule back-to-back matches or games.
4. If you have to schedule back-to-back matches or games, try to schedule the same for everyone.

First, create a master facility schedule based on your available facility reservation. See table 5.3 for a sample master facility schedule for the first day of the tournament (Monday) based on the doubles tennis tournament discussed previously. In this case, there are 12 contest slots per day.

Second, refer back to the formulas to determine how many contests each round-robin league will play in order to complete one round. Remember, in our doubles tennis tournament, there are two games per league in each round [(5 – 1) / 2 = 2], and there are six round-robin leagues.

Third, put your round-robin leagues into available contest slots on your master facility schedule. Each league will occupy two courts in each round. For our doubles tennis tournament, we can use the following league abbreviations:

- Men's league 1: ML-1
- Men's league 2: ML-2
- Women's league 1: WL-1
- Women's league 2: WL-2
- Mixed league 1: Co-1
- Mixed league 2: Co-2

Where you place the leagues on the schedule is up to you. You could do this based on the time preference of participants, the availability of tournament personnel, the desire to showcase premier games at attractive times, or any other factors that relate to the objectives of the tournament.

Fourth, create individual league schedules based on the scheduling matchups that you created. In a five-team league, the first round of matchups would be as follows:

Bye: 5

1 vs. 4

2 vs. 3

TABLE 5.3 Round-Robin Master Facility Schedule

Monday, 7/16	Court 1	Court 2	Court 3	Court 4
4:00 p.m.	ML-1 Pros vs. All-Stars	ML-1 Avengers vs. Supermen	ML-2	ML-2
5:00 p.m.	WL-1	WL-1	WL-2	WL-2
6:00 p.m.	Co-1	Co-1	Co-2	Co-2

Round robin tournaments are popular with participants. This lacrosse team is celebrating their championship, as they had the best win-loss record after playing everyone in their league once.

Imagine that the following five teams were registered to play in men's league 1:

- Team 1: Pros
- Team 2: Avengers
- Team 3: Supermen
- Team 4: All-Stars
- Team 5: Sharks

The first round of matchups for men's league 1 would be as follows:

Bye: Sharks
Court 1 at 4:00 p.m.: Pros vs. All-Stars
Court 2 at 4:00 p.m.: Avengers vs. Supermen

In order to schedule the entire tournament, repeat this process for each league, and do this for every round.

Round-Robin Tournament Summary

Round-robins are popular tournament designs. They are advantageous when the objective of the tournament is to maximize participation and when there are adequate resources and facilities to accommodate the number of contests that are required. They also provide a clear ranking of league teams at the end of the schedule by comparing win–loss records. Round-robins do have drawbacks, however. They are time and facility intensive and can create disincentives for losing teams to continue to participate over the course of a long season. One of the biggest drawbacks is the inability of round-robin tournaments to crown a true champion, particularly when there is more than one round-robin league where teams do not play common opponents. If determining a true champion is the objective, then an elimination tournament is usually necessary.

ELIMINATION TOURNAMENTS

Elimination tournaments are among the most well-known tournament designs. Because they determine a true champion by rewarding those who win and eliminating those who lose, they create excitement—each contest is critical. **Single-elimination tournaments** emphasize winning.

Teams that win advance and teams that lose are out. Popular single-elimination tournaments include the men's and women's NCAA college basketball tournaments, also called *March Madness*. Part of the excitement of these tournaments stems from the high stakes of every game and the upsets that often happen along the way. **Double-elimination tournaments** allow a team to lose a game and continue playing through an elimination or losers' bracket. Teams have the opportunity to play their way back to a potential championship even though they lost a game. The NCAA men's baseball and women's softball College World Series use a double-elimination format and have grown incredibly popular. Consolation tournaments are just single-elimination tournaments that provide the opportunity for losing teams to play another contest for exhibition or fun. They are typically used to determine third- and fourth-place teams.

In addition to being exciting, elimination tournaments are efficient and economical in that they typically do not require a lot of games to complete, and their scheduling process provides the opportunity to reward teams based on ability. Single-elimination tournaments in particular are easy for participants to understand, and they are perhaps the most used tournament format. They pair nicely with round-robin formats for use as postseason play-offs to determine a true tournament champion.

As with all tournaments, however, elimination formats have their disadvantages. They tend to focus on winners at the expense of losers and are not the best formats for encouraging long-term participation. Tournament matchups may be difficult to reschedule in case of team conflicts or weather problems because contests must be played sequentially. One positive feature of elimination tournaments, the excitement of needing to win to stay in the tournament (i.e., win or go home), can also be a drawback because it can create highly competitive environments that may not be suited for recreational sport. Additionally, the process of scheduling teams based on ability can be controversial if there is no objective way to determine tournament seeds. Finally, double-elimination tournaments can be difficult for participants to plan for because they need to consider schedules in both the winners' and losers' brackets, and they require far more games to complete than a single-elimination format.

Elimination Tournament Formulas

The scheduling process for single- and double-elimination tournaments is similar, particularly for the top half of the tournament bracket. A number of useful mathematical formulas and concepts make scheduling elimination tournaments easier. These are discussed next, and any differences between the two tournament types are noted.

Total Number of Games

One of the advantages of single-elimination tournaments is the relatively small number of games that it takes to complete them. Double-elimination tournaments, on the other hand, can take up to twice as many games to play, so they can be more facility intensive and unwieldy. To determine the total number of games in an elimination tournament, use the following formulas:

Single elimination: $n - 1$ = total number of games.

Double elimination: $2n - 1$ = total number of games (maximum).

Double elimination: $2n - 2$ = total number of games (minimum).

In a single-elimination tournament with 12 teams, it would take 11 total contests to complete the bracket and arrive at a champion, because $12 - 1 = 11$. A double-elimination tournament could take twice as many games to finish, because it is possible that the entry with one loss could beat the entry with no losses in the initial championship game. The 11-team double-elimination tournament would take a maximum of 21 games to complete because $22 - 1 = 21$. If the entry with no losses wins the first championship game, then the double-elimination tournament ends after only 20 games ($22 - 2 = 20$).

Total Number of Rounds

A round in an elimination tournament consists of all the contests that must be completed to determine who can advance in the tournament bracket. In single-elimination tournaments, rounds are determined by the following formula:

The power to which 2 must be raised to equal or exceed n = number of rounds.

ALTERNATIVE TO THE DOUBLE-ELIMINATION TOURNAMENT

Because double-elimination tournaments are so facility intensive, some recreational sport professionals instead use a combination of three-team round-robin leagues (guaranteeing teams 2 games) followed by a single-elimination tournament composed of league winners. In this format, for the round-robin tournaments it would take 12 games to complete the four leagues of three teams each: 3(3 – 1) / 2 * 4 = 12, where the formula is $n(n - 1) / 2$ * number of leagues for round-robin tournaments. Then there are 3 games to play the single-elimination playoff (4 – 1). The total number of games using the round-robin plus single-elimination format would be 15. This could save 7 games and still achieve the goal of guaranteeing teams at least 2 games. Saving these 7 games could be advantageous depending on the tournament objectives, facilities, staffing demands, and budget.

Using the previous example, it would take four rounds to complete a single-elimination tournament with 11 teams. This is because we need to multiply the number 2 four times to exceed the number of teams in the tournament—in this case, to exceed 11 teams. For example, $2 \times 2 \times 2 \times 2 = 2^4$. Two is multiplied four times, meaning it will take four rounds to complete this tournament.

Double-elimination formats follow a similar pattern, except it takes twice as many rounds to complete the tournament. In the previous case, it would take a minimum of eight rounds to complete a double-elimination tournament with 11 teams, because $2 \times 4 = 8$. In the event that it is necessary to play an extra championship game, it would take a maximum of nine rounds to complete this double-elimination tournament.

Total Number of Byes

As you can see, elimination tournaments are based on mathematical powers of 2. That is, when the tournament size is a power of 2 (e.g., 2, 4, 8, 16), it is considered to be a perfect tournament. This means that there are no first-round byes. Byes are advantaged positions in the bracket because they allow highly seeded teams to avoid playing a contest in the first round of the tournament. Participants who receive a bye play their first contest in the second round. To determine the number of byes in an elimination tournament, use the following formula:

Next highest power of 2 – n = number of byes.

For example, in a single-elimination tournament with 11 teams, there would be five byes, because 16 – 11 = 5. To schedule the tournament, the top five seeded teams would receive byes in the first round.

Number of First-Round Games

Figuring out the total number of first-round games in an elimination tournament follows a similar pattern. To determine the total number of first-round games, use the following formula:

n – next lowest power of 2 = number of first-round games.

In the 11-team tournament, only three first-round games will be played in the first round, because 11 – 8 = 3. Remember, there will be five first-round byes, so there will be more byes than games in the first round! That will not always be the case, because the number of first-round games and byes is dependent on the number of tournament entries.

Drawing Elimination Brackets

There are many methods for drawing accurate single- and double-elimination tournament brackets, and in many cases a tournament administrator may be able to access resources that provide ready-made scheduling templates for various tournament sizes. Byl's (2006) is one such resource, and a quick online search can yield countless others. However, there will undoubtedly be a time when you do not have access to your favorite tournament scheduling resources, which means it is important to know how to draw and seed elimination tournament brackets.

Single-Elimination Brackets

To draw a single-elimination bracket or the top half of a double-elimination bracket, always start from the end (the last game) and work backward. Continue to draw brackets on each available stem until you equal or exceed the number of teams in the tournament. Be sure that the brackets representing each round are lined up on top of one another to make it easy to read. Because large brackets are unwieldy and difficult to draw, it is preferable to keep bracket sizes to no more than 16 teams. For example, if you have 32 teams in a single-elimination tournament, rather than drawing one large (and messy) 32-team bracket, it would be wise to schedule the tournament in two 16-team brackets or four 8-team brackets with extra games provided to allow the bracket winners to play against one another to determine a true champion.

After drawing the bracket, it is time to seed the games. Again, it is advisable to start at the end and work backward. In a perfectly seeded bracket, the championship game should be a matchup between the two best entries—in this case, the #1 and #2 seeds. As a check to determine the proper matchups for each bracket, the seeds in each bracket in a round should add up to the number of entries in the round plus 1. This is the **magic number**. Because there are two entries in the final round, the magic number should be 3—in a perfectly seeded bracket, the seeds in the final round (#1 and #2) should add up to 3. Place the theoretical matchups on the bracket and move to the next round.

In the next round, there are now four entries. All bracket seeds should now add to 5 (number of entries in the round plus 1). Next, place the #1 seed on the top line of the top bracket and the #2 seed on the top line of the bottom bracket. Because the magic number is 5, the #1 team will play the #4 team, and the #2 team will play the #3 team. Again, place the seeds on the bracket and move to the next round.

There are now eight entries in this round. The magic number for seeding purposes should be 9, meaning that the seeds in all of the brackets in this round should equal 9. For this round, #1 plays #8, #2 plays #7, #3 plays #6, and #4 plays #5. Continue drawing and seeding brackets until you equal or exceed the number of teams in your tournament. Figure 5.2 shows an example of an eight-team single-elimination tournament.

Imagine you are scheduling an 11-team single-elimination tournament. After drawing and seeding your brackets, you should arrive at the following first-round matchups: #8 versus #9, #7 versus #10, and #6 versus #11. Because the highest seeds will always receive the byes, the top five seeds (#1 through #5) will not play in the first round. A single-elimination bracket that depicts the first-round bye games is called an **explicit bye bracket**. Many times, bye games are only

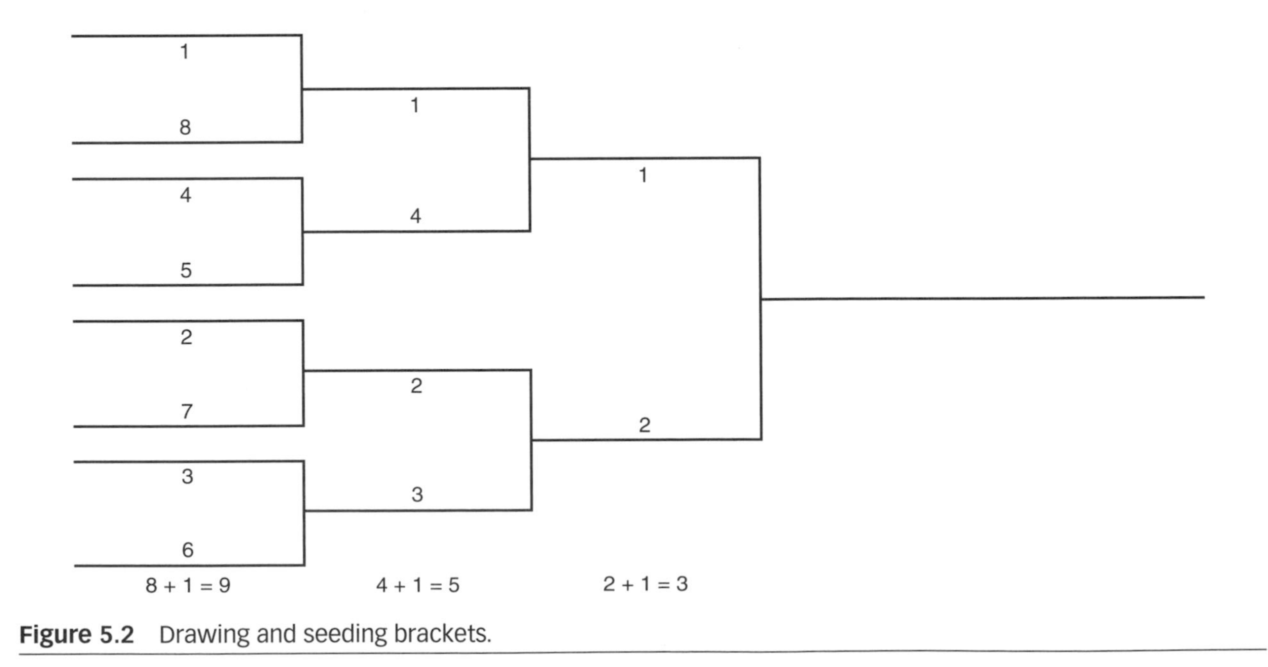

Figure 5.2 Drawing and seeding brackets.

indicated by a blank space on the tournament bracket. This is called an **implied bye bracket**. The formulas discussed earlier serve as a check on this process. Before drawing the bracket, the formulas showed that in an 11-team elimination tournament, there would be three first-round games and five byes.

After drawing and seeding, there are two final steps to complete the single-elimination scheduling. First, it is important to number each single-elimination game in the order that it appears on the tournament bracket. Start at the top of the round and work down, numbering sequentially, before moving on to the next round. In the case of the 11-team single-elimination tournament, the #8 versus #9 matchup should be game 1, followed by #7 versus #10 (game 2), #6 versus #11 (game 3), #1 versus winner of #8 versus #9 (game 4), and so on. Finally, after all contests are numbered, each bracket can be assigned a date, time, and playing location based on the available facility reservation.

Double-Elimination Tournaments

The process for drawing and seeding the top half (winners' or championship bracket) is the same for a double-elimination tournament. However, in a double-elimination tournament, every round played in the upper (winners') bracket requires two rounds in the lower (losers') bracket. Therefore, before the tournament can be scheduled, it is necessary to draw the lower bracket. There are various methods for drawing double-elimination brackets, but the easiest way is to stack the top and bottom halves of the brackets together. It is also important, particularly in double-elimination tournaments with more than three teams, to use **crossover scheduling** where the loser of a contest is matched up in an elimination contest against a team from the next major bracket (Byl, 2006). This prevents entries from playing one another in close succession. Although this is not always possible to control, crossover scheduling can minimize one of the major disadvantages of double-elimination tournaments. Figure 5.3 shows an example of a double-elimination bracket scheduled with this method.

Elimination Tournament Summary

Both single- and double-elimination tournaments are exciting for participants because of the high-stakes nature of the format (i.e., win or go home). Because of this, elimination tournaments are excellent choices for recreational sport programmers when the objective of the tournament is to determine a true champion or to maximize competition between entries. Although they are exciting and efficient, single-elimination tournaments can sometimes place too much emphasis on winning, and they are not always appropriate when the goal is to maximize participation or guarantee entries a certain number of playing opportunities. Double-elimination tournaments are good choices when the objective is to guarantee teams at least two games. However, double-elimination tournaments are time and facility intensive, and they can be confusing for participants to understand.

CHALLENGE OR EXTENDED TOURNAMENTS

Challenge tournaments, also called *extended tournaments*, are creative tournament formats that allow participants to challenge one another to play matches over an extended period of time. Challenge tournaments are participant centered; that is, the recreational sport programmer's job is to lay out a framework for participation, including a tournament structure, time frame for completion, basic rules, and contact information for each entry. The details related to scheduling matches, competing, and reporting results are left to the tournament participants.

Challenge tournaments tend to work best in sports where participants have a certain level of expertise or in activities where the rules, norms, and standards are fairly well known. These tournament formats are often used with individual, dual, and team sports where participants are highly motivated, have an interest in playing over an extended time, and need little direct supervision (Barcelona, 2008).

An almost unlimited number of creative challenge tournament formats exist, although two major types and their variants are used most often—the ladder tournament and the pyramid tournament. The idea is that participants challenge one another in contests that they schedule within parameters set by the recreational sport programmer. For example, participants might be required to play at least one contest per week and

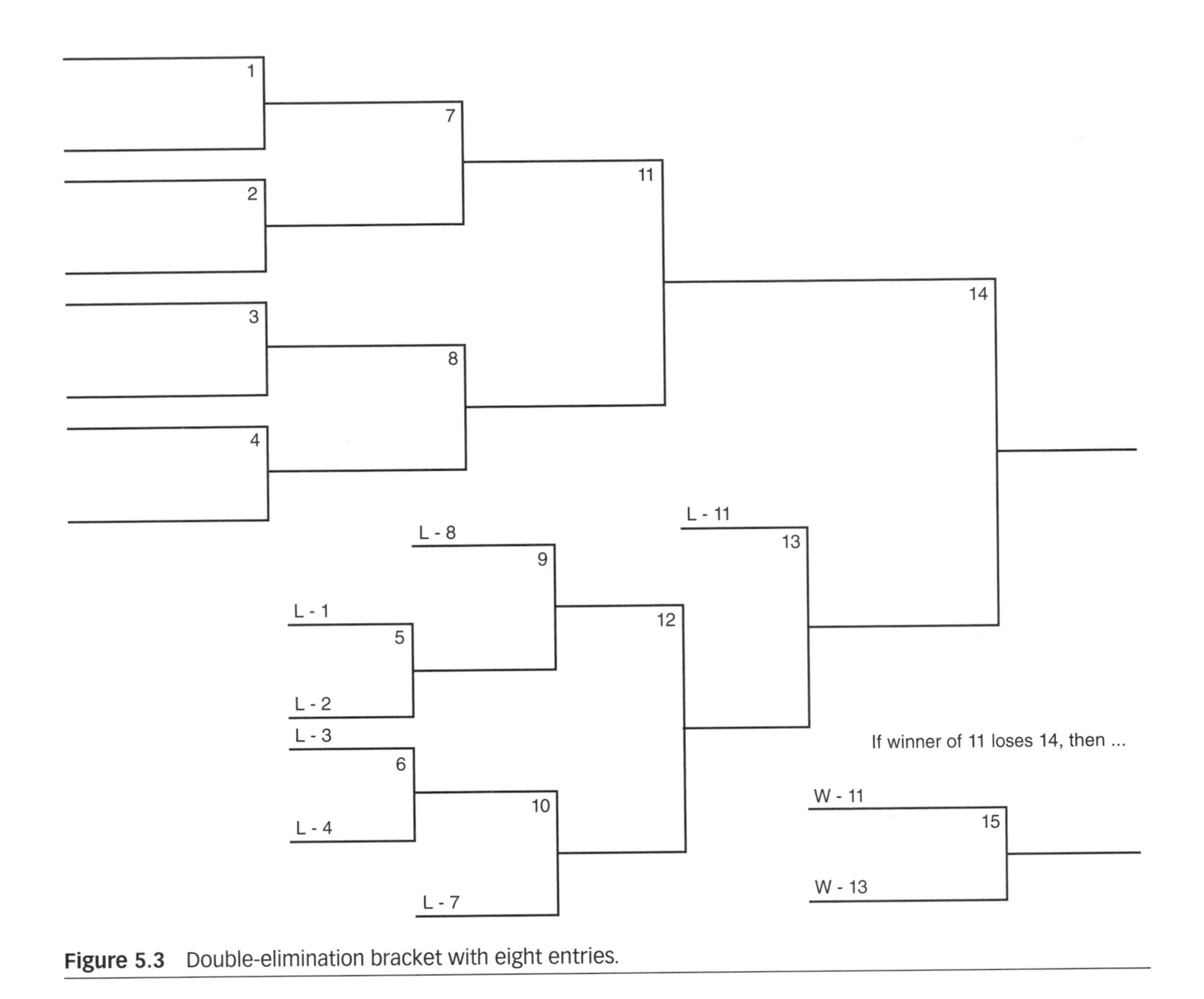

Figure 5.3 Double-elimination bracket with eight entries.

report the results. Winners of challenges either move up the tournament structure or defend their position. The person at the top of the ladder or pyramid at the end of a specified time period would be considered the winner of the tournament. Both ladder and pyramid tournaments are discussed next.

Ladder Tournaments

Ladders are easy for participants to understand and are useful for relatively small tournaments. Participants are placed in a position on a ladder before challenges begin. The placement of participants is at the discretion of the recreational sport programmer. If it is possible to know the ability levels of participants, then seeding entries based on ability makes sense. However, often this is not possible, in which case random assignment to ladder positions is appropriate.

After participants are placed on the ladder, they are typically given a time frame to schedule and play a match against an opponent who is one or two places away. If the lower-ranked participant wins, she trades places on the ladder with the higher-ranked participant. If the higher-ranked participant wins, she defends her spot and remains in place. The goal of the tournament administrator is to set up the ladder structure and monitor the tournament to make sure that contests are being played. Sometimes participants do not play as frequently as they should, and guidelines or incentives should be put in place to encourage challenges. For example, if a participant is not challenged in a certain time frame, then he should be encouraged to challenge someone else ahead of him on the ladder. Figure 5.4 shows an example of a ladder tournament for intramural racquetball.

Intramural Racquetball Ladder Tournament

Division: Women's Intermediate

League: Intermediate ladder 1

Place	Players	Place
1	Alicia Atwater	1
2	Betsy Brookover	2
3	Celeste Clem	3
4	Denise Donaldson	4
5	Emma Echenmeier	5
6	Fiona Ferdinand	6
7	Georgia Greenleaf	7
8	Harriet Hoffman	8
9	Ingrid Inhoff	9
10	Jacqueline Joyce	10
11	Kim Kilpatrick	11
12	Loraine Lamont	12
Place		Place

Rules:

1. Players have been assigned randomly to positions on the ladder.
2. In order to move up the ladder, you may challenge another player above you.
3. You may only challenge players who are up to 2 levels ahead (#4 may challenge #3 or #2).
4. Challenges are made by contacting opponents via their preferred contact method.
5. Go to www.intramurals.edu/racquetball to obtain contact information for opponents.
6. Challenges should be made early in the week for scheduling convenience.
7. Opponents have 1 week to accept a challenge and play a game.
8. Challenges not accepted within a 1 week time frame (or no shows) will be declared a forfeit.
9. Challenges must be played in order!
10. It is the winner's responsibility to notify the IM staff within 24 hours of contest results.
11. If the lower seed wins, positions are switched on the ladder.
12. If the higher seed wins, ladder positions stay the same.
13. You must play at least one game per week.
14. If you are not challenged in a week, you must challenge one of your opponents.
15. Official rules can be found at the IM website (www.intramurals.edu/racquetball/rules).
16. All questions or disputes will be settled by the IM staff - contact us at imstaff@im.edu.
17. The player at the top of the ladder on Friday, October 27 will be declared the winner.

Figure 5.4 Intramural racquetball ladder tournament.

Pyramid Tournaments

Pyramid tournaments are similar to ladder tournaments in that the participants' objective is to arrive at the top of the pyramid after challenging opponents and defending their own positions on the pyramid. The biggest difference is that in a pyramid tournament, multiple participants are on the same level. There are two main methods for conducting challenges. The first method is similar to the ladder, where challenges are made with participants at the next highest level of the pyramid. The second method provides a bit more complexity. Challenges must be made at the same level of the pyramid, with the winner then being free to challenge an opponent on the next highest level. An example of a pyramid tournament can be found in figure 5.5. The spiderweb tournament is a variation on the pyramid, except the goal is to get to the center of the web.

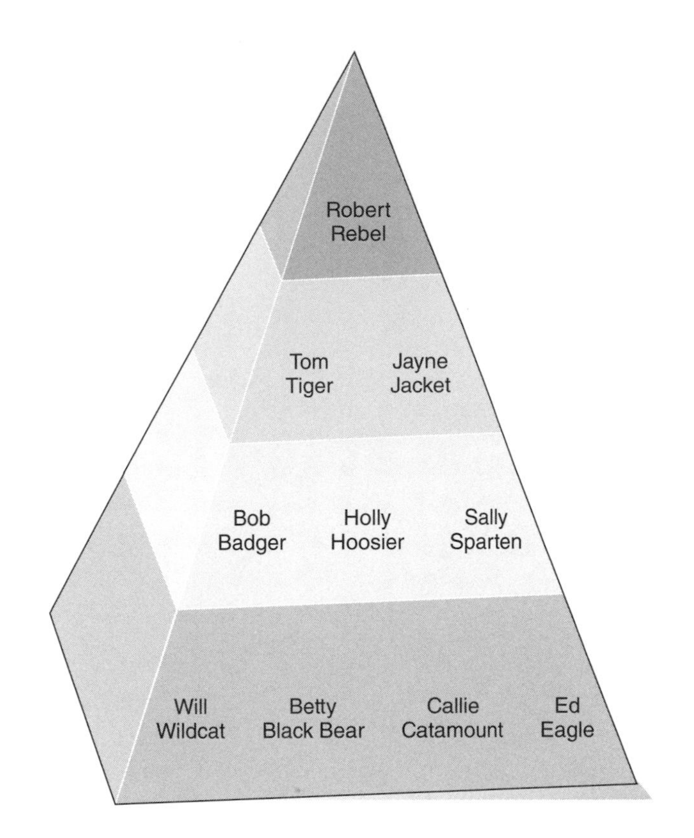

Figure 5.5 Pyramid tournament.

Challenge or Extended Tournament Summary

Participants like challenge tournaments because they are creative and fun and they provide a maximum amount of flexibility. They are advantageous for recreational sport programmers because they require few resources and generally run themselves with minimal supervision. As such, challenge tournaments work best with participants who are highly motivated and who need little direct oversight. As with all tournament formats, it is important to match the design with the objectives of the tournament and the characteristics of the participants.

CONCLUSION

Successful tournament design is the result of strategic decision making on the part of the recreational sport programmer. Many tournament formats are available, including round-robins, single and double eliminations, and a host of challenge or extended tournament formats, such as ladders, pyramids, and spiderwebs. Each has its advantages and disadvantages—there is no perfect design. The best format is entirely dependent on the objectives of the tournament, characteristics of the participants, sport-specific rules and regulations, facility, equipment, personnel needs and limitations, and number of tournament entries. Finally, good tournament design is as much art as it is science. Recreational sport programmers would be wise to make decisions with the three big-picture goals of tournaments in mind—to facilitate sport participation, promote cooperation, and provide a framework for just and fair competition.

RESEARCH TO REALITY

Popke, M. (2000, May). Tournament Time! *Athletic Business*, 69-73.

This article provides suggestions for effective tournament design and scheduling. One of the main points the author makes is that tournaments are showcase events, and participants have a variety of choices in the marketplace. Poorly designed tournaments do not attract repeat visitors. Even well-run tournaments that do not keep up with the times may find it difficult to attract the desired number of teams. Suggestions for effective tournament design include offering well-maintained facilities, creative and intriguing events, skilled officiating, quality concessions, adequate lodging, reasonable registration fees, creative marketing, tight security, partnerships with community organizations and corporate sponsors, media coverage, strict enforcement of game rules, and easily disseminated game information. The author suggests that to drive repeat customers, tournament administrators must continue to improve, making each tournament better than the one before.

The author suggests that with an increasingly crowded marketplace, recreational sport programmers must be aware of the quality of the tournaments that they run; otherwise they run the risk of poor participation. Think about what we have discussed in the preceding pages. How does Popke's research on well-run tournaments connect with our tournament goals of facilitating sport participation, promoting co-operation, and providing a framework for just and fair competition? What are the consequences of poorly run tournaments for participants, staff, and recreational sport organizations?

REFLECTION QUESTIONS

1. Describe what is meant by the idea that tournament design is as much an art as a science.
2. What are the advantages and disadvantages of round-robin tournaments, single-elimination tournaments, double-elimination tournaments, and challenge tournaments?
3. What are the major considerations that tournament administrators must take into account before the tournament scheduling process?

LEARNING ACTIVITIES

1. Do some research on your school's intramural sport program. What sports are offered? How are each of the sports scheduled? Does your school use one tournament design method more than others? Talk to the intramural sport director and ask why the sport is scheduled in the format that it is.
2. You are interested in running a flag football tournament for your school's intramural sport program. You are going to schedule games on the hour. The facility director has given you the following facility reservation: two weeks, Mondays through Thursdays, 4 p.m. to 10 p.m., three fields. How many total games are available for your tournament given the facility reservation? You are interested in scheduling your tournament with leagues of five teams. How many five-team leagues can you have in your tournament? How many total teams could you register if you were scheduling in five-team leagues? Provide a master facility schedule for all games in the tournament.
3. Draw and seed a 12-team single-elimination tournament. The regular season rankings are as follows: (1) Tigers, (2) Bulldogs, (3) Wildcats, (4) Devils, (5) Turtles, (6) Hornets, (7) Hurricanes, (8) Seahawks, (9) Bears, (10) Wolf Pack, (11) Eagles, (12) Rebels. The tournament will run for four days (Thursday through Sunday) and will be played every two hours on one court, with the following facility reservation available: Thursday: 1 p.m. to 9 p.m., Friday: 1 p.m. to 9 p.m.; Saturday: 1 p.m. to 5 p.m.; Sunday: 1 p.m. to 3 p.m. Teams should only play one game per day.

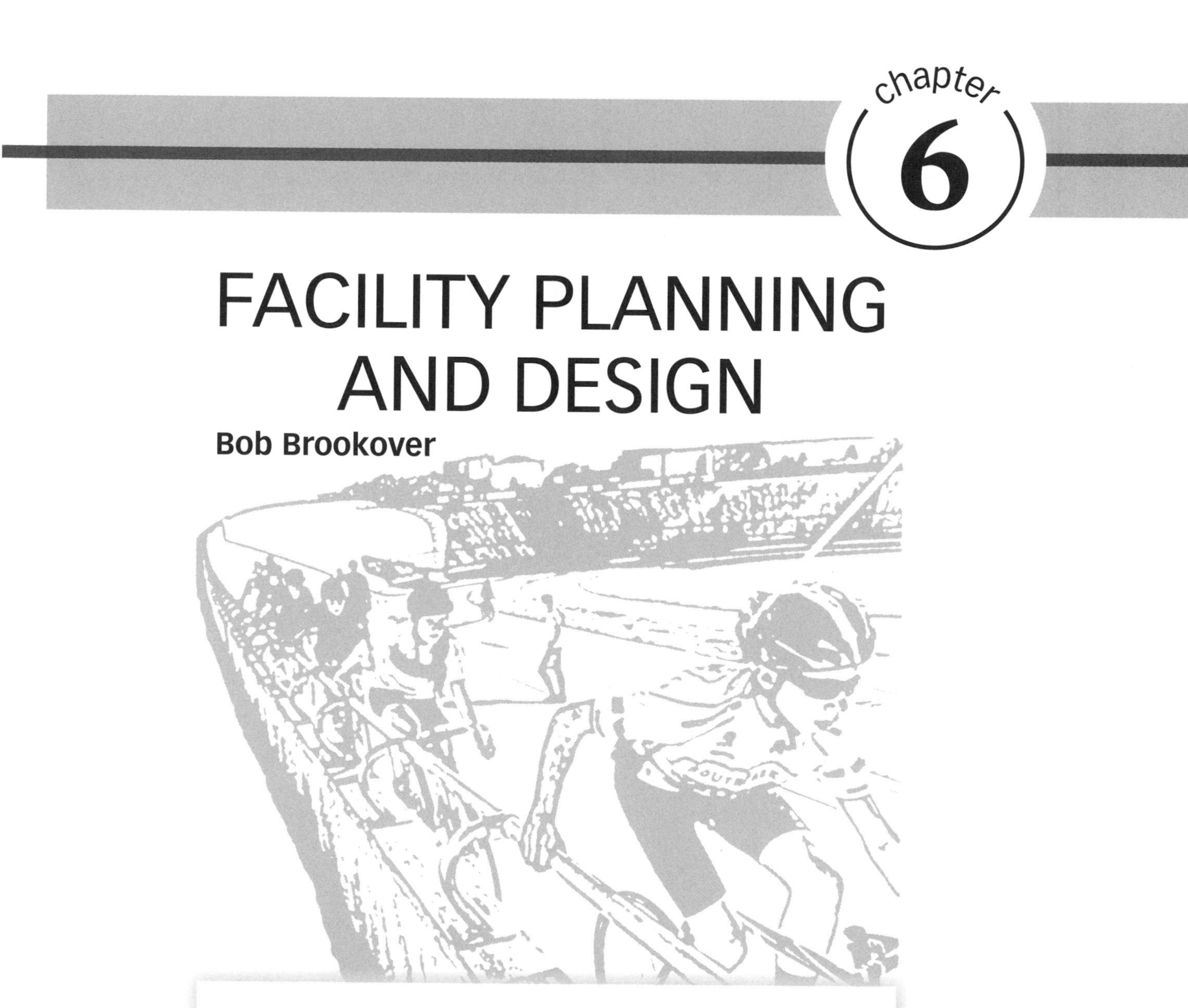

chapter 6

FACILITY PLANNING AND DESIGN

Bob Brookover

LEARNING OUTCOMES

By the end of this chapter, readers will be able to

- explain the importance of developing strategic and master plans and how the organizational vision, mission, and goals derived from planning efforts should drive the development and operations of recreational sport facilities and venues;
- describe the master planning process and how it relates to strategic planning;
- define and differentiate between the facility design and construction processes;
- outline project financing options and trends for recreational sport facilities; and
- articulate how sustainability, risk management, equipment, maintenance, and technology factor into facility projects.

Case Study

OUTDOOR CENTER AT RIVERWALK IN ROCK HILL, SOUTH CAROLINA

The City of Rock Hill's velodrome project is a small but transformational piece of an economic development project. This project, known as Riverwalk, is a 1,008-acre (408-hectare) tract of land on the Catawba River that was once owned and occupied by Hoechst Celanese Corporation. At one time this site was the largest cellulose acetate manufacturing facility in the United States. The plant began operations in 1948 and at its peak employed 2,500 people in Rock Hill. The facility closed in 2005 after 57 years in operation. Shortly thereafter, The Assured Group, a private equity firm, purchased the site and formed a local subsidiary known as The Greens of Rock Hill LLC. The Greens began demolition and environmental cleanup of the site in 2005, completing the initial phase in December of 2007.

The idea to construct a velodrome (a banked track used for cycling races and other events) began around this same time when a few cycling enthusiasts approached the developer with their dream of building a velodrome in Rock Hill. The velodrome was quickly identified as the catalyst for the future development of the site. The developer partnered with the City of Rock Hill by pledging 250 acres (101 hectares) of the site for public ownership and use. The development vision includes a river village and a planned vibrant community including housing, shopping, entertainment, offices, light manufacturing, and recreational amenities. Employment at the site is projected to bring 4,000 jobs to Rock Hill. Along with construction of the velodrome, facilities such as an Olympic-specification BMX supercross track, a cyclo-cross course, and trails to host professional mountain-bike races are planned for the site. In addition to the cycling-related facilities, 6 acres (2 hectares) of open green space; fields for soccer, football, lacrosse, baseball, and softball; and river access including a canoe and kayak launch site will be developed on the site.

In the spring of 2010, construction cost estimates for the velodrome came in at $4,000,000. The city considered all forms of financing, including general obligation bonds, tax increment financing (TIF), revenue bonds, New Markets Tax Credits, and recovery zone bonds. Regardless of the type of financing, a local hospitality tax was identified as the best source for funding eventual debt repayment. The city's finance department then began studying the most economical means of financing the project as well as determining when the city's hospitality tax revenues would increase sufficiently to support the additional debt. Financial projections identified $375,000 as the annual amount necessary to fund a $4,000,000 project financed over 20 years. A time frame for achieving that revenue was projected.

City finance staff began researching and learning the specifics of a form of financing called the *New Markets Tax Credit (NMTC)*. Congress established the NMTC Program in 2000 to incentivize new development in low-income communities by permitting investors to receive a tax credit against their federal income tax return in exchange for making equity investments in specialized financial institutions called *community development entities*.

The City of Rock Hill found that with an NMTC, approximately 25 percent of the project costs could be forgiven after seven years. Rock Hill finance staff called various financial institutions but ultimately worked with TD Bank in Greenville, South Carolina. Additionally, city staff learned that various previously awarded but unused stimulus funds were available for reallocation by the State of South Carolina. The city quickly submitted an application for the reallocated funds and put together an application for a recovery zone designation, which provided a 45 percent interest rebate.

Next, city staff learned that the NMTC process involved many legal steps. It was determined that the break-even point on legal and issuance costs was a project cost of at least $5,000,000. In other words, for any project less than $5,000,000, the 25-percent saving achieved would be spent in legal and issuance costs. At that time the project became known as the Cycling and Outdoor Center of the Carolinas. BMX supercross, cyclo-cross, and mountain-biking facilities were added to the scope of the project to expand the $4 million velodrome project to a $5 million project.

The City of Rock Hill entered into an NMTC agreement with TD Bank to fund the $5 million project. The project was funded as two interest-only loans for seven years. Loan A was negotiated for $3.8 million at a taxable rate of 5.75 percent. Loan B was for $1.2 million at a tax-exempt rate of 2.25 percent. At the end of the seven-year interest-only term, the NMTC would be granted to an investor and loan B, or $1.2 million in principal, would be forgiven in exchange for the tax credits. Also after year 7, loan A would convert into a traditional loan.

With the $375,000 in hospitality taxes already identified and budgeted annually, the city began annual interest payments of $223,000 on loan A and $27,000 on loan B, leaving $125,000 per year to set aside annually for an $875,000 principal payment on loan A in year 8. Additionally, the recovery zone designation was approved, reimbursing 45 percent of the annual interest cost, or $112,500 per year, to the city. These funds, amounting to $787,500, are being set aside in escrow for the principal reduction of loan A in year 8. Sponsorship dollars (Giordana, the Piedmont Medical Center, and Presbyterian Sports Medicine purchased naming rights to several of the facilities) are also being set aside for the future principal reduction of loan A.

In year 8, the city will be required to convert the $3.8 million loan A to traditional principal and interest financing, and over $1.8 million in funds will have accumulated in the escrow account ($875,000 in hospitality taxes, $787,500 in recovery zone dollars, and $140,000 in sponsorship dollars). Paying down the principal balance reduces the $3.8 million loan in year 8 to less than $2.0 million, which will require approximately $250,000 in annual payments over a 10-year term. At the same time, loan B will be forgiven in exchange for the NMTC. In summary, in year 8, the City of Rock Hill will owe less than $2.0 million on $5.0 million in amenities.

Financed as a general obligation or tax increment loan, this project would have cost the City of Rock Hill $7,500,000 ($375,000 per year × 20 years). Financed as an NMTC deal with a recovery zone designation, this project will cost the City of Rock Hill $5,125,000 ($375,000 × 7 years + $250,000 × 10 years). Plus, the city is gaining a BMX supercross, a cyclo-cross, and mountain-biking trails in addition to the development catalyst, the velodrome.

Case study developed by Anne Harty, CFO for the City of Rock Hill, and John Taylor, operations supervisor for the City of Rock Hill Department of Parks, Recreation, and Tourism.

Think about some of your favorite places and make a list. Now consider how many of those places have some relationship to your leisure, recreation, or sport interests. It is likely that most of the places on your list have something to do with how you spend your leisure time. Sport and recreational facilities and venues are extremely important to us as individuals and as a society. They can contribute to individual and community health, create a sense of place, play important roles in community and economic development, and give people a place to escape to. Whether you enjoy joining 80,000 of your closest friends at a college football game or spending quiet time reflecting in a local park, the facilities and venues where we spend our leisure time are essential to us as human beings and in some cases even become part of our personal identity. Imagine what your life would be like if the places you listed did not exist.

For the purposes of this chapter we will define **recreational sport facilities** as any indoor, outdoor, natural, or human-made structures, areas, or spaces that are designed, managed, or used for recreation, sport, and leisure activities. The facilities can be public or private, active or passive, and formal or informal in nature. This definition is so broad because the range and types of facilities in our field are extremely broad, from open space to trails to ball fields of every variety to aquatic facilities to major stadiums to recreation and fitness centers.

In addition to the many types of facilities within our field, there are several other reasons why it is important that recreational sport professionals understand the principles of planning and management as they relate to facilities and equipment. Facilities and equipment create impressions—good and bad. Facilities are the vehicle many organizations and businesses use to generate significant portions of their operational revenues. There are federal, state, and local laws and regulations that have an impact on facility design and operations. Regardless of your position in the field, you will deal with some type of facility or be involved in decisions about facilities. Without facilities, we cannot provide programs or services. But as usual, the bottom line is the bottom line. For the majority of organizations, facilities and equipment are the most valuable and most expensive assets. Here are a few examples of facilities and their costs:

- The Ohio State University's Recreation and Physical Activity Center—$140 million
- The Fenlands Banff Community Recreation Centre Renovation and Addition—$26 million (Canadian)
- Tyger River Park in Spartanburg, South Carolina (12-field baseball and softball complex)—$20 million
- Commonwealth Community Recreation Centre Renovation and Addition—$96.8 million (Canadian)
- The median cost for a typical community center falls between $140 and $150 per square foot (.09 m^2) or $1.4 to $1.5 million for a small facility of 10,000 square feet (929 m^2) (Dalvit, 2010)

People and programs are important, but without facilities, spaces, and equipment, people cannot create programs to serve the needs of their communities. Facilities and equipment are obviously an essential part of what recreational sport professionals do.

The purpose of this chapter is to provide an overview of the planning processes related to developing and operating recreational sport facilities. Organizations in the public sector use revenues derived from the people through taxes and have a higher burden (or should have a higher burden) of responsibility for using those resources in a responsible and efficient manner in meeting stakeholders' needs. In the private sector, if organizations miss the mark with their planning, they risk losing their own and their investors' money. Many of the common problems in facility design and operations are a result of poor planning; in fact, poor planning is often the reason programs and services fail, budgets do not work, and liability issues arise.

The chapter is organized around the planning and operations model shown in figure 6.1.

The focus of the chapter is the ongoing process of **strategic planning**, where organizations take a step back and assess, evaluate, develop, change, or refine their vision, mission, and goals. This process drives the organization's **master plan**, which verifies that existing facilities and programs are appropriate and creates concepts for new or improved facilities, venues, and spaces (and programs and services). Once selected, concepts go through a design and construction process, and upon completion, they enter the operations phase. Throughout this cycle, the organization and designers should ensure that the concepts they pursue through the design and construction process, as well as the operations of their current

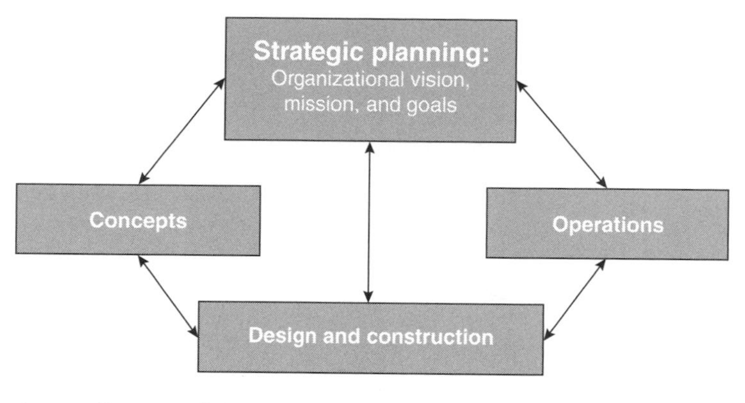

Figure 6.1 Planning and operations model.

and future facilities and venues, support goals that ultimately result in the achievement of the mission and realization of the vision.

DEVELOPING AND REFINING STRATEGIC AND MASTER PLANS

A common practice in developing strategic or master plans has been to create a 10-year plan with at least one evaluation point built in around year 5. Although this approach has worked well for many organizations in the past, there is a trend to create and revisit these plans on a 5-year or shorter time frame due to the fact that conditions change much more rapidly today than they did even 10 or 15 years ago. Turnover on boards, commissions, and city and county councils that make decisions and set priorities for public agencies may necessitate change. Technological advances in equipment, building systems, and management information systems are providing new opportunities and abilities to create operational efficiencies that should not wait for the next plan to be developed before implementation. It is ultimately up to the organization to determine the appropriate frequency and timing of the strategic planning process based on its operating environment, context, and conditions.

Strategic Planning

Strategic planning is often one of those simple yet complex processes. A common framework for planning includes three relatively simple questions that get at complex issues: (1) Where are you now?, (2) Where do you want to be?, and (3) How do you get there? (Daly, 2000). In other words, an organization conducts a situational analysis (where you are now), conducts an opportunity analysis (where you want to be), and develops an implementation strategy (how you get there). The purpose of a situational analysis is to determine an organization's capabilities, and it should include a comprehensive examination of internal and external factors that influence those capabilities. Taking a look at resources, demographics, history, future trends, competition, the political environment, and other factors should be part of a situational analysis.

Using the information gathered during the situational analysis phase of the strategic planning process, an organization can then outline opportunities for creating new programs and services to meet the needs and demands of its stakeholders during the opportunity analysis phase of the planning process. Opportunity analysis involves developing and vetting multiple concepts, ideas, and strategies to pursue.

Finally, the implementation strategy should focus on creating a vision for where the organization wants to be, a mission statement that describes what the organization is about and does, and goals and objectives outlining the actions the organization should take to pursue the concepts, ideas, and strategies chosen in the opportunity analysis. Obviously, these concepts, ideas, and strategies should be in line with the mission and should assist in realizing the vision of the organization.

Although a multitude of detailed strategic planning models have been developed, most can be organized within these three basic questions. Some organizations choose a generic model and

© Bob Brookover

Strategic planning can help determine the needs for specialty facilities like this BMX bike track.

some create their own model or adapt a generic model to fit their needs. Again, it is ultimately up to the organization to decide which approach best meets its needs.

Strategic Plans Drive Master Plans

Once a strategic plan has been developed outlining the big ideas, concepts, and strategies, organizations typically develop **master plans** that outline how they can use their existing facilities and resources and the types and locations of new facilities and resources to be developed to support the plan. Sometimes used interchangeably with *strategic plans*, master plans typically focus on large- to small-scale planning related to the development of entire communities or large areas down to what specific sites within a community might be used for. Your school most likely has an overall master plan that starts from a big-picture perspective and gets into finer and finer levels of detail that outline plans for currently unused sites; potential expansions, renovations, and retrofits of existing facilities; traffic flow; and even parking. The master plans may even begin to get into specifics about where facilities such as intramural complexes, athletic facilities, and future indoor recreation centers may be located and how they connect to each other, to where students live, and to the rest of campus.

Another example might be a municipal recreation agency deciding that as part of a strategy to increase sport tourism, it should develop tennis facilities capable of hosting large regional and national tournaments. In this case, the recreation staff should work with the planning department of the municipality to determine if any previous planning efforts included developing tennis amenities. If so, then the planning process may begin with a simple update to an existing plan. If not, then the agency may create, or hire consultants to create, a master plan that outlines the size, scope, location, and design concepts for a tennis complex.

Input in Strategic and Master Planning Processes

In any planning effort it is vital for both public- and private-sector organizations to receive input from customers, staff, administrators, decision

© Bob Brookover

Master facility plans help to determine the overall layout of sport facilities like this clover leaf softball complex.

makers, and other stakeholders. Some organizations choose to undertake planning projects on their own and some choose to hire consultants. Regardless of whether it is an in-house effort or you hire a consultant, the success of the plan will ultimately be up to your ability to make the input process as participatory as possible. This means that you should provide all possible interested parties with opportunities to make their voices and opinions heard. Any good input strategy employs multiple methods of data collection, several of which are described next. Again, the main goal should be to give everyone an opportunity to provide input through some channel.

Needs assessment surveys have been and continue to be a primary method of receiving input. These surveys can be an invaluable source of information. However, the traditional method of getting input from a random sample of the target population using a mail survey has become extremely difficult due to low response rates. Many researchers and consultants hoped that the ability to create online surveys would increase response rates, but this has not typically been the case. When considering the use of surveys, it is important to develop an aggressive plan to encourage people to participate. In addition to traditional incentives to entice people to complete and return traditional mail surveys, you might identify organizations and events (e.g., civic groups, churches, social organizations, youth leagues, community festivals) in the community whose participants provide a representative cross-section of your constituents and go to a meeting or event and conduct surveys on-site as part of a multiple-methods approach to achieving a representative sample.

In addition to surveys, focus groups are a popular input method for strategic and master planning. Small to medium-sized groups are interviewed using questions and input activities to get them to think about what they believe is important for the recreational sport organization to provide. Some input activities for focus groups might include exercises such as what-iffing and using headlines. What-iffing uses what-if scenarios, such as "What if there were no recreational sport facilities or programs in your area? What would your top three to five priorities be if you were charged with developing those services?" The headlines activity asks participants to create headlines or stories they would like to see in the local newspaper in 5 and 10 years that outline the major accomplishments of the recreational sport agency over that time. In both cases, the group is given time to come to a consensus and record its priorities and headlines. Staff or consultants then categorize that input and analyze the results to determine top priorities.

With a variety of user-friendly polling systems readily available, it is possible to create large-format, hybrid-input sessions. Polling software and systems allow you to invite hundreds of people to sessions and conduct traditional surveys using the software and input devices. The interesting feature of these systems is that results can be posted immediately. As soon as the participants have finished entering their answers, researchers can display the results. Once the polling session is complete, the larger group can be broken up into groups of 8 to 12 for traditional focus-group sessions and activities. Another advantage of this method is that the research team can create new questions on the fly to enter into the polling software and follow up with additional questions at the end of the session to create a finer level of detail in the data.

Random sampling is still the gold standard, but it has become more and more difficult to achieve. Using multiple methods and casting as wide a net as possible to ensure that you are receiving input that is representative of the population you are serving should be the primary goal.

Master Planning Process

The master plan provides a finer level of detail about concepts for facility projects at both the system level and individual project level. The design process will be discussed later in the chapter, but the first step in the design process is conceptual design (creating ideas or concepts of what a facility or amenity may be). Master plans provide conceptual designs for one or more projects depending on the scope of the plan and therefore can save time once an organization decides to move a concept forward into the more detailed levels of design. The master planning process typically involves five or six steps:

1. Select a consultant. Unless the organization has great planning resources and capabilities, hiring a consultant is in its best interest. In addition to being able to spend a great deal of time on the project, consultants provide an outside perspective that can be invaluable.
2. Complete the preproject coordination. This step includes creating a schedule or timeline of when steps in the project will be completed and formulating goals and objectives for the master plan.
3. Conduct an inventory and analysis of the current situation. This step is the meat of the process. It's where an organization assesses the current situation and begins to formulate ideas about future directions. Reviewing strategic planning outcomes (vision, mission, goals), looking at the organization's history, understanding the programs and services the organization provides, inventorying current facilities, assessing potential sites for development, reviewing previous master planning efforts, and conducting public-input activities are all part of this phase.
4. Create a draft plan outlining possible projects and alternative solutions. This stage should include feedback from staff, administrators, decision makers, and the public in deciding which projects and solutions move forward into the final draft.
5. Complete the final draft, including final reviews and revisions by staff.
6. Submit the plan for final approval and adoption by the appropriate decision-making body.

Once adopted, the master plan is ready to be presented to the public and media. See figure 6.2 for a flow chart.

BENCHMARKING AND SPACE STANDARDS

A number of organizations have published space and safety standards that can be useful for determining facility needs and benchmarking an agency against other similar agencies. The National Recreation and Park Association (NRPA), National Intramural-Recreational Sports Association (NIRSA), and American College of Sports Medicine (ACSM) are three such groups that provide benchmarking and space standards.

NRPA has developed a system called *PRORAGIS* that allows public recreation agencies to mine operational and performance data and GIS (geographic information system) data from agencies throughout the United States. These data can be used to make comparisons between your agency and similarly sized and structured agencies or

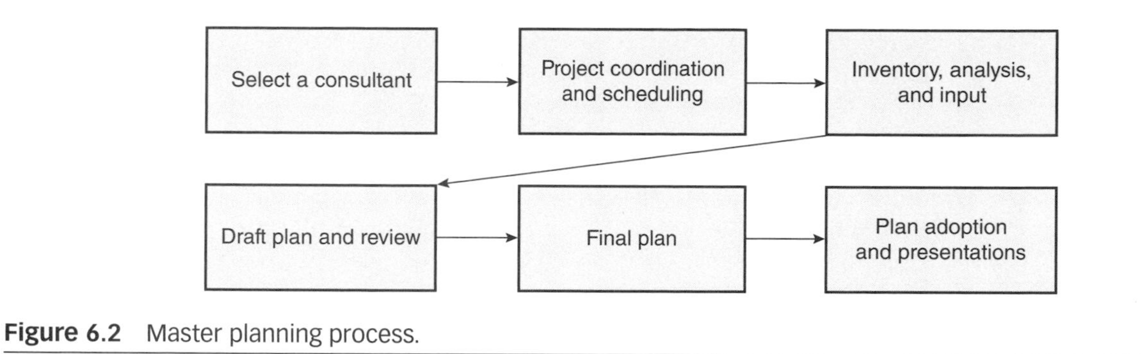

Figure 6.2 Master planning process.

agencies you aspire to emulate. NIRSA (2009) publishes *Space Planning Guidelines for Campus Recreational Sport Facilities*. The guidelines provide benchmarking information for total indoor space, fitness spaces, outdoor adventure spaces including climbing walls and aquatic facilities, and outdoor spaces such as intramural fields. These standards were derived from a survey of more than 200 campus recreation administrators in the United States and Canada. Finally, the ACSM's *Health/Fitness Facility Standards and Guidelines* (Peterson & Tharrett, 2012) gets into specific details about activity spaces, auxiliary areas, specialty areas, safety, programming areas, organizational structure and staffing, signage, emergency procedures, equipment, environmental considerations (e.g., temperature, air turnover), lighting, and cleaning.

Using accepted published standards and benchmarking information is extremely useful, but it is also important to create your own list of peer organizations and facilities and benchmark yourself against those. NRPA's PRORAGIS system makes this easier for public recreation agencies to accomplish without having to contact individual agencies directly. However, PRORAGIS relies on agencies uploading and updating their own data. Until that system hits a critical mass, you need to make sure it is providing sufficient and timely information. The good news is that it is relatively easy and can be fun to create a list of agencies (10 to 15 are plenty) and talk directly to your peers about their facilities, programs, and services. Be sure to create a basic outline of the information you want to gather and the level of detail you need for each area you are trying to benchmark. An online survey can be an effective tool if you need more detail than can be obtained in a phone interview. At a minimum, basic information about square footage and acreage of various spaces, programs and services offered (if this information cannot be attained by looking at the agency's website), fees charged, and population served should be gathered from each peer for benchmarking.

PROGRAM STATEMENTS

Initially, a program statement can be developed to outline and gain support for a specific project or concept derived from the strategic or master plan. It can act as an important or even a required part of the project approval process. Once an organization decides to move forward with the project, a program statement is the written document that acts as a principal method of communicating the idea to planners and designers. The program statement should cover the following:

- Description of the organization and its vision, mission, and goals
- Current and proposed programs that will take place at the proposed project, including specific goals or outcomes as well as expected participation levels
- User demographics and characteristics
- Comparisons with similar agencies and facilities as well as accepted standards
- A description of current space (e.g., what square footage or acreage is available and its condition, what programs and activities take place in current facilities) and proposed space needs (e.g., types of spaces needed to accomplish or expand programs, services, and activities; what you plan to have happening in the new facility or area); this section should also include a description of support and auxiliary spaces such as offices, locker rooms, maintenance areas, concessions, and storage

- A detailed description of the furniture, fixtures, and equipment needed for those spaces; for example, if you are designing a weight room, you should outline the types and quantities of equipment needed, specific clocks you might put in the weight area so users can time workouts, and benches or couches for people for resting between sets
- Critical relationships between specific spaces, such as locker rooms having direct access to the pool or having offices accessible before entering a controlled area of the building
- Any other important considerations such as environmental conditions, site conditions, and availability of potential sites, to name a few

Developing the program statement is a critical step in the planning process. Program statements should be comprehensive and may be more than 100 pages. Well-written and detailed program statements can save time and money during the design stage of project.

DESIGN AND CONSTRUCTION PROCESS

Once an organization has decided to move a concept forward, one of the first decisions to make is the design and construction method it will use. There are three common processes and relationships that can be entered into with designers and contractors. In the private sector, organizations can choose any method they deem appropriate. However, public-sector agencies may be required to use a particular method based on local and state laws and regulations.

A project committee, design committee, or both should be formed early in the process. The purpose of this committee is to assist in selecting a design or a design and construction team depending on the design and construction method chosen (discussed next) and to work with and approve the design as it moves through the three to four phases of the design process. Oftentimes a project committee is the smaller core group consisting of key administrators, staff, and decision makers (e.g., city or county council members, board members) and a representative or representatives of user groups. This group should consist of a maximum of six to eight people. A larger design group can be an extension of the project committee. A design committee can be quite large and may include a broad range of staff, maintenance workers, custodians, users, code enforcement officials, public safety representatives (e.g., fire and rescue, fire inspector, police), and consultants such as interior designers, lighting specialists, and flooring specialists. Even with a well-written program statement, architects will typically conduct a series of design **charrettes** to receive input from the design committee and other stakeholders and potential users of the proposed facility.

The three construction methods are as follows:

1. **Design–bid–build or competitive bid.** In the design–bid–build method, an organization hires a designer, the facility is designed, and the project is put out for bid to contractors. Contractors bid on the project based on what they think it will cost to build and realize an appropriate profit. There is no overlap between the design process, development of construction documents, and construction process. An advantage of this method is that it is a common and relatively easy process to manage. It also creates a competitive environment during the bidding phase and theoretically should yield the best price. However, because there is no overlap during the three phases (design, bid, and build) of the project, this method can take longer. You are also often required to take the low bid and may risk hiring a contractor who is not capable of completing the job, you will not know the final price of the project until the bids come in, and any changes after construction begins must be negotiated and can be costly.

2. **Design–build.** In a design–build situation, the designers and contractors are hired together as a team at the beginning of the project. Typically a maximum price for the project is established early in the process. The advantages of this process include being able to choose a contractor based on qualifications and experience and having the designer and contractor work through the design process together throughout the project, which saves time and ensures that the design can be built within the budget. However, there can be some difficulty in making changes once construction begins, and it is sometimes hard to determine if you are getting the best price because there is no competitive bid.

3. **Construction manager at risk.** A middle ground between the design–bid–build and design–build methods is the construction manager at risk. An organization chooses a designer and then hires a construction manager before the bid documents are fully completed, which means the construction manager can work with the design team to estimate costs. A maximum price is agreed upon with the construction manager relatively early in the process. The construction manager is responsible for hiring and overseeing subcontractors who complete the project. Construction can be fast-tracked using this method, you are choosing a contractor based on qualifications and experience, and having the designers and construction manager work together during the design phase should help avoid the need for change orders during the construction project. The disadvantage of this method is that it is difficult to assess whether you are getting the best price for the work completed ("Getting the best value for our construction dollars," n.d.).

Design Process

Once architects or designers are hired, the design process consists of three to four phases depending on the level of conceptual design that has been completed. If no conceptual design has been done on a particular project in the master planning process, the design process typically starts with conceptual design. During this early phase of design, the architects consult with the design committee and hold a series of design charrettes, as discussed earlier. Conceptual designs begin to show the types of spaces and relationships between spaces and can be as simple as bubble diagrams. Once the design committee and architects have reached an agreement on the basic spaces and amenities to be included in the project and begin to understand the potential relationships between those spaces, the process moves into schematic design.

If a schedule has not been established during the conceptual design, it should be established at the beginning of the schematic design phase. During this phase, consultants are brought on board to assist as the design begins to become more detailed and refined. If the project needs to be completed in phases, plans to phase the project are completed during schematic design. Concepts for the design are overlaid on the site and initial cost estimates are completed. The architects provide more detailed drawings of the facility or site for approval by the design committee and review by decision makers, and then the process moves into the design development phase.

During the design development phase, key details are developed, materials are selected, specifications are outlined, cost estimates are refined, and further revisions to the design are completed. During this phase it may be necessary to send plans to agencies (e.g., code enforcement) for preliminary approval. Upon completion, the updated design work is approved again by the design committee and reviewed by decision makers.

The final stage of the design process is the construction documents phase. Construction documents include working drawings and specifications. **Working drawings** are the blueprints that include the information for building and completing a project, and **specifications** are the written companion to the blueprints. These documents are important for several reasons. First, if you are using the design–bid–build method, the working drawings and specifications are what contractors use to determine the bid they will offer for the project. Second, if the drawings or specifications are inaccurate or contain errors, you will have to either use costly change orders to fix those mistakes after construction has begun or live with the errors. Third, the drawings and specifications are what the architects use to ensure that the building is being built as intended. Details are important, but too much detail can make contactors nervous and lead to higher prices. The rule of thumb is to include the amount of detail needed to have the project completed accurately.

Again, specifications are the written portion of the construction documents, and they include three parts: bidding and contract requirements, general requirements, and construction specifications. This part of process can be tedious because of the extreme amount of detail and time it takes to complete. However, it is probably the most important part of the process. As with working drawings, you need to include everything you want to see in the final constructed project but only include information necessary to the specific project. Including unnecessary information can lead to higher prices during bidding. Make sure the general requirements include the contractor providing as-built drawings, catalogue cuts, and, where appropriate, operations manuals and training of operations and maintenance staff. As-built drawings replace the blueprints and show exactly how the building has been built. Contractors may have a more efficient way of completing

The final project, when fully built out, is the end result of a long process of facility planning.

something than what is shown in the drawings or may run into issues during construction that require changes. Whenever a change is necessary, it should be approved by the architect or project manager. Catalogue cuts show how and where electrical, plumbing, HVAC, and other systems are included in the facility. Construction specifications are written using the 2004 MasterFormat from the Construction Specifications Institute (CSI). This format includes 50 divisions outlining how materials and products are used in construction. (See www.csinet.org for more information.)

Once construction documents are produced and approved, the bid package is prepared, which includes the construction documents. The specifications outline the bid process and requirements for potential bidders. In the public sector, bid opportunities are advertised for a period of time (usually at least 30 days for major projects). A prebid conference is held to address questions from bidders and the bid may be amended to address questions and issues. Once the time period has passed, bids are opened and typically the low bidder is awarded the contract to complete the project.

Construction

Before the actual construction begins, a preconstruction conference should be held to finalize the schedule and coordinate the process. During the construction phase, the architect or the project manager should visit the site at least every other week depending on the scope of the project. The bigger and more complex the project, the more visits will be required. The project manager and architect are responsible for preparing change orders when necessary, observing the process and determining if the contractor is adhering to the schedule and performing at the expected level, reviewing and approving material samples, and accepting or rejecting work that does not conform to the working drawings and specifications.

As a project nears completion, the project manager, architect, contractor, and building owner should complete a walk-through inspection and create a punch list of items to be fixed or completed. A final walk-through to confirm that the punch list has been addressed is followed by acceptance of the project. It is important to be satisfied with the work before accepting the project. Once the project is accepted, it can be difficult to get the contractor to return to address issues in a timely manner.

Two things can help protect the building owner during the construction process and once the building is complete and accepted. One is a **performance bond**, which is an insurance policy guaranteeing that the contractor will perform the work in accordance with the construction documents. If the work is not completed in a satisfactory manner or the contractor goes bankrupt, the project will be completed by the insurance company. The second is a **warranty**, which is a guarantee the contractor provides for the building and usually covers the period from occupancy to 12 months. Warranties cover defects such as pooling water in parking lots, leaky roofs, and major system failures. If the warranty period is 12 months, the building owner should schedule a warranty inspection for 11 months. This inspection should lead to a warranty punch list that outlines problems to be addressed that are covered under the warranty.

FACILITY CONSIDERATIONS

There are a number of key considerations to take into account when designing recreational sport facilities. Some of these considerations include financing, sustainability, risk management and safety, equipment, maintenance, and technology. Each of these is discussed in the following sections.

Financing

The financing of recreational sport facilities has changed over time. In the public sector, traditionally appropriations were made from a city or county's general fund or municipal bonds were issued that were guaranteed by property taxes. It was even possible that an agency might receive grant money to help cover the cost of a new facility or amenity. However, the political environment changed, making it increasingly difficult to get city and county councils to approve increases in property tax rates. Additionally, most grant-making agencies have shifted the focus of their funding to programs and do not allow grant funds to be used for the construction or renovation of facilities.

Although it is still possible to fund recreational sport facilities through property taxes and guaranteed bonds, public-sector agencies have been creative in positioning themselves to take advantage of other options. Popular trends in financing facilities include using local option taxes such as sales tax, hospitality tax, and accommodations tax as well as taking advantage of government programs such as the NMTC Program that was part of the American Recovery and Reinvestment Act of 2009. As the case study at the beginning of the chapter demonstrated, it is vital to be informed so your organization does not miss an opportunity, and leveraging multiple financing mechanisms is often necessary to complete and possibly enhance projects.

Many states allow municipalities and counties to add local option taxes. Some recreational sport agencies have successfully secured funding for facility projects from a portion of revenues derived from a local option sales tax (where cities and counties charge a 1 percent sales tax on top of the typical sales tax for that state). Some states allow municipalities and counties to charge an accommodations tax (additional tax on hotel and rented rooms) and a hospitality tax (additional tax on prepared food and beverage). The legislation allowing these types of taxes typically restricts the use of the tax revenues to fund projects and agencies that promote tourism. Public recreational sport agencies have made the case that the development of their facilities can generate tourism. For example, a local soccer complex might attract a regional or national tournament to be held in the city where it is located and therefore will attract participants to stay in local hotels and eat in local restaurants, generating accommodations and hospitality taxes as well as having an additional positive economic impact on the city.

The two types of bonds issued by state and local government agencies are general obligation bonds and revenue bonds. A **general obligation bond** is backed by the full faith and credit of the agency. For example, if a city issues general obligation bonds to build a new aquatic complex, that city is backing the bonds based on its ability to collect and raise general taxes (e.g., property tax, local option sales tax) and raise more funds through additional credit. A **revenue bond** is paid back using fees collected by the project being funded. The same city might issue a revenue bond for the aquatic facility and pay the bond back using revenues generated by the facility. Another example of a project that might use revenue bonds is a parking garage where the fees to park in the garage are used to pay back the principal and interest on the bonds. Campus recreation and athletic programs at public universities also use these two options depending on the type of facility, state regulations, and funding sources. Campus recreation fees dedicated to the development of a new indoor recreation center could be used to guarantee a revenue bond, or the state where the university is located might fund the facility using general obligation bonds backed by state tax revenues.

In the private sector, financing has remained relatively stable. Although it might be a bit more difficult to obtain private financing since the recession that began in 2008, a private business can obtain traditional bank financing, get money from investors, or sell sponsorship opportunities and naming rights (public agencies do this as well) to generate funds for a project.

Regardless of whether the agency is public or private, facility finance works as follows. If an agency or organization borrows money from a bank, from an investor, or through bonds, it is obligated to pay someone back on some type of payment plan. A simple rule of thumb to follow in estimating the payment for a facility project is that if you are paying back a loan over the course of 15 years, the yearly payment will be approximately 10 percent of the total amount borrowed (this will fluctuate based on interest rates but is still useful for getting a ballpark figure). So, if you borrow $10 million to build a facility, you will pay back approximately $1 million per year for 15 years for a total repayment of $15 million. Similar to people purchasing a home, organizations and businesses must determine how they will generate enough revenue to cover the payments.

Agencies and organizations most often leverage a variety of funding options on a single project. There are guaranteed bonds (backed by property taxes) and nonguaranteed bonds (backed by revenues produced by the facility), naming rights (a company pays money to have its name included in the facility name), sponsorships, in-kind contributions (donations of equipment or supplies), donations, vendor and concessionaire exclusivity (caterer or vendor pays a fee to be the sole provider in the facility), bequests, parking revenues, and seat licensing fees (requiring patrons to pay an upfront fee that gives them the right to purchase that seat for a set period of time), to name a few. We have not gone into a great deal of detail about finance mechanisms for facility development in this book; however, you will most likely take a course in finance that will provide you with the foundational knowledge you will need in the field of recreational sport.

Sustainability and LEED

According to the U.S. Department of Energy, buildings in the United States consume more than 36 percent of the total energy used in the United States and 65 percent of electricity each year (United States Department of Energy, 2015). A typical commercial construction project generates up to 2.5 pounds (1 kg) of solid waste per square foot (.09 m^2), and 5 billion gallons (19 billion L) of potable water are used to flush toilets every day. In large part, sustainability is about increasing efficiency and reducing waste. Both the private and public sectors are beginning to embrace the idea of sustainability in daily operations and capital projects. The case is being made that sustainable practices can lead to reduced costs and increased profits. Even Walmart has gotten in on the act and has a goal of being a zero-waste company by 2025. A pilot program implemented in California by Walmart that includes three major points (recycling, donation, and creation) has already achieved the 80 percent mark. In the public sector, where the emphasis has traditionally been on efficiency and legislative compliance, the trend toward saving money and resources by implementing sustainable practices is gaining traction. States, local governments, and public agencies have created goals and policies geared toward implementing or requiring sustainable practices. Many public agencies have set goals to have all new capital construction projects gain LEED certification.

LEED (Leadership in Energy and Environmental Design) is one of the most well-known programs that is directly related to capital construction projects and the operation and maintenance of existing buildings. Created by the U.S. Green Building Council, the LEED program is "a voluntary, consensus-based, market-driven program that provides third-party verification of green buildings" (www.usgbc.org/leed). Buildings can earn LEED certification by satisfying all prerequisites and earning a minimum of 40 points on a 110-point rating scale. Rating systems have been developed for new construction and major renovations, operation and maintenance of existing buildings, commercial interiors, core and shell development, retail, schools, homes, neighborhood development, and health care. Projects and buildings earn points in the areas of sustainable site credits (minimization of impact on ecosystems and water resources), water efficiency credits (smarter use of water, inside and out, to reduce potable water consumption), energy and atmosphere credits (promotion of better building energy performance through innovative strategies), materials and resources credits (use of sustainable materials and reducing waste), and indoor environmental quality credits (promotion of better indoor air quality and access to daylight and views).

Risk Management and Safety

Risk management and safety are crucial to consider when designing and operating any recreational sport facility. Risk management and safety considerations include the things you can reasonably do to make a facility safe and minimize the risk of being named in a lawsuit. Many risk management and safety concerns can be dealt with and mitigated during the design process. Security, access, use of space, traffic flow, signage, surfaces and finishes, environmental control, lighting, and technology are a few of the things to consider in the design phase of a project that can be difficult and expensive to remedy once a building is complete.

Here are some general questions to consider when thinking about risk management during the design process. They are also useful when performing a risk management assessment for a currently operating facility.

- **Access.** How do people access the facility? Is it open access or controlled access? Are there sufficient and appropriate entrance and exit points that meet fire and local and state building codes? Are emergency exits and paths to exits clearly marked? In the event of an emergency or due to the type of facility and program you operate, do you need the ability to keep people in or out of the facility?
- **Use of space.** Are there activities that people may use a particular space for that were not intended in the original design, and are those other uses safe and compatible with the intended use? If not, what can you do to mitigate any risks this situation may pose? Are there appropriate spaces designed for spectators?
- **Traffic flow.** Is there adequate space for traffic to, from, and through activity areas? Is there sufficient safety space around equipment and activity areas?
- **Signage.** Is there adequate signage at the facility that lets people know how to enter, move through, and exit (especially in the case of emergencies)? Is there signage that tells people what they should do in the case of emergencies? Are rules and regulations clearly displayed?
- **Materials, finishes, and surfaces.** Are the materials, finishes, and surfaces appropriate and safe for the activities taking place in the facility? For example, are there safety mats on the walls surrounding the basketball courts in the event that a player runs into the wall? Do locker rooms and other potentially wet areas have antislip surfaces?
- **Environmental control.** Will proper temperatures (not too hot to exercise), humidity levels (can cause maintenance problems and malfunctions with electronic equipment), and air quality (stale air can make it harder to breathe during exercise) be maintained? Is HVAC (heating, ventilation, and air conditioning) adequate to heat and cool the space and provide sufficient fresh-air turnover in the facility?
- **Lighting.** Are lighting levels appropriate and adequate for the activities conducted in the space? Can repairs be done easily and safely to lighting systems in high-bay spaces such as gymnasiums and natatoriums? Are fixtures in gymnasiums able to withstand being hit by a basketball or volleyball?
- **Technology.** How will you use technology such as card-reader systems, security systems, camera systems, fire detection and suppression systems, lighting control systems, and emergency communications systems to meet code requirements and make the facility as safe as possible?

Equipment

Recreational sport facilities require a wide range of equipment. Managers and front-line personnel may deal with everything from weed trimmers and basketballs to scoreboards and fitness equipment to HVAC and pool filtration and control systems. Regardless of your position, your ability to understand, evaluate, operate, and maintain a wide variety of equipment and systems is essential. Fixed (e.g., HVAC system, fire suppression), administrative and support (e.g., office furniture), and major equipment essential to the operation (e.g., scoreboards for field complex or indoor basketball courts) are included in the budget for most major projects as furniture, fixtures, and equipment (FFE), which is one of the divisions in standard construction specifications. However, nonpermanent or expendable equipment such as softballs or other supplies typically are not included in capital project budgets and are purchased from other budget categories.

Determining Equipment Needs

Whether you are purchasing equipment for an existing facility or creating equipment specifications for a new facility, a renovation, or a retrofit, research is the first step in the process. A needs analysis should be conducted to determine the most appropriate types and quantities of equipment necessary to serve customers and operate the facility in the most efficient and effective manner. The purpose of the equipment needed will determine the best method for the needs analysis. If you are purchasing fitness equipment for an expansion of a fitness center, the needs analysis might include performing usage counts at peak hours and conducting a survey or focus group to determine the perceived needs of customers. If you are writing equipment specifications for a building or area that you have not operated before, the research process might include an initial Internet search for available options followed by discussing the function, quality, customer service, and price of those options with peers who use that equipment. Many manufacturers offer onsite trials or will suggest facilities you can visit to see equipment in use. But remember, when you are dealing directly with a company, you are dealing with salespeople who are trained to get you excited about their products. Be sure to do ample research and consider multiple options.

Purchasing Equipment

Depending on whether you work for a private or public agency and the size of the purchase, you may be required to go through a bid process in order to buy equipment and supplies. Public agencies typically have a process that involves filling out a purchase requisition that includes a section for specifications (e.g., type, size, quantity, features, warranty, delivery, setup, payment) of the desired equipment. Specifications can even list a desired vendor or brand. As with the bidding process to hire a contractor to complete a construction project, the bid is typically advertised for a period of time, bids are received from suppliers, and the low bid that meets the specifications is accepted. However, not all purchases necessarily have to go through the complete bid process. For example, in South Carolina, purchases may be made without going through a bid process at all if the price of the equipment or supplies does not exceed $2,500. For purchases between $2,500 and $10,000, a department or agency can secure quotes from three suppliers and accept the lowest quote without going through the full bid process. Once the $10,000 threshold is exceeded, the bid opportunity must be advertised. In the private sector, a bid process is typically not required, but using one may lead to lower prices because it creates competition among potential suppliers.

Leasing Equipment

Options exist to rent or lease equipment. Renting may be an attractive option when a piece of equipment is only needed for a short time or on a periodic basis, such as renting a large tent to host meals at tournaments. Leasing should be considered for items that require maintenance, have short life cycles, or require replacement on a regular basis. When equipment leases include scheduled maintenance and replacement in the event of a breakdown, it may actually be less expensive to lease than to purchase once the maintenance cost is factored into the equation. Examples might include leasing grounds maintenance equipment such as mowers or fitness equipment such as treadmills. Commercial treadmills can cost in excess of $10,000 each and may need to be replaced every few years depending on the frequency and intensity of use.

Maintenance

Maintenance is a key issue to address during the planning stages of a facility project as well as a daily issue for facilities that are operational. Well-maintained facilities are generally safer and create a positive organizational image. Poorly maintained facilities not only pose safety concerns, but they also do not attract high-quality programs.

During the design process in the planning stage for a renovation or new construction, it is important to include the people who will be maintaining the facility. Custodians, grounds crew members, electricians, and plumbers have unique perspectives and skill sets that add value to the design process and can lead to design features that allow the building to be maintained in the most efficient manner possible. Custodians can provide input on the location of custodial closets, grout color in tile floors, and necessary equipment and maintenance requirements for various types of flooring. Members of the grounds crew can provide input on the landscape plan. Electricians can look at lighting plans and suggest systems such as remote ballasts that make it easier to maintain lights in high-volume spaces such as gymnasiums. Using colored, textured block on the lower portion of walls rather than drywall or painted cinderblock can eliminate black marks and streaks that need to be cleaned or painted over on a regular basis. The technicians or staff who will maintain the fitness equipment can provide input on the space, equipment, and fixtures necessary for an equipment repair room.

Once a facility is operational, maintenance falls into two categories: routine and nonroutine. **Routine maintenance** is everything that has to be done on a daily basis to keep a facility running and includes cleaning, garbage removal, and field lining. **Nonroutine maintenance** includes things that are done on a periodic, preventive, or emergency basis. Periodic maintenance may occur on a regular but infrequent basis. Overseeding baseball fields in the winter with a cool-season grass is an example of a periodic maintenance task. Preventive maintenance is done to keep something from wearing out. Changing the oil in mowing equipment or cleaning the chlorine pumps on a pool would fall into the preventive maintenance category. Finally, emergency maintenance covers unexpected events such as a broken chlorine pump or a leaky roof.

A recreational sport organization should have a method of planning for and scheduling maintenance tasks. Maintenance planning should begin by completing an inventory of everything the organization is responsible for maintaining and assigning responsibility to the appropriate staff or contractor (if the organization outsources some maintenance tasks). This inventory should lead to the development of a maintenance manual with specific task lists that outline who is responsible for the task, how frequently the task is performed, and how the work is reported and recorded. For nonroutine maintenance, a system of work orders is often used that describes the work to be done and who does that work. A system to track and

Ongoing maintenance and repairs can save money in the long run and can help to ensure a safe and quality facility.

record both routine and nonroutine maintenance tasks should be developed.

Unfortunately, deferred maintenance is a significant concern for many organizations; for instance, it is a $10 billion problem for the U.S. National Park Service. **Deferred maintenance** is the practice of postponing maintenance due to budget constraints. This practice can lead to serious deterioration of facilities. The longer maintenance problems are deferred, the more costly they become to remedy, and they can ultimately shorten the useful life span of a facility.

Technology

Because chapter 10 addresses technology in recreational sport, in this section we will only briefly discuss technologies that can assist in the planning and operation of recreational sport facilities. During the design process, CAD (computer-aided design) and other design software allow the designer to create three-dimensional models and can even allow the end user to simulate facility use in a virtual environment. Maintenance tracking systems allow an organization to program tasks that will automatically send reminders to the responsible person's phone and allow him to track the workflow through to task completion. Pool controllers can send text messages to the aquatic facility supervisor, alerting her to changes in pool chemistry. Artificial turf technology has improved to the point that it is sometimes difficult to tell the difference between real and artificial turf. Some fitness equipment has been designed to produce electrical current as it is being used that goes back into the grid or is stored in order to power other parts of the building. Again, there is a lot of technology out there (and more being updated or released every day) that has been specifically designed for or can be leveraged to enhance the management of recreational sport facilities. It is important to keep yourself informed and up to date on the technologies available.

CONCLUSION

Facilities are essential to the success of recreational sport organizations. Without quality spaces and equipment, it can be exceedingly difficult to create quality programs and a positive public image. Whether you are creating new recreational facilities or renovating, retrofitting, or continuing operations of existing ones, it is essential to employ a planning model or process that continually reflects on, evaluates, and assesses how facilities, programs, and services are helping the organization achieve goals and realize its mission and vision. As a future recreational sport professional, a primary focus of your professional development should be keeping informed of technological advances, innovations in equipment, efficiencies of systems available to enhance operations, and trends in finance, maintenance, and sustainable practices related to facilities and venues.

RESEARCH TO REALITY

Lee, K.Y., Macfarlane, D., & Cerin, E. (2013, Winter). Objective evaluation of recreation facilities: Development and reliability of the Recreation Facility Audit Tool. *Journal of Park and Recreation Administration, 31*(4), 92-109.

This research describes the development and testing of a recreation facility audit tool called *RecFAT* (Recreation Facility Audit Tool). RecFAT is a 111-item tool that is meant to objectively evaluate recreation facilities across 10 domains using trained raters. Auditors determine the context (indoor or outdoor) and the nature (public, residential, or commercial) of the facility. Then they evaluate the 10 domains, which include availability of sports facilities, accessibility to the facility, availability of supportive amenities, conditions of changing rooms, conditions of toilets, management, policy, environmental safety, aesthetics, and social environment.

Tools such as RecFAT are an important part of both the planning stage of facility development and the operation of new and existing facilities. For example, a facility analysis that used a tested facility audit tool such as RecFAT would add significant value to a comprehensive program statement to demonstrate need. It is also important to have an evaluation plan for new and existing facilities. A primary goal of an evaluation plan is to determine if facilities are being used in the most efficient and effective manner possible. Again, a tested audit tool provides a consistent method and valuable data to use in making decisions about allocating resources to achieve an organization's goals.

REFLECTION QUESTIONS

1. What are the similarities and differences between strategic and master planning processes?
2. Which design and construction process (design–bid–build, design–build, or construction manager at risk) would you prefer to use to develop or renovate a recreational sport facility and why?
3. How would you go about gaining input from the public or the potential customer base when undertaking a planning process?
4. If you own and operate a private, commercial recreational sport business, what financing options are available for developing facilities?

LEARNING ACTIVITIES

1. Find the campus master plan for your college or university. See if you can find references to your school's vision, mission statement, goals, or other plans or planning efforts and if it is obvious within the plan how those things are tied together and support each other. Find out what leisure, recreation, and sport amenities are planned for your campus. Does your school have anything in its stated mission, goals, or plans that is related to or supported by the provision of leisure, recreation, and sport activities and facilities?
2. Make a list of all the equipment you might find in a typical recreation center. Then interview a staff member at a local recreation center and show him your list. Ask the staff member to point out anything you missed and to discuss equipment and systems you did not include. Finally, ask for an estimate of what it would cost to replace all of the equipment in the facility.

chapter 7

FINANCING AND MARKETING RECREATIONAL SPORT

LEARNING OUTCOMES

By the end of the chapter, readers will be able to

- identify sources of income for a typical recreational sport agency,
- determine typical expenditures for a recreational sport agency,
- find sources of outside funding, and
- implement effective marketing techniques for multiple mediums.

Case Study

BAD CUSTOMER SERVICE LOSES CUSTOMERS

Kathleen is a mother of three children who wants to sign up her oldest, Maryclare, age 6, for beginning tennis lessons. When she goes to her local tennis club to register, the man at the front desk is rude and impatient. Furthermore, as he is trying to charge her credit card, he enters the information incorrectly, accidentally charging her double for the lessons. He then goes on to claim that Kathleen had asked him to do so despite the fact that there would be no reason to pay for two sets of lessons because her other children are too young to take part. Instead of apologizing and correcting the mistake, the clerk tells her she will have to come back some other time to appeal the charges when his manager is back from vacation.

When Kathleen gets home, she immediately leaves a message on the manager's voice mail explaining the situation and asking him to remedy it. While she waits to hear back from him, however, she vents to her friends about the problem and tells them that she will be withdrawing Maryclare from the program completely as soon as she has the chance and will enroll her in lessons at the competing tennis club. Because many of Kathleen's friends also have children Maryclare's age who are interested in tennis, they decide to enroll their children in lessons at the other facility as well. By the time the manager receives the message from Kathleen, he has already lost several customers without even realizing it, all due to the poor customer service of one person. Even though he offers Kathleen a full refund and a discount on future lessons in an attempt to remedy the problem, she declines and Maryclare, her friends, and eventually Kathleen's two other children all enjoy their tennis lessons at the competing facility for many years to come.

In the increasingly resource-restricted environments where recreational sport professionals often work, knowledge of sound finance, budgeting, and marketing strategies is key to the successful delivery of recreational sport programs. Chapter 7 introduces both finance and marketing concerns. This chapter covers major sources of revenue generation in recreational sport, with a focus on taxes, program fees and charges, corporate sponsorships, private donations and gifts, contracting out services, and grant funding. In addition, the chapter provides an understanding of the key expenditures associated with recreational sport programs. It also presents the concept of marketing and the importance of customer service for the fiscal health of the recreational sport organization. Finally, examples of effective promotional techniques are provided.

EXPENDITURES

The first step in the process of financing and marketing a recreational sport program or organization is usually to determine what costs are associated with the program. This means going through all potential expenses that may be incurred in delivering the desired services and experiences to participants.

Direct Versus Indirect Costs

When looking at a program, the average person will typically see many costs that are involved in production. For example, an observer may notice that a swim team needs to account for costs associated with paying a coach, purchasing timing equipment, and renting pool times for practices

Running a recreational sport facility, event, or program includes a number of both direct and indirect costs.

and meets. However, many more costs exist that are easily overlooked in the initial budgeting process, such as the electric bills of an office. Consequently, it is necessary to understand the difference between direct and indirect costs to ensure that both are accounted for in the budget.

Direct costs refer to those expenses necessary for the program itself. For example, for a hockey program, it is necessary to buy hockey pads, rent ice time, and pay for a coach. These are all direct costs because without the hockey program there would be no need for them. However, other relevant costs are necessary for the program to exist even if there is not an obvious direct relationship to the hockey program (Rossman & Schlatter, 2008).

Many **indirect costs** exist and are present whether or not a specific program is offered. One example of these is the costs associated with running an office. Any recreational sport organization of a certain size needs to either buy or rent office space and pay for electricity, water, heating, cooling, and phone service in that office. In addition, budgeting must account for employees such as administrators, executive assistants who draw a salary and benefits even if they are not involved with one specific program. Those costs exist whether or not specific programs are offered, and they must be considered when it comes to determining prices and raising revenue from other sources (Rossman & Schlatter, 2008).

Facilities

Facilities are necessary for all recreational sport agencies and may include fields, office space, gyms, ice rinks, pools, and tracks, among others. Whether these are owned, rented, or borrowed in partnerships, the costs of using them should be specified. In addition, budgets need to account for maintenance of the facilities. All facilities will require repairs at some point, and a good budget includes funds to make sure any necessary repairs can take place in a reasonable and timely manner.

Equipment

Equipment expenses are related to more permanent structures used in activities, such as basketball hoops, soccer goals, and pool lane lines. These usually do not need to be replaced at a frequent rate, but the budget should make room for upgrades and repairs. In general, it is important to thoroughly understand the sports being provided and the trends within those sports to make sure your equipment is appropriate and sufficient for running a good program. In addition, do not forget about equipment for the overall organization, such as computers, copiers, and a phone system to make sure that the office is running smoothly as well.

Supplies

In addition to equipment, budgeting should account for any necessary supplies that the organization uses. Supplies are those purchases that are frequently used and regularly replaced. For example, footballs, flags, and jerseys for a flag football league will likely need to be replaced at least yearly along with paint to line the field and gas for the lawn mower. The goalposts and lawnmower itself, however, would be considered equipment. Again, it is necessary to keep in mind the indirect costs associated with supplies. Any office will need to purchase things like cleaning supplies to maintain a neat and professional environment, and these need to be included in the overall budget.

Staffing

Any recreational sport organization must have highly qualified and trained employees to offer the best experiences to participants. Staff members may include people to work the front desk, people to take care of league registrations, coaches, officials, and recreational sport coordinators. Salaries are not the only expenses related to staffing; other costs include employment taxes, benefits, and expenses for any trainings and travel that are required by the organization.

Marketing

For any program to run successfully, marketing must occur, and these expenses need to be accounted for in the overall budget. Specific types of marketing are discussed later in the chapter.

Insurance

A final expense that needs to be considered in the budget is insurance. No recreational sport organization should operate without some sort of insurance policy, although the types and amounts necessary will vary according to the organization and its services. Types of insurance might include automobile, fire, flood, and liability. All insurance policy options should be thoroughly discussed with legal counsel and included as part of the overall risk management plan (see chapter 8).

MAJOR SOURCES OF REVENUE IN RECREATIONAL SPORT

After all the potential expenses of a program have been accounted for, it is necessary to determine how to cover those costs. This means a recreational sport organization must be familiar with all its options for sources of revenue. These include public funding, program fees and charges, corporate sponsorships, donations and gifts, partnerships, and grants.

Public Funding

One of the unique aspects of working for a public recreational sport agency, such as a community recreation center, is having public funding as a source of revenue. Public funding includes any tax dollars that might be raised through property taxes, local taxes, and bonds. In addition, funding might come in other forms. For example, a community recreation center probably won't have to retain its own insurance policies and legal counsel for risk management, and it may have access to public-works employees to help with the care and maintenance of its facilities. These benefits drive down the overall costs of a public agency, and as a result individual programs can frequently be offered at lower prices than those offered by private organizations.

Program Fees and Charges

Private organizations and public organizations that are not fully subsidized by the government may also cover expenses by charging participants program fees and other expenses. For example, athletes in a league are often required to pay a registration fee in order to join a team. Most recreational sport organizations use this source of revenue, and professionals need to know how to make sure the fees are appropriate. This can be done through a system of analyzing costs and then determining prices.

Analyzing Costs

When analyzing costs, it is first necessary to ensure that all expenditures have been accounted for. Many expenditures have already been discussed in previous sections of this chapter. It is important to account for all costs so that the organization is fully aware of what needs to be paid to whom as a result of the program. For example, as mentioned previously, costs may include equipment, supplies, facility space, coaching fees, insurance, administrative salaries, and employee benefits.

Determining Prices

After accounting for the costs of the program, it is necessary to determine the overall price to charge participants. The first step in this process is to decide on the organization's philosophy for cost recovery. Several options exist, including no cost recovery, partial cost recovery, and full cost recovery. Each of these is fairly self-explanatory. In no cost recovery, services are provided at no charge to participants. Instead, other sources of funding such as grants and sponsorships cover expenses. In partial cost recovery, programs are partially subsidized by other services, and full cost recovery means that the entire cost of the program is paid for by the participants (DeGraaf, Jordan, & DeGraaf, 2010). These options all have their strengths, and the philosophy that the organization chooses should partially depend on its other sources of funding, the overall costs associated with the program, and the demographics of the customers.

Another price consideration should be whether to use differential pricing, which means charging different prices to different groups based on factors such as participants, quantity, and incentives. Price differentials based on participants provide discounts to certain groups of people such as senior citizens or children whose families have less disposable income. A price differential based on quantity might be for two or more people from the same family. For instance, if one child signs up for a soccer program, the family might be charged $75, but each additional child will only result in a charge of $30. This encourages families to sign up more of their children, meaning there can be more teams, more games, and hopefully less hassle for parents trying to take all their children to activities. Finally, price differentials as incentives are discounts given to encourage trying something new. This might mean that first-time participants get a discount or that if a parent is willing to sign up as coach, her child will receive a discounted registration (DeGraaf et al., 2010).

Finally, psychological variables should be considered when pricing a service or experience. For example, many people associate the price of a service with its quality. This is one reason recreational sport organizations often charge at least a minimal amount rather than providing an experience for free. The belief is that people perceive a free program to be of lower quality than one that costs money and will choose to participate in one for a fee over one that is fully subsidized (DeGraaf et al., 2010).

Corporate Sponsorships

Another source of revenue popular in recreational sport is corporate sponsorships. This refers to private corporations exchanging money, materials, or **in-kind gifts** for free marketing. For instance, many youth sport sponsors supply jerseys in exchange for having the sponsor's name on them. This allows the business to earn a tax deduction and a favorable perception in the community while reducing the costs for the sport organization. Though it may seem that corporate sponsorships are always a good idea, this is not necessarily the case. Make sure that the sponsor you are working with makes sense from the standpoint of your mission. An easy example would be a cigarette company wanting to sponsor a baseball team. Advertising cigarettes to 10-year-olds and their families may not be the image the league wants to present, so it would be best to turn down that sponsorship and focus on others that may be more appropriate, such as nutrition bars or sport drinks.

Private Donations and Gifts

Private donations and gifts could include money, equipment, supplies, and in-kind contributions. These may come from individuals, groups, or businesses, but unlike the case of corporate sponsorships, there is no associated agreement for advertisement in exchange for the donations. However, it is still necessary to be careful when receiving gifts. Although they may seem to be free, this is not necessarily the case. For example, a donated car may be needed to transport a team

© Mary Sara Wells

Appropriate corporate sponsors can be used to help finance recreational sport events and programs.

from meet to meet, but the organization needs to be careful in what type of car it accepts. A car that requires higher insurance and maintenance costs than the organization is able to spend may not be such a wise gift in the long run. In this case, the organization needs to look at the long-term ownership cost of the car being donated and determine if the maintenance of this particular vehicle is within the budget of the organization.

Partnerships

As the costs associated with recreational sport programs continue to increase and the means to provide them continue to become scarcer, partnerships between organizations are becoming more and more common. In a partnership, two or more organizations join together and form an agreement based on mutually beneficial goals and objectives. For example, a school district may have access to soccer fields that are primarily used during the school day and immediately after school but not on weekends. A local soccer club might form a partnership for access to the fields and in return provide some coaching and instruction to the school team. In this case, both groups receive necessary resources to run their programs because they work together, reducing both their costs. Another example of a frequently underused partnership opportunity lies in college and university campuses. Many college and university sport management programs are full of faculty and students looking for chances to gain experience or conduct research. It could be helpful for both parties to create a partnership where students serve in coaching, instructional, or administrative positions in exchange for service learning opportunities, internships, and data collection.

Grants

One final option for additional revenue is from grants. Many nonprofit agencies provide financial grants to organizations that match their mission. For example, the Nike Foundation supports efforts to increase the health and safety of adolescent girls throughout the world (Nike Foundation, n.d.), while the Robert Wood Johnson Foundation works to curb childhood obesity

Partnerships between multiple entities can help increase recreational sport opportunities while lowering costs.

(Robert Wood Johnson Foundation, n.d.). Both of these may or may not relate to recreational sport programs. In addition to national and international nonprofit organizations, there are also many localized programs and foundations that support community initiatives. Recreational sport organizations would benefit from exploring options both locally and nationally for external funding that lines up with the mission, goals, and objectives of the program.

MARKETING TECHNIQUES AND CONSIDERATIONS

Marketing is one area of recreational sport management that highly relates to both revenue and expenditures. Without good marketing, a business will not gain optimal revenue, and good marketing requires funding. Many techniques for promoting programs exist, including broadcast media, print and display media, and electronic media. By appropriately mixing the messages provided through these sources, a recreational sport organization should be able to promote its services and programs in the best possible way.

Broadcast Media

Broadcast media include messages that are transferred over the airwaves. This typically refers to all radio and television messages and can include both advertisements and news stories. Radio can be an effective way to reach an audience if the target market is one that listens to the radio, which is becoming less common with the advent of other means of accessing music such as online music streaming and MP3 players. Television can be a slightly more expensive option, but technology has created ways to avoid advertisements through DVR systems that allow users to fast-forward through commercials. For this reason, it might be beneficial to view broadcast media as a means to promote through press releases and other news stories. For example, you might try to recruit participants to a 5K run by engaging with a local morning news show rather than just buying advertisement time. This will keep production costs

One of the keys to marketing is making sure that the method used matches the program and the target market.

lower and ensure that more viewers or listeners receive the message (DeGraaf et al., 2010).

Display and Print Media

Display and print media are common tools used to market recreational sport programs and organizations. Options can include billboards, exhibits, posters, brochures, fliers, magazines, and newspapers. All of these are valuable ways to present a message, but they must target the right audience. For example, most magazines target readers with a specific interest and billboards target visitors to a specific geographical area.

One potential downside of these methods is an increasingly paperless society. As more newspapers and magazines convert to online editions, however, it creates an opportunity to connect the concept of print and display media with electronic media. Advertisements can now be more creative with direct links within the ad to the organization's website or registration forms, but this creativity requires commitment, expertise, and financial resources (DeGraaf et al., 2010). Because of the turn away from print media, it may benefit recreational sport programs to look at alternatives within the online versions of paper-based products. For example, if a community recreation center used to print and distribute seasonal guides to recreational sport opportunities with a local newspaper, perhaps it should now look into having an ad in the online version of that newspaper with a link that takes potential customers to an online version of the seasonal guide and further links within the document that direct people to the registration website.

Electronic Media

The opportunities to market a recreational sport program or organization through electronic media are vast and ever changing. Although not everyone has access to these types of marketing messages, when a target market does, it can be highly valuable. Electronic media promotion could be any kind of electronic communication, but it mostly involves the Internet and more specifically social media. Social media are a type of outlet where "news, photos, videos, and podcasts are made public via social media sites" (Evans, 2012, p. 33). The popularity of specific social media sites continues to change, but current ones include Twitter, Facebook, YouTube, Instagram, and Pinterest. In addition to these social media websites, electronic media marketing may take the form of online reviews, blogs, text messaging, and even e-mails.

Perhaps the most unique facet of electronic media marketing is the fact that it is word-of-mouth publicity that is more quickly accessed by a greater number of people. This creates a challenge where the marketer is no longer in complete control of the message that is being provided (Sterne, 2010). Consequently, it is necessary for recreational sport organizations to monitor social and other forms of electronic media to adjust services, provide feedback to consumers, and address negative reviews and concerns (Evans, 2012; Sterne, 2010).

Social media are continuing to have a great impact on people's lives and choices. This includes the choices people make regarding which recreational sport programs they choose to be involved in. Many people look for important information regarding a program on Facebook or other sites, and when they do not find it they simply begin looking at another organization or activity. Consequently, recreational sport organizations need to have a plan for effectively using social media in ways that are desired by their customers. This could include posting updates regarding new sport or league registration deadlines on Twitter, having a regularly updated Facebook page that provides links to websites for new tournament offerings, or posting videos and pictures from summer sport camps on YouTube and Instagram.

Whoever is responsible for the content on social media pages must recognize the rights of participants and refrain from posting any information, pictures, or videos of those who do not wish to have a presence on these websites. Consequently, registration materials need to include photo waivers, which should be considered as a part of the risk management plan and should be designed by legal counsel.

Other Marketing Considerations

Though the method of presentation is an important consideration, several other aspects of marketing also play a role in how the message is received by consumers. To begin with, professionals need to consider the difference between marketing a product and an experience. For the most part, recreational sport agencies provide experiences, which differ from products in several ways (Akyildiz, Argan, Argan, & Sevil, 2013; Mullin, Hardy, & Sutton, 2007; van der Smissen, Moiseichik, & Hartenburg, 2005). Unlike tangible products, experiences cannot be separated from the organization providing them, and they tend to be more labor intensive and perishable and have a more fluctuating demand. In addition, the relationship between the experience and the provider means that there is more inconsistency in service (van der Smissen et al., 2005). For example, when marketing shoes, it is likely that each shoe that comes off the assembly line is identical. In experiences, however, the actual experience depends on not just the person leading it but also the person engaged in it, interactions with other participants, and many other uncontrollable factors such as the weather. In recreational sport, this typically means that what is being sold includes the facility, program administrators, coaches, officials, other team members, and even spectators. The uniqueness this provides can be a good thing, but the lack of control over factors related to the experience can create a challenge for a marketing team.

Another consideration in recreational sport marketing is the target market (Dees, 2011; Mullin et al., 2000). A **target market** is the population that an organization wants to receive a marketing message and can be classified by many demographic variables, including age, sex, socioeconomic status, geographic location, education level, desired benefits, and interest in the program. Each of these has an impact on the message and the method used to provide it. For example, if an organization is trying to promote a skateboard competition at the local skate park, the marketing strategy will vary significantly from one designed to increase participation in a senior fitness program. In each case it is appropriate to use marketing techniques that appeal to the people the organization is trying to attract, and those techniques should be implemented in areas where the target market will find them. The organization trying to promote a skateboard competition might try posting fliers in the local skate shop with information about the website and Facebook page, and it could further promote the competition through the organization's Twitter account using the hashtag #skaterockstourney. For the senior fitness program, on the other hand, including a message or advertisement in the newsletter of the local senior center or assisted living community might be a more appropriate means of reaching the target market.

Finally, market research should be conducted to help the organization understand a variety of facets related to the marketing strategy. First, it is important to know what competition exists in the market. This can help an organization specify its message to compare services and experiences with those of a competitor. Making programs and facilities sound better or more intriguing than others on the market has the potential to increase users (Mullin et al., 2007).

CUSTOMER SERVICE

A primary means of publicity is by word of mouth from either satisfied or unsatisfied customers. A major contributor to whether this marketing is positive or negative is the experience the customer had with the organization. Through good **customer service**, recreational sport organizations can help ensure the positive promotion of their programs.

Why Customer Service Matters

Customer service is a crucial aspect of any business. It is not only about keeping current participants happy, but it is also a major marketing tool. Current customers are more likely to come back and are more likely to recommend your services to others (Howat, Murray, & Crilley, 1999; Lee, Lee, & Yoo, 2000; Sureschchandar, Rajendran, & Anantharaman, 2002; Tian-Cole, Crompton, & Wilson, 2002; Yoshida & James, 2010). When considered this way, good customer service can actually save an organization money. Maintaining customers is more cost efficient than recruiting new ones, and people who receive a recommendation from someone they know are more likely to use that business than one they found through other means.

Customer Service Techniques

Several techniques can be beneficial when dealing with customers, including honesty and sincerity, listening, questioning, personal contact, and saying thanks. By engaging in each of these techniques, the experience is more likely to be a positive one for all involved.

One of the most important core values of any customer service policy is to always be honest and sincere with everyone. Honesty implies that employees tell customers the truth and that customers can trust the organization. This is crucial to any business. Within this concept lies the implementation of any rules or policies within the organization. All employees should know the reasoning behind the rules and policies that are in place and which rules are unbreakable and which ones can be bent. For example, in youth sport, if there are specific age groups for participants and there is one player who is younger than the others in his class, it might make sense to let that young athlete play up a year so that he can be with his friends. However, if that rule is in place to maintain the level of competition between teams, it might make less sense for an older player to play down a year and other accommodations might be necessary. The bottom line is to make sure that the decisions fit in with the organization's mission and benefit both the customers and the organization.

Many times what customers want most is to feel as if they are being heard. Consequently, listening can be one of the most effective means of ensuring good customer service. Unfortunately, however, listening is not always as easy as it appears. Professionals of all types are often busy, and recreational sport facilities offer many distractions, including noise, other customers, and technology. Furthermore, the way a person is approached can lead to further distractions as a result of stereotyping and attitudes. Although it can be difficult, employees need to use active listening techniques to make sure that customers know their opinions, concerns, and questions are valid. This might include restating any problems, taking notes, and providing feedback and answers when appropriate. In some instances, simply listening might help alleviate customers' concerns, reducing the likelihood that further customer service issues will arise.

Questioning is a customer service technique that takes listening to the next level. If a professional asks a customer appropriate questions, it is likely to enhance the customer's experience. Three types of questions may be beneficial: background, probing, and confirmation. Background questions can provide information regarding the facts and help both parties to see the situation more clearly. Probing questions, both open and close ended, can then go deeper into the issue.

The importance of providing excellent customer service in recreational sport cannot be underestimated.

Finally, confirmation questions help to check that the correct information is understood and that customers are certain their concerns are being heard and understood. It is important, however, to not ask questions just for the sake of asking questions, because it can come off as insincere. This might include asking questions at the wrong times, asking too many questions, or asking questions that are too personal. In every case, try to be judicial about how and what questions are asked so that they will contribute to a positive customer experience.

Providing personal contact is another technique that can enhance customer service. In an era when automated answering systems and online services are becoming increasingly common, customers appreciate dealing with real people, whether over the phone or in person. Again, however, these contacts need to be handled professionally to ensure a positive rather than negative experience. Nonverbal messages can be just as powerful as verbal cues, so it is necessary to be cognizant of the tone being used and the image being presented. In both cases the employees should try to be as professional as possible in their use of gestures, expressions, and overall appearance.

It would behoove all recreational sport professionals to find the appropriate time and place to say thank you much more often. When it comes down to it, customers make it possible for our services to exist, and no matter who they are, they deserve some level of appreciation. For this reason alone, a thank-you is appropriate, but there are other specific instances where saying thanks can enhance the customer service experience. Try to remember to thank customers when they compliment staff members or the organization as a whole, when they offer suggestions for improvement, when they recommend the organization to others, when they are patient, and when they make you smile. In addition, thanking other employees, supervisors, volunteers, and vendors can go a long way.

Solving Difficult Problems

Even when providing excellent customer service, issues will arise that are difficult to deal with. When this happens, the first step should always be to offer a sincere apology and a thank-you. This shows customers that you empathize with the situation and that you are taking their concerns seriously. Then attempt to fix the problem as quickly and fairly as possible, and if necessary offer some sort of compensation for their trouble. For example, in the case study at the beginning of the chapter, the employee would have been much better off if he had immediately recognized his contribution to the problem and tried to correct it rather than attempting to place blame on the customer and making her wait to resolve it.

When solving problems, it is important to remember not to overpromise in terms of solutions. Offer the best that you can, but be careful—going back on solutions later because they were unrealistic will do much more harm than offering a slightly lesser compensation. Finally, always make sure to follow up on the experience either by updating the customers on any changes that have been implemented or by contacting them to see if their experiences have changed at all. A well-timed and sincere follow-up helps customers to know that their concerns have been taken seriously, and in some cases it can turn a negative experience into a positive one.

Dealing With Difficult Customers

The common saying is that the customer is always right, but in actuality, that is not always the case. There may be times when you have to deal with customers who are wrong, who are belligerent, or who may cause more problems than benefits to the organization. If this is the case, it may be in the best interest of the agency to lose that customer. However, this does not mean that the process should not be handled with good customer service. It is important for employees to maintain their composure and professionalism at all times when dealing with irate customers. In these situations, try to avoid fighting fire with fire; resorting to their level does not help anyone. What might be of help, though, is speaking with a supervisor. This does not suggest a lack of competence on the employee's part; rather, the break in conversation along with the mere concept of speaking to a superior may help the customer relax somewhat. Finally, although they should remain professional, employees should not allow themselves to be bullied. Just because a customer is being inappropriate does not mean it must be tolerated.

CONCLUSION

This chapter has explained how recreational sport professionals can finance and market their programs. The foundation of a good budget lies in accounting for all expenses and revenue. Professionals should understand the numerous types of expenditures that exist, including direct and indirect costs, facilities, equipment, supplies, staffing, marketing, and insurance. They should also be aware of opportunities for revenue, such as public funding, program fees and charges, corporate sponsorships, private donations, partnerships, and grants. Finally, those who hope to work in the recreational sport field need to understand the many elements of a good marketing plan and the importance and components of good customer service. Through this knowledge, recreational sport professionals should be able to budget and implement programs in hopes of maintaining fiscal sustainability, thereby allowing continued service to participants.

RESEARCH TO REALITY

Osman, R.W., Cole, S.T., & Vessell, C.R. (2006). Examining the role of perceived service quality in predicting user satisfaction and behavioral intentions in a campus recreation setting. *Recreation Sports Journal, 30*, 20-29.

Osman and his colleagues wanted to determine if service quality dimensions had an impact on campus recreation users' satisfaction, intent to continue participation in the future, and intent to recommend campus recreation services to others. This is important information for campus recreation professionals because it is always beneficial to demonstrate accountability and efficacy of programs to campus administration. The researchers collected from students at a Midwestern university 249 questionnaires that asked questions about facility ambiance, operations quality, staff competency, overall satisfaction, and behavioral intentions.

Results from this study suggest that service quality was indeed related to user satisfaction. However, there was no relationship between service quality and intention to reuse campus recreation facilities. The authors felt this was a unique lack of relationship based on the fact that campus recreation services are already paid for by student fees, and therefore quality might not have the influence that it would in other situations. More importantly, though, satisfaction was related to users' intent to recommend services to their friends. This means that the better the service, the higher the satisfaction and the better the word-of-mouth advertising.

REFLECTION QUESTIONS

1. Think of a negative customer service experience from your past. How could it have been handled differently to create a better experience from both the customer's and the employee's standpoint? Be specific.
2. If you are running an adult ultimate Frisbee tournament for your region, what promotional tools do you think would be most effective for your target market? Why? How would you implement these tools for the greatest impact?

LEARNING ACTIVITIES

1. Pretend you are putting on a 5K run as a fund-raiser for your agency. Begin the budgeting process for this event by making a list of all of the expenses and resources. Make sure you include direct and indirect costs and all potential resources.
2. Think of the type of recreational sport agency you hope to work for some day and then think of an event you might put on for that agency. Research a granting agency through the Internet that might be willing to provide funding for that event. Why do you think this particular agency aligns well with your program? What requirements does the granting agency have in order to apply for funding?
3. Create a press release for a youth soccer tournament being put on by the local soccer club. How would you adapt this press release to market the tournament through broadcast media, display media, social networking, and so on?

RISK MANAGEMENT

LEARNING OUTCOMES

By the end of the chapter, readers will be able to

- define key legal terms that relate to potential liability;
- identify the potential risks involved in organizing and executing a sporting event;
- differentiate between the frequency and severity of the risks for employees, participants, and spectators; and
- determine the treatment of risks and develop a plan for an organization to manage risk to the extent possible.

Case Study

WHO IS LIABLE?

Wayne is the director of a youth hockey club for 8- to 14-year-olds at a community ice rink. Before the beginning of the season, he makes sure that all of the young athletes and their parents sign a waiver stating that they recognize the risks involved in playing hockey and they release the city from liability for any injury that is a direct or indirect result of participation. On one Saturday in December, 11-year-old Sidney is participating in some drills before a game. The league administrators who are supposed to be supervising the drills are late and the young athletes are by themselves on the ice when another player hits a puck directly into Sidney's forehead, causing a concussion. Despite the waiver they signed, Sidney and his father sue the city and Wayne for negligence based on the fact that the hockey drills were improperly supervised. Can Wayne, the city, or both be held liable for Sidney's injury? Why or why not? What risk management steps should Wayne take in the future to protect his young hockey players and decrease his liability for such injuries?

Over the last three decades, our society has become increasingly litigious. Because of this phenomenon, recreational sport professionals must develop, implement, and manage an organized plan to help control or mitigate program and financial risks. The information in this chapter is designed to assist recreational sport professionals in understanding the physical, financial, psychological, and political risks in their organizations and programs, including negligence, intentional torts, constitutional rights, and other hazards. With this knowledge, professionals should be able to assess and evaluate potential liability problems and then develop and implement plans for treating them.

In the scenario at the beginning of the chapter, Wayne and the city may both be held liable for Sidney's injury. Collecting waivers can help notify participants of the dangers involved in sporting opportunities and protect employees and agencies against lawsuits, but the practice of risk management is a lot more complicated than that. The laws guiding risk management procedures are intricate and may vary considerably by state and country. Because of this, it is always advisable for an organization to have legal counsel when making certain decisions. However, it is still important for organizations to be informed about laws, policies, and guidelines so that they can work with counsel in developing the most appropriate risk management procedures. This chapter is designed to provide recreational sport professionals with the basic knowledge of legal and risk management issues so that they will be able to work with legal counsel to provide safe, quality experiences for participants.

It is the responsibility of recreational sport professionals to ensure that the participants in their programs are safe. Not only is this morally the right thing to do, but it is also required in order to protect against future lawsuits to the extent possible. Professionals need to be aware of what the risks are in their facilities so that they can properly manage those risks to the best of their abilities. To create a plan for managing risk, it is first necessary to have a basic understanding of the legal system and how it relates to recreational sport agencies. A thorough understanding of the legal system as well as potential risks means that professionals can turn their attention to developing a risk management plan. To create such a plan, it is also necessary to understand the risk management process along with how to address workplace risks and hazards that are common in the industry.

LIABILITY AND RISK

Recreational sport is inherently risky. Any type of sport activity involves some sort of risk to participants as well as to employees and spectators. Before creating a risk management plan, an organization must first know what the risks are. It may be easy to watch a baseball game and realize that one risk is the potential of getting hit in the head with the ball, but understanding the risks involved in managing sport at any level is much more complicated. Furthermore, in order to adequately protect participants, spectators, employees, and the organization as a whole, recreational sport professionals must have a basic understanding of potential legal issues and risks.

First and foremost, recreational sport professionals should realize that anyone can sue anyone else at any time for any reason. Many of these lawsuits are the result of actual negligence on the part of someone, but in other cases they are frivolous and an attempt to make some easy money. Any recreational sport organization can become the defendant in a lawsuit and most will at some point. Defending an organization and its employees against a lawsuit can cause considerable or even catastrophic damage to the reputation and financial viability of the organization. Although an organization can never fully protect itself from the potential of being sued, it can provide itself with the best defense possible for the lawsuit. In order to do this, it is first necessary to have a basic understanding of some key legal terms. The majority of these terms are defined using *Black's Law Dictionary* (Garner, 2009), which is considered one of the standards for legal definitions.

What Is Liability?

Liability is a term that is frequently tossed around in recreational sport organizations as something to be avoided, but it is most often impossible to eliminate. Instead, understanding it will help professionals minimize it to the extent possible. **Liability** refers to a relationship in which a legal obligation exists to another individual, to another entity, or to society (Garner, 2009, p. 997). This obligation might be held by a specific person or by an organization as a whole. For example, in the case at the beginning of the chapter, Wayne and the city he worked for both had a legal obligation to protect the participants in the hockey program from injury. Similarly, in most recreational sport organizations, there is a legal obligation to protect participants from harm to the extent possible.

It is obvious that recreational sport professionals and agencies have an obligation to participants, but this is not the only category of people they have a responsibility to. Organizations also have a legal obligation toward all employees to ensure that they are able to perform their jobs safely. In the United States, every state has regulations approved by the Occupational Safety and Health Administration (OSHA) to ensure a safe working environment. Furthermore, in recreational sport agencies there are unique categories of people to whom there is a legal obligation that many other businesses do not necessarily have to deal with: volunteers and spectators. Many recreational sport organizations would not run effectively without volunteer help, and they have a legal obligation to ensure that volunteers are as protected as employees. In addition, previous court cases have ruled that sport agencies have a duty to ensure that all who are watching a game or match, such as parents, friends, or grandparents, also remain safe. Various levels of obligation exist to each of these groups depending on many factors, including age, type of involvement, and classification of the user.

Risk and Types of Risk

Knowing recreational sport professionals have a legal obligation to protect people from harm is important, but it also necessary to understand the types of harm they are protecting against. People engage in recreational sport partially because of the fun that is derived from having risk. However, it is still the responsibility of the agency to keep those involved in the activity as safe as possible without compromising the integrity of the activity. Because it is impossible (and also undesirable) to eliminate all risk, it is the responsibility of the organization to manage risk appropriately based on the activity itself and the people involved in it. To do this, a clear understanding of risk is necessary. A **risk** can be defined as the possibility of harm occurring (Garner, 2009). Most everything we do involves some sort of risk, and these risks can usually be classified into four areas: physical risk, financial risk, psychological risk, and political risk.

Physical Risk

Physical risks can include concussions, broken arms, torn ligaments, burns, drowning, and any other physical injury. These types of risks are common in the recreational sport industry and can never be completely protected against. To some extent, they can even be expected. Few athletes have never received any type of injury as the result of sport participation. People twist their ankles, trip and scrape their knees, get bruises, or even break fingers on a fairly regular basis. For the most part, these injuries cause minor

Denis Pepin/fotolia.com

Even though risk is an expected part of recreational sport, safety precautions still need to be present to help prevent liability.

damage and are accepted as part of the risk of sport involvement. A recreational sport organization needs to be concerned when those injuries become severe, such as a blown-out knee or a concussion, especially when the injuries occur because of improper care by the organization or one of its employees. Examples might be if the water in a pool is not deep enough at a swim meet and a young swimmer dives too deeply, causing a spinal cord injury, or if the unpadded wall surrounding a basketball court is too close to the basket, causing a player to break her arm on impact after a fast break.

Financial Risk

A quality risk management plan needs to minimize financial risks to the extent possible. Financial risks can include the potential for a lawsuit, costs of starting a new business or program, embezzlement, or anything that might lead to a financial loss. For a recreational sport agency, this issue most often arises in terms of protecting itself against liability. Lawsuits can be expensive regardless of who wins. This is the reason many cases are settled before going to court—cash settlements are frequently less than the plaintiff is asking for and are also less than what the defendant feels he would end up paying in legal costs if the case were to go to trial. Whether the case is settled or not, the organization needs to have an effective plan for preventing financial loss. Much of this entails the minimization and management of physical and psychological risks to prevent lawsuits from occurring in the first place.

Psychological Risk

Recreational sport agencies also need to concern themselves with any potential for psychological damage. Any sort of trauma is likely to affect a participant psychologically, and the effect could be either minor or extreme depending on the situation. A common example of psychological risk is becoming more frequent in youth sport settings. It is difficult these days to attend any type of youth sport tournament without hearing at least one parent berate a player, often her own child. This type of treatment obviously has an impact on the child, but it can also damage the psyches of the rest of the children playing. In extreme cases, this can even lead to a lawsuit.

Another psychological risk that is gaining more attention is the result of physical or sexual abuse. In multiple high-profile cases, sport organizations have been implicated in the sexual abuse of minors. To protect participants from this trauma and to prevent the liability of an organization in such matters, risk management plans should involve reducing these risks by monitoring programs and performing background checks on all adults working with children.

Political Risk

Political risks involve the potential for damage to one's reputation or any other type of political damage that might occur. It may seem that political risk is most relevant to public entities. After all, a community park and recreation department is at least partially dependent on the political climate to determine its resources. Political risk, however, also applies to private organizations for multiple reasons. First, private sport organizations frequently rely on public sport facilities for games, practices, and other team activities. For example, a travel soccer club may rent the county's fields for a tournament. Any lack of resources felt by the county might have an impact on the fields, such as a lack of maintenance. In addition, political risk may also refer to the reputation of the organization in general. Negative stories in the media based on organizational policies or the behavior of people representing the organization can have a negative political impact, thereby affecting the organization as a whole.

Clearly, it is possible to have multiple risks from the same activity. The recent case involving the Pennsylvania State University athletic department in which a former coach was convicted of sexually abusing several minors serves as an example. The abuse had physical and psychological effects on the children (physical and psychological risks), and the university is now facing several financial and political risks as a result. Multiple lawsuits are likely to be filed and donors may choose to stop donating to the university (financial risk). In addition, many people have lost their jobs and have faced severe public scrutiny, and the athletic department and university as a whole may face sanctions from the government (political risk). Although this case covers each of the four types of risk on a large scale, even small organizations should be aware of how they could face risk in each of these areas and how they interrelate. For example, any time there is a serious physical injury, such as an athlete breaking a leg or a spectator getting hit in the head with a puck (physical risks), there is usually the potential for the hurt person to file a civil lawsuit against the organization (financial risk).

Real Versus Perceived Risk

One final note about risk involves the difference between perceived risk and real risk. Perceived risk involves what others think is likely to cause them harm, whereas real risk involves what will actually cause them harm. In many cases these may be the same, but they can also be different. When a difference between the two exists, it is necessary to protect people from both to the extent possible. For example, if a young athlete receives a minor head injury during a football game, the perception of many adults is if the child feels fine, he is fine. There might not be much of a perceived risk in letting him back in the game if he did not lose consciousness and he says that he is okay. However, the real risk at this point is significant. Secondary impacts to head injuries are frequently much worse than initial ones, and a second head injury immediately after a minor one can be catastrophic, leading to permanent brain damage and even death. For this reason, a quality risk management plan would include protocol for ensuring that anyone who receives a head injury is not allowed back into a game until he has been cleared by a physician. The real risk must be protected against in spite of any perceptions to the contrary.

On the other hand, there might also be cases where there are perceived risks with minimal actual risks. For example, parents of youth rugby players might be excessively concerned about head injuries resulting from the fact that players do not wear helmets. This is a much greater perceived risk than real risk due to the way rugby players accommodate their unprotected heads through their style of tackling, among other adaptations. Consequently, although parents may perceive that the lack of helmets makes rugby players significantly more at risk for head injuries than football players, this is not actually the case. In such instances when real risk is lower than perceived risk, recreational sport professionals should use education as a tool for addressing participants' concerns.

LIABILITY CONCERNS

Now that some of the basic legal terms are clear, it is necessary to look at the liability concerns that most recreational sport organizations face. In other words, what should recreational sport professionals be concerned about in terms of risk and potential lawsuits? Each of these concerns, including negligence, intentional torts, constitutional rights, hazards, and background checks, is equally present for employees, participants, and spectators. All three groups deserve to be treated with concern and have a safe environment in which to be involved with the organization.

Negligence

Many of the cases that recreational sport organizations are likely to encounter involve negligence. **Negligence** can be defined as "the failure to exercise the standard of care that a reasonably prudent person would have exercised in a similar situation" (Garner, 2009, p. 1133). In other words, negligence involves failing to do what the average person would do to prevent harm. It is typical to consider the standards of the industry as guidelines for what should be done to prevent negligence (Spengler & Hronek, 2011). Of course, what a reasonable person would do to prevent harm in a given situation varies by the industry and even by context. For example, although there are specific standards in the ski industry, expectations may differ based on the location of the ski resort. A ski resort in North Carolina is likely to have different terrain and ski conditions than a ski resort in Utah. Consequently, what is considered a reasonable behavior to prevent risk may also vary. This means that a ski coach in Utah who is attempting to prevent a negligence lawsuit may want to consider the industry standard as well as compare her practices with those of coaches who work at similar resorts and with similar clientele.

Elements of Negligence

Legally, proving negligence requires the presence of four elements: duty, breach, cause, and injury. All cases must demonstrate that these elements are present in order to be successful.

Duty refers to a "legal obligation that is owed or due to another and that needs to be satisfied" (Garner, 2009, p. 580). An individual or an organization must provide some level of care or service to an individual. For example, if Emma owns and operates a tennis club, she has a duty to ensure that her facilities and equipment are well maintained and usable or to provide ample notification when this is not the case.

Breach occurs when the duty held by the individual or organization is violated in some way (Garner, 2009). So, if Emma knows about a ball machine that is malfunctioning or a court with a leaky roof and she allows her patrons to use them without providing a warning, she likely has breached her duty.

Cause refers to the fact that whatever happens is a result of the breach. Breaching the duty is what caused a particular effect (Garner, 2009). This cause can be further broken down into two categories: cause in fact or proximate cause. **Cause in fact** means "the cause without which the event could not have occurred" (Garner, 2009, p. 250). This typically refers to a direct result of the action. For example, in the case of Emma and her tennis court, if she intentionally aims the ball machine at a client's head and a ball causes a head injury, it would likely be considered cause in fact.

Proximate cause means that "a cause that is legally sufficient to result in liability; an act or omission that is considered in law to result in a consequence, so that liability can be imposed on the actor" (Garner, 2009, p. 250). This means that people can be held liable if their action or lack of action in a matter eventually leads to an incident. For Emma, this might mean that by neglecting to maintain the roof, a leak developed, causing a puddle of water to form on the court. Although she did not physically pour the water on the court and shove someone into it, she is still responsible for the water being there because she did not maintain the facility. Usually to show proximate cause there needs to be some degree of **foreseeability**, or the ability to see that something is likely to happen (Garner, 2009). Emma should know that improper roof maintenance is likely to lead to leaks, and if she sees a puddle on the court, she could easily foresee that a tennis player could get hurt.

Finally, in order for the incident to be negligence, there needs to be some sort of **injury**. This can be defined as "the violation of another's legal right, for which the law provides a remedy" (Garner, 2009, p. 856). Injuries relate somewhat to the four types of risk that were previously discussed. In the case of Emma and her tennis club, a participant who falls due to an unexpected pool of water could easily tear a knee ligament (physical injury), which would require knee surgery and could cost not only medical expenses but also time off work (financial injury).

Remember, in order for negligence to exist, all four elements must be present. If, for example, Emma adequately warned her patrons as they came in the door that a particular court was closed because it was under a leaky roof and she blocked that court off, she might not be found negligent if a tennis player decided to jump over the barrier and play on the court anyway. If that person slipped and fell, tearing a knee ligament, he would find it difficult to prove that Emma was negligent. She had a duty and there was an injury, but the injury in this case was not caused by a breach of duty on Emma's part.

Other Important Factors

Additional factors can come into play when trying to minimize the potential of a negligence suit through risk management. These include the physical characteristics, mental characteristics, skills, and knowledge of participants. Dealing with a variety of participants may mean that you have various concerns when aiming to minimize risk while creating the best possible experience.

The physical characteristics of the participants is one such concern. When it comes to safety and sport, size does matter. Consequently, it might be beneficial to match participants according to size. For instance, children develop at different rates and hit growth spurts at different times. When creating youth leagues, it thus might be a good idea to consider size when matching opponents, particularly in collision sports. This would ensure that in football, a 50-pound (23 kg) child is not across the line from a child twice his size, which could easily lead to serious injury once the ball is snapped.

The mental characteristics of participants can also be a factor when designing programs to prevent negligence. Mental ability and capacity can affect both the ability to understand instructions and the requirements for supervision. Though it may be easy to assume that mental characteristics follow a simple progression based on age, this is not always the case. Recreational sport programs are popular among people with developmental disabilities as well as among older age groups for whom diseases such as dementia might be an issue. Consequently, recreational sport professionals need to understand their participants' mental abilities and concerns in order to provide the safest programs possible.

Finally, skills and knowledge should come into play when designing sport programs. Again, these factors can influence not only what is taught but also how it is taught and the level of supervision required for instruction. For example, in teaching swim lessons to a class of beginners, no matter what the age or mental ability of the participants, it would be advisable to have small classes in a small area with the instructor in the water in order to minimize risk and reduce the chances of a negligence lawsuit. This allows the instructor to teach without worrying as much about a swimmer drowning. As the ability of the swimmers improves, however, it is likely that the instructor can handle larger numbers in the class, that the class will take up more space so that the swimmers can swim farther, and that the instructor will begin to spend more time out of the water where he can see the swimmers' technique more clearly. Because of the swimmers' advanced skills, the likelihood of drowning has decreased, so the expectations for what is acceptable within the program have changed as well.

Intentional Torts

Negligence may be the most common type of **tort** in which recreational sport agencies are involved, but consideration should also be paid to preventing intentional torts. An **intentional tort** is "a tort committed by someone acting with general or specific intent" (Garner, 2009, p. 1626). In other words, whereas negligence may occur due to a lack of concern or care, intentional torts do not simply occur. Instead, they happen because someone intended them to happen. When talking about intent, we are referring to the act itself, not the result of the act. So the person who engages in an intentional tort may not have intended to harm someone as a result of her action, but the action itself was intentional. For example, a baseball pitcher may intentionally throw a pitch at a batter's head out of frustration. Whether or not he meant to cause damage with the throw is irrelevant. If injury were to occur because of that pitch, such as damage to the optic nerve resulting in permanent blindness, the pitcher could be held liable for an intentional tort because the action itself was intended.

Two issues related to intentional torts particularly need to be considered when preparing a risk management plan. First, with intentional torts, there may be criminal charges. Criminal law and civil law are two aspects of the U.S. legal system that can overlap in some cases. **Criminal law** involves wrongs committed by individuals against the state, is typically prosecuted by the government, and results in imprisonment and fines. **Civil law** involves wrongs committed by individuals against individuals and can result in compensated losses (Garner, 2009; Spengler & Hronek, 2011). For the most part, risk management is concerned with civil law, but in the case of intentional torts, issues might arise involving both. For example, if a staff member loses it during an adult league softball game and gets in a physical confrontation with one of the players, the player could press battery charges against the staff member (criminal law) and also sue the individual and organization for any damages resulting from the battery (civil law).

The second issue that needs to be considered is type of intentional tort. Intentional torts can be divided into two categories: persons and property.

Intentional Torts to Persons

Intentional torts to persons generally involve things that directly affect the person (Garner, 2009). Types of intentional torts to person that risk managers should prepare against include battery, assault, defamation of character, and intentional infliction of emotional distress.

Intentional Torts to Property

Intentional torts to property differ from those to persons in that they involve damage to physical property, or some type of possession that can be owned (Garner, 2009). The most likely property tort involving a recreational sport agency is trespass to land, or unlawful entry onto another's land that is visibly enclosed (Garner, p. 1643). In other words, if young adults break into a community pool for a midnight swim, the organization could sue them for trespass to land. Although generally it is illegal to gain access to an organization's land without paying or obtaining specific permission, certain conditions might change the situation. For example, if the land includes an attractive nuisance, it could limit the liability of a trespasser and an organization could be held liable for any damages that result from this nuisance as a potential form of negligence.

An **attractive nuisance** is any type of human-made, dangerous condition that may entice children to visit the property, putting their safety at risk (Garner, 2009). If an organization is aware of a feature on its property that might attract children and can foresee that feature being a risk to children, then it is the organization's duty to take reasonable precautions to prevent children's access and harm (Spengler & Hronek, 2011). Features at recreational sport facilities that are commonly perceived as attractive nuisances include swimming pools. It is easy for the average adult to perceive how a swimming pool would attract young children to play in it, regardless of whether or not the children have legal access. It is also easy to see how a swimming pool could be highly dangerous to children who access it after hours and without proper supervision. For this reason, a good risk management plan will take into consideration the need to reduce access to such an attractive feature through the use of fences, locked gates, and so on. This will increase the safety of children and reduce the likelihood of a lawsuit.

© Mary Sara Wells

Recreational sport facilities can often be considered attractive nuisances and extra efforts should be used to protect unintentional users.

Constitutional Rights

One additional group of potential torts that a recreational sport professional may need to be concerned about is those involving constitutional rights. All citizens of the United States are guaranteed certain rights by the U.S. Constitution and the constitution of the state in which they live (Garner, 2009). Recreational sport agencies need to have policies and procedures in place to ensure that they do not infringe on these rights. Specific constitutional concerns that might affect recreational sport professionals include discrimination and the right to privacy.

Right to Privacy

Although the U.S. Constitution does not specifically mention privacy, the Supreme Court has consistently ruled that it is a guaranteed right supported by aspects of the Constitution (Garner, 2009). Privacy applies to many areas related to recreational sport, including athlete injuries and medical records, physical exams required before sport participation, locations of security cameras throughout facilities, accommodations for overnight trips with athletes, and the ability of an organization to have access to gym lockers. One of the problems in maintaining a right to privacy in recreational sport is when privacy concerns conflict with safety concerns. For example, an injured athlete has a legal right not to disclose medical information to a coach. That withheld information, however, might directly influence what the coach expects of the athlete and how he designs the athlete's training. Because of the complex nature of the laws and regulations, an organization should work directly with legal counsel to ensure that the risk management plan does not violate privacy rights.

Discrimination

A second important constitutional concern for recreational sport organizations is preventing discrimination. Several municipal, state, and federal statutes, along with the 14th Amendment

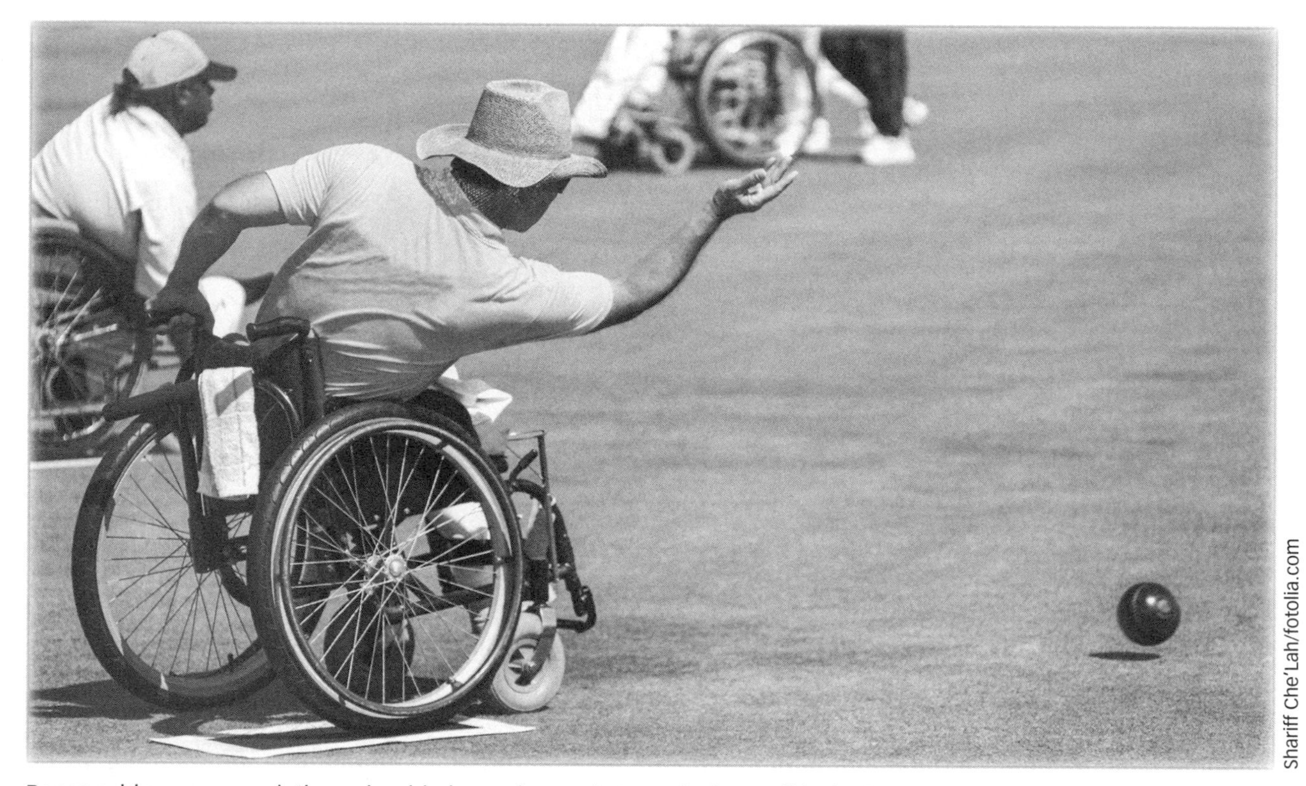
Sharriff Che'Lah/fotolia.com

Reasonable accommodations should always be made to make it possible for individuals of all types to participate.

to the Constitution (ratified July 8, 1968), make it illegal to discriminate against people for a variety of reasons. *Discrimination* refers to any type of differential treatment based on specific categories such as race, age, sex, religion, and disability (Garner, 2009). In addition, several municipalities have added sexual orientation to the list of categories. In each of these instances, the law requires that an organization treat all people equally when no reasonable distinction can be made between them. A reasonable distinction might include specialized training, experience, education, or skill level, all of which could affect the ability to either play a sport or supervise people playing a sport.

A somewhat unique situation exists in the sport industry when it comes to discrimination against people with disabilities. Although it is important to accommodate people when reasonable, the nature of the sport itself does not necessarily need to change in order to make those accommodations. The Americans with Disabilities Act of 1990 (ADA) makes it necessary for organizations to provide reasonable accommodations for people with disabilities to ensure nondiscrimination in the workforce and in access to public programs. This means that a recreational sport organization is required to provide reasonable access to individuals with disabilities both for participation and hiring purposes. However, exceptions can be made to this policy. For example, if the organization is looking for volunteer coaches for a youth basketball league and a woman using a wheelchair volunteers to coach her daughter's team, accommodations should be made to ensure she can do so. Making sure that courts are accessible and navigable by a wheelchair is a completely reasonable accommodation. If, however, a young person who uses a wheelchair wants to register for the league, it is not necessary to change the league from basketball to wheelchair basketball. That accommodation would change the nature of the sport the other participants had agreed to play and would therefore be unreasonable. In this case, the organization needs to talk with the child's parents regarding how he can participate to the extent possible without changing the activity itself.

Hazards

Additionally, recreational sport professionals and organizations should pay attention to specific hazards that present liability concerns. Particular concerns to consider include emergency medical preparedness and bloodborne pathogens, natural features, weather and natural disasters, and transportation.

Emergency Medical Preparedness and Bloodborne Pathogens

The inherent risk in sport means that any recreational sport agency should have proper procedures in place to deal with medical emergencies. This could range from basic first aid all the way up through lifesaving procedures related to the use of automated external defibrillators (AEDs). Standards in these areas are partially determined by industry standards. At a minimum, however, staff should be trained in first aid and CPR (cardiopulmonary resuscitation) for the population with whom they are working, and staff working in any waterfront sports should be trained in the proper lifesaving techniques.

In addition, preventing the transmission of bloodborne pathogens such as hepatitis and HIV requires several precautions that should be used when bodily fluids are present. Athletes frequently get injured during games, and staff who deal with injuries should know how to minimize exposure to and appropriately dispose of anything blood related. This includes using barriers such as gloves and breathing masks, sanitizing exposed areas, and using biohazard waste dispensers when necessary.

Natural Features

Many sport activities take place outside, exposing people to risks associated with the natural environment. Sun exposure alone presents several risks, including sunburn, dehydration, heat exhaustion, and heatstroke. Sunburn can also be an issue for outdoor winter sports such as skiing, and hypothermia may be a concern for athletes in many sports, including most water-based ones. Furthermore, there may be concerns related to terrain, altitude, and surface quality. Every organization should be aware of the environmental conditions in which all activities are taking place to best ensure the safety of participants.

Weather and Natural Disasters

Recreational sport professionals also need to be aware of how weather and natural disasters might influence the risk involved in an activity. Outdoor activities are regularly affected by weather conditions. Lightning should be of particular concern; exposing athletes, coaches, and spec-

Staff at recreational sport facilities should always be trained in how to appropriately handle potential emergency situations.

tators to lightning is dangerous and completely unnecessary. Sport leagues and organizations have specific procedures for game or meet delays and evacuation rules for spectators in the case of lightning, and these should always be followed in order to reduce the organization's liability if an injury should occur.

Natural disasters are frequently related to weather, and certain regions are more prone to certain types of disasters than others. Training all staff and educating all participants on the procedures to follow in the case of such disasters is necessary to maintain the safety of participants.

Transportation

Transportation is another frequent concern for recreational sport organizations. Many employees in these organizations are responsible for transporting groups to events and matches. Again, proper training and safety procedures such as using defensive driving techniques and seatbelts should always be followed to minimize liability in the case of an accident. This is often an issue for groups requiring larger vehicles such as 15-passenger vans. Recreational sport professionals should always ensure that the drivers of these vehicles have completed the proper training to do so.

Another transportation issue may result from injuries that occur during games or practices. For example, if a young baseball player gets hit by a pitch and seemingly has a concussion, the coach or a league official might offer to drive the player to the hospital to save time rather than calling an ambulance. However, doing so may open the organization to liability if anything unexpected happens. If the parent or responsible party is not able to give consent in such situations, it is generally better to let health care professionals handle the situation from the beginning.

Background Checks

A final issue involving the safety of participants in recreational sport programs is **background checks**. This is particularly a concern when programs involve youth or other vulnerable populations. Due to high-publicity legal cases such as in the Penn State child sex abuse scandal, the risk of children being harmed by trusted people associated with sport has become more recognized. This has increased the need to ensure that all volunteers and employees working directly with youth (e.g., coaches, officials) do not have a history of criminal behavior and are not registered sex offenders. In addition, completing background checks also helps protect organizations from lawsuits by demonstrating that the organization has done what is within its power to ensure the people working with young athletes are as safe as possible. All recreational sport professionals should be concerned with the safety of their young participants and need to do what is reasonably possible to maintain their well-being. Although a background check will not always catch unsafe people, particularly if they have not previously been charged with a crime, it is an important step in maintaining the safety of a program and its participants.

The right to access the criminal records of people who will be working with children is based on the Volunteers for Children Act of 1998 (VCA), which amended the National Child Protection Act of 1993 (NCPA) to authorize organizations to complete fingerprint-based background checks in order to ensure the safety and well-being of children. These acts apply to all public, private, not-for-profit, or voluntary organizations that work with youth. Such organizations are not required to perform background checks; however, doing so is often in the best interest of the organization and the children it serves. Background checks and the depth of information provided can vary, so it is up to each recreational sport organization to decide what checks it will complete based on its resources and the services requested by the stakeholders.

CREATING A PLAN TO MANAGE RISK

Recreational sport professionals should use their knowledge of liability and risk to create risk management plans designed to protect their organizations to the extent possible. The intent of a risk management plan is not to eliminate risk. However, it is the moral and legal responsibility of all recreational sport organizations to keep their participants and employees as safe as reasonably possible from any known dangers. Following a risk management process helps agencies to provide safe services in an effective manner.

Risk management can be defined as "the procedures or systems used to minimize accidental losses, especially to a business" (Garner, 2009, p. 1442). Every recreational sport organization should have a plan in place for preventing loss. This plan should detail the procedures and policies of the organization for minimizing the physical, financial, psychological, and political risks of participation, employment, and spectating. Determining how best to do this entails a four-step process: risk identification, risk evaluation, risk treatment, and plan implementation (Spengler & Hronek, 2011; see figure 8.1).

To begin the risk management process, recreational sport professionals should first be aware of the responsibilities of their organization. It is the agency's responsibility to provide a reasonable amount of care in keeping the area safe and to warn of any known dangers. The specific amount of care that is required is what "a prudent and competent person engaged in the same line of business or endeavor would exercise under similar circumstances" (Garner, 2009, p. 240). In other words, recreational sport organizations should look to current industry standards and to similar agencies as examples of the minimum expectations for safety. Industry standards tend to vary by the type of services being provided but can frequently be determined with the help of insurance companies, national associations, and even comparison with similar organizations. Keep in mind that if an organization sets up its own risk management plan with higher standards, courts are likely to hold it accountable to those written policies even if they exceed what other organizations are doing. This should not discourage organizations from setting higher standards than what is expected, but they should be cautious in doing so. If the standards are unreasonably high, it could set the organization up for failure and damage the long-term financial health of the organization.

Risk Identification

The first step in the risk management process is to identify potential risks that may be encountered by participants, employees, and spectators. Earlier sections of this chapter have already discussed several risks and concerns, including negligence, intentional torts, constitutional rights, and hazards. Other areas to consider include equipment, participant attributes, and supervision procedures.

Equipment used for some sports can be dangerous, especially when it is used for something other than its intended purpose. A tennis ball machine, for example, has inherent risks that may increase when the machine is left unsupervised with a group of teenagers. Consequently, when risk managers are identifying risks, they should not limit themselves to the most obvious ones. To help in this process, it is important to receive information from as many parties as possible. The best risk identification occurs when multiple perspectives are represented. Recreational organizations should empower employees, athletes, coaches, parents, and other interested parties to express safety concerns so that as many reasonable and unreasonable risks can be identified as possible. A risk management plan that does not address all the major concerns will not be nearly as effective as one that does (Spengler & Hronek, 2011).

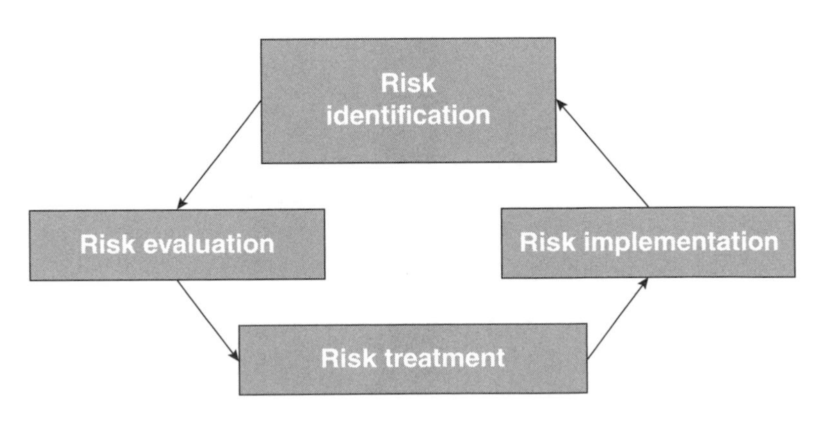

Figure 8.1 Risk management process (Spengler & Hronek, 2011).

© Mary Sara Wells

Risk management in recreational sport should include concerns of players, coaches, officials, employees, and spectators.

Risk Evaluation

Now that the risks are identified, it is important to determine their potential impact on people and the organization. Typically, there are two ways of evaluating a risk: the potential frequency of the risk occurring and the potential severity of injury as a result of the risk occurring (Spengler & Hronek, 2011). Separately, neither provides a full picture of a facility or program. As an example, one of the most frequent accidents at a pool occurred when small children jumped in water that was over their heads and needed to be fished out by a lifeguard. It happened fairly regularly, but the consequences were never severe. On one occasion, however, a life-threatening injury occurred. A swimmer on the swim team accidentally dove in too deeply in the shallow end, hit her head on the bottom, and floated to the top. In the end, she recovered fully, but the severity of that accident was significantly greater than any of the other accidents. If recreational sport professionals only looked at the frequency of occurrences, they would assume that the deep end of the pool was the most dangerous part of the facility and might overlook the severe danger that could occur in the shallow end. It is only in analyzing the whole that the best risk management plans are developed. Risk managers must consider where events occur, how often, and what the consequences are in order to bring risks to an acceptable level.

Every organization has access to multiple devices to help in evaluating risks. Accident reports, organizational policies, and inspection forms can all be used to help understand what is happening in an organization. For this reason, it is beneficial to keep records on everything. Not only will these records provide immediate assistance in the continual development of a risk management plan, but they will also provide evidence of actions in case of a lawsuit. In addition, it is useful to look at similar organizations and industry standards. Other businesses might have valuable experience and insight into the risks that a particular recreational sport organization faces.

Risk Treatment

The third step in the risk management process is to treat the risks that have been identified and evaluated. There are three options for treating every risk: Retain the risk, transfer the risk, or avoid or eliminate the risk. Retaining the risk simply means that you keep it. When the risk is unlikely to happen or the potential harm from the risk is minor, most agencies opt to retain it. For example, there is a risk for participants in almost any sport that they will stub a toe. Although this is highly likely to happen, the potential harm from it is minor and therefore most organizations will keep that risk. Remember, risk is a vital component of almost any activity in recreational sport, and in a lot of cases keeping that risk is important. If every agency had signs warning people of every possible risk at every point, it would make a cluttered landscape, but more importantly people would likely be so desensitized to the warnings that they might ignore the ones that are the most important.

The second option in treating the risk is to transfer it. Transferring the risk means that the risk is still present but that someone or something else takes over responsibility for that risk. This is usually done through insurance policies, lease agreements, and exculpatory documents (e.g., agreements to participate, waivers).

One of the most common methods for transferring risk is insurance. When purchasing insurance, an organization agrees to pay a certain fee on a yearly or monthly basis, and in exchange the insurance company pays for damages that are covered by the policy. Essentially the organization budgets a certain amount of money to ensure that it will not have to make a large payout at an unscheduled time. Most people have some sort of insurance policy, whether it is medical, dental, life, home, or auto. Responsible organizations also must maintain certain policies to ensure that they are covered in the case of an emergency. Types of insurance to consider include accident, automobile, inclement weather, travel, event, and liability. The organization should also consider what specific things need to be covered, such as certain facilities and events, categories of people, and time periods. Every recreational sport organization has unique needs, so an insurance agent should be consulted to make sure that the organization has optimal coverage for its needs (Spengler & Hronek, 2011).

A second way to transfer risk can be done if an agency is leasing property to another organization. The liability of the leasing entity may be transferred to the organization using the facilities through the lease agreement. This method of risk transfer is frequently used when private organizations use facilities for practices, meets, or tournaments if they do not have the necessary facilities themselves. For example, a travel soccer team may regularly rent a field from the city park and recreation department for practices and games and then schedule a group of fields in order to host a tournament. In this case, the city park and recreation department would likely include a clause in the lease stating that the soccer club has agreed to be responsible for the liability for the participants during the times specified on the agreement. However, a lease will not necessarily absolve an organization from all liability, such as if there is an accident caused by poor field maintenance (e.g., a hole in the middle of the field that the city knew about but failed to fix). For this reason, it is important for both sides to have legal counsel review any leasing documents so that everyone understands their potential liability in the case of an accident.

Another option in transferring risk is to transfer the risk back to the participant—in other words, making the participant assume responsibility for any injury that might occur. This is typically done through the use of exculpatory documents, which are documents that free a person or an organization from blame or accusation (Garner, 2009). These documents remove the liability from the organization and place it on another person or entity. Exculpatory documents generally include **waivers**, agreements to participate, and releases (see figure 8.2 for an example). Because every sporting event involves some inherent risk, making participants sign waivers results in a written contract outlining the fact that they know and understand the risks and that they are willing to participate in spite of them.

There are six points to remember about waivers. First, the participant needs to know that the document is actually a waiver (*Johnson v. Rapid City Softball Association*, 1994). Many times waivers are printed in places where participants do not know they exist, such as on the back of

Figure 8.2 Sample Waiver

University of Utah Participant Agreement, Release, and Acknowledgment of Risk for Mountain-Biking Courses

(Please print your name on the line below.)

I,________________________________ (herein referred to as "Participant"), understand this is a legal document and, in consideration of the services provided by the University of Utah, its officers, employees, agents, or representatives (herein referred to as "the University of Utah") as part of ________________________(course title, herein referred to as "Field Trip"), hereby agree to release and discharge the University of Utah on behalf of myself, my heirs, assigns, personal representative, and estate as follows:

1. In consideration of the University of Utah's sponsorship and direction of this field trip, I hereby state that I have read and understand the terms and conditions of the University of Utah Policy and Procedure 1-10 and specifically agree to be bound thereby.

2. I understand and acknowledge that the field trip I voluntarily expect and intend to engage in as a participant bears certain known and unanticipated risks from avalanche, falling objects, animals, insects, and broken or improperly used equipment that could result in damage to or loss of property, illness or disease, physical or mental injury, or death to myself or other persons. Injuries that may occur from participating in this field trip include, but are not limited to, cuts, bruises, sprained joints, broken bones, psychological trauma, loss of extremity, infection, gastric disease, animal/insect bites, hypothermia, heat injury, and death while participating in scheduled and unscheduled activities related to the outdoor environment, vehicular/foot travel, terrain, weather, food, and/or colliding with objects. My participation in this field trip is purely voluntary and I elect to participate in spite of the risks.

3. Being aware that this field trip entails known and unknown risks of injury to myself or other persons as a result of my actions, I expressly agree, covenant, and promise to accept and assume all responsibility and risk of injury, illness, disease, or death to myself or damage to and destruction of property arising from my participation in this field trip.

4. I hereby voluntarily release, forever discharge, and agree to hold harmless and indemnify the University of Utah, its agents or employees, and all other persons or entities from any and all liability, claims, demands, actions, or rights of actions that are related to, arise out of, or are in any way connected with my participation in this field trip, including but not limited to the negligent acts or omissions of the University of Utah, its agents or employees, and all other persons or entities, for any and all injury, illness, disease, or death to myself or damage to my property. In signing this document, I fully recognize that if anyone is hurt or property is damaged while I am engaged in this field trip, I will have no right to make a claim or file a lawsuit against the University of Utah, or its officers, agents, or employees, except where such injury, illness, disease, or death is caused solely by the negligent acts or omission of the University of Utah.

5. I certify that I am physically and mentally capable of participating in this field trip as described in the course outline.

6. I certify that I have sufficient health and accident insurance (e.g., hospital/medical insurance, student health insurance, University short-term accident insurance, etc.) to cover any bodily injury or property damage I may incur while participating in this field trip.

7. I agree and understand that I will comply with all reasonable directions and instructions by the instructor/trip director during the field trip.

8. I understand that the instructor/trip director reserves the right to refuse my participation or dismiss me from the field trip if I am judged by the instructor/trip director as physically or mentally incapable of meeting the requirements of participating in the field trip.

9. I agree not to possess, use, or be under the influence of alcoholic beverages, nonprescribed controlled substances, or illegal substances during the field trip. I understand I will be dismissed from the field trip and course by the instructor/trip director for violation of this agreement.

My signature below indicates that I have read this entire document, understand it completely, understand that it affects my legal rights, and agree to be bound by its terms. *(Sign in ink.)*

Signature of participant:____

Date: ______________ **20**___

Print name: ____

Student ID number: _________________

tickets. If someone purchases a ticket to a basketball game and then attends the game without seeing the small print on the back of the ticket, he may never realize that his rights have been waived. It is always better to make this clear both to ensure the safety of participants and to protect the agency from lawsuits by clearly stating that the participants have agreed to the waiver. The easiest way to do this is by placing a statement in noticeable type at the beginning of any document that says *Waiver of Liability* (*Dombrowski v. City of Omer*, 1993; Spengler & Hronek, 2011).

For a waiver to be effective, it should be clearly written and easily understandable. A person entering a contract needs to be fully aware of what she is agreeing to, and that is difficult if the contract is full of jargon or language that is too complex. To construct a clear and understandable waiver, it is beneficial to understand the target market for your agency and write the waiver at the appropriate reading level for that market. Younger participants generally require a lower reading level. In addition, if you serve a population that primarily speaks another language, you should make sure that waivers are available in that language (Carpenter, 2008; Dougherty, Goldberger, & Carpenter, 2007; Spengler & Hronek, 2011).

Because a waiver is considered a legal contract, it needs to be signed by a legal adult (Carpenter, 2008; Spengler & Hronek, 2011). This gets tricky for organizations that primarily work with a youth population. An organization working with youth typically requests waivers from both parents and their children. However, although the waiver or participation agreement signed by the parents will likely hold up in court, the waiver signed by the child probably will not. A child cannot legally sign away his rights, and the parents of a child cannot legally sign away his rights either (Carpenter, 2008; *Scott v. Pacific West Mountain Resort*, 1992). For example, in the case at the beginning of the chapter, Sidney signed a waiver agreeing to participate. Because he was a minor, the waiver was not legally valid and he has the potential to win the lawsuit as a result.

Does this mean that there is no need to present waivers to youth? Absolutely not. It is still important for every youth-serving organization to provide some sort of exculpatory document to young athletes outlining the risks of participation. Although it may not provide extensive legal protection for the agency if a case goes to court, it is at least morally prudent to provide children with the information they need to make an informed decision regarding whether or not they want to participate.

In addition to paying special attention to youth participants, the fact that waivers need to be signed by a competent adult is also a concern for anyone working with people with cognitive impairments. People with cognitive impairments, such as developmental disabilities, dementia, or even chosen cognitive impairments such as being under the influence of drugs or alcohol, could all lead to questions regarding the legality of a waiver in court. Therefore, if you are working with people who may not be fully competent, it is important to either follow the same rules as with young participants or wait until the person has regained competence before allowing her to sign any documents.

As a legal contract, a waiver also needs to be specific regarding what the person is agreeing to. In other words, make sure it specifies the most predominant and most dangerous risks (Dougherty, et al., 2007; Spengler & Hronek, 2011). Although it is impossible to cover all potential risks, participants should be fully aware of what is likely to occur and the extent of potential damage. For example, in the case of swimming, participants should know that they could easily be hurt multiple ways while slipping on the deck (e.g., mild scrapes, broken bones). These types of injuries happen frequently on a wet pool deck and are most often minor. Injuries that happen less frequently but that can be catastrophic include spinal and head injuries, drowning, and even death as a result of an improper dive into the pool. No one wants to scare away participants, but athletes of all ages should be aware of the risks they face so that they can make an informed decision as to whether or not that risk is worth it.

After the document is written clearly, the participant must not be under any duress when signing it (Carpenter, 2008; Spengler & Hronek, 2011). As stated earlier, participants should be able to make their own informed decisions about the extent of risk in which they wish to engage. This can only be done when the participants choose freely for themselves without feeling undue pressure from others, including agency officials, peers, and even parents. Recreational sport agencies should attempt to ensure that participation agreements are signed in advance and away from people such as coaches and teammates as a way to minimize these pressures. For example, when collecting waivers from players in an adult softball tournament, do not wait until right before the first game. Players might then feel the pressure from the team and coaches to sign, and the immediacy of the situation may also have an impact. It is always a better idea to include any waivers or participation agreements with initial registration packets. This allows players to make their own risk decisions without the undue influence of others.

Finally, waivers must not be against public policy (Spengler & Hronke, 2011). They need to follow all the laws in the state where services are provided. For this reason, it is always a smart business practice to seek legal counsel when constructing exculpatory documents. Lawyers familiar with the industry and the specific laws in a state are an invaluable resource for constructing documents that will hold up in court if a case is ever brought against an organization.

As a final note, a waiver will never completely absolve an agency from all liability concerns (Carpenter, 2008; Dougherty et al., 2007). All representatives of an organization must still refrain from acting in a negligent manner. Although the participants are agreeing that there is some level of inherent risk in participation, they are still participating under the assumption that you will do everything possible to minimize that risk. For example, a batter in a baseball game can assume there is potential for getting hit in the head by a ball, but if an agency has agreed to supply batters' helmets, that batter can also assume that the helmets will meet a minimum safety standard. In this case, by either not supplying the helmets or by supplying faulty ones, the agency opens itself up to liability despite the fact that participants have willingly signed a waiver.

Finally, when considering how to treat risks, if the risk is simply too big of a concern it is most likely in the best interest of the organization and the people involved to close or avoid the risk. This will likely happen if both the frequency of an event occurring and the consequences of that event are too high.

Plan Implementation

The final step in the risk management process is implementation. Keep in mind that no plan is perfect. For this reason, every risk management plan should include some schedule for evaluation. This allows recreational sport professionals to determine whether the policies and procedures are effective and reasonable for minimizing risk. As the plan is evaluated, it will likely continue to be adapted and hopefully improved. Furthermore, one of the most important aspects of a risk management plan is the implementation itself. Actions to avoid, minimize, or transfer risk should occur in the timeliest manner possible. A delay of any kind can have serious consequences that lead to extensive damages both to participants and the agency.

CONCLUSION

Recreational sport professionals should be concerned about protecting their participants, employees, and spectators to the extent possible, but not at the expense of eliminating all risks. Risks are an inherent and valuable part of the experiences provided in these programs. Consequently, quality programs have good risk management plans to ensure that safety is a priority without changing the nature of the activity that is being offered. To develop this plan, professionals need to first understand the physical, financial, psychological, and political risks involved in their programs along with any concerns about negligence, intentional torts, constitutional rights, and hazards. They can then create a risk management plan through a four-step process of identifying, evaluating, and determining treatment for risks and then implementing the plan. This should help recreational sport professionals to continue offering high-quality, safe programs with risks that are enjoyable to participants and manageable by the organization.

RESEARCH TO REALITY

Lowe v. California League of Professional Baseball, 56 Cal. App. 4th 112 (1997).

In this case, John Lowe was hit in the face by a foul ball when he was at a professional baseball game. Just before he was struck, he was distracted by the team mascot. Because of this distraction, he was unable to protect himself from the foul ball. Lowe claimed that the mascot's actions increased the inherent risks of attending the game and that this was a breach in duty by the league to keep spectators safe. The court agreed with Lowe that despite the fact that spectators accept certain risks by attending baseball games, because the mascot's antics were not an integral part of the game, it could be considered a breach of duty to increase the risks associated with attendance.

In a world where there is increasing pressure for entertainment at sporting events, this case is highly relevant. Although this case involved a professional rather than recreational sport organization, multiple aspects can apply to both situations. Distractions such as music, games, T-shirt tosses, and mascot interaction with the audience are becoming an expectation for spectators of sports at all levels, including recreational sport. And although these extra pieces of entertainment tend to be fun, recreational sport professionals need to recognize the heightened risk that comes with them. As this case demonstrates, distracting viewers from potential dangers, such as a flying baseball, as the game is in progress can lead to increased liability and therefore must be considered in the risk management plan. Professionals need to be aware of the risks these distractions present and try to ensure that they occur during breaks in play in order to better protect themselves and their spectators.

REFLECTION QUESTIONS

1. Whom can your participants sue if something goes wrong? When can they sue? Why can they sue?
2. What are the four types of risk to address when developing a risk management plan?
3. What is negligence and what are its components?
4. What are the four steps in the risk management process?
5. What are some specific concerns you should pay attention to when constructing and distributing a waiver?
6. What level of standard of care should be provided by any recreational sport organization?

LEARNING ACTIVITIES

1. Take the following checklist to your favorite sport facility (e.g., gym, tennis courts, swimming pool, track, soccer complex). Spend a half hour walking around as you try to find all the potential risks (i.e., physical, financial, psychological, and political). Also write down the probable frequency and severity of each risk along with how you would treat them (see figure 8.3).
2. What are the components of a good waiver? Looking at figure 8.2 from earlier in the chapter, can you identify each of these components?

Figure 8.3 Risk Checklist

Risk	Type of injury	Frequency (1-5)	Severity (1-5)	Treatment
1.				
2.				
3.				
4.				
5.				
6.				
7.				
8.				
9.				
10.				

chapter 9

HUMAN RESOURCES IN RECREATIONAL SPORT

LEARNING OUTCOMES

By the end of this chapter, readers will be able to

- describe the major personnel types and positions within a recreational sport organization;
- assess the key human resources processes involved with managing recreational sport personnel, including job design, recruitment, selection, hiring, training, and evaluating staff;
- articulate the similarities and differences involved in managing full-time, part-time, and volunteer staff; and
- explain the importance of employing competent staff and the impact they have on creating positive recreational sport outcomes for participants.

Case Study

COMPETITION VERSUS COMPASSION IN BOUNTIFUL

In Rick Reilly's August 8, 2006, You Make the Call column in *Sports Illustrated*, the author writes about a decision by a youth baseball coach to issue an intentional walk to the opponent's best hitter in order to pitch to the weakest hitter when the outcome of a championship game was on the line. This sounds like conventional baseball strategy. However, the details surrounding the game make this a complex and compelling case. Although the facts are detailed here, the presentation of those facts has been changed, and some information has been added to provide greater context for the purposes of this case study. However, the essential story came from Reilly's coverage of the incident. As you read, think about how you would respond to this situation if you were the athletic director in charge of community sport in Bountiful. Specifically think about personnel and human resources in recreational sport. What should the policies be for recruiting, selecting, training, and evaluating recreational sport personnel and volunteers?

Each August in Bountiful, Utah, just as in many other places across the United States, young baseball players take to the diamond to play their final games of the long summer. Leagues hold tournaments, crown champions, and give out trophies to the winners—even in recreation-focused programs, where the emphasis is on learning, skill development, and fun. The 9- and 10-year-old baseball league in Bountiful is an example of this fusion of winning on the one hand and development on the other. For example, the rules of the league are set up to create at least a somewhat level playing field—every player gets to hit and must play at least two innings in the field, there are limits on how many pitches a pitcher may throw, there is a maximum number of runs that a team may score in an inning, and there is a mercy rule that ends a game when one team is ahead by more than 10 runs after four innings. On the other hand, the league keeps score in the games, records which teams win and which ones lose, and holds a double-elimination tournament at the end of the 15-game season to determine a league champion. The local paper even covers some of the games in the sport section.

The two values of winning and development came into conflict during the league championship game between the Yankees and the Red Sox. The Yankees were beating the Red Sox by a score of 5–4 in the bottom of the sixth inning—the last inning of the game. The Red Sox were hitting with two outs and the tying run on third base. The player up at bat was Jordan, the best hitter on the Red Sox. Waiting to hit next was Romney, the worst Red Sox hitter. Romney had cancer at the time, was underweight for his age, took human growth hormone, and had a shunt in his brain, which required him to wear a helmet when playing in the field. Romney's parents had made the league administrators aware of his cancer due to the heightened potential for injury. In addition, Romney had been featured in the local paper, so the community was aware of his condition.

Regardless of these facts, the opposing coach elected to intentionally walk Jordan so his team could pitch to Romney. After all, conventional baseball strategy holds that the best coaching move in this situation would be to intentionally walk the best hitter and pitch to the weakest hitter. The idea is that the weakest hitter has the greater chance of making an out and ending the game. This was the league championship and both teams had worked hard to make it to that point. However, these were 9- and 10-year-old kids playing in what was billed as a recreation-oriented, development-focused league.

There is perhaps no greater influence on the outcomes of recreational sport experiences than the people who work to make those experiences happen. Recreational sport personnel—the paid and volunteer staff who work directly for or on behalf of the organization in the design and delivery of recreational sport programs—play critical roles in the success or failure of recreational sport. This is evident when you think about the people who had the most impact on your own sport experiences. When asked this question, most people talk about their coaches or sport instructors. In many cases, their memories are positive ones. These experiences may positively influence their view of sport or the outcomes that they attribute to the sport experience. Unfortunately, for some people the actions of former coaches or instructors created a negative experience, leading them to discontinue playing the sport or worse.

Although the impact of key influencers on the sport experience, such as coaches and parents, is most evident, a host of professional staff members who work behind the scenes is largely responsible for designing and delivering recreational sport programs to participants. Consider the opening case study. How might the circumstances of the case change depending on the personnel policies and procedures of this particular youth sport program? How might better staff selection, training, supervision, or evaluation help to alleviate some of the issues in the case? How do these processes help recreational sport managers build a highly skilled and competent staff—what management author Jim Collins (2001) refers to as *getting the right people on the bus*? These questions help to frame our discussion on human resources management in recreational sport.

Much of what recreational sport professionals do each day is manage and support the staff members who are necessary to run successful programs. Successful personnel management plays a large role in the efficiency and effectiveness of the organization. However, for the participant, the quality of the people who are charged with delivering recreational sport programs goes beyond management efficiency. It speaks to the memories that are created from participation and whether those memories are positive and healthy or negative and harmful.

This chapter discusses the importance of sound personnel management practices and procedures. It outlines the key staff positions found in recreational sport organizations; the procedures for recruiting, selecting, and retaining both paid and volunteer staff; and the impact that recreational sport staff have on participants. As you read the chapter, think about how you might have applied some of these practices and procedures and how the facts of that case might have changed if you were in charge of the youth baseball program in Bountiful, Utah.

RECREATIONAL SPORT PERSONNEL

As with most leisure services managers, much of what recreational sport professionals do in their day-to-day jobs revolves around **personnel**. For example, job or volunteer positions need to be conceptualized, planned, and outlined so that they reflect the needs of the organization. Employees need to be recruited, hired, trained, and evaluated for performance. Full-time, salaried staff members need to be adequately supported to do the jobs for which they were hired, including making sure that their professional and personal needs are met. Part-time staff members need to be scheduled to ensure that shifts are covered so that facilities are adequately supervised and programs can be provided. In many cases, volunteers are needed to coach or officiate games, run concession stands, or provide assistance and support to programs. Volunteers need to be supported and recognized for their contributions to the organization.

The four main functions of management involve planning, leading, organizing, and controlling work processes (Hurd, Barcelona, & Meldrum, 2008). As you can see from the examples in the previous paragraph, managing recreational sport personnel encompasses all four of these functions. As noted throughout the text, there is a good amount of diversity in the types of recreational sport organizations that exist. The exact type or title of positions will vary from organization to organization depending on factors such as the organization's mission, budget, or scope of services. Positions may also differ based on the management sector of the recreational sport organization (e.g., public, not for profit, commercial; see chapter 1). However, there are some general frameworks that help to understand the larger picture of organizational structure from the standpoint of personnel management. These are discussed next.

Five Sectors of Recreational Sport Organizations

Recreational sports organizations typically comprise five organizational sectors—upper-level administration, middle management, program staff, contingent staff, and business and support operations. Volunteers also play a role but will be treated separately. Figure 9.1 depicts this model of recreational sport organizations. Each sector contributes to the overall mission of the recreational sport organization in different but complementary ways.

As you read about each of these job sectors within recreational sport organizations, think about how they work together to carry out the mission of the organization. Look at the sample organizational chart depicted in figure 9.2. Can you find examples of each sector within this fictional organization?

Upper-Level Administration

This sector consists of the upper-level administrators who operate within the recreational sport organization. These positions focus on the big picture, including helping to shape the mission of the organization, developing and securing key resources such as funding and facilities, and working closely with external stakeholders. In recreational sport organizations, upper-level administration would consist of the executive director and the leadership of the organization. People in this role may hold the title of director, chief executive officer, senior manager, or unit head. However, titles can be deceiving, because they can mean different things in different organizations. Regardless of title, upper-level administrators are primarily tasked with leading the overall organization as opposed to managing specific divisions, departments, units, or programs.

In addition to executive-level staff members, many recreational sport organizations in the public, not-for-profit, and commercial sectors

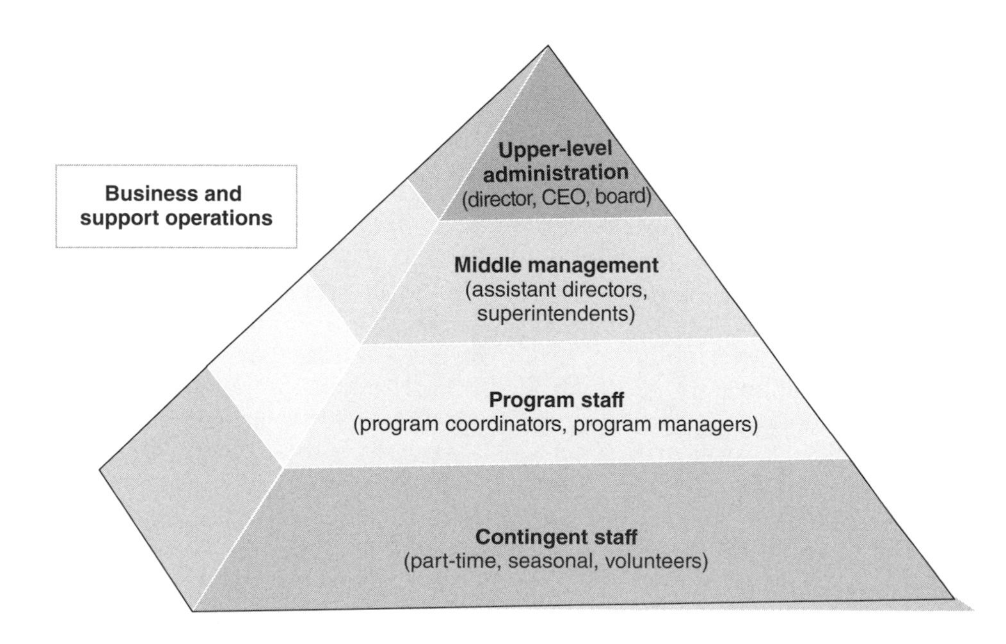

Figure 9.1 Five sectors of recreational sport organizations.

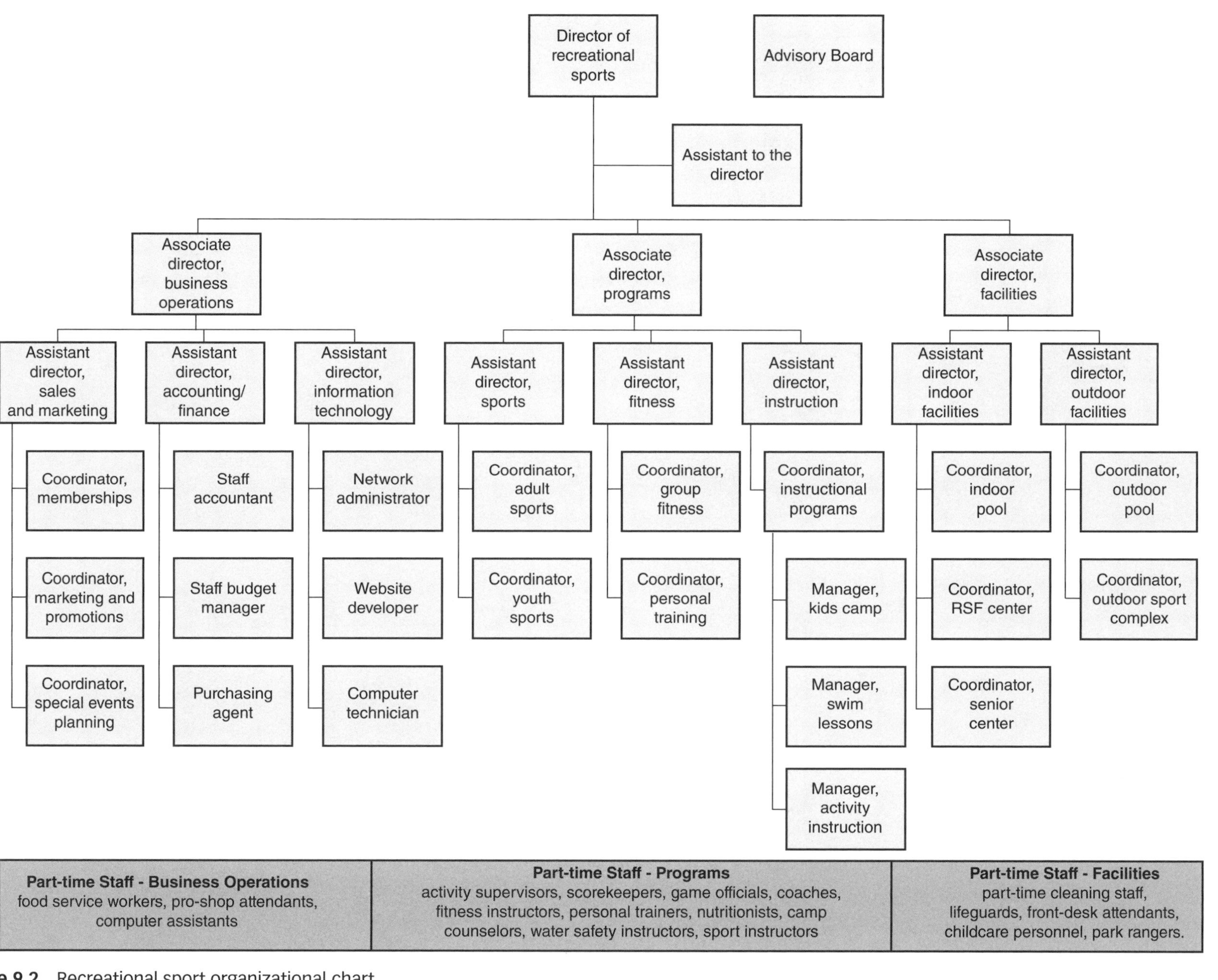

Figure 9.2 Recreational sport organizational chart.

have **boards**, or governing bodies within agencies (Hurd et al., 2008). Boards are typically composed of external stakeholders who are either elected or appointed. Strong independent boards may be tasked with duties such as policy formulation, strategic planning and decision making, financial oversight, and supervision of executive-level staff, and in some cases they may have taxing authority. Because so much authority is vested in independent boards, they are usually considered to be part of upper-level administration. Other types of boards, including semi-independent and advisory boards, do not typically have decision-making authority and are not part of the upper-level administration but are accountable to them. Semi-independent boards, typically found in public-sector organizations such as city park and recreation departments, often have governance roles but rely on a higher-level board (independent board) for final governing authority. Advisory boards provide advice and counsel to the organization's leadership, and board members may be selected because of their connections in the community, their ability to raise needed resources, or their ability to represent the interests of key constituents and organizational stakeholders.

Middle Management

Middle management comprises the heads of program areas or other units within the recreational sport organization. Middle management personnel generally are responsible for managing program budgets, supervising personnel, setting and carrying out program-specific goals, and evaluating unit effectiveness. In recreational sport organizations, middle management is typically composed of unit heads and middle managers. Titles may include associate or assistant director, area supervisor, and superintendent. In large organizations, middle management may be on more than one level of the organizational chart. For example, middle managers may include both associate and assistant director levels, as seen in the organizational chart in figure 9.2. Middle managers typically spend little time doing face-to-face, on-the-ground program delivery; instead they supervise, control, and provide resources for those who do (Bolman & Deal, 2008).

Program Staff

Program staff are full-time personnel responsible for delivering the basic work of the organization, including leading day-to-day activities, managing and overseeing facilities, and providing leadership for recreational sport programs. In the United States, organizations (and in some cases states) define what it means to be a full-time worker. Although there is no standard definition, full-time personnel typically work between 30 and 40 hours per week, and they may receive some form of fringe benefits package, such as health insurance, vacation or sick leave, and retirement savings (McGlone & Rey, 2012). The program staff typically have a high degree of contact with the core customers and are often the vital link in shaping customers' perceptions of the organization.

In recreational sport organizations, full-time personnel might include professional staff members, such as program coordinators or managers who are tasked with supervising programs and facilities. Even though program staff are often depicted at the bottom of the organizational chart, these staff members and volunteers are critical to the success of the recreational sport organization. Investment in staff development processes such as sound personnel recruitment, screening, selection, training, development, and evaluation is as important at this level as it is at higher levels of the organization.

Contingent Staff

Contingent staff are typically part-time, seasonal, or volunteer workers in recreational sport organizations. Volunteers are discussed in more detail in a later section. Part-time employees typically work fewer hours each week compared with full-time staff, or they may work inconsistent hours depending on participant demand for programs and facilities. They also may be employed seasonally. Part-time employees offer many advantages for recreational sport organizations, including

- providing work at a lower cost,
- providing workforce flexibility because staff can be hired (and let go) easily based on program availability and participant need, and
- providing experience and training for staff who might be hired full time in the future.

However, there are challenges with using large numbers of part-time staff members to carry out the day-to-day work of the organization. These challenges may include difficulties in recruiting high-quality part-time staff members, retaining part-time staff when they are presented with better opportunities elsewhere, and carrying out effective communication and coordination of work. In addition, competing priorities may distract part-time staff from giving 100 percent of their effort to their work duties.

Business and Support Operations

The organizational levels mentioned previously—upper-level administration, middle management, program staff, and contingent staff—are concerned with carrying out the core mission of the organization. The final two components—support staff and business operations—provide support and technical assistance in order to achieve the core mission. In recreational sport organizations, **support staff** help to facilitate the work of others in the organization. This could include secretarial support and administrative assistance, facility maintenance, transportation management, concessions, and food service. The **technostructure** includes personnel who manage processes critical for organizational information and accountability. In a recreational sport organization, this might include business operations staff such as accountants, purchasing and procurement agents, marketing and evaluation specialists, and technology specialists. As you study the organizational chart in figure 9.2, think about how ineffective this organization would be if it did not have support or technical staff.

Volunteers

Volunteers are people who perform work through or for an organization for no pay except expenses (Corporation for National and Community Service, 2012). In the United States, approximately 64.3 million people over the age of 16, or roughly 26.8 percent of the total population, engage in volunteer efforts. Similarly, in Canada, 13.3 million people aged 15 and over, or approximately 47 percent of the population, volunteer their time to a variety of charitable causes. Recreational sport organizations rely heavily on the help of volunteers. Official statistics on the rate of recreational sport volunteering are difficult to pin down precisely. However, in 2011 approximately 2.4 million Americans volunteered their time to work with sport, hobby, or cultural arts organizations (Bureau of Labor Statistics, 2011), and in 2010, almost 3 million Canadians volunteered for a sport and recreation organization (Imagine Canada, 2010).

Recreational sport volunteers come in many shapes and sizes. Volunteers may be in positions that require high degrees of technical knowledge

Volunteers are critical to the success of most recreational sport organizations.

and skills or that require significant investments of time and resources. These include positions such as volunteer sport coaches, league administrators, and agency board members. However, volunteers are also needed for short-term programs and events and for work that requires little in the way of technical skills or sport-specific knowledge. These positions might include swim-meet timers, open gym supervisors, and 5K race volunteers.

Volunteers give their time, energy, and talents for a variety of reasons, including feeling personal satisfaction, sharing their knowledge with others, making a difference in their community, connecting with other people, accomplishing goals, and strengthening neighborhoods and communities (Corporation for National and Community Service, 2012). Many of these motivations are true for paid staff as well as volunteers. However, recreational sport professionals must ascertain what motivates volunteers to give their time and how the organization can best structure positions so volunteers receive the benefits that they seek.

Volunteers are vital to the mission of most recreational sport organizations. In many cases, volunteers are the public faces of the organization. They may have the greatest impact on a participant's assessment of program quality, or they may play critical roles in helping to ensure safe, healthy, and positive sport experiences. For example, consider the impact that the volunteer coaches had on the young baseball players in the opening case. The actions of volunteers—positive or negative—have the potential to create memories that live in participants' minds long after the event is over.

The temptation among recreational sport professionals may be to take volunteers for granted, providing them with little training, supervision, and recognition. For example, one study found that only 40 percent of recreational sport organizations required background checks on their volunteer coaches, and less than 25 percent required volunteer coaches to go through a mandatory coach training program (Barcelona & Young, 2010). The primary reason given for this lack of volunteer management was that most recreational sport organizations lacked the resources to manage volunteers effectively. Even though most people who volunteer in recreational sport settings do so with good intentions, those who lack training, support, and supervision place participants and organizations at risk for a range of negative outcomes. Recent high-profile cases of child abuse in sport have certainly raised questions about the hands-off approach to volunteer management. Moreover, good volunteers who give their time for the right reasons want to be supported in the jobs that they do. Unfortunately, attrition rates among volunteers are often high, with more than one-third of volunteers failing to give their time the following year (Eisner, Grimm, Maynard, & Washburn, 2009).

Investing in the organizational capacity and infrastructure needed to effectively use and manage volunteers is a key to reducing risk, increasing the positive contributions of volunteers, and mitigating volunteer turnover. This can be done in five primary ways:

1. Matching volunteers' skills with appropriate assignments
2. Recognizing the contributions of volunteers
3. Measuring the impact of volunteers on the agency's mission each year
4. Providing volunteers with training and professional development
5. Training paid staff to work with volunteers

Unfortunately, research shows that more than half of the nonprofit organizations that use volunteers do not follow these practices regularly (Eisner et al., 2009). Recreational sport professionals must continue to not only pay lip service to the importance of volunteers but also take steps to implement good volunteer management practices.

HUMAN RESOURCES PROCESSES

The first section of this chapter has dealt primarily with the kinds of personnel that are typically found within recreational sport organizations and how these positions are classified and categorized. This next section provides a strategy for managing the human resources within an organization. Of course, it is impossible to cover the entire range of human resources management in one textbook chapter, and the range and diversity of recreational sport organizations is so great that much of what might be written would be subject to organization-specific approaches. However, one of the commonalities among recreational sport organizations is that they tend to be values driven, and their outcomes tend to be influenced greatly by the people they employ (Watson & Abzug, 2010). As discussed earlier, the experiences that are created through participant interactions with recreational sport personnel are often critical to the success of an agency. This means that the people within the recreational sport organization are perhaps the most important elements in delivering quality programs and services.

Human resources perspectives focus on people. In other words, human resources approaches to management attempt to understand the symbiotic relationship between employees (and volunteers) and their organizations, and they are composed of systems that meet the needs of both. As such, human resources approaches are built on a set of four core assumptions (Bolman & Deal, 2008):

1. Organizations exist to serve human needs rather than the reverse.
2. People and organizations need each other.
3. When the fit between individual and system is poor, both suffer.
4. A good fit benefits both.

These assumptions focus on what is known as **person–job fit**, which is the idea that people want to work for organizations where there is a tight alignment between the organization's goals and their own values (Kouzes & Posner, 2008). Thus, personnel decisions, including job design, recruitment, selection, training, supervision, and assessment, should be filtered through these fundamental questions:

- Are the goals of our organization clear?
- Are the actions of management consistent with our goals?
- Do we hire people based on their fit with our organization's goals and values?
- Do we provide people with the necessary resources, supports, and opportunities to meet their needs for personal and professional development?
- Do these resources, supports, and opportunities further our organization's mission?
- Are we learning from mistakes?

The remainder of this chapter focuses on fundamental human resources processes that can be applied to recreational sport organizations, particularly in regard to the hiring, development, and supervision of recreational sport professionals.

What Is a Professional?

Before we can begin to think about a process of human resources management, it is necessary to take a step back and examine what makes a recreational sport professional. Typically, there are five main characteristics that define a profession:

1. It is a vocation where accountability is primarily to those served or to the larger society as a whole.
2. The core element of work is based on mastery of a distinct body of knowledge and set of skills.
3. Knowledge and competence can be obtained through relevant academic preparation programs and through professional training and development opportunities.
4. Governing or other professional associations of like-minded professionals exist to help set standards, certify competence, formulate ethical principles, and so on.
5. A code of ethics or set of acceptable ethical standards exists and is adhered to and valued by members.

Examples of these five characteristics can be found among campus recreational sport professionals. These professionals work on behalf of the students and (sometimes) faculty and staff of their schools. The programs and services that they provide are designed to meet the needs of their clients. Most campus recreational sport programs are delivered through student life or student affairs divisions, and they emphasize student development outcomes that accrue through participation in purposeful out-of-class activities. The National Intramural-Recreational Sports Association (NIRSA) is a professional association that exists to support and advocate for its members, including providing opportunities for its members to receive training and continuing education related to recreational sport. NIRSA has a code of ethics for professional practice, and it has identified eight core competencies that guide its work:

1. Philosophy and theory
2. Programming
3. Management techniques
4. Business procedures
5. Facility management, planning, and design
6. Research and evaluation

7. Legal liability and risk management
8. Personal and professional qualities

These eight core competencies were outlined to be inclusive of all aspects of the recreational sport industry and were informed by the research on broad recreational sport management competencies (Barcelona & Ross, 2004). Finally, NIRSA has outlined a process for recognizing competence through the Registry of Collegiate Recreational Sports Professionals. However, the field of recreational sport is highly differentiated in terms of job duties and functions, and there are multiple ways to enter the field. Figure 9.3 shows the NIRSA core competencies.

This example is unique to campus recreational sport. However, recreational sport delivery occurs in diverse settings and contexts, and it is inclusive of a wide variety of program types that might lend themselves to more specialized bodies of knowledge. Take the following examples:

- The assistant director for aquatics would need to know about water safety instruction, lifeguarding techniques, and pool maintenance.
- The assistant director for community and youth sport would need to know how to schedule tournaments, maintain facilities, and train sport officials.
- The assistant director for fitness would need to know about personal training, fitness equipment trends, and training for group fitness leaders.

Competency	Description
Philosophy and theory	Professionalism and ethics, health and wellness theories, student development theory, campus recreation standards, issues of equity and diversity
Programming	Effective program development, scheduling, and delivery, as well as programming for special populations, or for specialized areas
Human resources management	Customer service principles, motivational skills, leadership development, staff selection and training, conflict resolution, governance structures, group facilitation
Business management	Good written and verbal communication, establishing partnerships, strategic planning principles, public relations and marketing principles, resource acquisition and allocation, sustainability
Facility management, planning, and design	Facility operations and management, development of policies and procedures, event management, equipment knowledge, facility planning and design
Research and evaluation	Program assessment, best practices in benchmarking, assessment and evaluation techniques or applications, applied research, sharing results in writing
Legal liability and risk management	Risk and crisis management, injury liability, sports waivers, the legal process, insurance coverage and plans
Personal and professional qualities	Problem solving strategies, goal and resource prioritization, adaptability, meaningful networking

Figure 9.3 NIRSA core competencies.

From NIRSA. Available: http://nirsa.net/nirsa/registry

Although each of these three people work in the same organization, their professional needs and identities are very different. Their jobs require different knowledge, skills, abilities, and competencies; they belong to different professional groups or associations; they might have different academic backgrounds; and they have different requirements for certification and continuing education. In short, although it is important to think about recreational sport employees as professionals, it is likely that people employed by the organization have very different professional identities and professional needs. Recreational sport is a diverse field that encompasses a variety of allied professions, including recreation, fitness and exercise science, human development, and business administration. What unites these diverse professions in the context of a recreational sport organization is a core set of values that focuses on the provision of active, participant-focused sport opportunities for all. Knowledge of this has a profound impact on the various human resources processes that will be discussed, including designing jobs and recruiting, selecting, and training staff.

Personnel Planning

Thinking intentionally about personnel needs is a critical first step in the human resources process. Bolman and Deal (2008) suggest that the first step in the human resources process—after building a human resources philosophy that emphasizes employee needs and the importance of person–job fit—is to hire the right people. In his book *Good to Great*, Jim Collins suggests that the most important thing for any organization is to get the right people on the bus, so to speak (Collins, 2001). This process of hiring the right people starts with knowing exactly what the organization wants and needs in terms of staffing. This needs assessment process for human resources includes the following:

- **Personnel costs.** These costs are often thought of in terms of salary, wages, and benefits, but they also include investments in training, professional development, office space, and computers. In addition, the time that it takes to adequately supervise and support staff needs to be taken into account in the personnel planning process.
- **Personnel levels.** An adult basketball program could probably operate with only one on-court referee and save money by doing so. However, what would the consequences be for participant safety or quality of game play? Similarly, although three-person officiating crews might lead to better officiated games, the added cost for the third official might not offer enough of a return on investment to be worth it.
- **Personnel types.** The pros and cons of using full-time, part-time, or volunteer positions were discussed earlier in the chapter. In addition to these, many recreational sport organizations use contingent or seasonal staff—personnel who are hired for short-term job assignments or on an as-needed basis. This provides flexibility. For example, if summer camp enrollments are high, then more camp counselors can be hired to help cover the responsibilities. The reverse can be applied when enrollments are low. In some cases, certain positions may be outsourced through a contract with a third-party vendor that handles staff selection, training, and scheduling. For example, leagues often contract with officiating associations that make sure games are covered. Similarly, recreational sport organizations might contract with a local sports medicine group to provide athletic training services and game-day medical coverage. This provides flexibility for the organization and eliminates the need for sunk personnel costs in positions that are extremely specialized and outside of the agency's core mission.
- **Personnel skills.** Some recreational sport positions are highly specialized. Lifeguards, fitness instructors, turf managers, athletic trainers, and sport officials require specific technical skills that are unique to their job functions. **Technical skills** are the job-specific knowledge and techniques that enable an employee to do a job effectively. Other recreational sport positions may place a higher premium on conceptual or human relations skills. **Conceptual skills** include the ability to analyze situations, determine causes and effects, come up with solutions to challenges, and see the big picture. **Human relations skills** include the ability to work with, lead, and understand other people, including both individuals and groups (Hurd et al., 2008). Supervisory positions, or positions that require staff to work directly with the public, might place a higher premium on these softer skill sets.

Staff who possess the right mix of technical, conceptual, and human resources skills are more valuable to an organization in the long run because they provide more flexibility. Staff with a range of skill sets may be easier to train to perform the tasks associated with multiple jobs within the organization. This is called **cross-training**, and it puts the organization in a position of strength in times of shifting demand. For example, if lifeguards are cross-trained (and properly certified) to also provide swimming lessons, which requires a specific set of technical skills, then they can be scheduled to work according to the needs of the organization at the time. This may also meet employees' needs for more work hours or variability in their job duties. A group fitness instructor who is skilled at leading fitness classes but who also possesses strong problem-solving ability and the ability to work well with others could be trained to work in membership sales or in a supervisory position. If the organization values a specific set of conceptual and human relations skills—for example, working collaboratively, taking initiative, solving problems creatively, and relating well to others—then hiring decisions based on these values may take precedence regardless of technical skills or abilities.

Hiring based on these kinds of values can be difficult to put into practice in recreational sport organizations where certain positions require specialized technical skills, talents, and abilities. However, organizations rarely take an either–or approach. Sport coaches, for example, need to have technical skills in the area of coaching, yet they also need the ability to solve problems and work effectively with others. It is a rare case when an effective group fitness instructor lacks human relations skills. Recreational sport organizations need to clearly assess and define the critical knowledge, skills, and abilities that their employees must possess and then make hiring decisions based on the areas that the organization most values.

Employee Recruitment

After the recreational sport organization assesses its human resources needs and capacities, it needs a plan for recruiting candidates for open positions. The scope of the search effort, as well as the specific techniques used to identify potential candidates, will vary depending on the nature of the position, the type of organization, and the specific legal or regulatory requirements that an organization is subject to follow. For example, the recruitment process for volunteer youth coaches or part-time fitness instructors differs substantially from that used to find a full-time coordinator of intramural sport or a full-time fitness and wellness director. Recruitment processes for volunteer or part-time positions tend to be more local in scope and less complex, and they use fewer agency resources. Similarly, it is likely that the human resources processes in large government agencies, such as municipal park and recreation departments, require a longer time frame to recruit full-time professional staff compared with the time that a private-sector, for-profit sport and fitness facility would take to recruit a similar position. For the most part, the discussion that follows is limited to positions involving contingent staff and entry-level program staff.

Job Announcements

Typically, the first step in the recruitment process is the development of the job announcement. **Job announcements** are written statements that provide information for job seekers about open positions within the recreational sport organization. Job announcements may be more detailed for full-time, salaried positions. Typically, job announcements for professional staff include the following information:

- Job title
- Brief description or overview of the organization and its mission
- Summary of the position, including the scope of responsibilities as well as supervision received and exercised
- Academic and professional qualifications, including education levels, degrees, areas of study, licenses, certifications, years of experience, or other qualifying credentials
- Specific job competencies, including those that are required for the job and those that are desirable but not critical
- Compensation range or some other statement regarding salary or pay grade
- Instructions for how to apply, required application materials, deadlines, and contact information for questions regarding the position or process
- Diversity statement, including the organization's commitment to ensuring a fair and equitable hiring process that meets federal, state, and organization-specific equal employment opportunity guidelines

- Supplemental information that is attractive to job seekers, including information about the area where the job is located, lifestyle amenities, and other perks

It may not be necessary to include all of this information, particularly for part-time, volunteer, and contingent positions, where the recruitment effort is primarily local or where there is no job-related reason to include the statements. In some cases, it might be necessary to include more information about required certifications, skills, or experiences. For example, it may be necessary for a part-time personal trainer to hold a certification from a recognized national organization such as the American Council on Exercise (ACE) or ACSM and have professional experience as a trainer. However, other academic qualifications might be unnecessary.

One other point about job announcements—typically, the more requirements they list, the smaller the applicant pool will be. For example, a position that requires a master's degree in recreation, physical education, sport management, or a related field will typically attract a smaller, less diverse candidate pool than a position that requires only a bachelor's degree. The same is true for requiring more years of experience, specific certifications, or other requirements that make the job more appealing to a smaller target audience. This may be advantageous, because putting the words *sport* or *recreation* in a job title may attract hundreds of applicants, only a few of whom are qualified for the position.

The decision to keep job announcements broad so as to attract a wide variety of applicants or narrow so as to limit the number of people who apply speaks to the importance of personnel planning, as discussed earlier. A useful strategy is to highlight the absolutely necessary elements of the job that are required for successful job performance. Then, list those elements of the job that are preferred but are not absolutely necessary. This allows an organization to develop a deeper candidate pool by not eliminating good candidates because the position is so narrowly targeted. At the same time, it sets parameters that can help candidates assess whether they meet the minimum requirements of the position and thus can help limit the number of potential candidates.

Recruitment Scope and Methods

As with the job announcement, the scope and methods used to recruit candidates for open positions will vary considerably depending on the position. Recruiting for part-time, hourly, contingent, and volunteer positions generally takes place locally, whereas recruiting for full-time, professional positions happens within a larger geographical range. To put it simply, it is unlikely that a person living in Walla Walla, Washington, would move to Clemson, South Carolina, just to take a part-time, hourly job as a recreation facility supervisor at the Central-Clemson Recreation Center. This is an extreme example, but it is an important one to consider when developing a recruitment plan. The idea is to develop a process that attracts the best possible candidates based on the needs of the organization and the demands of the job. This may be achieved with a highly targeted, local search effort, or it might require a wide-ranging, national strategy.

Recruiting volunteer or paid recreational sport staff generally follows two tracks—recruiting personnel from within the organization or developing a process to attract qualified people from outside the organization. Both strategies can be advantageous. For example, agencies might look to their existing part-time staff members when full-time job openings become available. This can save the agency time and money because fewer resources are needed for recruitment, orientation, and training. In addition, offering opportunities for staff to move up within the organization can provide a powerful incentive for volunteers and part-time staff to perform well in their jobs, particularly if they are looking for more permanent work or to move up the career ladder. Too often, good employees are forced to move out to move up because organizations are reluctant to recruit from within. On the other hand, recruiting from outside the organization can bring in new ideas and perspectives, promote diversity, and fill skill gaps.

Recruitment efforts can range from targeted, personal approaches to wide-ranging, shotgun strategies. Each method has advantages and disadvantages. Not all of these approaches must be used for every open position. However, combining approaches, particularly when searching for permanent, professional positions, can help mitigate the disadvantages associated with an overreliance on any one approach. Some of these methods include the following:

- Asking trusted friends, mentors, and former employees to recommend potential candidates

- Recruiting through professional organizations and trade associations, with a particular focus on reaching out to traditionally underrepresented groups
- Working closely with colleges, universities, and trade schools
- Recruiting at career fairs
- Using third-party search firms
- Using electronic methods for posting job announcements such as posting on the organization's website, e-mail databases, LISTSERVs, online discussion boards, and social networking sites such as Facebook and Twitter
- Disseminating job announcements through newspaper advertisements
- Advertising on generic job-search websites

These recruitment strategies range from personal, one-on-one approaches that rely on professional networks to broad, generic search strategies designed to get the word out to as many people as possible. The approaches that you choose will depend entirely on the position that you are recruiting for. A good recruitment plan and strategy designed up front will help make these decisions easier.

Employee Selection

Selecting the most qualified candidate for the position requires an intentional strategy and process designed before the job search begins. The employee selection process typically consists of the following:

- Determining the staff who will take part in the hiring process
- Screening the candidates
- Interviewing the candidates
- Conducting reference and background checks

As stated throughout this section, the exact steps of the selection process depend on the position. Hiring part-time facility supervisors requires a less involved process than hiring a full-time facility maintenance supervisor. Each organization will have its own internal human resources processes to fulfill as well, so all decisions should take this into account. The process described next focuses on hiring full-time, entry-level staff and offers some suggestions for adapting the process for part-time, contingent staff or volunteers.

Determining the Search-and-Screen Committee

A useful first step is to determine who will be in charge of the hiring decision. In the case of part-time, contingent positions that are hired frequently, the immediate supervisor typically makes hiring decisions. Sometimes the supervisor might consult others in the process, but when a large number of hires must be made, such as facility supervisors, lifeguards, group fitness instructors, or sport coaches, limiting the amount of input in exchange for speed in the decision-making process is usually prudent. However, for full-time professional positions, the organization should use a search-and-screen committee consisting of the person responsible for supervising the position along with three to five committee members representing various organizational interests. Using a committee for full-time positions or positions that are hired much less frequently is useful, particularly when others in the organization will be affected by the hire, because it includes multiple voices in the process. The drawback of using a committee is that it takes time to obtain input from committee members and to convene meetings. The key is to develop a process that makes sense based on the job opening and to move through the process as quickly as possible for the benefit of the candidate and the recreational sport organization.

Screening the Candidates

During the recruitment process, the job announcement specifies the methods that candidates will use to apply for the position. These methods might include some combination of the following:

- **Completion of an agency-specific job application.** This can be unique to the position itself, and it typically includes the candidate's contact information, employment or volunteer history, and qualifications for the job. It may also include a list of potential references. Job applications are most often used for contingent or part-time positions, but sometimes they may be required for full-time positions.
- **Submission of a letter of interest and résumé pertaining to the position.** This is usually a requirement for full-time positions. Letters of interest typically include a candidate's interest in the job, credentials, and current contact information. A standard résumé includes contact information, education history, and employment

history along with key areas of responsibility, certifications or other credentials relevant to the position, honors or awards received, and potential references.

- **Submission of proof of required credentials such as certifications or minimum education levels.** In some cases, it would be wise to have potential candidates include proof that they actually possess the required credentials. This might include providing photocopies of certifications or copies of college transcripts. This step helps the person or committee in charge of hiring immediately verify the information that is included in the application or résumé.
- **Completion of an affirmative action checklist, including information pertaining to the applicant's sex, age, ethnicity, and race.** In most organizations, completing the affirmative action checklist is voluntary on the part of the candidate. However, it helps the organization ensure compliance with federal, state or provincial, and organization-specific employee anti-discrimination legislation. In the United States, federal laws prohibit discrimination by private employers, state and local governments, and educational institutions based on the following factors: race, color, religion, sex, national origin, disability, and age. States often broaden these protected classes through their own laws and statutes, including sexual orientation, marital status, or veteran status. In Canada, protected classes include race, national or ethnic origin, color, religion, age, sex, sexual orientation, marital status, family status, disability, and conviction for which a pardon has been granted. Antidiscrimination laws are complex, and su.pervisors should be well aware of what they can and cannot do legally during the hiring process. It is highly recommended that supervisors consult their human resources department or legal counsel before embarking on the hiring process.

After application materials are received, the screening process can begin. A useful method for narrowing a large applicant pool is using a stage-based screening process that sets specific benchmarks for applicants based on requirements for the position (Hurd et al., 2008). The stage-based screening process can be used for a wide variety of positions, including volunteer, part-time, and full-time jobs. In a stage-based screening process, a candidate's application materials are assessed based on the required and preferred qualifications of the job, and the benchmarks for each stage become more stringent.

The goal of the screening process is to narrow the candidate pool down to the most qualified candidates for the position. For positions where only one hire is being made, such as permanent full-time professional staff positions, the goal is to narrow the list down to the top three to five candidates. For part-time or volunteer positions, the goal is to identify as many candidates as possible who meet the qualifications for the position and who would be good fits for the organization. A general rule is to have two or three potential candidates for every open position. For example, if you are interested in hiring five new group fitness instructors, you would ideally have between 10 and 15 good candidates to choose from.

Interviewing the Candidates

After identifying the top candidates, most organizations use an interview process to arrive at their final hiring selections. Interviews can take place in many formats using a wide variety of media. They can take place in person, over the phone, or using Web-conferencing technologies. As with almost all of the decisions discussed in this section, the format used will depend on the position. Examples of interview formats and media include the following:

- **One-to-one interviews.** These are classic interviews that take place between a candidate and the direct hiring supervisor or other key members of the organization. These interviews are useful for a wide variety of positions in the organization because they provide personal knowledge of the candidate and allow the candidate and interviewer to establish rapport. They can also be time consuming and expensive, particularly if there are many interviewees.
- **One-to-group interviews.** In this format, the candidate interviews with a group or committee of key stakeholders within the organization. This saves time because only one appointment must be made for each interview. It is difficult to get to know a candidate in a group setting, so there may be other scheduled times for one-to-one interaction between the candidate and the supervisor or other key members of the organization.
- **Group-to-group interviews.** A more novel approach is the group interview, where several candidates interview with the search committee at the same time. This can be advantageous, particularly if multiple hires need to be made at the same time, as is the case with many part-time or volunteer positions. It also allows a search

Candidate interviews can be done in many ways, including one-to-one, one-to-group, and group-to-group. Each approach has its own advantages and disadvantages

committee to assess candidates' answers to questions or scenarios in the context of other candidates' answers. Group interviews can provide the opportunity for candidates to demonstrate flexibility, creativity, and the ability to differentiate themselves from others.

Interviews may also take the form of practical, hands-on exercises or demonstrations of skills. These might involve simulated in-box exercises, where candidates are asked to work through a fictional set of tasks that are designed to help employers understand a candidate's approach to work, including the ability to prioritize tasks and make decisions. Demonstrations may also be used to help employers see a potential employee in action. This is especially important for positions where technical skills are a core component of the job. Lifeguards, swim instructors, group fitness instructors, personal trainers, and sport officials may all be asked to perform their jobs in simulated situations as a component of the interview process.

In all cases, interviews should highlight a candidate's technical, conceptual, and human relations skills. Interview questions or scenarios should be developed that elicit all three components. Asking candidates to restate their qualifications for the job is redundant, because a good screening process will have already revealed many of the technical qualifications for the job, such as proficiency in job-specific skills, certifications, or years of experience. Approximately 89 percent of hiring failures happen because of problems with an employee's attitude rather than a lack of skill (Murphy, 2012). Because of this, the interview process should help to highlight a candidate's attitude, analytic ability, decision-making processes, willingness to receive and act on constructive feedback, and ability to work with others. Table 9.1 shows a list of traditional interview questions and a corresponding set of questions designed to address the qualities described.

Conducting Background and Reference Checks

Before extending offers to candidates, it may be prudent to conduct background checks and checks of professional references. Background checks of criminal behavior often take place in connection with state and local law enforcement agencies, and they can be limited or wide ranging. Organizations must provide candidates with a written consent form that is signed and dated to allow the agency to conduct background checks

TABLE 9.1 Competency-Based Questions

Traditional interview questions	Competency-based questions
Can you tell us about your experiences recruiting and retaining volunteers?	Our volunteer base is not as large as we need, and we are having difficulty retaining the good volunteers that we have. If you were hired, what are three things that you would do to recruit more volunteers, and what would you do to keep them?
What is your experience working with budgets?	If you were hired and were asked to cut 10% of your operations budget, how would you react, and what actions would you take?
What marketing techniques do you think are most effective?	Right now, our social media presence isn't what it should be. Give us your plan for building and maintaining a social media presence for our agency so that we can better engage our customers.
What experiences do you have in designing and building a new recreational sport facility?	We have needs assessment data showing that 70% of residents want a new indoor recreational sport facility to be designed and built within the next 3 years. Tell us what you would do to help make that vision a reality.
What is your managerial philosophy with staff?	You have a staff member who is talented but unmotivated, and her negative attitude is starting to have an effect on her coworkers. She has been with the agency for more than 10 years. As her new supervisor, how might you deal with this situation?

for the purposes of employment. The National Alliance for Youth Sports (NAYS, 2012) suggests that criminal-history background checks should consist of the following:

- Social security number and name verification
- Sex-offender registry search
- National criminal database search
- County and statewide criminal search (used when an agency's geographic area is not included in the national criminal database)

Background checks can provide information about the applicant's history, but ultimately the recreational sport organization must determine potential disqualifiers for its job positions. For example, NAYS recommends that a candidate be disqualified for a position working with children if the candidate has a record of sex offenses and misconduct, violent felonies, other violence- or non-sex-related felonies in the past 10 years, child abuse or domestic violence convictions, or misdemeanors within the past seven years (NAYS, 2012). In addition to criminal background checks, organizations should contact a candidate's professional references to confirm employment history and qualifications for the job.

Employee Retention

It might be tempting to think of the hiring process as the culmination of the human resources process. However, the goal of human resources management is not to just find the right people but also to keep them (Bolman & Deal, 2008). The leisure services industry as a whole has experienced an 87 percent increase in job openings since 2009, and the recreational sport industry experiences relatively high monthly turnover compared with other industry segments (Bureau of Labor Statistics, 2012). There is little doubt that retaining quality employees and volunteers is beneficial—it saves time and resources, and the organization also benefits from the human capital that a highly qualified workforce provides. **Human capital** refers to the value that is created from an employee's knowledge, talents, skills, abilities, and creativity (Hardy, Barcelona, Hickox, & Lazaro, 2006). Frequent turnover of key staff members and volunteers decreases human capital and forces the organization to spend more resources on searching for and selecting new people.

Employee retention strategies focus on developing and keeping good people. Employee retention starts as soon as an employee is hired through new staff orientation and initial job training. It is an ongoing process, and it includes providing opportunities for continuing education and training, job-performance feedback, and recognition and promotion.

Orientation and Training

After new employees are hired, it is important to properly orient them to the recreational sport agency. New-employee orientation programs are designed around a number of key components with the purpose of helping new employees fit into the organization. There is no reason why orientation programs cannot be offered to all new employees regardless of whether they are full time, part time, or volunteers. The scope might change, but the goals of employee orientation remain the same regardless of position—to provide employees with information about their new organization and job and to help them fit in. Employee orientation programs can include the following (Hurd et al., 2008):

- Values, mission, goals, and objectives of the organization
- Organizational structure and how the new employee fits into the overall agency
- Work-related policies, procedures, and rules specific to the job
- Facility tours and access policies for secured facilities
- Compensation and benefits
- Social networking opportunities with other staff members and supervisors

Employee orientation programs should be offered in multiple ways to meet the needs of new employees. Information overload can become a problem, particularly when new hires are given too much information to handle at one time. An effective way to avoid information overload is to offer a range of activities over an extended period of time. These activities could include large group workshops, one-on-one meetings, individual time, and informal social gatherings.

Employee and volunteer training programs are more specific than orientations and focus on preparing new hires to do their jobs effectively. An agency typically develops a training program for its staff members based on its needs. Typically, employee training programs focus on the following main areas:

- **Preparing employees to operate within specific organizational protocols or systems.** This includes knowledge of basic tasks and functions relating to the job. For example, facility supervisors need to know the systems and protocols for opening, securing, and closing facilities, while lifeguards or aquatic supervisors need to know how to operate bulkheads or conduct water tests.
- **Providing specific knowledge and skills to accomplish job responsibilities.** This includes developing or refining the specific competencies that staff need in order to do their jobs safely and effectively. This aspect of training is typically reserved for part-time or contingent staff; full-time staff members are generally hired because they already possess the requisite job-related competencies. Examples include requiring coaches to attend a coach training program, such as the one offered through the National Youth Sports Coaches Association (NYSCA), or providing training for staff to obtain key certifications necessary to do their jobs. Such certifications may be required for personal trainers, water safety instructors, or youth sport administrators.
- **Developing broad-based competencies that address key organizational concerns (e.g., risk management, team building, conflict management, diversity).** This includes training workshops that focus on areas such as effective communication, team building, diversity management, or technology use.

Recreational sport organizations may also provide opportunities for staff to receive continuing education and ongoing employee development. Staff development tends to be employee driven compared with training, which tends to be organization driven. For example, a group fitness instructor might need support to attend yearly conferences to earn **continuing education units (CEUs)** to maintain certifications to teach fitness classes. CEUs are points that certified or licensed staff earn through professional continuing education. Generally, one CEU equals 10 contact hours of participation in organized experiences for continuing education, such as those offered by qualified instructors at professional conference sessions or workshops (International Association for Continuing Education and Training [IACET], 2012). A recreational sport organization might provide financial support for staff to attend conferences or workshops to receive ongoing professional development and education in their particular areas of interest. Other ideas for staff development might be providing tuition reimbursement for higher education or enriching jobs by providing employees with more responsibilities or professional experiences.

Performance Appraisal

Performance appraisal (or assessment or evaluation) is a method for providing feedback to employees on their job performance. Performance appraisal is used for a variety of reasons, including to provide opportunities for staff to improve their job performance, to identify areas that need further education or professional development, and to allow for recognition or discipline. Without adequate information on how employees are doing in their jobs, it is difficult to improve performance or fill in gaps in knowledge or training. Further, it is difficult for supervisors to recognize staff through promotions or other forms of incentives or to discipline or terminate staff if they are not evaluated regularly. Frequent performance evaluations are necessary because they provide a documented record of job performance, and they open the door to dialogue about performance between the employee and supervisor. Performance evaluations should be provided for all recreational sport staff members—full time, part time, and volunteer. This is important because contingent staff members and volunteers often receive little or no feedback from their supervisors on their job performance.

Performance evaluations are generally based on job responsibilities. Job parameters and responsibilities should be clearly communicated to staff and volunteers before they start working. For example, if the membership services coordinator for a recreational sport facility is responsible for generating new memberships to the facility, he needs to know that he will be evaluated on his ability to fulfill this responsibility. In addition to evaluating employees directly on the responsibilities associated with their position, evaluation may also be based on the ability of employees to meet their job-related goals. This method is known as **management by objectives** (Drucker, 2001). In this method, employees document their job-related goals for the evaluation period. Then they discuss these goals with their supervisor and negotiate them when appropriate. For example, the intramural sport coordinator in a campus recreation department might have a goal of increasing team sport participation by 10 percent. At the end of the evaluation period, the employee reviews her goals and documents whether the goal has been achieved. If she has not achieved the goal, she is given an opportunity to discuss the reasons why.

Performance appraisal may be formal, informal, or both. Formal performance evaluations generally occur at regular times and use a standard format that includes both written and verbal information for the employee based on preset performance indicators. Performance evaluations may be based on objective indicators, such as the number of teams that register for an intramural contest, the amount of money raised in league sponsorships, or the number of new members who join a recreational sport facility. Objective indicators are easily measurable and should be tied to job responsibilities or job-related goals. Subjective indicators are those areas that are not objectively measurable. These might include criteria such as communication ability, initiative, or creativity. Informal performance appraisal occurs more frequently. It might include meetings with the supervisor to touch base on performance, pats on the back for a job well done, or other forms of informal, ongoing feedback. Supervisors should use both formal and informal performance appraisal.

Work Motivation

Herzberg (1966) suggests that six key characteristics underlie work motivation—achievement, recognition, the nature of the work itself, responsibility, advancement, and growth. Herzberg's research holds true for a wide range of disciplines and job categories. These motivators are fundamental human needs. When managers neglect to recognize employee performance or forget to acknowledge achievement, employees become dissatisfied with their jobs. As discussed earlier, the lack of recognition of volunteers' contributions is one of the primary reasons behind high volunteer turnover. The same is true for full- and part-time paid staff. Taking opportunities to recognize the performance of individuals and units is a key part of employee retention.

Managers can use the six key work motivators as a guide for thinking about employee motivation and retention strategies:

1. **Achievement.** Managers should implement systems that allow recreational sport staff and

volunteers to set and reach goals and see how their work affects the people they serve.

2. **Recognition.** Managers should provide frequent means for recognizing the performance of outstanding employees and units, including full-time, part-time, and volunteer staff. Examples are developing awards that are regularly given out to high-achieving staff and holding regular events to recognize the service of staff and volunteers.

3. **Work itself.** It matters how work is designed and how it is described to an employee. All staff members need to see how their jobs connect to the larger mission of the organization. This is true of the highest-level recreational sport administrator, and it is also true of the person working the equipment desk in the basement of the facility. Is the job challenging? Does it allow employees to take initiative and own the day-to-day duties? Is the job adequately matched to the employee's skills and interests? These are critical questions when thinking about job design and how it influences employee motivation.

4. **Responsibility.** As noted earlier, motivation can be enhanced when there is an opportunity to own the job. One way to encourage this is to provide opportunities for progressive leadership within classes of jobs, allowing outstanding employees to earn more responsibility within their jobs. For example, a sport official might start out officiating games in the less competitive leagues or divisions but have the opportunity to work more competitive games as she gains confidence and skill. As time goes on, she may be given the responsibility of leading an officiating crew as a crew chief or officials' supervisor.

5. **Advancement.** Remember the discussions earlier in the chapter about providing opportunities to hire staff from within the organization? Providing internal opportunities and pathways for advancement based on job performance can motivate staff to do their best.

6. **Growth.** How can organizations best support the continued learning and growth of their staff members? Investing in ongoing continuing education and development is one way to fulfill this need for growth within positions. This is true for all levels of the organization, including volunteers.

Progressive Discipline

In some cases, staff and volunteers may fall short of desired performance levels, or they may commit actions in their job that undermine organizational effectiveness or put the organization at risk. This could be due to a variety of reasons, including poor job motivation, a lack of fit between the individual and the organization (or the job), inadequate support or supervision, a lack of professionalism, or improper training or education. In some cases it may be necessary to take steps to correct undesirable behavior on the part of employees, and in extreme cases it may be necessary to terminate employees or volunteers. Organizations have their own policies regarding the process for disciplining or terminating employees, and it is necessary to consult the human resources department for explicit steps. Regardless, it is always advisable to thoroughly investigate the specific personnel problem and document both the process and results of the investigation. Investigation and documentation are critical steps in almost all employee discipline cases.

Progressive discipline is a system for correcting employee behavior or addressing poor performance. The underlying goal is to change behavior or performance by using the least severe action that can accomplish the goal. There are generally four steps in progressive discipline:

1. Counseling
2. Written warning
3. Suspension (usually without pay)
4. Termination

In some cases, it may be necessary to repeat one or more of the steps. For example, repeated counseling sessions might be needed to correct a problem with work performance, particularly if progress is being made. In other cases, there may be no choice but to immediately terminate an employee because the behaviors or actions are so severe that they do not warrant intermediate steps. This could involve situations where the employee puts the lives or well-being of others in danger, commits a major breach in ethics, or willfully and callously ignores the basic respect and dignity owed to others. In all cases it is important to thoroughly investigate and document the problem.

CONCLUSION

Staff and volunteers are perhaps the most important resource that dictates the success or failure of the recreational sport organization. Recreational sport staff have a profound impact on participant experiences because they are the ones who directly influence the quality of programs and activities. Recreational sport staff hold a variety of positions in the organization, ranging from administration to program management to direct service to participants. They hold full-time, part-time, and volunteer positions, and they come from a variety of professional backgrounds and disciplines. Recreational sport managers can mold and shape their workforce by employing sound human resources systems. This includes developing an intentional approach to personnel planning, recruitment, selection, and retention.

RESEARCH TO REALITY

Mulvaney, M.A., McKinney, W.R., & Grodsky, R. (2008). The development of a pay-for-performance appraisal system for public park and recreation agencies: A case study. *Journal of Park and Recreation Administration, 26*(4), 126-156.

Performance appraisals are important for staff development for a number of reasons. They provide opportunities for recreational sport staff to improve their job performance, they identify areas that need further education or professional development, and they allow for recognition or discipline. However, developing a sound system for performance appraisal is a challenge, and getting buy-in from employees and staff can be difficult. Perhaps even more difficult is devising a performance appraisal system that effectively and fairly links pay with performance.

The authors of this study conducted a case study focused on the development of a pay-for-performance system in a public recreation agency. The results of the study provide insight into the development of a sound performance appraisal system, including employee assessment instruments, management training, and a system for tying pay increases to performance. Recreational sport managers can use the results of this study to design similar systems for their agencies.

REFLECTION QUESTIONS

1. What are the five components of the recreational sport organization?
2. What are the advantages and disadvantages of hiring or promoting staff from within the organization?
3. What is the connection between high-quality recreational sport staff and positive participant outcomes in sport?
4. What are some ways that organizations can improve volunteer management practices?
5. What are the differences between staff training and staff development? Provide examples of each in recreational sport.

LEARNING ACTIVITIES

1. Find an organizational chart of a recreational sport organization that you are familiar with. Conduct an organizational analysis based on the five components of the recreational sport organization discussed in the chapter.
2. Develop a job description for a full-time position in a recreational sport organization based on the parameters discussed in the chapter.
3. Think about a recreational sport position that you might supervise someday. Develop a staff training and development plan for that position. Consider including elements of both job-specific training and ongoing professional development.

chapter 10

TECHNOLOGY IN RECREATIONAL SPORT

LEARNING OUTCOMES

By the end of this chapter, readers will be able to

- describe the role of technology and how technology has advanced within the recreational sport organization,
- articulate the steps involved in the technology planning process for recreational sport organizations,
- compare and contrast hardware and software as well as differentiate between traditional and cloud computing, and
- analyze the major technology applications used in recreational sport organizations.

Case Study

SCIENCE FICTION MEETS RECREATIONAL SPORT

"But we've been online since 1996. Everything that someone would want to know about our programs and facilities is on the website, available 24–7. We use Facebook and Twitter. We have automated card readers at all of our indoor facilities. How much more technology do we really need?" At their weekly program staff meeting, a spirited exchange was taking place between Nathan Epping, the director of parks and recreation, and members of his sport programming and facilities staff, led by Emily Walters. Nathan was an open-minded boss who encouraged new ideas from his staff. At this meeting, Emily was advocating for implementing a biometric-based access system for the city's $1 million unstaffed skate park.

"Vandalism and loitering have been huge problems for us, and we can't get the city's legal unit to allow us to staff the park because of the liability issue," Emily argued. "Technology can allow us to supervise the park without actually putting our people on-site. And if this works, we could replace all of our automated card readers with biometric access systems that read members' fingerprints. That would eliminate the time and money involved in issuing ID cards to all of our members."

Nathan was intrigued. A new facility access system could solve several problems by enhancing facility safety, curbing vandalism, and lowering the costs associated with the ID process. Plus, the system could eliminate the problem of customers forgetting their IDs. He asked Emily to give him some additional details on her plan.

Emily obliged. "We'd start with the skate park, implementing a biometric access system that would allow registered users to access the skate park with their thumbprint. Patrons would need to register their name, address, and phone number with us so we can verify their residence eligibility. Then we scan their thumbprint, which creates a unique identifier. All the patrons need to do to access the facility is scan their thumb when they enter and exit. To reduce vandalism and loitering, we can install cameras that continuously record the activities at the park. These are already being used at busy intersections and in other public places downtown by the police department, and they have given the police a big advantage in both deterring and investigating crime. If this works, then we can look at implementing a similar system in all of our controlled-access facilities."

Nathan was almost sold. But he had one nagging concern. "Isn't this whole thing a bit too sci-fi? What about protecting people's privacy?" he asked.

Emily explained that they would need to do some educating on the new system, and that would take time. They would need policies in place to assure the public that no personal data would be used for any purposes except for controlling facility access or investigating security issues associated with the facility. Emily assured Nathan that once people got used to the new system and saw its advantages—for example, not having to carry an ID card, faster facility access times, and lower costs—they would choose to scan their fingerprints.

In the end, Nathan agreed to move forward with the process of researching vendors. Sci-fi or not, the management upsides of this new technology seemed to be a good solution to the agency's safety, security, vandalism, and budget-efficiency challenges.

New technologies have forever changed the way organizations and systems operate. From supercomputers to personal computing, desktop software applications, and the Internet, technology has transformed the way goods and services are produced. Technology has also had an impact on systems of organization, influencing how work is structured, how people are managed, and whether or not human resources are even necessary in the first place. Most of us see technology as an unbridled positive, forging new possibilities for production and management. Technology can be a paradox, however—it can yield great promise, but it can also create unforeseen implications for privacy, service quality, and human resources management. Nevertheless, organizations and individuals continue to reap benefits from the technological innovations that have emerged throughout history.

This chapter discusses the intersection of technology and recreational sport, specifically focusing on the role that technology plays in how recreational sport professionals do their jobs. While reading the chapter, consider the many ways that technology can improve or contribute to the various aspects of recreational sport that you have read about in this book. How does technology affect recreational sport program design, tournament administration, facility and equipment management, risk management, personnel, or any of the other areas discussed in the preceding pages? What types of technology are available to recreational sport organizations? How are organizations taking advantage of technology to improve their practices? How is the recreational sport industry using technology to innovate and change the way it does business? How can technology be used to improve management practice, and how can professionals minimize or eliminate some of the potential negatives of technological dependence? These are some of the questions that will be explored throughout this chapter.

UNDERSTANDING THE SCOPE OF TECHNOLOGY

When most people think of technology, the things that come to mind are usually electronics, computers, and data. This chapter primarily discusses computer-based **technology tools** and other electronic devices as they are applied in recreational sport settings. However, in the field of management, which recreational sport is a part of, technology is seen in a broader context. The term *technology* can be broadly defined to encompass not only computers and computing systems but all of the tools that managers use to get things done. Technological tools consist of a combination of skills, knowledge, abilities, techniques, materials, computers, and other equipment (Jones, 2004).

The idea of technology as a set of tools that we use to meet our managerial goals is an important one. Technology is something that we control. Just because a technology exists doesn't mean we have to use it. Consider the opening case study. Biometric-based systems are just one means to control access to a recreational sport facility. Other methods include automated card readers or just stationing staff members at the entrance and manually checking membership cards. The recreational sport agency in the case had specific reasons for considering the use of an advanced biometric-based ID system coupled with video surveillance cameras at the skate park. This specific technological solution was a tool to obtain desired managerial outcomes—to control facility access more effectively, to reduce costs of producing membership identification cards, and to reduce vandalism and other facility-based crime. Technology should be thoughtfully integrated into the overall operations of the agency via a technology plan. The idea is that, as with any other tool, technology is something we use to accomplish a specific organizational objective.

Why Technology?

There are three big questions that managers must answer when assessing the role of technology and its contribution to organizational effectiveness:

1. How does technology help us do the things we do better?
2. How does technology help us better manage our customers and external environments?
3. How does technology help us fundamentally change the way we do things for the better?

According to Jones (2004), each of these questions helps to address the three processes that managers use to assess organizational effectiveness—efficiency, control (over customer relationship management), and innovation. Managers may adopt technological approaches to increase effectiveness in one or more of these areas.

Efficiency

Organizations use technology to help reduce costs, increase staff productivity, raise production levels, routinize work processes, and standardize product delivery. Though it may seem that these goals are unique to industrial or manufacturing organizations, recreational sport organizations benefit from increased efficiency and can use technology to improve organizational functioning in much the same way.

Consider the example of the automated identification system installed in a commercial sport and fitness center. Installing such a system affects the goals of efficiency listed in the previous paragraph. Organizations with these systems have fewer needs for front-desk staff to manually check members' identification cards and control facility access, which means they may be able to reduce costs. These systems routinize the process of facility control by taking subjectivity out of the process—the member either has a functioning identification card allowing access or she doesn't. In addition, facility control is standardized—no longer can people gain access because they know the front-desk attendant who works the night shift or because the attendant did not want to engage in conflict with a potential user by strictly controlling facility access. Through this technology, access policy is consistently and routinely enforced. By routinizing and standardizing what once required manual labor (checking identification and manually controlling access), facility management staff can focus their time and energy on more pressing customer service issues or perform other tasks that help the organization meet its goals.

Incorporating management technology like this automatic card-scan reader can increase the recreational sport organization's efficiency and effectiveness.

Customer Relationship Management

Organizations can use technology to increase their control over the customer relationship process by improving customer service. They can also use it to increase their marketing potential by influencing supply and demand. In the public sector, government agencies may use technology to shape and influence stakeholder perceptions of the value and worth of what they do, as well as provide more opportunities for constituent involvement in the services that the agencies provide. For example, technology can increase communication between participants and recreational sport staff, and customer feedback can be acted on more immediately. In this way, technology can enhance the position of a public agency in the community.

Providing customers with easily accessible information and relatively easy interactivity represents an opportunity for increasing customer satisfaction, improving organizational performance, and increasing constituent empowerment. Organizations may also use technological functions such as databases to collect, warehouse, and analyze customer data. Consider the possibilities of a database with the following information on recreational sport participants:

- Who is using the organization's services? (Consider demographic data such as such as customers' age, sex, race or ethnicity, income, education level, geographic location, and number of children.)

- What services are customers using? (Consider use of facilities, specific programs, and other services as well as program skill levels.)
- How often are customers using the services? (Consider usage frequency and specific times and days.)
- Are customers using the services alone or with others? (Consider family use patterns and social networks.)
- What are customers' perceptions of the quality of the services? (Consider evaluation of the quality of the service, staff, location, or price.)
- What new participation opportunities are customers interested in? (Consider existing programs, services, and facilities as well as new possibilities for program, service, and facility development).

Data on each of these questions alone would be valuable for an organization to have. For example, being able to call up a list of participants in yoga classes in the last month can provide useful data for market segmentation. Knowing that the majority of the yoga participants are women would allow for a targeted marketing approach and a specific message strategy that appeals to future female participants. In addition, consider the possibilities of being able to integrate data and look at patterns and relationships in the database. A fitness organization that can identify the specific women who took part in a beginning yoga class on Wednesday nights (linking several pieces of data together) can create a more tailored marketing message to drive participation to a future intermediate yoga class that also takes place on Wednesday nights.

Innovation

The recreational sport field is both a beneficiary and driver of innovation. **Innovation** refers to the development and implementation of new ideas, structures, processes, products, systems, or services that increase efficiency and productivity (Jaskyte, 2010). At a minimum, technological innovation allows us to do existing things better than we did before.

Transformative technologies change society in profound ways. For example, the crowded field of commercial suppliers of recreation products, equipment, and apparel requires organizations to innovate in order to maintain (or gain) competitive advantage and growth. Technological innovations in field lighting have enabled companies to provide recreation organizations with more efficient and less expensive lighting solutions that also limit light pollution and overall community impact. These solutions provide organizations with greater light control as well as more efficient operations and management options. The development and proliferation of geospatial technologies and computer mapping and analysis programs (e.g., GIS) has provided recreational sport organizations with vastly improved planning, management, and analytical abilities. In these and many other ways, technologies developed outside the field have greatly benefited recreational sport.

Although innovation is a hallmark of the commercial sector, public and not-for-profit organizations must also innovate to continue to fulfill their missions. Consider the importance that high-tech cardio equipment plays in the promotion of fitness. A recumbent bike in a fitness facility might offer a screen that uses **virtual reality**—a computer-generated simulated world—to allow the bicycle enthusiast to complete a stretch of the French Alps during a workout. Key statistics such as time, pace, calories burned, and laps completed help the virtual cyclist to keep track of her experience. In this case, technology is used in an innovative way to produce the fitness experience. Another example of innovative technology use is the biometric-based facility access system discussed in the opening case study.

Using Technology

Remember, technology is a tool that helps the organization to achieve its goals. It is not necessary to adopt every new piece of technology just to appear innovative or unique. Organizations should match their specific goals or needs to the specific technology application that they are thinking of using. Examples of technology applications in recreational sport are discussed later in the chapter. As you will see, these technologies can range from the complex, such as biometric access systems and virtual reality, to the relatively simple, such as social media. As you read the following sections, think about how each technology example could be used to enhance the goals of the recreational sport organization.

COMPUTING TECHNOLOGY AND RECREATIONAL SPORT

This section discusses some of the major examples of computing technology that can be used in recreational sport. This is by no means an exhaustive list of technology products and vendors; such a list would be impossible because of the ever-changing nature of technology capabilities and commercial vendors. However, recreational sport professionals can use these major technology categories to determine how they might incorporate them into their organizations. Specific products or vendors are highlighted as examples rather than endorsements. There are many technology products and vendors in the marketplace, and recreational sport professionals should take the time to research the ones that are best for their specific needs.

Desktop and Mobile Computing

Substantial technological advances have made personal computing easier and more accessible over the past 20 years. It would be difficult to find a recreational sport organization that is not using personal computing for basic office functions such as word processing, spreadsheets, presentations, desktop publishing, and database management. It is safe to assume that most recreational sport agencies are using personal computers to access the Internet, send and receive e-mail, transfer and store electronic files, and maintain a website. As we move into the second decade of the 21st century, these basic technology functions are taken for granted in most organizations.

The hardware and software that are available to recreational sport organizations for some or all of these functions have changed dramatically over the years. **Hardware** refers to the physical components of a computing system or electronic device. In other words, hardware comprises the things that can be seen. It might include the monitor, hard drive, keyboard, mouse, and webcam of a computer. Hardware also includes the physical components of peripheral electronic devices that help extend computing capability, such as printers, fax machines, and digital cameras. **Software** is what powers the physical components of a computer or electronic device. Examples of software include computer **operating systems**, or the software that drives the computer (e.g., Microsoft Windows, Mac OS, Linux). Software also includes the tools that make computers useful for everyday work, such as word processing programs, spreadsheets, or databases. More specific recreational sport software includes sport scheduling, facility scheduling, recreation registration, and fitness and wellness applications. Software is virtual because it refers to the programming code and scripts that computer programmers write that tell the computer what to do. Software may be preinstalled on the computer or electronic device that is purchased from the manufacturer, or it may be installed manually by CD-ROM, DVD, USB flash drive, or direct download from the Internet.

There is now a tremendous amount of choice in the marketplace for personal computers. These choices include desktop, laptop, and tablet computers and smartphones.

Desktop Computers

Desktop computers, or desktops, are personal computers that are generally fixed to a single location, such as an employee's office, front desk, or equipment counter. They have advantages in that they typically have a large amount of computing power, can handle a multitude of computing tasks, and can be purchased at a relatively low price compared with other personal computing options. The disadvantage of desktops is that they are fixed to one location and cannot be moved easily. They also tend to be larger and take up more space, although recent advances in design technology have made desktops more streamlined. Desktop computers come in two major categories—PCs (personal computers) that use Microsoft Windows for an operating system and Apple computers (Macs) that run on Mac OS. The choice between PCs and Macs is largely a personal one. Historically, PCs have greatly outsold Macs; however, recently that gap has been closing. Currently, it is estimated that PCs outsell Macs by a 20-to-1 ratio (Gross, 2012).

Laptop Computers

Laptop computers, or laptops, are portable computers that typically weigh between 2 and 10 pounds (1-5 kg; PCMag.com, 2012). Laptop computers have batteries that allow them to be used anywhere. Recreational sport staff who work in multiple facilities or in multiple offices might find laptops to be advantageous because they can

Mobile computing using laptops, tablet computers, and smartphones has revolutionized the way recreational sport is delivered and evaluated.

take all of their files and information with them. The speed, memory, and disk space available on laptops have grown rapidly over time, and many high-end models compare favorably with desktop options. However, for true mobile use, smaller, lighter laptops weighing between 2 and 6 pounds (1-3 kg) may be the best. These smaller laptops may be referred to as *notebooks*, *netbooks*, or *mini laptops* in the marketplace. Typically, there is a relationship between the size and weight of the laptop and its performance capabilities. For example, netbooks or mini laptops that weigh around 2 pounds (1 kg) will not have the same computing power and capabilities as a larger notebook model. Similar to desktops, laptops come in two major categories—PCs and Macs.

Tablet Computers and Smartphones

Tablet computers, or tablets, are personal computers that use a single panel and a touch screen for navigation. The largest selling and most popular tablet computer is the Apple iPad. However, other vendors have also entered the tablet market using the Android operating system, including the Google Nexus, Samsung Galaxy, and Amazon Kindle Fire, among others. The Microsoft Surface tablet entered the market using the Windows operating system.

Smartphones are cellular telephones that include digital voice service as well as a variety of built-in applications and Internet access. This allows the user to browse the Web, listen to music, take and share pictures and video, send text messages and e-mail, and access thousands of free and paid third-party **apps**, or software applications, that turn the phone into a mini computer (PCMag.com, 2012). Apps have been developed in a variety of categories, allowing users to turn their tablets or phones into calculators and computing devices, to play games, to get information and news, to check the weather, and to engage in social networking.

Apps that would be helpful for recreational sport professionals are starting to be developed as well. For example, TeamSnap is a Web-based service and app designed to help manage recreational sport teams, leagues, and participants. It helps manage team and league schedules, provides networking and communication opportunities for coaches and participants, and provides a platform for viewing and posting photos. Another app that could be useful for recreational sport professionals is E-QYP (Equipping Quality Youth Professionals; see figure 10.1). The app delivers information about child and youth development, including resources and sample activities, directly to mobile devices such as an iPad or iPhone. Other apps, such as MyFitnessPal, allow users to track nutrition and physical activity information such as daily caloric intake, nutrient balance, weight, and physical activity participation. As mobile devices become more popular, more and more apps focused on recreational sport will undoubtedly be developed.

Mobile phones run on a variety of operating systems, including Android, iOS (iPhone), Blackberry, and Windows. Market research shows that smartphones are used by almost 6 out of 10 Americans and by more than 75 percent of U.S. consumers under the age of 44 (Snider, 2012). More than one-third of users use their smartphones to make calls, send or receive text messages, browse the Internet, and use social networking sites several times a day (Hayden, 2012).

Tablets and smartphones have the potential to change the way recreational sport agencies do business. For example, mobile technology can be used to communicate in real time with participants in order to provide up-to-date information about schedules, registration deadlines, or facility closures. Staff can take and immediately share pictures and videos of programs and events and post summaries of sport performances or tournament championships. Participants with smartphones or tablets can get information and register for programs or events wherever they happen to be. They can also provide immediate feedback on their experiences with programs and facilities, and they can report unsafe or dangerous situations to recreational sport personnel in real time. However, this technology can also create problems for recreational sport professionals. For example, many agencies now have policies preventing smartphones from being used in locker rooms, near pools, and on gym floors because of privacy issues, particularly concerning the ease with which users can take and share pictures and videos (Saint Louis, 2011).

Internet

Many of the advantages of personal computing are due to the development of the Internet. The **Internet** is a worldwide network of computers that store and share information. It encompasses a range of features, including the World Wide Web, e-mail, instant messaging, and file transfers. Over 70 percent of U.S. households have Internet access inside the home, and over 80 percent have access outside the home (U.S. Census Bureau, 2012). As discussed previously, a large percentage of U.S. consumers access the Internet through mobile devices such as smartphones and tablets.

Most people are familiar with the **World Wide Web** (or Web for short). This a subset of the Internet and consists of pages that are accessed by their unique address using a browser such as Explorer, Safari, Chrome, or Firefox. The Web has gone through at least two generations—what O'Reilly (2005) has termed *Web 1.0* and *Web 2.0*. Although Web 1.0 and 2.0 are different, they are an integrated system—that is, they are used for different purposes, but they can and should complement one another.

Web 1.0 strategies use a top-down approach to disseminate content to others. They use tools such as e-mail newsletters, LISTSERVs, and websites to communicate information to customers and agency staff. A hallmark of Web 1.0 technologies is that they are low in two-way interactivity—that is, information is pushed from the agency to the end user. More advanced Web 1.0 functions allow for a little more interactivity, although interaction is structured by the organization. For example, advanced Web applications allow users to register and pay for programs online, reserve facilities, check out equipment, or submit questions to staff through online forms. Staff may use the agency's **intranet**—a private, password-protected Web available only to authorized users—to accept or decline shift schedules, clock in and out of work, make purchase requisitions, submit budget requests, and update personnel records.

Web 1.0 technologies are advantageous in that they can communicate a large amount of material to consumers quickly and cheaply. For example, sport equipment vendors can put their products on their website with pictures and specifications along with online ordering and payment functions. This saves companies money because they don't have to print catalogues or pay people to take phone orders. Communication and information distribution can also be tightly controlled and managed. Web 1.0 technologies can be easily combined as well, such as using e-mail LISTSERVs to distribute agency newsletters or reminding repeat customers to visit the website to get information on new programs or activities.

A big disadvantage of Web 1.0 technology is that it is low in dynamic interactivity. Communication

An App for Recreation and Leisure Managers, Staff and Volunteers.

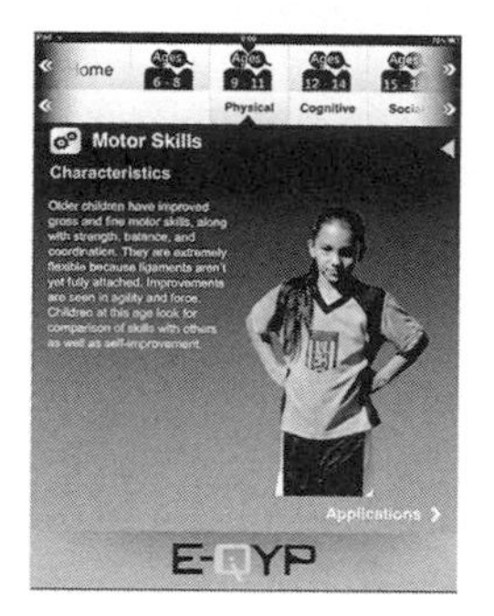

E-QYP™ is the leading tool harnessing smartphones to place answers and resources in your hands when planning youth recreation programs, including sports and camps. E-QYP places activities and resources in the context of child and youth development theory to develop understanding of age-appropriate developmental needs and how to work appropriately with young people at different ages.

E-QYP is organized by four school-age groups: 6 - 8, 9 - 11, 12 - 14 and 15 - 18, and four developmental areas with easy-to-follow subareas:

- Physical (with 4 subareas),
- Cognitive (with 5 subareas),
- Social (with 6 areas) and
- Emotional (with 3 subareas).

E-QYP was developed and reviewed by practitioners to make it practical information and realistic activities and resources.

E-QYP is designed for the full range of recreation and leisure personnel that support the development of young people:

- Counselors and activity aides,
- Part-time, on-call and seasonal staff,
- Program directors,
- Coaches, volunteers and mentors, and
- Parents that contribute to program activities.

E-QYP is an especially useful resource for supervisors and administrators. It provides a shared coaching tool and training supplement to quickly focus areas of development for individual staff or volunteers, in an easily accessible format.

E-QYP supports standards of quality programs and services, such as:

NRPA Council on Accreditation for Recreation, Park Resources, and Leisure Services Education:

- 8.08: Understanding of the importance of maintaining professional competence and the available resources for professional development
- 8.14:01 Assessment of Needs
- 8.14:03 Selection and coordination of programs, events, and resources
- 8:15 Understanding of group dynamics and processes

Commission for Accreditation of Parks and Recreation Agencies:

- 2.4.1 Recreation Programming Plan
- 4.1.4.4 Training, career development
- 4.2 Volunteers

For more information and to access E-QYP, go to: www.E-QYP.net.

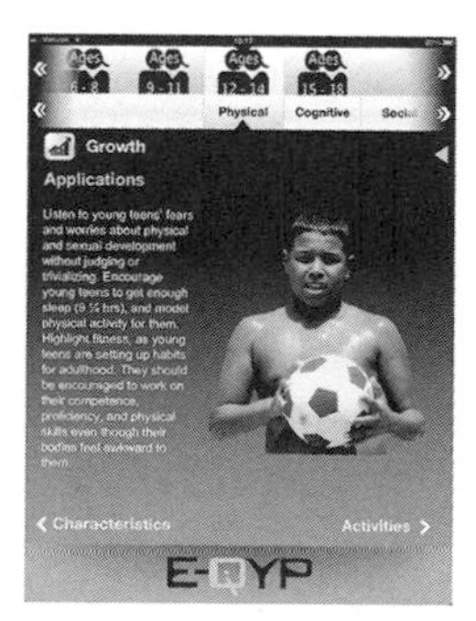

Figure 10.1 E-QYPing Quality Youth Professionals.

is top-down and structured by the agency. Web information can become stale if it is not changed frequently, and users may not visit websites that do not have new information or updates. Finally, many users are turning to other Internet-based systems to communicate, such as text messaging and social networking, prompting some to suggest that the e-mail era may be coming to an end (Parker, 2012).

Web 2.0 technologies include tools that focus on sharing and collaboration. They promote interaction between users, meaning they are less top-down than Web 1.0 systems. Examples of Web 2.0 technologies include social networking sites, blogs, wikis, cloud computing, and Web conferencing. One way of describing Web 2.0 tools is that they provide users with the opportunity to "work together in creating content through multiple authoring, whether in text, audio, or video" (Moore, 2007, p. 179). The following are some examples of Web 2.0 tools and how they might be used by recreational sport agencies. This is not meant to be an exhaustive list or an endorsement of the vendors but merely an illustration of how Web 2.0 applies to recreational sport.

Social Networking

Social networking takes place in online virtual communities that allow people to share up-to-the-minute information with others within their network (PCMag.com, 2012). Social networking is hugely popular, with 69 percent of U.S. adults using a variety of social networking communities (Brenner, 2012). Popular social networking sites include Facebook, LinkedIn, Twitter, Pinterest, Instagram, Flickr, and YouTube.

The value of social networking is the community that is created among users. One of the advantages of social networking is that it allows instant interaction and the ability to share information among networks. A recreational sport agency might use Facebook or Twitter to post information, pictures, or video. This information can travel not only from the agency to its users but also among users themselves as they share and reshare information that they find useful. This has tremendous power for marketing, because users can quickly transmit information and assist the agency in spreading the word about interesting activities and events. For example, one study showed that virtual social networks are at least partially credited for increased participation in triathlons and adventure racing (Popke, 2011). At the same time, users can make online, public comments and create discussions about the information that is shared. The public nature of information shared through virtual social networks can also be a disadvantage, however, because agencies cannot control what is made public by their online friends. It is possible that public feedback on social networking sites can be negative or derogatory toward the agency. In addition, staff can sometimes use social networking sites carelessly, potentially harming the agency's reputation through negative posts or comments.

Two popular social networking tools include Facebook and Twitter. Most people are familiar with personal accounts on Facebook, which allow users to connect with one another through social networks of friends. However, Facebook also offers organizations and businesses the opportunity to set up Facebook pages, or accounts that can be used to connect with clients by sending information, updates, and pictures and by soliciting comments. Facebook pages provide organizations with statistics on how many people they are reaching, how many people "like" the content, and how many people share the organization's information. Recreational sport organizations might use their Facebook page to provide updates of nightly game scores, to recognize individual performances, or to post pictures or videos of classes, programs, or events.

Twitter is another popular social networking utility that helps people connect with one another through developing a network of followers. This system allows users to read, send, and share short messages of no more than 140 characters to their followers. Messages sent through Twitter are referred to as *tweets* and can be grouped or categorized using hashtags (#). Recreational sport organizations can use Twitter to remind followers about upcoming deadlines and drive traffic to their website for registration, provide links to pictures or videos, or provide up-to-the-minute information on weather delays or event cancellations. Twitter can be used to connect more personally as well. For example, a popular fitness leader might tweet the following: "About ready 2 teach Zumba at 5. Who's coming? #rockvillefitness." In this way, a two-second tweet can reach countless people instantly and is recognized by recipients in a personal way. Recipients of the message can also respond in real time, giving the instructor a sense of who might attend. Imagine how long it would take the same message to reach the same number of people using traditional communication forms.

Blogs and Wikis

Weblogs, or **blogs**, are websites that provide an ongoing series of information in the form of text, images, video, and user-generated comments. One way to think of a blog is to think of a diary. Blog publishers (bloggers) create posts, or articles that are arranged in chronological order and categorized by topic. In addition to these features, blogs typically contain a mechanism for readers to leave comments on posts, allowing for a discussion on the topic. Blog posts typically contain Web links to other sites of interest that pertain to the topic, and these links are embedded in the text itself. Many commercial blog platforms are available that allow users to start blogging quickly and cheaply. Popular sites include Blogger and WordPress, both of which offer free and fee-based systems.

Recreational sport organizations can use blogs to generate content that their customers might find interesting and to provide links to other sites of interest. For example, a fitness and wellness professional might create daily blog posts about healthy meal ideas, simple stretching exercises, or stress reduction techniques. The fitness professional might use social networking sites such as Facebook or Twitter to get the word out about new posts and drive traffic to the blog site. Blogs are more interactive than traditional websites, particularly for creating and sustaining dynamic interaction between the recreational sport agency and its customers.

Wikis are shared Web spaces that allow multiple users to author unique content and edit the work of others (Barcelona & Rockey, 2010). In this way, wikis are collaborative and can greatly increase interunit coordination and efficiency. For example, rather than having staff members work individually on a document such as a policy manual and then trying to integrate all of their work at the end, wikis allow people to work together on the same document, often at the same time. What is seen on the screen is always the most up-to-date version of the group's work. Wikis can be open to the public or they can be set to higher levels of privacy. There are many free wiki applications, including Google Docs and Wikispaces, that recreational sport organizations can easily access. Recreational sport organizations might use wikis among their staff to create and edit policy manuals, create event plans, develop meeting agendas, or share resources.

Cloud Computing

Cloud computing refers to a system of shared computing resources such as networks, servers, storage, applications, and services that can be easily accessed by users (National Institute of Standards, 2011). In cloud computing, data are stored on the servers of third-party vendors that serve as hosts. Data and software then can be accessed directly from these third-party servers without taking up space on the agency's own network or computing system. One of the advantages of cloud computing for recreational sport organizations is that data storage can be centralized and shared by multiple users across multiple computers. In the past, sharing large files was burdensome and inefficient. E-mail systems often have difficulty sending and receiving large files, requiring users to share files using external storage devices such as USB flash drives or external hard drives. However, with cloud-based file storage systems, users can save files in shared folders that can be accessed by anyone who has permission.

One cloud-based storage system is Dropbox, which provides both free and fee-based options depending on how much storage space is needed. Other examples of cloud-based computing services include Google Docs, a Web-based office suite that offers the ability to create, save, share, and collaborate on documents, spreadsheets, and presentations. As users or groups of users use these applications, they are automatically saved on Google servers, so the version that appears on the screen is always the most updated version of the file. In this way, Google Docs functions like a wiki.

Sport and Facility Management Software

The previous examples show how publicly available Web-based applications can be used by recreational sport organizations to communicate with, connect, and build community among participants. However, many of the day-to-day programming and management responsibilities in recreational sport can be enhanced through technology capabilities built specifically for the recreational sport professional. The complexity involved in managing and scheduling sport leagues and tournaments, scheduling recreational sport facilities, and managing recreation registrations and memberships can be simplified using available technology.

Many sport and facility scheduling software and Web-based programs are available. There are commercial products that focus on specific recreational sport functions, such as league and tournament scheduling, facility scheduling, and membership and registration management. However, many vendors have developed integrated systems that provide organizations with an all-in-one solution to their software needs or allow recreational sport professionals to choose among a list of solutions that they offer. The following is a list of technology solutions that vendors provide to recreational sport professionals:

- **Activity registrations.** This solution allows the recreational sport organization to manage activity, event, and program registration. Features may include the ability to let participants register and pay online, to generate program rosters, and to manage refunds and waitlists. Features may also allow the agency to track customer information, including usage patterns, and obtain program demographic reports.
- **Facility reservations.** This solution allows the recreational sport agency to book and reserve facilities. Features may include providing information about available facilities to potential customers, such as details related to cost and other policies. Other features may include calendars, online payment options, specific maintenance and setup requests, and the ability to track reservation overlaps and prevent double bookings.
- **Membership and pass management.** This solution helps the recreational sport agency manage, process, and track facility memberships. Most systems provide the ability to create personalized photo identification cards with a scannable bar code that allows the agency to track usage statistics. Features may also include the ability to place restrictions on certain membership types or suspend access privileges for certain people. Some vendors offer other identification solutions, including the use of biometrics such as finger- or hand-scanning systems.
- **League and tournament scheduling.** This solution helps to minimize the inefficiencies and errors involved in scheduling large tournaments, leagues, and events by hand. Features generally include the ability to schedule a variety of tournament formats, including round-robin, single- and double-elimination, and challenge tournaments. Desirable features include the ability to develop and view team, league, and master game schedules; access all schedules online; assign players to teams; assign teams to leagues; generate player rosters; designate home and away teams; and track game results. Some systems also feature the ability to track sportsmanship ratings for players and teams.
- **Other solutions.** The solutions described thus far are typically the most used among recreational sport agencies. However, many large commercial technology vendors also offer other solutions depending on the specific needs of the recreational sport organization. Examples of other software solutions include point-of-sale payment processing for use in pro shops and equipment stands, golf course management, incident reporting, and child care management. Large commercial vendors such as Active Network and Vermont Systems offer integrated solutions, removing duplication and redundancies between systems. For example, Active Network's league management software fully integrates with their activity registration and facility registration programs to prevent duplicate entries and scheduling conflicts (Active Network, 2012). Vermont Systems' RecTrac system also offers fully integrated park and recreation software (Vermont Systems, 2012).

Other Technology Advances in Recreational Sport

In addition to computer hardware, software, and the Internet, the field of recreational sport has benefited from the technology revolution in other ways. Many of the technological advances over the past 250 years have affected manufacturing and the production of physical goods, but the services industry, of which recreational sport is a part, has also been affected by these innovations. Other technology advances that have directly benefited recreational sport include improved sport and fitness equipment, higher-quality playing areas, controlled facility and program access, and improved facility and program safety.

- **Improved sport and fitness equipment.** New materials and physical design technology have improved recreational sport facilities and equipment. Playground equipment, for example, has benefited from improvement in materials construction, including advanced plastics. These new construction materials allow for increased participant safety (no more exposed metal or sharp edges) and less expensive playground options. New materials technology can also limit the impact of vandalism through increased durability.

- **Higher-quality playing areas.** Technology advances in materials and physical design have also enhanced the facilities where recreational sport takes place. Innovations such as durable and disease-resistant turf grass, as well as the development of organic pesticides for golf courses, parks, and athletic fields, have increased the efficiency and quality of turf maintenance. High-quality outdoor lighting solutions extend facility availability and provide better and safer places to play. Finally, new composite and rubberized flooring materials and outdoor synthetic turf have increased durability for facilities that experience frequent use.

- **Controlled facility and program access.** Technology allows recreational sport organizations to more effectively control access to facilities and programs. For example, organizations have been able to issue identification cards to facility members that they run through a bar code reader at facility entry points, allowing eligible members access. Technology advances have also used biometrics to increase the efficiency and effectiveness of recreational sport agencies. **Biometric recognition** refers to the identification of people by their anatomical traits, such as fingerprints, palms, or eyes. Biometric identification systems allow organizations to save money printing and issuing identification cards and allow customers to avoid worrying about remembering to bring their ID every time they come to the facility. Similar to bar code ID readers, biometric systems also link to databases that contain information about each user. These databases allow organizations to mine useful data about participants for evaluation and reporting purposes.

- **Improved facility and program safety.** Technology advances have also led to the improvement of recreational sport facility and program safety. As discussed previously, advances in materials technology have made equipment and facilities safer through higher-quality and more durable sport equipment, such as playing surfaces, lighting, helmets, and other protective gear. In addition, advances in video technology have allowed organizations to provide around-the-clock video surveillance of program areas and facilities from a centralized control station. This can save time and resources, and it provides evidence when incidents occur at recreation facilities. This is particularly useful when vandalism or other crimes occur, allowing for follow-up investigation by police or authorities.

Technology Challenges

Technology has many advantages for an organization, as can be seen in the previous examples. However, there are also challenges associated with implementing technology and many considerations for recreational sport organizations to take into account. Technology can be seen as a paradox—on the one hand, it offers real advantages for organizational efficiency and effectiveness, but on the other hand, it can also have drawbacks. Some of these considerations and drawbacks are discussed next.

- **Moore's law.** Recreational sport professionals need to keep up with the prevailing technology trends because they change quickly. **Moore's law** suggests that technological capabilities—speed, memory, storage capacity, computing power—double every 18 months. Rapid technological advances make it difficult to stay up on the latest trends. Attending trade shows sponsored by professional associations such as NIRSA, NRPA, or Athletic Business can provide recreational sport professionals with up-to-date information on new technology, products, and vendors. Websites such as CNET (www.cnet.com), *PC Magazine* (www.pcmag.com), and Slashdot (www.slashdot.org) provide information on new technology applications and discussions about products and vendors.

- **Market churn.** Many technology companies have considerable market attrition, and companies that exist today often do not exist tomorrow. This is referred to as *market churn*. Some of the strongest technology companies that were in existence a decade ago are no longer providing services or provided services that have been rendered obsolete. For example, pioneering tournament scheduling software companies such as Intramural Participation Systems (IPS) and Web-based systems such as Intramurals.com are no longer in business today and have been replaced by others in the marketplace. Market churn makes it even more important for recreational sport agencies to conduct considerable research to choose the right application based on their specific needs.

- **Resource expenditures.** New technology products can be expensive. Some agencies might not see a strong enough justification for spending scarce resources on technology products and applications. This is compounded by market churn and constant evolution of products in the marketplace. **Planned obsolescence** refers to a business strategy in which the usability of a product is planned to diminish or disappear over time (Hindle, 2008), encouraging customers to update or replace old products. This is evident in the ever-increasing versions of smartphones and computer operating systems. Recreational sport organizations need to take into account not only the initial cost of purchasing new technology but replacement or upgrade costs as well.
- **Privacy and security.** Privacy and data security are important to consider when adopting new technology solutions. This is true at both the individual-user and organizational levels. For example, the individual user needs to know that his personal information is secure and will not be shared with others without his permission. Consider the opening case study and the potential for abuse of video surveillance systems or facility access systems that collect biometric data. At the organizational level, network security needs to be in place to ensure that computer systems are difficult to breach by third parties. In addition, staff need to be trained and made aware of what they can and cannot do with the data collected from participants.
- **Knowledge and expertise.** In addition to the costs associated with purchasing technology systems, organizations need to consider the capacity of their staff to install, work with, and maintain new technology. Too often, expensive software or technology systems are purchased but are not used to their fullest potential due to inadequate staff training. In other cases, staff may be reluctant to adopt the new technology systems because they have not been fully consulted or oriented to the potential of the technology to improve their day-to-day work.
- **Equity and access.** Much has been made about the digital divide—the gap between those who have full access to computers, the Internet, and other forms of technology and those who do not. In 2000, approximately 51 percent of American households had a computer and 42 percent had home Internet access (U.S. Census Bureau, 2012). A decade later, these numbers had risen: By 2010, more than three-fourths (77 percent) of households had a computer (U.S. Department of Commerce, 2011) and more than 70 percent of households had access to the Internet inside the home (U.S. Census Bureau, 2012). As mentioned earlier in the chapter, most people have access to the Internet either at home or in public places such as libraries. However, there is still a sizable number of people who may not have easy access to technology. Recreational sport organizations should make sure that redundant systems are designed so that people without Internet access can still fully participate in programs, services, and facilities. In addition, recreational sport organizations can make public computer and Internet access available in their facilities through stationary kiosks and Wi-Fi hotspots to help promote access.

CONCLUSION

Keeping up with technological advances is a key competency for recreational sport professionals. Technology is used by recreational sport agencies to improve efficiency, manage customer relationships, and drive organizational innovation. Many technology applications are useful in the recreational sport field, including hardware, software, and Internet-based services. However, technology should be viewed as a tool to accomplish organizational goals, and careful planning is necessary to ensure that technology is being adopted and implemented wisely. Finally, although technology offers definite advantages for recreational sport programming and management, it also has disadvantages and concerns that must be addressed to mitigate wasteful spending, protect user privacy, and ensure equal access for all participants.

RESEARCH TO REALITY

Blunt, G.H., & King, K. (2011). Developing a fitness center-based, self-guided instructional program using MP4 player technology. *Recreational Sports Journal, 35*(1), 61-69.

One of the challenges that fitness professionals face is the lack of knowledge that participants possess. This lack of knowledge extends to how to properly use fitness equipment and how to perform exercises safely and correctly. The authors provide a discussion on how MPEG-4 (MP4) video technology might be used to help orient and train fitness-center participants on the safe use of equipment and exercise. Specifically, the authors focus on how to develop and edit self-guided training videos, how to download these videos to MP4 players, and how to evaluate participants' fitness experiences after watching video content.

Think back to the opening discussion in this chapter about the idea that technology is a set of tools that can help recreational sport professionals reach their desired goals. The authors of this paper demonstrate how digital video, desktop editing software, and MP4 players can be used to solve a common management challenge—orienting and training recreational sport participants to use fitness equipment. Think about how this process might have been done before this technology. How has technology made the goal of improving participants' knowledge of fitness equipment more efficient for the recreational sport professionals in this case? How might it create a better experience for customers? Do you see any potential drawbacks to using technology in this way?

REFLECTION QUESTIONS

1. What are the three ways that technology contributes to organizational effectiveness?
2. What are the steps in developing a technology plan for a recreational sport organization?
3. How can recreational sport organizations use Web 1.0 and Web 2.0 strategies to meet their goals?
4. What are the major recreational sport software applications on the market, and what are some of the key vendors that provide this software?
5. Identify and describe some of the pressing technology challenges that recreational sport organizations need to consider when implementing technology solutions.

LEARNING ACTIVITIES

1. Imagine that you have been tasked with developing a technology plan for a recreational sport organization. Identify a management challenge that could be addressed using a technological solution. Address each step of the technology planning process as you put together your plan.
2. Do some research on vendors that provide technology solutions for recreational sport organizations. Choose examples of vendors that supply various types of products (e.g., computer software companies, facility access and control systems, recreation equipment or products). Provide a description of the products that are offered, the costs of purchasing the product, and the costs involved in training and implementation.
3. Develop a social media policy for the staff in a recreational sport organization. What is acceptable use of social media? What types of things should staff be allowed to post? What happens when users or others leave disparaging or negative comments about the agency in public forums? Where is the line between personal and professional social networking? What responsibilities should staff have for the content posted on their personal social networking sites? What boundaries or rules should be in place for using social networking to communicate with participants who are minors? These questions should be used as a starting point when developing your policy.

RECREATIONAL SPORT SETTINGS AND CONTEXTS

chapter 11

RECREATIONAL SPORT IN THE COMMUNITY

LEARNING OUTCOMES

By the end of the chapter, readers will be able to

- identify the relationship between community and recreational sport,
- differentiate between the types of opportunities available in community recreational sport management,
- describe the unique benefits of community recreational sport in nontypical communities, and
- describe creative ways of dealing with the challenges of community recreational sport in nontypical communities.

Case Study

BENEFITS OF MWR PROGRAMS

Greg and Joy work for a Morale, Welfare, and Recreation (MWR) program in Germany overseeing tournaments among service members and their families. They are in charge of the organization and implementation of several recreational sports for the community. Their bosses have received word from base administration that the budget for recreational sport is likely to be cut significantly due to the downturn in the economy and the resultant decrease in funding by the government. Greg and Joy's bosses have asked that they create a proposal justifying why their budget should not be cut based on the impact of their department on the base.

In the first step of the process, Greg and Joy discover that their department is not directly bringing in revenue to the base. However, further research demonstrates that there are several other benefits they need to emphasize. They find that the service members and their families who use their services are happier and better adjusted to living on the base than those who do not use their facilities and programs, which means that in an indirect way, funding the MWR program provides a significant benefit to the base. In other words, the services their program provides to the community are not necessarily directly profitable, but they do create a number of benefits in terms of community development. With this information in their report, they are able to convince the administrators that budget cuts to their department would result in more harm than good to the base community and the health and wellness of those living in it.

Recreational sport and community have a reciprocal relationship. A **community** can be defined as a group of individuals whose members share a general location, government, culture, or heritage. The community affects recreational sport and recreational sport affects the community. In general, the recreational sport provided in a community will match the location of the community, the interests of the residents, and the support the residents are willing to provide. For example, many communities in the American Mountain West have ski teams. This is in direct relationship to an environment that produces snow on mountains. Similarly, many communities in other areas of the West support rodeo teams due to a history of interest in the sport among its residents. In the Southeast, on the other hand, car racing might be a bigger draw, with community members willing to attend races in droves. This does not mean that community recreational sport managers cannot introduce new sporting opportunities to communities but simply that a history of interest and support makes these traditional opportunities easier to provide.

This chapter provides an overview of recreational sport within the community and the relationship between the two. It discusses the community benefits of recreational sport and the various types of community recreational sport, such as municipal, commercial, and alternative sports. Furthermore, the chapter addresses some unique community environments, such as military bases, college and university campuses, and senior living communities. The benefits of community recreational sport and the unique challenges these environments present are also addressed.

COMMUNITY BENEFITS OF RECREATIONAL SPORT

It is clear that a community can influence the types and formats of recreational sport in which people engage. In addition, involvement in community recreational sport can provide many benefits to the community itself. Many community leaders have begun to see recreational sport as having a role in community development (Coaffee, 2008; Glover, 2004). Recreational sport opportunities can help to strengthen the bonds of a community, provide a healthier environment and population, and have a positive economic impact. All of these benefits create a strong case for why these programs should be available.

One of the first ways recreational sport can benefit a community is by strengthening it. Residents of many neighborhoods believe that recreational sport can facilitate improvements in infrastructure and quality of life within the community (Autry & Anderson, 2007). This is partially related to the concepts of **social capital** (Burnett, 2006; Skinner, Zakus, & Cowell, 2008) and social inclusion (Cortis, 2009). The belief is that through recreational sport, participants will interact, and those interactions will lead to bonding. They will then know people they can rely on for needs ranging from information to support in a crisis. The more connections people have with others, the healthier they will be. And the more people have improved their social capital within a community, the more the community will improve as well (Autry & Anderson).

Communities can also benefit from recreational sport through its influence on physical health. To begin with, social capital is crucial in health promotion (Draper, Kolbe-Alexander, & Lambert, 2009). This means that as they are making social connections, participants are likely to experience physical improvements as well, including an increased level of physical fitness (Lyle et al., 2008). Consequently, the overall health care costs in the community could decrease.

Finally, positive economic impacts can be derived from community recreational sport. Small-scale recreational sporting events such as tournaments, matches, and meets can bring in tourists, which is important to the economy of most communities (Cela, Kowalski, & Lankford, 2006; Wilson, 2006). These types of tournaments, matches, and meets will be discussed more thoroughly later in the chapter.

COMMUNITY RECREATIONAL SPORT MANAGEMENT IN TYPICAL COMMUNITIES

A plethora of methods and organizations exist for providing community recreation services. Many people view **municipal recreation** as the sole or primary type of recreational sport opportunities, but several other types of organizations and

Municipal recreation programs are one of the most common ways people are introduced to recreational sport.

programs can also benefit a community. Resort and commercial recreational sport provide a for-profit outlet for many athletes, and tournaments, matches, and meets present a chance to connect the community with tourists and outside athletes. Additionally, alternative sports are gaining popularity and should not be overlooked by recreational sport professionals.

Municipal Recreation and Sport Management

Municipal recreation and sport management is at the core of community recreational sport. Other than through families, municipal recreation programs are how most people begin their lifelong participation in recreational sport. Consequently, municipal recreation departments play a crucial role in recreational sport management. Recreational sport opportunities range from introductory leagues for youth through adult recreational leagues and typically cover a variety of recreational sports. Although many municipalities focus primarily on traditional recreational sports, it is becoming more common to provide facilities, if not actual programs, for alternative options.

The qualifying standard for a municipal recreational sport organization is that it is part of a local government. This includes cities, counties, and special recreation tax districts. These agencies all provide recreational sport programs that are largely supported by tax dollars, although they may be supplemented by participant fees.

Resort and Commercial Recreational Sport

Although municipal recreation departments tend to be the primary focus of community recreational sport management, resort and commercial recreational sport also play an important role in the community. The types of opportunities can vary greatly by the area where you live, but golf clubs, ski resorts, sailing clubs, rock-climbing gyms, and many others can all have an impact on the community at large and members within it in significant ways.

Commercial recreational sport is offered by for-profit recreational sport organizations and can include a variety of recreational sports. A common example of this across the United States is golf clubs. Most golf clubs are run by organiza-

Denis Pepin/fotolia.com

Community recreational sport can also involve for-profit organizations such as ski resorts.

tions independent of the government and are designed to make a profit through club fees, course fees, rentals, and other spending opportunities. Other examples include ski resorts, tennis clubs, climbing gyms, and even bowling leagues. Any recreational sport opportunity that is run by a private organization fits into this category. Resort and commercial recreational sport offer many of the same benefits as municipal recreational sport because the benefits depend on the opportunity itself rather than who is providing the opportunity.

Not-for-Profit Recreational Sport Programs

Charitable organizations in the **not-for-profit sector** can also provide a multitude of recreational sport opportunities. These organizations are typically supported through donations, grants, and member fees and include well-known entities such as the YMCA and YWCA, Jewish Community Centers, Boys and Girls Clubs, and many more local organizations. Although many think of these organizations as primarily supporting youth recreational sport, they often also provide recreational sport for all ages and abilities through recreational leagues, instructional programs, and facilities for drop-in or pickup games and activities. They key determinant for not-for-profit organizations is that the revenue they generate returns to the organization itself. Typically these organizations either have or are working toward a special tax designation (501c) that exempts them from some federal income tax responsibilities.

Tournaments, Matches, and Meets

Among the more common trends in community recreational sport management is the attempt to attract tournaments, matches, and meets to the community (Kellett, Hede, & Chalip, 2008). Cities, counties, and even private organizations are attempting to update fields and other facilities to bring in small-scale recreational sporting events. The hope is that these will provide tourism dollars that have a positive economic impact, but serious consideration needs to be given to what events are selected and how they are conducted in order to provide the maximum benefit to the community.

Communities that put on these tournaments, matches, and meets receive several benefits (Cela et al., 2006; Wilson, 2006). Evidence has shown that small-scale recreational sporting events such as age-group swim meets or adult softball tournaments can have a positive economic impact on communities, particularly when they are multiday affairs. Visitors for these events tend to come for the primary purpose of attending the meet, and they spend money on accommodations, food, and other entertainment expenses while there. This can have a positive impact on the town as a whole and particularly on the tourism industry (Dixon, Hegreness, Arthur-Banning, & Wells, 2007).

In addition to the positive economic impact, many other benefits can result from small-scale recreational sporting events. These events have the potential to enhance the image of a region by presenting it in the best light and by drawing new visitors to the area (O'Brien, 2007). Furthermore, news coverage can serve as free marketing to those who are not attending the event.

In order to gain the greatest economic impact from these types of events, certain strategies should be followed. First, it is necessary to determine the appropriate events and programs. This makes it possible to attract the highest number of visitors and participants. To go along with that, professionals should try to encourage out-of-town participation in order to maximize tourism. This could be done by offering discounted registration rates for those who are traveling more than a certain distance. Professionals should also try to maximize the length of stay, because accommodations are one of the greatest expenditures. A longer stay means a higher influx of revenue for local merchants. It might also be good to partner with local businesses to encourage spending on food and souvenirs. Finally, it is important to connect with the community through support and good communication. Without community support, the event is unlikely to be a success, and community support can only be accomplished with good communication throughout the entire process (Dixon et al., 2007).

Alternative Sport

Although many people think of traditional sports such as baseball and soccer as the primary type of community recreational sport, several other options provide similar benefits and opportunities to communities. Alternative sports such as skateboarding and ultimate Frisbee are frequently overlooked by recreational sport professionals but attract many people looking for an experience beyond the typical recreational sport offerings. In 2003, 5 of the top 10 sports in the United States were considered to be alternative, including in-line skating, skateboarding, snowboarding, BMX biking, and wakeboarding (Thorpe, 2009).

Alternative sport refers to sports outside the traditional realm of team and individual sports. A lot of these sports would also be considered action or risk sports because of their high injury rates. Examples of alternative sports include skateboarding, snowboarding, ultimate Frisbee, and parkour. These sports have recently been gaining popularity, and as a result they have become more regulated and organized through events such as the X Games and the Dew Tour. Some, such as snowboarding and mountain biking, have become so established that they have even become Olympic events.

Benefits of Alternative Sport

Participation in alternative sport has many of the same benefits as participation in traditional sport, including the physical, psychosocial, and cognitive benefits discussed in chapter 2 of this text. An added benefit of providing these programs is the opportunity to reach a new audience. Though many enjoy traditional sports, many others avoid them as a result of negative experiences, a lack of peer involvement, or simply a lack of interest. For this reason, providing alternative sport programs and events may reach people who otherwise would not be involved in sport. Furthermore, alternative sport could provide some of the same opportunities for community development as traditional sport, such as the economic impact that can be gained from putting on an ultimate Frisbee tournament.

Addressing the Unique Challenges of Alternative Sport

One of the greatest challenges in providing community opportunities for alternative sports is the contradictory nature between designed programs and the sports themselves. Because alternative sports tend to emerge from a desire to distinguish oneself outside the establishment, making the sport a part of the establishment goes somewhat against the nature of the sport (Coakley, 2004). Although competitions and classes in sports such as skateboarding, rock climbing, BMX racing, and even parkour are becoming more common, recreational sport professionals should be careful not to regulate these offerings too much because it may be detrimental to participation in the program.

Philippe Devanne/fotolia.com

Alternative sports such as snowboarding have been increasing in popularity and are becoming more mainstream.

COMMUNITY RECREATIONAL SPORT IN NONTYPICAL COMMUNITIES

When talking about community recreational sport, most people generally think of their hometowns or neighborhoods that are similar to many other cities and towns across the country. Each of these municipalities is unique and presents its own challenges in recreational sport management, but there are several other types of communities that present even more differences. These nontypical communities are places where people live in unique circumstances compared with the average family. Nontypical communities include military bases all over the world, college and university campuses, and senior communities.

Military MWR Programs

U.S. military bases throughout the world house **Morale, Welfare, and Recreation (MWR)** programs to enrich the lives of soldiers and their families (U.S. Army, 2010). These programs can be found on bases within the United States, in foreign countries, and even on aircraft carriers (Miller, 2003). Military bases are nontypical environments for a wide variety of reasons. For all bases, there is a concern about deployment for both the soldiers and the families they leave behind. In bases on foreign soil, there is an added element of isolation from the outside community or distance from home, and this sense of isolation can be further compounded when serving on an aircraft carrier in the middle of an ocean. MWR programs are used by soldiers and their families who are dealing with some serious challenges in addition to the everyday problems of a normal life. As a result, these programs can provide some unique benefits, and recreational sport professionals working in these programs must overcome some unique challenges (U.S. Army, 2010).

Benefits of Community Recreational Sport

MWR programs were created for soldiers and their families under the belief that recreational sport is an essential service. Specifically, MWR supports combat readiness and effectiveness, supports recruitment and retention of qualified personnel, supports quality of life, promotes and maintains mental and physical well-being, fosters community pride and morale for soldiers and their families, and eases the impact of military life (U.S. Army, 2010).

Addressing the Unique Challenges

The challenges involved in providing quality MWR programs are partially the result of the environment on a military base and partially a result of the location of the base itself. In terms of the general environment on a base, MWR participants are somewhat transitory. This means that throughout a recreational sport program, participants may change as some personnel are relocated and others are deployed or return from deployment. MWR professionals need to be flexible to ensure that military personnel and their families are able to use their service regardless of when they are able to enter or exit a particular program. This could mean providing more single events than long-term programs or rotating rosters of participants.

MWR professionals also need to be aware of issues related to deployment. This involves both the needs of family members of deployed soldiers and the needs of soldiers who have returned from deployment. For family members, it is important to understand that they are dealing with the lack of a parent or spouse in addition to the very real fear that their loved one might not be coming back. Adapting programs to address these needs provides a vital service to improve their health and well-being. Soldiers returning from deployment may face a variety of issues ranging from post-traumatic stress disorder (PTSD) to physical impairment as the result of combat. Professionals should be cognizant of these issues and when possible work with doctors to ensure the soldiers' needs and abilities are being met.

Finally, the location of the base can affect what recreational sport programs and events are offered. Bases located in the United States may have fewer limitations than those that are overseas or on an aircraft carrier, for example. Programs should be adapted whenever possible to ensure they fit their location. In all cases, MWR professionals need to be flexible and work with base leaders to understand what services can be provided and how best to do so.

Campus Recreation

Another type of nontypical community that has recreational sport services is found on the campuses of colleges and universities. The population tends to be student oriented, and many of these students are 18- to 22-year-olds living away from home for the first time. The focus is more on young single adults without children or many outside responsibilities rather than on a family atmosphere. Although some students may be older than this age group or may have families, this is not the norm for most college or university settings. The priorities for most students tend to be school, jobs, and the college or university community in which they live. In the following section, we discuss the benefits and challenges of campus recreation; see chapter 13 for more information about this nontypical community.

Benefits of Community Recreational Sport

Campus recreation programs provide significant and unique benefits to college and university communities (Forrester, Arterberry, & Barcelona, 2006). Most schools hope to attract and retain students, and research suggests that campus recreation is one of the primary attractions for students and helps them feel a connection with their school (Becker, Cooper, Atkins, & Martin, 2009; Miller, 2011). This sense of connection or bonding leads to an increased likelihood of remaining at school (Hall, 2010). Furthermore, research has shown that academic performance in higher education is related to campus recreation (Belch, Gebel, & Maas, 2001); students who engage in activities such as intramurals are more likely to be successful. All of this means that colleges and universities should have the best campus recreation facilities and programs possible in order to benefit both the school and the individual students (Hall, 2010; Henchy, 2011).

Addressing the Unique Challenges

The benefits of campus recreation are clear, but participation by students is far from guaranteed. Campus recreational professionals have some unique challenges to overcome in order to provide optimal programs to participants, including finances, availability, and marketing.

Financial limitations affect campus recreation in two ways. First and foremost, students tend to have fewer financial resources for engaging in recreational sport. Although a gym membership may be free to students, costs may exist for individual programs along with equipment and supplies. Campus recreation centers need to be aware of students' financial limitations and provide services as inexpensively as possible. However, these centers are also affected by the funds they receive from the institution. Colleges and universities across the United States are currently undergoing budgetary crises related to the economic downturn. Budgets for most departments, including campus recreation services, are being cut, but student expectations typically remain high (Hall, 2010). This means departments are expected to do more with less. Consequently, campus recreation professionals need to be creative in providing services in a cost-effective manner to maintain their bottom line while not passing on too many of their expenses to participants.

Another challenge facing campus recreation professionals relates to availability of programs and facilities. Scheduling athletic facilities can be difficult in this environment. Even though many colleges and universities have state-of-the-art facilities, a number of groups can lay claim to access, including intercollegiate athletic teams, club sports, classes, intramurals, and drop-in sport opportunities. Furthermore, because most participants share similar schedules, they typically desire these resources at similar times. Campus recreation professionals need to work with representatives of each group when scheduling facilities and programs to ensure that needs are filled according to priority and demand while also making sure that all groups are at least somewhat satisfied with the outcome.

Finally, marketing presents a challenge for campus recreational professionals. Although it seems as if a college or university campus presents a captive audience of participants, many students decline to participate in campus recreation services. Professionals need to determine which students are not participating, why they aren't participating, and how to target those markets (Cooper, Schuett, & Phillips, 2012). This may involve creating innovative programs, adapting the marketing used or the message presented, or making sure these students understand the benefits of participation. No matter what solution is chosen, however, encouraging greater participation is good for the students, the campus recreation department, and the school as a whole.

Senior Communities

As the U.S. population ages, there is a trend of seniors moving together into communities for either active lifestyles or for progressive levels of care ranging from full independence to long-term care or hospitalization. In some ways, recreational sport opportunities resemble campus recreation programs. The participants are at a point in their lives where they have fewer outside responsibilities because they are at or near the age of retirement and their children are independent. However, many seniors remain insufficiently active (Bergman, Bassett, & Klein, 2008). Therefore, a variety of health concerns can create a unique environment that needs to be addressed.

Benefits of Community Recreational Sport

Community recreational sport participation presents a range of benefits to seniors. Many of these were presented in chapter 2 of this text, including the several physical health benefits, cognitive benefits, and psychosocial improvements that can result from physical activity. Together, these benefits mean that recreational sport could be crucial to senior living communities. Unfortunately, although recreational sport programs are becoming more common, not every senior living community has made it a priority.

Addressing the Unique Challenges

Perhaps the main reason senior living communities do not emphasize recreational sport participation is because of the many challenges involved in doing so. Among these challenges are financial concerns, health problems, and lack of available facilities. Related to each of these is the wide range of ages and abilities in these communities. Residents could be anywhere from early retirement age and physically fit with few health concerns to upper ages and physically dependent on outside care. This makes it difficult for recreational sport professionals to plan programs, but it is a difficulty that can be overcome.

Finances are a real concern in senior living communities. Many seniors have restricted financial resources and have limited funds to spend on extraneous activities. For this reason professionals should try to provide recreational sport programs, equipment, and supplies at little to no cost for participants.

Finances definitely influence participation, but of greater concern are the health issues of this population. Although recreational sport participation provides significant health benefits, the reality is that health problems can limit, prevent, or present the need for adaptations in recreational sport participation. Recreational sport professionals working in senior living communities should know the limitations of their participants in terms of cardiorespiratory ability, flexibility, balance, and cognitive functioning to ensure that

Monkey Business/fotolia.com

Recreational sport can be an important component of healthy senior communities.

participants can remain active in their programs. For example, knowing that Teddy is experiencing balance problems allows a professional to adapt her program in order to improve Teddy's balance while not placing him at risk for a fall, which could break his hip, leading to more serious health consequences.

A final concern when providing recreational sport to senior communities is the availability of facilities. Some of this is related to a long-standing model in the medical field of providing services to recover from injury and illness rather than focusing on prevention. Consequently, organizations may focus more on providing physical therapy facilities over recreational sport facilities, leaving residents with little physical activity available other than walking the halls. Recreational sport professionals in these environments should take initiative to become involved in the design process when new facilities are being created or old ones are being updated. This would provide an opportunity to present the benefits of providing gym space, tennis courts, weight rooms, trails, and other sport areas where participants can engage in lifelong fitness and recreational sport.

It is clear that in each of these nontraditional communities, recreational sport opportunities are a crucial service to residents. Recreational sport professionals in these environments should be cognizant of how best to approach the challenges in these environments in order to produce the best experiences.

COMMUNITY RECREATIONAL SPORT FOR PEOPLE WITH DISABILITIES

One final population group that has unique benefits and challenges when it comes to community recreational sport is people with disabilities. This is not a population that is isolated from others; instead, people with disabilities should have access to recreational sport programs in all communities. Consequently, all recreational sport professionals should be aware of the benefits of participation for these individuals as well as how to address the unique programming challenges they may present.

Benefits of Community Recreational Sport

The benefits of recreational sport participation for people with disabilities are quite similar to the benefits received by all people. These include many of the physical, psychosocial, and cognitive benefits of physical activity mentioned in chapter 2. In addition, benefits from participation might include a reduction of secondary health conditions and the opportunity to develop an identity outside of the person's disability. Because a disability is prevalent in the person's life, she might begin to see it as a core part of who she is. Developing an athletic identity may contribute to a greater sense of confidence and competence that will promote healthier long-term development (Piatt & Wells, 2012).

Addressing the Unique Challenges

Although the ADA (Americans with Disabilities Act) ensures that all services should be available to people with disabilities, it does so with the caveat of reasonable accommodations. This means that community recreational sport organizations should do their best to provide services whenever possible, but it is not always required. For example, if one teenage girl who uses a wheelchair wants to play rugby, it is not necessary to convert a preexisting rugby league to a wheelchair rugby league. However, if a few people who use wheelchairs wish to reserve a court to play a rugby game, they should be allowed to do so using the same court reservation system that others use.

Community recreational sport professionals can make several adaptations to ensure that they are serving people with disabilities who wish to participate in their programs. To begin, when it comes to building and updating facilities, universal design methods should be used. This will allow, for example, people who use wheelchairs to access trails and courts without changing the nature of the activities themselves. Also keep in mind when filling facilities that all individuals should have access. This may mean spacing weight equipment farther apart so a wheelchair can get through or providing railings between a locker room and a pool so that people who are blind can easily go for a swim. Finally, all personnel within these organizations should receive training on how best to approach situations where adaptations are required so that no one feels intentionally excluded from participation (Piatt & Wells, 2012).

CONCLUSION

This chapter has presented information that should assist recreational sport professionals working in any community environment. These services are important for many reasons and result in strengthened communities, healthier participants, and positive economic effects. Professionals should also have a good sense of what opportunities are available for providing services to typical communities as well as nontypical communities such as military MWR programs, campus recreation services, and senior communities programs. Finally, community recreational sport offers benefits for people with disabilities, and it is important to allow all individuals to participate in programs. Overall, this information should help recreational sport professionals as they design, market, and implement their services in whichever community they serve.

RESEARCH TO REALITY

Cela, A., Kowalski, C., & Lankford, S. (2006). Spectators' characteristics and economic impact of local sports events: A case study of Cedar Valley Moonlight Classic soccer tournament. *World Leisure Journal, 48*(3), 45-53.

Because there is a trend toward focusing community development on sport tourism and much of the current sport tourism research is on large-scale sporting events, Cela and colleagues studied the economic impact of a smaller, localized soccer tournament on a community. Researchers distributed a questionnaire to 116 spectators at the tournament with questions on topics such as the spectators' residence, primary reason for the trip, accommodations, spending patterns, and demographic information.

Results from the study demonstrated a significant economic impact of approximately $137,000 to the community. This was based on the average spending of $286.56 within the city itself and was comparable to money spent by visitors who came to the area for other reasons. Although the results of this study are not necessarily generalizable to other communities, they do present evidence that small-scale sport tournaments can have a positive effect on a community. Other cities hoping to support sport tournaments in their own communities should be encouraged by these results and collect data to provide further evidence for the benefits of such events. This information supports bringing recreational sport tournaments to a community as an opportunity for economic development. Future recreational sport professionals could use this information to support bringing tournaments to their own facilities.

REFLECTION QUESTIONS

1. Describe the relationship between recreational sport and a community. What impact can a community have on sport, and what impact can recreational sport have on a community?
2. What are the benefits of large-scale recreational sporting events in a community in comparison to small-scale events?
3. What are some benefits of recreational sport in nontypical communities such as military bases, college and university campuses, and senior communities? How would you program to ensure these benefits in these unique environments?

LEARNING ACTIVITIES

1. As the president of your local swim club, you want to host a weekend swim meet at the community pool and need approval from the city council in order to do so. You have already completed the necessary paperwork for your application and just need to present your proposal at the next city council meeting. Write the speech you will make to the council members, including all the potential benefits of the meet to the community along with how your organization will attempt to maximize the positive and minimize the negative impacts of such an event.
2. You have just been hired as a recreational sport coordinator in a nontypical community and you've been asked to complete a project priority list. For one of the three types of communities mentioned in the chapter (military MWR, campus recreation, or senior communities), develop a list of your top 10 priorities for programs or events. For each of these programs or events, make sure you provide justification for its placement and rank on the list.

chapter 12

RECREATIONAL YOUTH SPORT

LEARNING OUTCOMES

By the end of the chapter, readers will be able to

- describe the current environment in recreational youth sport,
- differentiate between the needs of youth and adults,
- explain the potential positive impact of others on the recreational youth sport experience,
- describe how to change the recreational youth sport experience in a positive manner, and
- describe what opportunities are available for future careers in recreational youth sport.

Case Study

IMPROVING A RECREATIONAL YOUTH SPORT PROGRAM

Judge and Beth have been working as recreational youth sport coordinators at their local park and recreation center for the past five years. Each year their basketball league has become increasingly problematic. Although they rarely have problems with the children in the youngest age group, the older players have become more challenging in terms of behavioral issues, and parents of all age groups have had to be escorted out of multiple games because of their behavior toward the referees. Because of the increasing risk the program presents both in terms of liability to the organization and the well-being of the participants, Judge and Beth decide they either need to cut the program or revamp it. They choose the latter and start researching ways to develop a better youth basketball program. Then they use the information they gathered to change their program to better fit the wants and needs of the players. They do this by improving the structure of the program along with focusing many of the environmental elements on developing sportsmanship and teamwork.

As the first season of the redesigned program begins, there is some initial resistance from parents who are used to the status quo. However, as the season progresses, the parents start to realize that their children are having more fun. More importantly, Judge and Beth notice that they are dealing with fewer overall complaints. Whereas last season they had several calls a day from parents who were upset about one issue or another, now it is a rare week when they get more than one or two phone calls total. At the end of the season, no parents have been kicked out of a game, and both the players and parents rate it as a better season than the year before. The next season there is even an increase in the number of registrations because others have heard of this unique program and want to be involved. Judge and Beth realize that because they were willing to look at their recreational youth sport program a little differently, they were able to design something that better suited their young athletes, and as a result a program that was almost eliminated is instead thriving.

The picture of recreational youth sport today is different than it used to be. It has gone from an unorganized activity done with minimal supervision in local neighborhoods to a highly structured and financed business in many areas. Rather than playing in neighborhoods, many young athletes are traveling hundreds of miles each weekend to compete against other specialized teams before they are even 10 years old. With these changes in program structure come questions regarding program quality. Although many programs provide excellent opportunities for children's growth, development, and athletic achievement, this is not always the case.

The case study at the beginning of the chapter is one that is all too common in recreational youth sport. More and more programs are on the verge of being cut because of parents or coaches who are out of control. In other situations, young athletes are burning out or suffering career-ending injuries before they have even finished high school. This chapter addresses many of the issues surrounding recreational youth sport. It begins with a description of the current recreational youth sport environment, including the status of recreational youth sport today along with the many of the benefits. This leads into a description of the unique nature of young people and how sport programs need to adapt to their needs. Finally, techniques are suggested for designing recreational youth sport programs to better serve young athletes.

RECREATIONAL YOUTH SPORT EXPERIENCE

The changing structure and dynamic of recreational youth sport means that young athletes engage in a far different experience than before. It is important for recreational youth sport professionals to be aware of exactly what participants are experiencing in order to provide optimal programs. This includes an understanding of children's participation and the benefits they receive from these programs.

Youth Sport Participation

Youth have been participating in sport since long before people kept track of youth sport statistics. That participation has changed significantly both in terms of who is participating and what they are doing. Since 1972 and the introduction of Title IX, for example, far more girls have been involved in youth sport. Between the years of 1972 and 1978 alone the numbers increased by 25 percent, and since then the numbers have continued to grow even more (Stevenson, 2007). Furthermore, the types of sports have changed as well. A number of new sports have become more popular including kayaking, yoga, paddleboarding, snowboarding, and rock climbing.. In addition, the style of participation is vastly different than it was even 20 years ago. Today, leagues tend to be far more structured and there is more pressure on children to choose one or two sports at an early age rather than participate in many. All this describes a youth sport environment that is continuing to grow and change. This section will discuss why young people participate in sport and how to keep them involved.

Reasons Youth Participate in Sport

More than 44 million youth participate in sport each year (National Council of Youth Sports, 2008) and the easiest way to find out why is to ask them. The vast majority of young athletes say they take part in a sport program for one of five reasons: to have fun, to have something they are good at, to stay in shape, to learn or improve new skills, and to be part of a team (Hedstrom & Gould, 2004). Children like to enjoy themselves and sport provides an excellent avenue for fun. They also have a need to feel they are good at something, and they like learning new things in order to do this. Sport is an excellent opportunity for them to learn new skills and then to show them off to parents and friends during practices or games. A connection to others is crucial to the development of young people. The team atmosphere of most sports allows children to gain the sense that they belong to something. Finally, because all sports involve some element of physical activity, athletes have the potential to gain physical fitness in a way that more passive activities do not allow.

Although each of these reasons is important, it is essential to also note what the young athletes did not say—winning was not in the top five reasons they play sports. Although many of us perceive winning to be fun, most children do not see winning as a priority in playing.

Becoming Lifelong Participants in Sport

Participation rates in youth sport are high; however, one troubling fact is that the dropout rate is also high. Some research has suggested that nearly 70 percent of all young athletes stop participation in a sport before the age of 13 (Engh, 2002). Other studies suggest that approximately 95 percent drop out of at least one sport before the 10th grade (Butcher, Lindner, & Johns, 2002) and dropout rates increase between 7th and 10th grades (Butcher et al.; Seefeldt & Ewing, 1996).

Perhaps the best way to prevent young people from dropping out of sport and to help them become lifelong participants is to understand why they stop. Many children reduce their participation in sport because of negative experiences such as being yelled at or insulted by coaches and spectators in games (Engh, 2002). Other young athletes feel they lack competence and are unable to perform well. Whether or not these athletes are actually competent is less relevant than how they feel; even if a child is an excellent athlete, if she feels that she is not any good, she is more likely to start devaluing the activity to compensate for her poor self-esteem and then quit (Rodriguez, Wigfield, & Eccles, 2003). Finally, one of the most important reasons children stop participating in sport is because they no longer find it fun. This could be because of any number of reasons, including the fact that they are not playing enough (Mandigo & Couture, 1996), they do not feel they have enough say in what they do in the sport (Mandigo & Couture, 1996), or the internal rewards such as excitement are replaced with external ones such as trophies or ribbons (Scanlan, Russell, Beals, & Scanlan, 2003).

Benefits of Sport Participation

As recreational sport professionals, it is easy to feel that sport is an important experience for children and that it is our responsibility to keep them interested and involved. What might be less clear are the specific benefits that can be gained as a result of participation. A common conception is that sport participation is good for children. Contrary to popular belief, however, recreational youth sport does not inherently build character. Although this idea is highly touted by many people who promote sporting events and agencies, it simply is not true. First, the term *character* is vague, making it difficult to measure and ensure that it is improving. Second, and perhaps more important, recreational youth sport in itself is not inherently good or bad. Rolling a ball onto a field and telling a 10-year-old to kick it into a goal does not automatically lead to increased positive qualities in that 10-year-old. Instead, it is through quality recreational youth sport programming that children can benefit from sport participation. These benefits may occur in four areas: physical, cognitive, psychosocial, and moral.

Physical Benefits

Several health benefits are related to participation in recreational youth sport, including a reduced risk of future chronic illness, improved body composition, healthier cardiovascular and immune systems, and a stronger musculoskeletal system (Storm & Jenkins, 2002). Children who are more physically active tend to be healthier in general; however, there comes a point when too much physical activity can actually be harmful. The recent trend of early specialization has young athletes training in a single sport throughout the year. This has led to an increase in overuse injuries in young people, which are particularly damaging in bodies that are still developing (Stricker, 2006; Tye, 2001). Therefore, it is important to remember that although sport can provide positive benefits to physical health, too much sport can do more harm than good.

Cognitive Benefits

Children may also receive certain cognitive benefits as the result of recreational youth sport participation. In particular, less structured sports

© Mary Sara Wells

Youth sport has the potential to lead to numerous physical, cognitive, psychosocial, and moral benefits.

such as those played during free time with friends and without adult intervention may improve creativity due to their unorganized nature (Coakley, 2004). This provides children with opportunities to develop their own strategies while adapting to continually changing situations. Unorganized sports have also been linked to chances for youth to demonstrate cooperation, organization, negotiation, problem solving, flexibility, planning, and improvisation. As an added benefit, when young athletes practice and develop these skills in an environment with few severe long-term consequences, such as through unorganized sport, they are then able to engage in them in more crucial environments such as the classroom.

Psychosocial Benefits

One of the primary ways youth benefit psychosocially from sport participation is through identity development (Barber, Eccles, & Stone, 2001). **Identity development** is one of the important developmental milestones for youth in general and adolescents in particular, and many elements of sport can contribute to this process. Athletic performance frequently provides a clear context for self-evaluation of abilities and competence that is necessary for identity development (Coatsworth & Conroy, 2009). Other ways sport can promote identity development include the social interaction involved and the nature of sport as a freely chosen and popular activity. The social interaction that occurs with teammates and with coaches and other adults can provide the crucial supportive relationships and social belonging that lead to the formation of a healthy identity. Furthermore, because sport is typically an activity that is chosen rather than compulsory (e.g., school), athletic performances are usually a place where youth are freer to explore and express their chosen identities (Eccles, Barber, Stone, & Hunt, 2003). The fact that sport is a popular activity in most school settings and in society as a whole also promotes identity development as many adolescents seek to identify with popular groups (Crain, 2000).

Another aspect of psychosocial development that might be influenced by sport participation is interpersonal skills. In recreational youth sport, athletes have the opportunity to learn how to interact with both children and adults in a variety of relationships (Martens, 1993). Youth have peers who are teammates and opponents and can engage with adults who are coaches, officials, parents of teammates, and even other spectators. In each of these engagements children are learning how to interact appropriately and play their role in such interactions. In addition, sport serves the crucial function of introducing children to each other so that friendships can develop. Considering that sport is one of the most common activities for young people, it becomes clear that certain aspects of recreational youth sport can have a significant impact on friendship patterns with peers (Weiss & Smith, 2002). As children age and peers start to have a greater influence on development, this may lead to greater significance of the relationships developed through sport.

Moral Benefits

Many parents who register their children for sport express a desire for them to learn **sportsmanship**. Although there is potential to learn sportsmanship and other moral behaviors through a sport experience, it is by no means guaranteed, and in fact moral benefits have a controversial relationship with sport. Some research has suggested that children are exposed to mixed moral messages in recreational youth sport and this confusion can limit moral development (Eitzen, 2003). The behaviors observed by the young athletes can have a particular impact on whether they engage in more prosocial or moral behaviors. Coaches especially have been shown to influence the sportsmanship of their players (Wells, Ellis, Arthur-Banning, & Roark, 2006).

NEEDS OF YOUNG ATHLETES

Achieving the benefits of participation requires meeting the unique needs of young athletes. This means recreational youth sport professionals should understand the young athletes themselves. Physical, cognitive, and psychological development are still occurring at a rapid rate for these young athletes, and good professionals will understand these changes and adapt their programs to best serve their participants' needs.

Differences Between Youth and Adults

One of the most important things to remember when working in recreational youth sport programs is that young people are not just miniature adults. Children are still growing and developing in all areas. Because of this, it is necessary to understand where children are developmentally in order to match programs to their needs (see table 12.1). Running adult programs for children does not do anyone any good. Coaches who ask too much of their young athletes get frustrated because the athletes are not doing things correctly, and the athletes who want to please their coaches get frustrated because they cannot do what is asked of them. In the end, it is a negative experience for everyone involved. Children need the chance to grow into their activities, including sport. For example, in the education system, first graders do not do long division because their brains are not ready for it, and young athletes should not be asked to do things in sport before they are developmentally ready, either.

Part of the problem in recreational youth sport is that coaches and others who work with children are volunteers who typically have knowledge about the sport being taught rather than a solid expertise in child development. Being able to provide this information about child development is crucial to the success of recreational youth sport programs and the positive experiences of the youth involved.

The three prime areas where youth are still developing that might affect their ability to learn in sport are physiological, cognitive, and psychological. The following sections discuss each of these areas. It is important to note that development is most often discussed in terms of the average child. There will always be some children who develop more quickly and some who develop more slowly, but it is easiest to program for where the average young athlete will be in the developmental process.

Physiological Development

Every sport requires some sort of physical skill and movement. Many of these seem so natural to adults that they are done without thinking. However, they are not completely natural. Standing up, walking, jumping, tracking the motion of an object—at some point in everyone's lives these were all skills and movements that were learned. Furthermore, they were all learned at differing points along the developmental continuum. Consequently, where children are in their **physiological development** will have a significant impact on how they perform in every sport. Although it is important to push all athletes to develop their skills, trying to push them beyond their developmental level is likely to do much more harm than good. Going back to the academic example, it is completely unreasonable to ask a child to write an article for a scientific journal if she does not yet know how to read. She has to have the capacity and basic skill sets before she can go on to advanced levels. Similarly, it is unreasonable to ask a child to dribble a basketball into a layup without traveling if she is still struggling with her basic balance.

Among the first physical movements children learn are the gross motor skills such as running, jumping, throwing, and catching. Recreational youth sport professionals may assume that the 5-year-olds they are working with are fully capable of performing these skills without question, but the reality is that many children at this age have to actively focus on maintaining their balance, and less than one-third of all 2- to 5-year-olds can throw and catch a ball effectively (Stricker, 2006). The implications of this are fairly evident. If the young athlete is having trouble staying upright while running, trying to kick a ball on top

TABLE 12.1 Developmental Concerns in Youth Sport

	Types of Development		
	Physiological	Cognitive	Psychological
Developmental concerns	Gross motor skills Balance Visual skills Fine motor skills Strength Aerobic capacity Flexibility Heat tolerance	Attention span Abstract thought Learning style	Self-concept Self-confidence Stress management

of that can become frustrating, especially if the ball is in motion before it is kicked and if it has to be kicked directly to another player who is also moving. This is one of the reasons why beehive soccer works so well for young children. Although overenthusiastic parents and coaches may try to get their players to break out of the beehive and pass the ball to teammates to score, the reality is that within the beehive, children are able to practice kicking the ball on their level.

Related to gross motor skills is balance. Children and youth continue to have issues with balance throughout their development because balance is a skill that is related to multiple developmental factors. First, balance is related to the inner ear, which is not fully developed in young children and relates to their difficulty standing and running. After the inner ear has fully developed, however, many youth will continue to have balance issues because of changes in their center of gravity (Stricker, 2006). Minor changes in height can result in a period of adjustment while a child is attempting to adjust to his new body. This means that growth spurts of many inches in a year can have significant effects on a young athlete's ability to remain upright. Though most sports involve some element of balance, some rely on it more than others, such as hockey, cycling, and gymnastics. For this reason, growing athletes may need a period of adjustment for their performance at various times throughout their careers to account for developmental changes.

Visual skills are also highly important for sport performance and vary according to developmental stage. In particular, it is difficult for children to appropriately track objects until the optical center of the brain is fully developed (Stricker, 2006). This is one of the reasons tee ball is a developmentally appropriate step in playing baseball. Children who play tee ball generally have not developed the ability to follow a baseball as it is coming through the air and to make accurate judgments regarding when and where it will arrive in relationship to where they should swing the bat. Consequently, having the ball remain stationary as the child is learning the correct swinging technique enables the child to improve her skills while minimizing frustration. Other sports could follow similar patterns. For example, in hockey young children should be taught first to hit a stationary puck, then how to handle the puck themselves, then to receive a pass, and finally to hit a puck that has been passed to them. Even leaders of sports that may not normally be associated with tracking ability should consider this developmental issue. Swimming,

Tee ball provides an opportunity for young children to learn proper swing techniques that are appropriate to their physical development.

for example, uses flip turns, which require the ability to judge distance from the wall in relation to speed of the approach.

Other physiological development concerns to be aware of in recreational youth sport include fine motor skills, strength, aerobic capacity, flexibility, and heat tolerance. Fine motor skills typically develop after gross motor skills and become more automatic after the preteen years (Stricker, 2006). This means that introducing complex actions will be difficult up to this point. Instead, it is beneficial for the young athletes to learn complex actions in stages so that they become familiar with one element to the point of doing it automatically before the next part of the skill is introduced. For example, when learning the breaststroke in swimming, a young athlete might learn the kick first, followed by learning the arms. Once both movements were automatic, the athlete would work on doing them at the same time.

Both strength and aerobic capacity tend to develop later in children (Stricker, 2006). In both cases, it is good for young athletes to have a solid base, but coaches and parents should not expect too much change before puberty. For the most part, training children in either area before they have developed the capacity will lead to minimal improvements, and adults should not become concerned if training is not yielding the results they expect. In this case, more training is not the answer. Instead, it is appropriate to maintain a base so that when the child is physiologically ready she can train to improve.

Flexibility is similar to balance in that it changes throughout a person's life. In this case, however, many of its changes are related to hormone levels. Certain hormone outputs lead adolescents to suddenly become more flexible, and this is not necessarily a good thing (Stricker, 2006). Whether athletes demonstrate too much or too little flexibility, care must be taken to prevent injury.

Finally, heat tolerance should be a consideration when working with young athletes. Although it is obviously a concern for outdoor sport, particularly in the summer, any athlete can become overheated no matter what the season. When it comes to heat tolerance, children are different from adults. They tend to become hotter faster, and their bodies have not developed an efficient sweating system yet so they cannot cool themselves off as easily. Furthermore, they are less likely to ask for a water break both because the thirst drive has not fully developed and because most children do not like to stop having fun just to take a drink (Stricker, 2006). All this creates a dangerous combination in which children are more likely to overheat than adults. Recreational youth sport professionals and parents should make sure that adequate breaks are in place to give young athletes an opportunity to regularly cool off before overheating becomes a concern.

Cognitive Development

Sport takes not only physical skills but cognitive ones as well, and children are different from adults in terms of their **cognitive development**. The brain generally continues to develop into a person's 20s (Keating, 2004). This means that a young person's athletic abilities will also continue to develop throughout this time. A 5-year-old has a different cognitive skill set than a 15-year-old, so it would be unreasonable to think that the same techniques would work for both. In order to improve the quality of recreational youth sport programs and meet young athletes at their developmental level, it is necessary to understand what differences exist between younger and older children and adapt what is required of them accordingly.

The development of three cognitive skills in particular are likely to affect sport performance: attention span, abstract thought, and learning style. One of the most notable cognitive differences between children and adults is the average attention span. Most people who have worked with children at some point realize that they can maintain focus for only short amounts of time and are easily distracted (Stricker, 2006). This is not necessarily because they are not enjoying themselves or are uninterested in what the coach has to say; it is simply a result of where their brains are developmentally. Having the most enthusiastic discussion about a fun topic like sport is not going to change that no matter how hard you try. When developing recreational youth sport programs, it is important to take this into account. Keep in mind that in general, the younger the child, the shorter the attention span. According to the age of the athletes, instruction should therefore take place where there is minimal outside distraction and instructional topics should change frequently.

Another cognitive skill critical to sport performance is the ability to use abstract thought. No matter what the sport, athletes improve their performance by automatically going through hypothetical situations in their minds and developing solutions. Until a certain point, however, children are unable to do this because their brains have not yet developed the capacity. Instead, concrete thought dominates their thinking (Stricker, 2006). This is why many youth basketball leagues have developed a system where all the children on a team wear different-colored wristbands. To determine whom they are guarding, all they have to do is look for the person on the other team wearing the same color of wristband.

Man-to-man coverage makes sense for the youngest athletes. Frequently, however, an overly enthusiastic coach will decide to implement zone coverage to improve his team's competitive advantage. Almost without fail, the players on the team nod and smile as the coach explains what to do. Then they go out on the court and either wander around confused or revert back to the man-to-man coverage that makes sense to them. The coach then gets frustrated that the players are not doing what he told them to, and the players get frustrated that the coach is yelling at them and they do not know how to fix what they are doing wrong. The problem is not that the young athletes do not care or that they are ignoring their coach; the problem is that the instructions they were given are beyond where their brains have developed.

A third cognitive development issue that is related to the ability to think abstractly and that might affect sport performance is learning style. Although learning style varies significantly from person to person throughout life, there are certain stages when one type of learning style is more prevalent than others. For example, young children tend to learn better physically (Stricker, 2006). This means that sport instruction should take the child through the physical motions as she is being told what to do. Feeling the process will last longer in her memory than listening to the instructions, partially because it is easier for her to understand concrete movements as opposed to abstract verbal instruction. As young athletes grow older, they are more capable of learning visually by seeing the proper technique and then finally by listening to simple verbal instruction.

Psychological Development

Youth also differ from adults in terms of their **psychological development**, and these differences should be accounted for by recreational youth sport professionals. Perhaps the most important psychological difference between children and adults relates to their self-concept or self-confidence. **Self-concept** refers to the overall beliefs people hold about themselves in terms of worth. This is often displayed through their **self-confidence**, or their belief in their general ability to perform.

To develop their sense of self, children usually compare their skills with those of others and interpret the reactions of those around them. In doing this, they tend to give preference to what people do over what they say—in other words, actions speak louder than words (Stricker, 2006). Consequently, a coach acting out frustrations when a child misses a goal will lead the child to feel as though the coach is disappointed in him. Because self-concept and self-confidence are still developing at this point, they tend to be more fragile. For this reason, it is important that young athletes are not placed into intense win-or-lose scenarios until they know that their own worth is not based on the outcome. Although competition is important for children in helping them to grow both as athletes and individuals, the athlete should not feel as if losing a competition means that she has no worth as a person. It might be easy for the adult to see that this is the case, but it is more difficult for a child whose self-concept is still fragile. All recreational youth sport programs, especially those designed for younger age groups, should be implemented with this in mind.

Another psychological concern that is related to self-concept and self-confidence, and one that is becoming increasingly common in recreational youth sport, is the need to manage stress. As pressures and expectations have increased for young athletes, so have the levels of stress they undergo in sport. Unfortunately, in many cases children are not developmentally ready to handle the higher stress load and it can become overwhelming (Stricker, 2006), leading to poor performance in the short term and eventually to burnout. Although an adult may be able to withstand the pressure of a win-or-lose penalty kick at the end of the game, and in some cases such pressure may actually improve performance, these situations may simply be too advanced for a child's current skill sets. Placing them in that environment then becomes detrimental not just to the outcome of the game but to the child's overall psychological health as well.

How to Adapt Recreational Youth Sport

Clearly, the expectations of young athletes and the environments in which they play should be different from those of adults. Although many sport purists will argue that children should experience any sport the way it was meant to be played, with a little creativity sport can be adapted to create better experiences for youth while still maintaining the integrity of the game. Among these are changes to the social interactions, physical setting, and equipment of the game.

Social Interaction

One of the most important elements of sport for youth is social interaction. This interaction is not only critical to healthy development, it is also one of the primary reasons they play sport to begin with. Recreational youth sport professionals should capitalize on this element in order to maximize enjoyment for their young athletes. To begin, opposing teams should never be treated as enemies. Rivalries are common in professional leagues, college athletics, and to some extent in high schools, but they are not healthy at younger ages. It is difficult for children to understand the difference between dislike in terms of a rivalry and dislike in general. Treating opposing teams as enemies at young ages could lead to psychological damage on both ends.

Instead it is important to begin teaching young participants that they can compete to the best of their ability against opponents and still be friends with them after the game is over. This can be accomplished through the use of introductions before the game or at socials afterward. For example, it is common in recreational youth sport for team parents to organize a system where a parent is responsible for bringing snacks and drinks for the whole team after the game. One league took this concept a step further and decided that to increase social interaction between teams, after each game the home team would have a parent responsible for drinks and the visiting team would have a parent responsible for snacks. This provided a chance for children on both teams to get together after the game was over and enjoy the opportunity to interact socially, which is one of the primary reasons children enjoy sport (Ellis, Henderson, Paisley, Silverberg, & Wells, 2004; Wells et al., 2008; Wells, Paisley, Ellis, & Arthur-Banning, 2005).

Providing opportunities to socialize with players on both teams can help young athletes enjoy their recreational sport experiences more.

Leisure Equipment and Supplies

Equipment and supplies can also be adapted in creative ways to better suit the needs of young athletes. For example, the use of tees in tee ball was previously mentioned as a way to help children who have not yet developed the ability to track objects. Other potential adaptations might relate to the size of the equipment used, such as using larger tennis balls that children can track more easily or smaller footballs to match the children's gripping strength. Finally, adaptations can be made by using the equipment on hand in a slightly different manner. If young people participate in sport because they want to be active and because they genuinely want to play, why not throw an extra ball into a scrimmage? If two balls are going at the same time in a soccer game, more children can be involved in the action at the same time, which means more children are practicing their skills and having fun.

CHANGING THE CURRENT CULTURE OF RECREATIONAL YOUTH SPORT

It would be easy to assume that the current nature of recreational youth sport needs to be accepted, and to some extent this is true. There are certain trends in recreational youth sport that are not going away, such as an increase in professionalism. It is still the responsibility of recreational youth sport professionals, however, to design and implement the best programs possible for youth. Sometimes all it takes are minor changes to the environment or training for the coaches and parents to show them why things are a little different in your program.

Changing the culture of recreational youth sport to better serve young people should involve focusing on what is best for the athletes in terms of their physical, cognitive, and psychological needs. Many programs do this naturally, but creative elements can also be added to already successful programs in order to make them even better. This means taking a look at the developmental stage of participants and adapting to those needs. The next few sections discuss specific methods that other programs have successfully employed to change the environment and work with administrators, officials, coaches, and parents to create the best experiences possible.

Ideas for Changing the Environment

Perhaps the most important idea for changing the recreational youth sport environment is to make the mission of the organization clear to all those who are involved in the recreational youth sport experience. Most administrators, parents, and children agree on the reasons for children becoming involved in sport. They include reasons such as spending time with their friends, learning new skills and sportsmanship, being physically active, and having fun. Problems arise, however, during games when people forget those reasons and start to focus on other priorities such as winning. Recreational youth sport professionals need to remind those involved about what is important, and they can do this by making the mission statement of the league clear in multiple ways throughout the season. They should make sure it is on registration forms and in all promotional materials, and they could place posters and signs around the entrances to the court or field and maybe even on the sidelines themselves. Finally, when dealing with immediate problems it could be useful to have business cards printed to distribute to spectators, coaches, or other offending individuals that reemphasize the mission and goals of the program. This will help spectators remember the purpose of the league and hopefully will influence their behavior in a positive direction (Ellis et al., 2004; Wells et al., 2005; Wells et al., 2008).

Ideas for Administrators

Administrators can also make adaptations to increase the fun for players. Current research suggests that children have more fun in close games (Wells et al., 2005). When a child is by himself hitting balls, he usually imagines that it is the bottom of the ninth, his team is down by 3 with a 3–2 count, and he hits a grand slam to win the game. He is not pretending that it is the bottom of the eighth and his team is already up by 5. Win or lose, close games tend to be more fun. Thus, programs would likely benefit from having teams that are as competitive as possible. This can be difficult when children are young and are still developing skills, but it is possible with creativity. If one team is leading the other by a significant margin during a game, there is no reason not to mix up teams in the middle of the game. This provides an opportunity to create more fun by evening out the score without compromising the skill development of the players. For older participants, it might make sense to institute a system of team selection whereby players are evaluated in a clinic before the season starts and then selected by coaches for teams. Though not a perfect system, it does allow a more level playing field and increases the likelihood that games will be competitive. Finally, there is no reason postseason play has to involve a play-off system with an ultimate winner. Instead, it could be a tournament where the closest teams (i.e., 1 versus 2, 3 versus 4, 5 versus 6, 7 versus 8) play each other in a single game.

Ideas for Officials

Another important but frequently overlooked contributor to the overall environment of a recreational youth sport league is the referee. Referees or umpires are often viewed negatively as enforcers of rules. However, referees can have a positive impact on the game environment when given the authority by recreational youth sport administrators. Leagues have successfully employed referees to enforce positive sportsmanship standards for the entire game environment by giving them control over encouraging and demonstrating positive sportsmanship, such as by encouraging players to help players up on opposing teams during breaks and play within the game itself and by calling sportsmanship infractions on the spectators (Arthur-Banning, Paisley, & Wells, 2007; Wells et al., 2008). These referees are involved not just in enforcing and encouraging sportsmanship expectations but also in correcting skills, thereby contributing to the overall positive environment of the program. For example, if a child double dribbled, the referee would call it, but then he would demonstrate what happened and how to correct it, giving the young athlete the opportunity to demonstrate it as well. This technique is not common, but it is beneficial. Research has shown that using referees in this manner can increase the fun and improve the overall sportsmanship in recreational youth sport.

Ideas for Coaches

For coaches, perhaps the most important thing is to focus on and meet their athletes' stage of development. Providing the best instruction means that it matches where young athletes are physiologically, cognitively, and psychologically. One of the challenges with this is that many recreational youth sport programs rely heavily on volunteer coaches who have more expertise in the sport being played than in the science behind youth development. Well-constructed training programs can assist in getting this information to coaches in an efficient manner. One such training program, the Score Big training program that has been employed in Colorado (Brooks, 2010), does a thorough job of teaching coaches the most effective methods of teaching sport to youth in an effective manner. It provides background information on what children need and the influence that coaches have on their players. In addition, it presents ideas for creating positive environments and for how coaches can have a good experience in the program by reducing their own stresses and pressures. Additional sources can be found from NAYS (www.nays.org) or the Positive Coaching Alliance (PCA; www.positivecoach.org).

Ideas for Parents

Recreational youth sport administrators do not have control over everything parents do or say to their young athletes. However, they can control what parents do in their programs. Parents can use several techniques to improve their children's experiences in recreational youth sport. The first is to evaluate the priorities they are demonstrating to their children. Parents frequently state that the experience their children have in recreational youth sport and the lessons they gain such as teamwork, sportsmanship, and work ethic are far more important than winning. However, the first question they ask after a game is often, "Did you win?" When this is the first question asked, young athletes perceive winning as the most important part of the game. Instead of asking if they won, parents might ask about other important outcomes of recreational youth sport, such as "Did you have fun?", "What did you learn?", "Did you enjoy playing with your teammates?", or "Did you reach any of your goals?" Focusing on these questions before getting to the topic of winning (if at all) will help parents to maintain a proper perspective on the desired outcomes of the program and help their children to not misperceive what their parents believe is important.

Parents can also engage in specific behaviors during the games to demonstrate the positive benefits of sport participation they are seeking for their children. For example, many parents and young athletes state that social opportunities and good sportsmanship are important benefits of recreational youth sport. Interestingly, one way to encourage both is for children to interact with members of the opposing team in a positive manner, and parents can demonstrate this behavior to their children by interacting with the parents of the opposing team. Typically the parents from each team all sit together, but there is no reason why parents from opposing teams cannot intermingle and enjoy the game together. Seeing the parents socializing with each other will likely lead the young athletes to have positive interactions with other players, thereby increasing the likelihood of a positive experience for all involved.

Another behavior that parents can engage in during games to encourage positive sportsmanship is to cheer for the positive aspects of both teams. Obviously parents want to cheer and encourage their own children, but there is no reason why that they cannot cheer when an athlete makes a good play for the other team. Respecting the good play of others does not take away from the children's experience. Rather, it demonstrates to them that playing hard and well along with showing positive sportsmanship are more valued outcomes than winning.

The main way to make each of these changes is through a combination of training and reminders. Parent training programs are available from multiple national organizations such as NAYS (www.nays.org) and PCA (www.positivecoach.org). Regardless of whether these programs are used or if an organization wants to create its own training, all parents should understand what the expectations are for their behavior and why. Although there may be some initial resistance, providing solid research for how this will benefit their child and the sport experience will hopefully make the transition to a new way of thinking easier. After parents understand the reasoning, however, they still need to be reminded. This could be done through the environmental changes mentioned earlier, or it could be the job of an organizational official at each game. An even better solution might be to make the parents police themselves by having a rotating sideline official monitor the sportsmanship behaviors of the spectators and ensure that expectations for behavior are being met by all who are present.

CONCLUSION

This chapter has presented valuable information for recreational sport professionals who design and implement programs for youth. Many aspects of the recreational youth sport experience should be clear, including the reasons youth participate in sport, how they become lifelong participants, and the many physical, cognitive, psychosocial, and moral benefits that can result from quality programs. Recreational youth sport professionals also should now be prepared to address the unique needs of young athletes according to their physiological, cognitive, and psychological development. Furthermore, many specific tools for changing the current culture of recreational youth sport can be implemented for administrators, coaches, and parents. By using the ideas, knowledge, and suggestions provided in this chapter, recreational youth sport professionals should be able to work with youth in way that results in the best experiences possible, thereby creating a lifelong enjoyment and love of sport for these young athletes.

RESEARCH TO REALITY

Wells, M.S., Arthur-Banning, S.G., Paisley, K.P., Ellis, G.D., Roark, M.F., & Fisher, K. (2008). Good (youth) sports: Using benefits-based programming to increase sportsmanship. *Journal of Park and Recreation Administration*, *26*(1), 1-21.

Wells and her colleagues used their knowledge of prosocial behavior theory to create a youth basketball program specifically designed to encourage fun and to increase positive sportsmanship behaviors and decrease negative ones among children, coaches, and spectators. They designed a study with three groups in which the first group had no intervention, the second group employed limited sportsmanship techniques, and the third group used the same sportsmanship techniques along with referees specifically trained to promote sportsmanship among the players, spectators, and coaches. Research assistants then gathered data through observation of all the positive and negative sportsmanship behaviors demonstrated in each game. Fun was also measured at the end of the games with a fun-o-meter where the players got to place a colored marble in a thermometer-type structure.

Results from the program showed that it was successful at improving sportsmanship in a youth basketball league. The lowest levels of positive sportsmanship behaviors and highest levels of negative sportsmanship behaviors were found at the site with no intervention. The highest levels of positive sportsmanship behaviors and lowest levels of negative sportsmanship behaviors were demonstrated by the group who had the sportsmanship techniques plus trained referees, and the third group (sportsmanship techniques only) fell in the middle. These results suggest that recreational youth sport professionals can successfully target sportsmanship outcomes and promote moral development through their programs. To do so, they should intentionally add elements focusing on these areas to their programs.

REFLECTION QUESTIONS

1. Think back to your own recreational youth sport experiences. What were your favorite parts of the programs? How can you make sure you are providing opportunities for athletes in your programs to experience these things?
2. What practical adaptations would you make to your favorite sport to teach children based on their current developmental stage?
3. How should recreational youth sport professionals promote sport opportunities that are less structured?

LEARNING ACTIVITIES

1. Outline a parent and coach training program for a recreational youth sport program at your local community center. This is an opportunity to provide information to parents and coaches on adapting sport programs to the needs of youth. What topics need to be covered in terms of what youth need in a sport program? How would you address these issues with each group (parents and coaches)?
2. Design two promotional fliers or other form of advertisement for a recreational youth sport program. Create one directed toward the athletes themselves and one toward their parents. How do these two fliers differ? What are the implications for how you design and run your program?

chapter 13

CAMPUS RECREATIONAL SPORT

LEARNING OUTCOMES

By the end of the chapter, readers will be able to

- articulate the historical perspective and philosophical orientation of collegiate recreational sport,
- explain the significance of campus recreational sport as a component of the higher-education mission,
- define and differentiate major campus recreational sport facility and program areas, and
- describe the scope of professional development in campus recreation and identify the main career pathways for campus recreational sport professionals.

Case Study

CAMPUS RECREATION MEETS STUDENT HEALTH

Growing enrollments and declining state funding were putting pressure on campus administrators at Edgewood State University to rethink the way student services were delivered. One of the dilemmas facing the student-life staff was what to do about improving student health and wellness. Institutional research studies were showing that fewer than half of Edgewood State students were meeting the Centers for Disease Control and Prevention (CDC) recommendations for moderate and vigorous physical activity, more than one-third had a recent experience with binge drinking, and—perhaps most alarming—almost half regularly experienced more than average levels of stress. Visits to the outdated student medical center for treatment of both physical and emotional health problems were up 150 percent over the past five years, and the strain placed on campus medical staff was becoming a real management issue. It happened that Edgewood State wasn't alone in experiencing these strains; data collected by the American College Health Association (ACHA, 2012) showed similar trends nationally.

Discussions were underway at Edgewood State to improve existing facilities for both campus recreation and student health. Existing plans called for separate facilities for both units. However, during these discussions, a coalition of student-life staff, including the director of campus recreation, dean of students, director of the student health center, and campus coordinator for Healthy Campus 2020 initiatives proposed a new idea—to think about student health and wellness at Edgewood State in a more holistic way. The idea would be to focus on health maintenance and improvement as an illness prevention strategy rather than waiting for students to become sick and seek treatment (Patton, 2009).

The centerpiece of this proposal was the development of a joint campus recreation and student health center that would leverage the resources of both units to help improve student health outcomes. Encouraging student participation in healthy, physically active pursuits through the campus recreation department had long been a priority for Edgewood State. However, the campus recreation program was known mostly as a place to play intramurals, lift weights, and do aerobics. An innovative partnership that would bring together these two formerly separate units would create a win–win scenario for students and staff, dramatically improving the services that could be offered.

For example, by locating the student health center in the campus recreation facility, campus medical professionals would have access to recreation activity spaces, fitness programs, and equipment that they had never had access to before. In addition, the campus recreation department would be able to better meet its mission of offering health-enhancing programs and physical activities for Edgewood State students by working closely with health center staff to better plan programs, facilities, and treatment modalities. They would be able to draw on the expertise of medical and allied health professionals to assist students with nutrition, exercise prescription, and medically supervised weight-loss plans. The new campus recreation center would also be a one-stop shop for student health and wellness, providing a place for active participation in healthy activities, a hub for information about healthy lifestyles including both nutrition and physical activity, a place to connect with fellow students and faculty, and a suitable treatment facility for illnesses. Programs and services offered by the two units could be integrated to a greater or lesser extent, depending on the level of student privacy required. To ensure privacy, students who were visiting the health center as a result of physical or emotional illness would be able to enter the facility through a separate entrance and have access to space dedicated specifically to treatment.

In doing some research on the new idea, the student health and wellness coalition at Edgewood State found that similar models already existed at schools such as South Dakota State University, Macalester College, Bradley University, and the University of Texas at San Antonio (Patton, 2009). As discussions continued, the idea of more closely integrating campus recreation and student health started to emerge. Rather than just creating a plan to share facility space, both saw benefits that would eventually lead to a full administrative merger of the two units. In addition, other campus units saw the potential of holistic thinking about student development. Final plans for the new facility included not only spaces for recreation, fitness, and student health but also dedicated spaces for studying and other forms of academic support. The facility plan that emerged was certainly a far cry from the old sport facility on campus and had the potential to turn around the alarming health trends that were negatively affecting student development.

The chances are good that if you are a college student, you have taken advantage of the recreation opportunities available on your campus. It has been estimated that approximately 8 out of every 10 college students access recreation facilities or participate in the many programs that are offered through campus recreation departments (NIRSA, 2012a). Intramural sport, sport clubs, fitness classes, instructional programs, informal or drop-in recreation, outdoor adventures, special events, and family and youth programs are just some of the many opportunities that are available to students and in many cases to college faculty, staff, families, and the general community as well. Over the past 30 years, many colleges and universities have built showcase indoor and outdoor recreation facilities designed to accommodate physical activity, facilitate social interaction, and promote student learning and development outcomes such as improved retention and graduation rates. At most colleges, campus recreation is now seen as a major contributor to the mission of higher education.

As you read through this chapter, think about the opportunities that are available on your college or university campus. What is their history? When did they become available to a wide variety of students? How many students participate each year? How does student involvement in campus recreation enhance their college experience? Who runs the programs and facilities, and how did these people get their jobs? This chapter will provide answers to some of these questions from a broad perspective. However, use the recreation program on your own campus as a laboratory to explore some of the answers yourself. Talk to the campus recreation director or interview some of the students who participate frequently in campus recreation programs and facilities to try to understand why campus recreational sport is among the most popular student activities. Find out how you can become more involved in your campus recreation program, either as a participant or as a student leader. In the process, you may find that these leadership experiences in campus recreation can provide much-needed résumé experiences as you start preparing for a career as a recreational sport professional.

FOUNDATIONS OF CAMPUS RECREATION

The term **campus recreation** encompasses all of the diverse recreation and leisure programs and facilities offered on college campuses (Hums & MacLean, 2008). More than 500 colleges and universities in the United States and Canada offer some type of organized campus recreation program or facility (Rockey & Barcelona, 2012). In some cases, these programs and facilities may be housed in one university department. Administrative names often differ by school; examples include the department of campus recreation and wellness, division of campus recreational sport, and department of recreational services.

Recreation and leisure programs and facilities are offered by a variety of departments, units, or groups on a college campus, and the scope of programs often differs. For example, certain kinds of recreation or leisure-oriented clubs and activities might be offered through the student union, student activities board, physical education academic program, or residence life. In a few cases, campus recreation programs and facilities are outsourced. **Outsourcing** refers to contracting out the management of campus recreation programs, services, and facilities to an external private vendor.

The size and scope of program offerings in campus recreation have changed dramatically over time. In the past 100 years, campus recreation has grown from informal groups of students gathering to play their favorite sport, to a component of the organized physical education and ROTC (Reserve Officers' Training Corps) curriculum, to an organized intramural athletic program for men and women, and finally to the diverse programs and facility offerings that are available today. Collegiate recreation programs and facilities have progressed from focusing primarily on physical fitness and military readiness to promoting a more holistic view of health and wellness, contributing to student recruitment and retention, and promoting student learning and leadership development. This historical and philosophical progression is discussed next.

Historical Perspectives

It has often been said that to know who we are and where we are going, we need to look at the past. Studying history has value above and beyond memorizing dates and facts. History can help us understand how things change over time as well as the causes and effects of those changes. Examining the historical evolution of campus recreational sport can provide insight into where the field has been and where it may be going in the future. In the process, it is easy to see that some of the current struggles, challenges, and philosophical debates about the place of organized recreation on college campuses have their roots in the historical development of the field.

Campus Sport in the Early Years (Late 19th and Early 20th Century)

In most colleges and universities today, there is a clear distinction between varsity intercollegiate athletic competition, physical education academic classes (where they still exist), and campus recreational sport programs and facilities. If this is not apparent to you, gather a few friends and try playing a pickup soccer game at the football stadium and see how long it takes for campus security to escort you off the field! Although the boundaries between athletics, physical education, and recreation are clear now, this was not always the case. In the late 1800s, most campus recreation and athletic programs were organized and run by students. Informal leisure activities, intramural games and contests, and extramural competitions between other colleges and community teams constituted the general scope of collegiate sport participation in the late 19th century. During this time, there was probably little distinction between what we now think of as student-athletes and the general college student body.

By the turn of the 20th century, collegiate sport participation generally took three primary forms:

1. Informal leisure activities that students organized for themselves with little outside assistance, such as hiking, paddling, or equestrian activities (Byl, 2002)
2. Organized physical activity and instruction programs focused on calisthenics, hygiene, and military training
3. Semiorganized games and competitions played against fellow college students, local club teams, or students from other universities

As mentioned, informal recreation and semiorganized games started out as primarily student-led activities. Over time, however, the popularity of intercollegiate athletic contests (driven primarily by American football) led to a more organized structure, particularly as coaching, formalized sport rules, league affiliations, and the popularity of college sport as a spectator event became more widespread (Rockey & Barcelona, 2012). The growing organization of intercollegiate athletics and the demand for winning teams, particularly in football, provided opportunities for those who were good enough to make the team. At the same time, physical activity and instruction programs were organized by college faculties into departments of physical education to promote exercise, health, and military readiness, particularly for men.

Physical education programs filled an important niche for the students who were not skilled enough to play on the increasingly competitive intercollegiate athletic teams, but many students wanted more fun and engaging activities rather than "rigid calisthenics, drilling, and exercise or gymnastics programs" (NIRSA, 2008, p. 23). Once again, college students took the organization of these activities in their own hands and started student-led sport clubs and various recreational sport activities. In the early 1900s, the growing popularity of recreational sport for the general student body led college administrators and faculties to create separate facilities for recreation apart from intercollegiate athletics as well as distinct departments of intramural athletics at schools such as Cornell University, University of Michigan, and Ohio State University (Lewis, Jones, Lamke, & Dunn, 1998; NIRSA, 2008). This structure of separate programs for intercollegiate athletics and intramural recreational sport, as well as for health and physical education, became the norm through the first half of the 20th century.

Intramural Sport Movement (Post–World War II)

The middle of the 20th century brought greater economic prosperity in the years following World War II. Partly as a result of the **GI Bill**, which provided U.S. servicepeople with financial assistance to attend colleges and universities, enrollment in higher education grew exponentially (Rockey & Barcelona, 2012). For example, in 1947, more than 49 percent of college students were veterans (U.S. Department of Veterans Affairs [USDVA], 2012). Eventually, the law was expanded to include veterans of the Korean and Vietnam Wars, so by 1956, more than 2.2 million veterans had received an education under the GI Bill, including almost 65,000 women (Solomon, 1986). The growing influx of college students in the postwar years started a national conversation about how best to deliver campus recreation programs and services.

By the late 1940s, there still was no distinct professional network for campus recreation professionals and no real consensus on how to offer campus recreation programs and services. Dr. William Wasson, a faculty member, coach, and intramural director at the historically black Dillard University, received a grant to study the intramural sport programs at other predominantly black colleges and universities. Wasson's *A Comparative Study of Intramural Programs in Negro Colleges* was the impetus for the first meeting of 22 African American intramural directors representing 11 colleges in 1950. At this meeting, the National Intramural Association (NIA), the predecessor of NIRSA, was born (Blumenthal, 2009; NIRSA, 2008).

The early effort to connect intramural sport professionals through a separate association apart from physical education and intercollegiate athletics was important for several reasons. First, the NIA helped intramural sport directors at colleges and universities to share ideas and discuss common concerns. Second, by choosing to stay separate from physical education and athletics, the philosophical orientation of intramural sport was firmly grounded in a commitment to participation and play rather than performance or winning. Finally, the NIA helped to grow and raise the profile of intramural sport participation among college students at member institutions.

From Intramurals to Campus Recreation: Growth and Diversity (1960s and 1970s)

The growth and diversification of intramural sport defined the 1960s and 1970s. By 1952, the NIA had grown beyond the original 11 historically black colleges and universities and had become an interracial organization. Growing membership as well as increasing professional services such as vendor trade shows, job placement services at the annual conference, research grants, and the publication of a professional member directory led the NIA to hire its first executive secretary to help lead the organization (NIRSA, 2012a).

One reason for the growth and diversity of campus recreation programs and services was the increasing influence of women. Beginning in 1960, a series of laws were passed to make discrimination based on race, sex, and religion illegal. This legislation, coupled with larger social movements directed toward gender equality, significantly affected women's access to higher education. The landmark 1972 educational amendment of Title IX opened the door for more women to participate both in intercollegiate athletics and in intramural and recreational sport (Blumenthal, 2009). As larger numbers of women enrolled in two- and four-year colleges, campus recreation programs began to offer more opportunities for women to participate in healthy activities. Perhaps not coincidentally, the popularity of aerobic programs was growing at this time with the publication of the book *Aerobics* in 1968 by Dr. Kenneth Cooper, a physician in the U.S. military. Taking the idea further, a dancer named Jacki Sorenson developed a set of dance routines and called it *aerobic dance* (Cassel, 2011). This growing emphasis on health and fitness provided additional programming opportunities for campus recreation professionals.

The growth in opportunities for women's participation in recreational sport, coupled with growing social concerns regarding gender equity, undoubtedly influenced the NIA in 1971 to revise its constitution and accept women as members. This move reversed the 1959 decision to eliminate women from professional membership in the association (NIRSA, 2012a). The growth of campus recreational sport during the 1970s mirrored larger national trends emphasizing sports, fitness, and healthy lifestyles. Diversification of student programming beyond intramural sport, including group fitness activities, instructional sport, aquatics, and special events, helped spur the organization to change its name in order to more accurately capture the range of services that member institutions offered. In 1975 the NIA changed its name to the **National Intramural-Recreational Sports Association (NIRSA)** to better reflect the depth and breadth of recreation opportunities available on college campuses. Although there have been several attempts to rebrand the association since 1975, including a move in the 1990s to eliminate the references to *intramural* and *sports* in the name, the membership has elected to continue to recognize and retain the association's historical roots. However, by the end of the 1970s, NIRSA was a growing professional association made up of members working in a diverse range of recreational programming areas and facilities.

Establishing the Recreational Sport Profession (1980s and Beyond)

The 1960s and 1970s helped to establish campus recreational sport as a growing contributor to collegiate life. The establishment of the NIA and NIRSA helped to lay the foundation for professionalism among campus recreation directors and staff. Further steps toward professionalization were taken as the 1970s came to a close and the 1980s began (NIRSA, 2012a). These critical steps included the following:

- The *NIRSA Journal* began in 1977, a peer-reviewed professional publication that provided a forum for disseminating research, program case studies, and discussing professional issues. The *NIRSA Journal* would subsequently be renamed the *Recreational Sports Journal (RSJ)* in 2001.
- The Certified Recreational Sports Specialist (CRSS) credential was established in 1981 to recognize campus recreation professionals who were able to demonstrate knowledge and work-related competencies related to recreational sport. The CRSS exam was phased out in 2005, and in 2011 the new Registry of Collegiate Recreational Sports Professionals (RCRSP) was implemented in its place.
- The Code of Ethics for Professional Members was adopted in 1984.
- Increased opportunities for academic and professional training were offered, including regular events such as the Sport Club Symposium (1986), School of Recreational Sports Management (1989), Executive Institute (1991), Sports Facility Symposium (1991), Outdoor Recreation Symposium (1996), Marketing Symposium (2000), Aquatics Symposium (2001), Fitness Institute (2003), and Intramural Sports Symposium (2008).
- The National Research Institute for Collegiate Recreational Sports and Wellness was established in 2005 as a partnership with the Ohio State University to promote and explore emerging areas of research in recreational sport.

The NIRSA Annual Conference and Recreational Sports Exposition continues to attract thousands of campus recreation professionals and students from the United States, Canada, and other parts of the world to network and to participate in professional workshops, educational sessions, and roundtables on topics related to campus recreational sport. In addition, recreation and fitness vendors exhibit their equipment, products, and services at the exposition held in conjunction with the conference.

Philosophical Orientation of Campus Recreation

The emergence, growth, and establishment of the campus recreation profession was influenced by a number of significant factors. These included the influence of larger social trends, such as the movement toward greater gender and racial equality, increased student diversity, the growing importance of fitness and healthy lifestyles, growth in higher education, and increased student demand for access to recreation programs and facilities on campus.

The campus recreation profession continues to evolve today. One of the biggest shifts in the field is the focus on student learning and development. Campus recreation programs are still primarily focused on providing recreational sport and fitness opportunities for the widest range of participants. However, there is a growing emphasis on using recreation as a modality for influencing key student development outcomes, such as "effective communication, healthy behavior, enhanced self-esteem, collaboration, appreciating diversity, meaningful interpersonal relationships, satisfying and productive lifestyles, intellectual growth, social responsibility, personal and educational goals, realistic self-appraisal, clarified values, independence, career choices, and spiritual awareness" (Blumenthal, 2009, p. 56).

Campus Recreation Administrative Structure

Similar to most human endeavors, the history of campus recreation programs and facilities shows a consistent process of continuity and change. One of the constants in campus recreation over time has been the provision of participant-focused recreation, sport, and fitness experiences for the widest range of students, regardless of gender or ability. This idea of sport for all is consistent with the philosophy of recreational sport and differs significantly from other campus-based sport experiences. For example, in intercollegiate athletics the focus is on providing competitive sport experiences for elite athletes and on staging high-level athletic competitions for spectators. University physical education departments today are mostly focused on preparing future teachers to work in K-12 educational settings and providing college-level coursework focused on coaching and athletics administration. In those schools where credit-based physical education classes still exist, the focus is primarily on skill instruction based on a set of physical performance standards. This philosophical divide between offering everyone sport and fitness opportunities for fun, enjoyment, and student development on the one hand and providing high-level athletics and sport instruction for a select few on the other has helped create a powerful argument for changing the administrative orientation of campus recreation away from athletics and physical education to a stand-alone campus organization with its own staff, facilities, budget, and programs.

Although the philosophical orientation of campus recreation has led it away from athletics and physical education, there has been a growing recognition of the commonality of campus recreation and other areas of campus student life, such as residence hall programs, student union activities, and fraternities and sororities (Rockey & Barcelona, 2012). A seminal report titled *Rationale for Independent Administration of Collegiate Recreational Sports Programs* argued that campus recreation facilities and programs play a significant role in contributing to student learning and development, similar to other educationally purposeful out-of-class experiences (Bryant, Anderson, & Dunn, 1994). The 1994 report outlined a direction for campus recreation that would lead to a closer alignment with student affairs divisions and away from intercollegiate athletics and physical education departments. Today, approximately 75 percent of campus recreation departments are housed within student affairs or student life rather than athletics or physical education (Haines, 2007).

Focus on Student Development

Those who champion a focus on student learning and development note that "transformative learning always occurs within the active context of student lives" (Keeling, 2006, p. vii). Campus recreation programs and services are significant parts of the student experience and are high-involving activities, meaning that large numbers of students participate in them. Students change as they progress through college as a result of their personal growth and past experiences as well as through their interactions with others and the institutional environment of which they are part. Student development theories focus on each of these elements, including both intrapersonal growth processes and college impact models. These theoretical models are useful in that they help campus recreation professionals to better align program priorities with the mission of the school—to have a positive impact on the growth and development of students. Some of these theoretical approaches are outlined here.

- **Psychosocial theories.** These theories focus on the way people change and grow across the life span as a function of both intrapersonal and interpersonal processes. Many psychosocial theories focus on a series of developmental stages that people progress through. Erickson's (1993) eight-stage theory of life-span development (see also chapter 3) and Chickering and Reisser's (1993) seven vectors of student development are two well-known applications of the psychosocial approach, and both have applications within campus recreation (Toperzer, Anderson, & Barcelona, 2011). The seven vectors build upon each other; however, it is not necessary to go through each vector sequentially, and students can often experience several vectors at once. Figure 13.1 shows these seven vectors of student development.
- **Cognitive theories.** These theories focus on how students think. More specifically, they help to explain how students perceive, organize, and reason through the experiences they have while attending college (Pascarella & Terenzini, 2005). A classic cognitive theory is Kohlberg's theory of moral development, which focuses on the formal reasoning processes that are part of the moral decision-making process. Student affairs and campus recreation programs can put Kohlberg's theory into practice by offering field-based learning experiences, where students experience moral dilemmas (Pascarella & Terenzini), and by scaffolding the developmental process such that students have a chance to reflect on the decisions that they make.

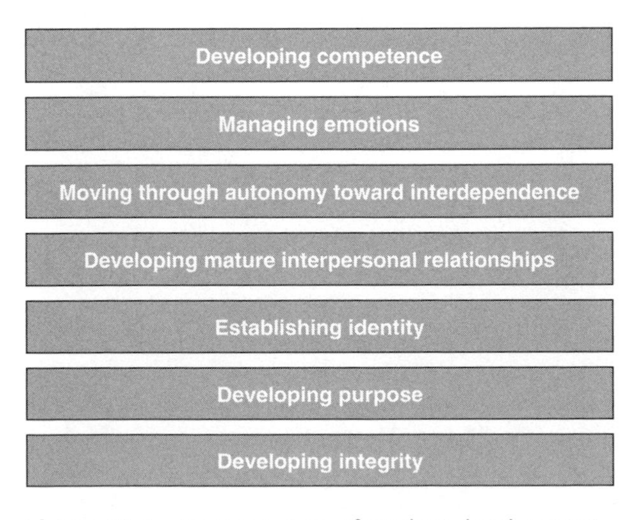

Figure 13.1 Seven vectors of student development.

- **Typological theories.** These theories examine individual differences that have an impact on student development. They generally focus on the individual characteristics or groups of characteristics that affect certain areas of development. Theories that focus on learning styles, for example, can tell campus recreation administrators the conditions under which certain staff members will learn best, and they can aid in the delivery of student orientation and staff training programs. An example of this type of theory is Kolb's experiential learning theory, which focuses on a four-stage model of learning: having a concrete experience (CE), observing and reflecting on the experience (RO), forming abstract concepts (AC), and actively testing and experimenting with new concepts in new situations (AE) (Kolb, 1984). Figure 13.2 illustrates this experiential learning cycle.
- **College impact models.** College impact models of student development focus primarily on the interaction between college students and their environments. These models hold that the most important indicator of student development is what students actually do while at college. For example, Astin's (1984) theory of student involvement holds that development is based on the quantity and quality of student engagement on campus, both inside and outside the classroom. The more time and effort that students devote to educationally purposeful activities, the more outcomes they gain from their college experience. Similarly, Tinto's (1975, 1987) theory of student departure focuses on the level of integration that students develop while at college. *Integration* refers to the sharing of norms with faculty and peers, as well as achieving a proper fit with the formal and informal structural requirements of the institution. Students who lack adequate integration are thus more likely to leave school. Campus recreation departments encourage students to use their programs and services because participation helps to integrate students within the institution. In fact, research shows that students who use campus recreation programs and

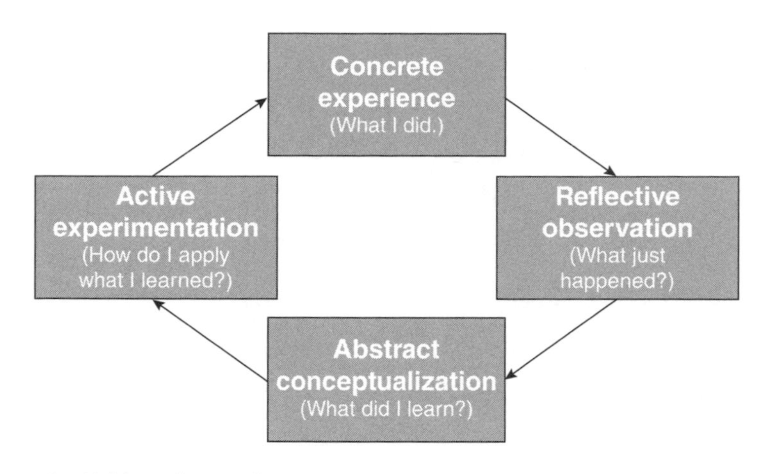

Figure 13.2 Kolb's experiential learning cycle.

facilities are more likely to stay in and graduate from college (Huesman, Brown, Lee, Kellogg, & Radcliffe, 2009).

Student Learning Reconsidered

One strength of campus recreation departments is that they can contribute to a whole-student approach to education, integrating both academic learning and student development (Keeling, 2006). The idea is that student experiences both inside and outside the classroom can provide a seamless web of learning, and educationally purposeful out-of-class experiences can be platforms for student learning and development (Kuh, 1993). This philosophical shift toward a student learning approach in campus recreation programs is in line with the broader focus on learning in out-of-class environments as articulated by student affairs divisions. NIRSA is one of seven partner associations in the Learning Reconsidered 2 initiative, placing campus recreation in the company of college student unions, residence life, campus activities, academic advising, and student affairs administrators in focusing on the learning outcomes associated with out-of-class experiences (Learning Reconsidered, 2004).

This student learning imperative provides a framework of learning outcomes in seven main areas (Komives & Schoper, 2007):

1. Cognitive complexity—focusing on critical and reflective thinking, reasoning, intellectual flexibility, and integration of cognition, emotion, and identity
2. Knowledge acquisition—focusing on understanding and integrating knowledge from a wide range of disciplines and relating that knowledge to daily experiences, pursuing lifelong learning, deciding on a career path, and building competence in technology
3. Humanitarianism—focusing on understanding and appreciating diversity, cultural competence, and social responsibility
4. Civic engagement—building a sense of civic responsibility, commitment to public life, engagement in principle dissent, and effective leadership
5. Interpersonal and intrapersonal competence—developing a realistic self-appraisal and understanding of self; developing attributes such as identity, self-esteem, confidence, ethics, and integrity; developing spiritual awareness; setting personal goals; and developing meaningful relationships, interdependence, collaboration and ability to work with others
6. Practical competence—developing effective communication skills, effective management of one's personal life, economic self-sufficiency, and vocational competence; maintaining personal health and wellness; prioritizing leisure pursuits; and living a purposeful and satisfying life
7. Persistence and academic achievement—developing academic and personal success, academic goal success, and degree attainment

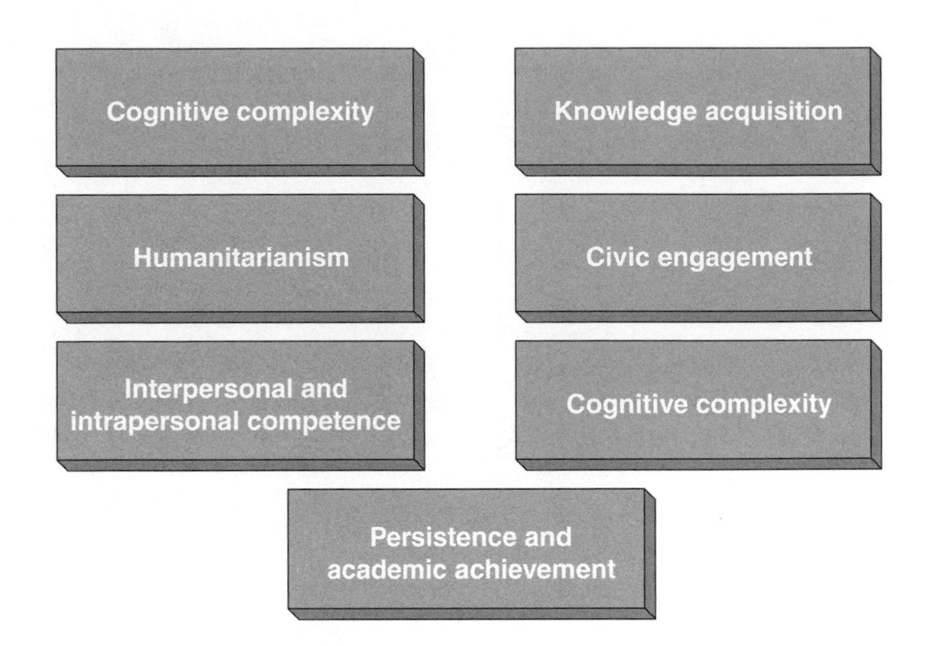

Figure 13.3 Student learning imperative model. How might campus recreational sport foster these learning imperatives?

The key for campus recreation administrators is to purposefully use these outcomes to guide program planning and to form the basis for interactions between professional staff and students. Figure 13.3 shows the student learning imperative model.

Significance of Campus Recreation

With their focus on student development and learning, campus recreation departments have become significant contributors to the mission of higher education (Barcelona & Ross, 2002). Although there are many areas where campus recreational sport contributes to student life, this section highlights four: contributions to health and wellness, competence building and skill development, student recruitment and retention, and student leadership and cocurricular learning.

Health and Wellness

The fitness and wellness boom that started in the 1970s helped to fuel the growth of campus recreation fitness facilities and programs. Decreasing physical activity among North Americans has had devastating consequences, including an increase in overweight and obesity, diabetes, high blood pressure, poor overall health status, and premature death (CDC, 2012). Obesity and physical inactivity have become important public policy priorities. Recent research shows that less than half of college students meet the CDC's recommendations for moderate- or vigorous-intensity exercise, almost one-third have had a recent experience with binge drinking, and almost half regularly experience higher than average levels of stress (ACHA, 2012). Because of this, health and well-being are one of NIRSA's six strategic values (NIRSA, 2012b). Campus recreation programs and facilities can have a significant impact on encouraging healthy lifestyles. Research has shown that regular participation in campus recreation programs and facilities can

- act as a moderator of stress (Kanters, 2000),
- help increase physical activity during and after college (Forrester, Arterberry, & Barcelona, 2006; Forrester, Ross, Hall, & Geary, 2007),
- contribute to obesity prevention and weight loss (Ferrara, St. Laurent, & Wilson, 2008), and
- reduce problem drinking and alcohol use (Jackson, Walling, & Thompson, 2007).

The results of these studies and others are encouraging; however, more research on the impact of campus recreation on student health and wellness is needed. This area is an emerging research priority for those interested in studying the impact of campus recreation on students (Sweeney & Barcelona, 2012).

Competence Building and Skill Development

Involvement in campus recreation programs can play a significant role in building physical skills and competence. As noted in the historical evolution of campus recreation, the physical development of students was once the mandate of physical education and hygiene (health) programs. However, credit-based physical education departments are less common in colleges and universities today. In many cases, physical education activity classes are only offered for physical education majors. Many campus recreation departments now provide noncredit instructional sport programs designed to fill this gap. Instructional programs in fitness, strength training, dance, martial arts, outdoor recreation pursuits, and even traditional sports such as tennis, bowling, and golf can be found at many colleges and universities. These programs are designed to teach the basics of the activity, and in some cases to provide opportunities for more advanced instruction, for the purposes of furthering the student's participation in the activity.

Student Recruitment and Retention

Many factors go into the decision-making calculus of students when choosing a college. Certainly, factors such as the availability of one's chosen major, quality of the faculty, distance from home, and cost of tuition are among the most important, but for many students, campus recreation programs and facilities also play a major role in their choice of school. A number of studies suggest that the quality and availability of campus recreation facilities is a key decision-making factor for up to one-third of potential college students (see Blumenthal, 2009, for a review). In addition, those students who participate most frequently in campus recreation programs and facilities are likely to say that these experiences are important in keeping them enrolled in their school. Recruitment and retention of students has long been a key concern for college and university administrators. In the increasingly competitive landscape of higher education, investments in

Dragan Trifunovic/fotolia.com

Non-credit instructional and fitness programming like this dance class helps to build physical resistance and social competence.

campus recreation facilities and programs can help school meet their recruitment and retention goals.

Student Leadership and Cocurricular Learning

From the earliest days, intramural sport on college campuses was a primarily student-led endeavor. Even as colleges and universities have moved toward the employment of highly educated, full-time recreational sport administrators, student leadership is still valued on a majority of campuses. Students are involved in leadership positions within various components of the campus recreation program, including facilities and programs. Student leadership may be exercised in a voluntary capacity, such as by serving as a team captain for intramurals, as an officer on a club sport team, as a fraternity or sorority intramural chairperson, or as a member of a campus recreation department's student advisory board. In many cases, campus recreation departments are laboratories for students majoring in exercise science, recreation and sport management, public health, and even business or communications. Students may find campus recreation departments to be useful places for engaging in internships or practicum experiences as a component of their academic major. Finally, perhaps the most visible student leadership positions involve paid employment within the campus recreation department. Campus recreation is often one of the largest employers of students on campus, with student employees working as facility supervisors, fitness leaders, outdoor recreation instructors, lifeguards, and intramural officials.

The training and mentorship that student leaders receive from professional staff members, along with the job-related competencies that they develop in their volunteer or paid positions, help to build **transferable skills**. These are the skills that students obtain through their jobs, volunteer work, and participation in out-of-class activities that are transferable to a variety of employment settings and that can assist in career development. Transferable skills that can be developed through student leadership in campus recreation include program design and event planning, activity leadership, personnel supervision, decision making, risk management, conflict resolution, marketing, communication, public speaking, technology applications, customer service, networking, facilities management, and budgeting.

CAMPUS RECREATION FACILITIES AND PROGRAMS

It is safe to say that the central mission of campus recreation is to provide programs and facilities that contribute to student learning and development from a holistic perspective. In a sense, the programs and facilities that campus recreation provides are the **modalities**—that is, the methods or facilitating agents—that help to produce these critical outcomes of the student experience. The quality and availability of recreation facilities and programs play a key role in student recruitment and retention. However, quality recreation programs and facilities are intentionally designed to maximize student development and learning outcomes. Campus recreation professionals start with the end result in mind and plan their programs and services in a manner that is best aligned with the outcome that they are seeking.

The following section discusses some of the key aspects and features of campus recreation facilities and outlines typical campus recreation programming options. As you read the sections that follow, see if you can find the places where student learning and development can be maximized through the intentional design of campus recreation facilities and programs.

Recreational Sport Facilities

The earliest campus recreation facilities were dedicated spaces where the student body was able to participate in intramural sport or informal recreation. In many cases, these facilities were shared-use spaces typically shared between student recreation, physical education classes, and in some cases intercollegiate athletics. As demand for student recreation services grew, the idea of shared-use facilities became less palatable for campus recreation administrators and participants, and new spaces for recreation were needed to accommodate the diverse needs of students. The following sections provide an overview of campus recreation facilities, including both indoor and outdoor recreation areas and current trends in facility design. Chapter 6 provides a more detailed discussion on the design of recreation facilities in a wide variety of recreation settings and contexts.

Indoor Facilities

The 1980s and 1990s ushered in a facility-boom era for campus recreation, one that saw the proliferation of new and modern campus recreational sport facilities dedicated almost exclusively to the recreation and fitness needs of the general student body (Blumenthal, 2009). Most of these recreational sport buildings are open-concept facilities that allow participants, staff, and visitors to see a variety of recreational and physical activities happening at the same time. This contrasts with the segmented, closed-off activity spaces that typified many earlier facility designs.

The new facility design is more appealing and inviting, is generally more accessible for participants, and is safer because of the lack of hidden spaces and greater administrative control over participant entry and egress. These indoor facilities provide opportunities for a wide variety of recreation, physical, and social activities. In addition to the typical gymnasium, jogging track, weight room, aquatic center, and locker rooms, student recreation centers often feature auxiliary gym facilities; fitness studios; spaces for cardio, selectorized, and plate-loaded fitness equipment; indoor rock-climbing walls; student meeting rooms, lounges, and study areas; and even places to eat, buy equipment, and watch television.

It appears that the facility boom of the 1980s and 1990s has continued, as colleges and universities are still investing considerably in signature campus recreation facilities. A **signature facility** is one that stands out in terms of its architectural form and usable functionality. Signature campus recreation facilities are showcases for colleges and universities, and they are usually high priorities on campus tours for prospective students. In 2011, the winners of the NIRSA Outstanding Sports Facilities Awards averaged approximately $39 million per facility for new campus recreation facility construction, not including land and design fees (Rockey & Barcelona, 2012).

Outdoor Facilities

The staple of the outdoor recreational sport complex for many campus recreation programs is still the multipurpose athletic field. Multipurpose facilities have an advantage in that they can be used for a variety of sport activities and events, such as flag football, soccer, lacrosse, rugby, or ultimate Frisbee. However, many campus recreation departments also provide single-purpose outdoor sport facilities such as tennis courts. Mississippi State University's RecPlex features multipurpose athletic fields for recreational sport, but it also features four lighted softball fields in a cloverleaf design, complete with control building and concession stand. In addition to facilities for competition-oriented sport, many campus recreation departments are developing diverse facilities such as outdoor fitness and hiking trails, sand volleyball courts, disc golf courses, and boat launches for paddling, sailing, and other watersports.

Campus Recreation Facility Trends

One of the key trends in the facility boom years was the construction of separate facilities that were primarily dedicated to campus recreation. Interestingly, today there appears to be a return to building campus recreation facilities with a mind toward greater integration with the broader goals of student and academic life. For example, some new facilities are returning to the mixed-use concept, providing spaces for indoor and outdoor recreation, academic classrooms, retail, student meeting areas, lounging, and informal games and activities. Portland State University's Academic and Student Recreation Center is a 100,000-square-foot (9,290 m^2) fusion facility that incorporates traditional campus recreation facility space with student learning areas, classrooms, and retail opportunities. In addition, it is a LEED building, meaning that it was built with sustainability in mind (see chapter 6). This focus on sustainability is reflected in a variety of new campus recreation building projects, including those at the University of Arizona, Cal State Fullerton, University of Richmond, University of Maine, Morehead State University, and University of Cincinnati (Hatch, Blumenthal, Accetta, Su, & Ling, 2011). Finally, in an attempt to meet students where they are, many campus recreation departments have developed satellite facilities, such as fitness and wellness centers located in student dormitories, while others have developed joint facilities and partnerships with campus-based student health centers.

Recreational Sport Program Areas

Campus recreation facilities are often showcases for schools and provide spaces for recreation activities to take place. From the perspective of program design and delivery, facilities are everything.

Without a suitable facility, recreational sport opportunities are limited or cannot be offered in the first place. The quality and availability of facilities dictates what programs are offered, when they occur, how they are delivered, and how many participants or teams can be accommodated. Although facilities are the foundation, it is the diverse activities and programs that are offered at those facilities that give life to campus recreation departments. The programs offered by campus recreation departments are the vehicles that allow students (and in some cases faculty, staff, and community members) to engage in healthy and developmentally purposeful activities.

Many diverse program areas are offered by campus recreation departments in the United States and Canada. It would be an interesting but impossible task to capture the depth and breadth of the creativity that campus recreation professionals employ every day to ensure that their offerings meet the needs of their participants. However, there are some common programming areas that are typically found in the vast majority of campus recreation departments. Many of these programming areas can also be found in other recreational sport settings, such as municipal, military, and commercial recreation. This is important because students are often introduced to new recreation activities while attending college, and the availability of similar activities in their community enables them to continue participating after graduation. As you read about the following program areas, think about what is available at your school and whether similar programs exist in your community.

Intramural Sport and Special Events

Intramural sport is arguably the most recognized campus recreation program. As discussed earlier, intramural sport opportunities were at the core of the development of campus recreation. *Intramural* literally means "between the walls" and refers to the competitive and cooperative sport opportunities available to students enrolled in a particular school. Most intramural sport programs limit participation to just those students who are enrolled full or part time, and in some cases faculty and staff may be allowed to participate. This keeps participation in intramural sport between the walls of the college. Intramural sport typically encompasses a range of team, individual and dual, and meet sports as

© Bob Barcelona

Creative sport events like this Quidditch tournament are gaining popularity on college campuses.

Flag football is a competitive sport, both on campus and off. There are many opportunities to compete in men's, women's, and co-recreational flag football at a high level.

well special events. Sports are usually offered in a tournament format and may use round-robin, single- or double-elimination, or challenge tournament designs. In most cases, strict eligibility guidelines are put into place to ensure that participants are not current or former professional athletes and are not currently participating on a varsity athletic team in the same sport. Intramural sport programs are typically offered at various competitive levels to provide maximum participation opportunities for students. Separate divisions for men, women, and coeducational participation are usually provided, and many schools offer point systems to encourage participation and healthy competition between residence halls, Greek houses, and student organizations.

Many colleges and universities offer special events on their intramural calendar. Special events tend to be one-day events that add elements that may not be available in the typical intramural activity. For example, special events may be designed to raise money for a charity, such as Indiana University's Jill Behrman Color the Campus Run, or they may include sponsorships, giveaways, or opportunities to compete in nontraditional games and activities. Often, special events are designed to introduce students to campus recreation and are offered as kickoff events. Clemson University's RecFest offers nontraditional games and activities, such as laser tag, pool Battleship, and cycling cinema, and students can register for a variety of campus recreation programs and activities.

Extramural Sport

If *intramural sport* means "between the walls," then *extramural sport* means "outside the walls." **Extramural sport** includes those competitive and cooperative sport opportunities that take place between students from different schools. Extramural sport opportunities have grown tremendously as state, regional, and national championship events are being offered in sports such as flag football, soccer, and basketball. In some cases, extramural sport opportunities are available to teams who win their college or university intramural championships in a given sport. Those winning teams then go on to represent their school in a regional championship, and, if they advance, a national championship. In other cases, regional contests are open to a variety of teams, and winners then progress to a national tournament. National championship events have attracted top-level corporate sponsors and even television coverage of tournament events. For example, the National Campus Championship Series (NCCS) Flag Football National Championships presented by NIRSA have been sponsored by Powerade and have been covered on television by the CBS Sports Network. The American Collegiate Intramural Sports (ACIS) Fitness Nationals, a separate national championship series outside of NIRSA, was televised by FOX College Sports (Rockey & Barcelona, 2012).

Sport Clubs

Sport clubs are typically organized by students, but they are recognized and supported by the campus recreation department in several ways. For example, campus recreation departments often provide facilities for student sport clubs to use, and they typically provide some funding for clubs to operate. Sport clubs provide students with opportunities to participate in a specific recreational sport in a deeper and more engaging way. They are among the more diverse sport offerings provided by campus recreation departments and can range from highly competitive to primarily recreational or instructional. In some cases, clubs may exhibit each of these elements. For example, the ballroom dancing club at the University of California at Berkeley offers instructional dancing lessons for the general student body, provides opportunities for club members to dance regularly, and has a competitive ballroom dancing team that participates in high-level dance competitions.

One of the distinguishing features of sport clubs is that they are almost universally student-led and student-run initiatives. Student leaders typically organize the club's activities, handle registration of members, work with campus recreation staff to schedule facilities and travel, and may even provide coaching or instruction. Sport clubs include traditional sports, such as lacrosse, soccer, volleyball, and ice hockey, as well as activities such as martial arts, fencing, dance, synchronized swimming, sailing, and rowing.

There has been tremendous growth in student sport clubs, particularly as varsity athletic programs are downsized and students need a home for their sport interests. For example, the University of New Hampshire eliminated men's baseball as a varsity sport, and it quickly reorganized itself as a campus sport club. This has happened with other varsity sports at UNH, including men's tennis and women's crew. However, in most cases, new sport clubs are driven primarily by student interest and student leadership. Campus recreation staff typically play a role as facilitators of student sport club experiences, working with student leaders to make the clubs successful.

Fitness and Wellness

Another growth area for campus recreation is in fitness and wellness programs. It may be tempting to think of fitness and wellness as just exercising or trying to lose weight, but these are only part of the concept. **Wellness** refers to "a state of optimal well-being oriented toward maximizing an individual's potential" (Patton, 2009). This definition points to a more holistic view of health—one that focuses not only on the physical aspects but on the emotional as well. This means that although physical conditioning is an important focus for campus fitness and wellness professionals, these programs also have broader goals, including stress release, relaxation, and disease and injury prevention.

A visitor to a campus recreation facility will likely see students lifting weights, jogging on an indoor track, or spending time on a stair-stepper machine or treadmill. However, closer examination of the fitness and wellness offerings at most campuses will reveal more diverse programs and activities. In addition to weights and cardio, fitness programs on campus typically offer instructor-led group exercise classes that are tailored to the fitness needs of participants at the beginner, intermediate, and advanced levels. Group exercise classes can include step, kickboxing, strength and flexibility, balance, dance (e.g., hip-hop, Zumba), high-energy boot camps, cycle spinning, and even group water exercise. Classes in yoga and Pilates, which can help with strength, flexibility, relaxation, and stress release, are becoming more common.

In addition to instructor-led classes, some schools offer personal training services and nutrition and weight-loss consulting. In many cases, campus recreation and fitness centers are developing joint partnerships with campus health centers and health care professionals to focus on a more holistic approach to student health. For example, Clemson University's campus recreation department participates in a partnership with other campus health professionals to help work toward achieving the goals of **Healthy Campus 2020**, a framework for improving the overall health on college campuses in the United States (ACHA, 2012).

Instructional Sport

Instructional sport includes activities that introduce participants to a particular sport or recreation activity or that help participants develop the skills needed in that activity. Instructional sport programs have their roots in the credit-based physical education classes that many schools used to require or encourage all students to take. However, as these credit-based classes have largely disappeared, campus recreation departments have been offering noncredit instruction in a variety of recreational sport activities. In many departments, instructional sport is embedded in the offerings of fitness programs, sport clubs, aquatics, and outdoor recreation programs. Northeastern University in Boston offers a range of instructional programs, including nutrition classes, martial arts, dance, fitness activities, and yoga. Some schools continue to offer credit-based instructional sport classes. For example, the leisure skills program at Clemson University offers 140 sections of one-credit activity courses that serve more than 2,500 students each semester.

Informal Drop-In Recreation

Informal recreation encompasses opportunities that are available to students in a format that allows them to participate in their own time and their own way. Examples include pickup basketball games, table-tennis matches, bowling, jogging, weightlifting, or any number of activities that can be done as long as a facility is available. Informal recreation opportunities may not require a tremendous amount of staff resources to plan and organize compared with programs such as intramural sport or sport clubs, yet these activities reach a tremendous number of students, faculty, and staff each year. Many students who may never sign up for an intramural sport or group exercise class can be seen tossing a Frisbee around the college quad, jogging around campus, swimming laps in the pool, or lifting weights in the fitness center. It is important for campus recreation professionals to make facilities available for informal drop-in recreation in order to accommodate the vast majority of student needs and interests.

Outdoor Recreation

Outdoor recreation is another major growth area for campus recreation departments as student interest in outdoor and nature-based adventure activities has increased. Many campus recreation departments have accommodated student interest in this area, offering instruction in outdoor activities such as hiking, backpacking, camping, bicycling, paddling, sailing, and rock climbing. In addition to instruction, outdoor recreation programs offer guided trips that allow students to experience the outdoors and to put into practice the skills that they learn in instructional settings. Many outdoor programs also provide equipment and information for students who want to camp, hike, or engage in outdoor recreation activities outside of the organized program. Some programs, such as Ole Miss Outdoors offered through the department of campus recreation at the University of Mississippi, provide opportunities to gain environmental awareness and courses for students to obtain certifications such as Wilderness First Responder.

Family and Youth Programming

Campus recreation departments tend to have different philosophies toward programs offered for nonstudents compared with those offered for students. This is because campus recreation departments typically receive funding from student activity fees—a tax levied on student tuition that funds a variety of campus activities, including recreation. Most campus recreation departments offer opportunities for faculty and staff to participate in their programs, however, and some departments provide programming opportunities for the general community. Many of these programs are offered to faculty and staff and their families, and they may include opportunities such as family nights or youth recreational summer camps. For example, Indiana University offers free family nights that are open to the public each month, including opportunities to swim, do arts and crafts, and participate in various recreational activities in the student recreational sport center. The campus recreation department at the University of New Hampshire offers Camp Wildcat, a day camp for children in grades 1 through 7. Several recreation activities, themes, and field trips are included in the summer camp offerings.

PROFESSIONAL DEVELOPMENT IN CAMPUS RECREATION

The administration of campus recreational sport programs and facilities is the work of highly educated and skilled professionals. Professional staff members combine their love of recreation and sport with specialty knowledge in various aspects of the campus recreation field. Depending on their position in the department, staff must have expertise in areas such as officiating, fitness, strength and conditioning, facility design, tournament scheduling, and outdoor skills. In addition to specialty knowledge areas, staff must possess general sport management competencies, including business procedures; marketing, promotions, and communications; technology applications and computer skills; facilities and equipment management; governance; legality and risk management; management techniques; philosophy and sport sciences; programming and event management; and research and program evaluation (Barcelona, 2004). Perhaps most importantly, campus recreation staff must be committed to college student learning and development. They must be able to integrate their programs and services seamlessly with other areas of student life, including residence hall programs, campus health services, Greek life, student union programming, and academic affairs.

If you are interested in a career in campus recreation, there are a number of critical areas to consider as you prepare for your future. Career development in campus recreation encompasses academic preparation, professional involvement in relevant organizations, specialty certifications, and active networking and seeking of career opportunities. Professional development should start now, while you are still in college, and continue throughout your career in the field.

Academic Preparation

A good place to start the career development process is through academic coursework and cocurricular experiences. Campus recreation professionals are highly educated. Virtually all full-time campus recreation professionals have obtained a four-year degree, and a significant majority hold a master's degree. Some even hold doctorates. This is one area of the recreational sport field where a graduate degree is considered an entry-level degree. As you begin to think about your academic career in campus recreation, it is important to consider how you can best position yourself for graduate school and beyond.

Undergraduate Preparation

There is no one ideal major for a student who is interested in a career in campus recreation. Often campus recreation professionals come to the field from a variety of undergraduate majors. For example, the lead author of this textbook has an undergraduate degree in political science. Other campus recreation professionals come from diverse majors, such as business, education, and the various liberal arts.

However, if you are interested in the recreation field, you may have the opportunity to major in recreation management, sport studies, exercise science, or a related field at your school. For example, more than 500 colleges and universities offer degrees in recreation management across the United States and Canada (Rockey & Barcelona, 2012). This is a good place to start in terms of receiving a focused academic degree within the field. If you are interested in fitness and wellness, then exercise science or kinesiology would be good majors to pursue. Some schools offer a focused area of study in campus recreation, such as the recreation studies program at Ohio University, which has long been a leader in this area. Others offer broader undergraduate study in recreational sport management, such as Indiana University. Regardless, choosing an appropriate undergraduate major and working hard in classes is an important first step.

Almost as important as the undergraduate major is involvement outside the classroom. As mentioned earlier in the chapter, co-curricular experiences offered through campus recreation departments are one of the best ways to prepare future recreational sport professionals. Students should get involved early and often in campus recreation activities as participants and, more importantly, as student staff members. Opportunities to work part time as a facility or intramural supervisor, fitness leader, intramural official, lifeguard, or outdoor adventures staff member help provide exposure to the various program areas and facilities in campus recreation. In addition to part-time work, students should try to obtain progressive leadership experience—it is important to build on experiences throughout the undergraduate career. This helps to build a résumé and provide more employment opportunities down the road. Students can also find opportunities for volunteer leadership, such as on student advisory boards. Most accredited recreation and sport management majors require focused practicums and internship experiences as part of the curriculum. These are critical in helping to build professional skills as well.

Graduate Preparation

Graduate school is usually a must for aspiring campus recreation professionals. Most professional staff members in campus recreation hold a master's degree, typically in fields such as recreation management, exercise science, business administration, or student affairs administration. Campus recreation departments often offer graduate assistantships that pay the full cost of tuition plus monthly stipends for living expenses in exchange for 20 hours of work per week in one or more campus recreation programs or facilities. This is an outstanding way for prospective campus recreation professionals to obtain both the education and practical experience that they need to position themselves for their first full-time job.

To be eligible for a campus recreation graduate assistantship, applicants should have strong undergraduate academic records, particularly in the last 60 hours of coursework; acceptable scores on the Graduate Record Examination (GRE); have a résumé showing progressive student leadership in some area of campus recreational sport; and have the drive and desire for graduate studies and the field as a whole. Students can find out about campus recreation graduate assistantships by visiting the NIRSA job search website, www.bluefishjobs.com. Typically, graduate assistantship opportunities are advertised in the spring and begin with the new school year in the fall. Interested students are usually advised to attend the NIRSA Annual Conference and Recreational Sports Exposition, usually held in March or April, where they can find out more about available positions. It is not unheard of to interview or actually be offered a graduate assistantship position at the conference. The NIRSA job search website also includes available full-time entry, midcareer, and executive positions in the field.

Involvement in Professional Organizations

Professional organizations such as NIRSA play a vital role in the development of campus recreation professionals. Involvement in national and, in some cases, state or regional professional associations can provide a number of benefits for professionals, including conferences and workshops, specialty symposia, training resources, access to research, career and job fairs, leadership opportunities, certification, continuing education credits, and, perhaps most importantly, networking opportunities. Most professional organizations offer student memberships at low or no cost and encourage student involvement at conferences. NIRSA offers student leadership positions at the state, regional, and national levels, and many states offer Student Lead On conferences that focus on building student leaders in campus recreation.

Although NIRSA is the leader in professional development for campus recreation staff, there are many other professional organizations that students and staff can get involved with in order to supplement their education and development. Organizations for students to consider include the following:

- National Intramural-Recreational Sports Association (NIRSA; www.nirsa.org)
- National Association of Student Personnel Administrators (NASPA; www.naspa.org)
- American College Personnel Association—College Student Educators International (ACPA; www.myacpa.org)
- Association of Outdoor Recreation and Education (AORE; www.aore.org)
- American College of Sports Medicine (ACSM; www.acsm.org)
- National Strength and Conditioning Association (NSCA; www.nsca.com)
- American Council on Exercise (ACE; www.acefitness.org)
- Aerobics and Fitness Association of America (AFAA; www.afaa.com)

These and other organizations are vital in promoting professional standards and continuing education for campus recreation staff, and they are excellent vehicles for students to get involved and learn more about their chosen profession.

Certifications

For some jobs in campus recreation, certifications are important or necessary to be hired or to continue employment. **Certifications** are credentials given by a governing body or professional association that acknowledge a recipient's qualification to perform a specific job. Certifications may be earned after studying and passing an exam, or they may be based on demonstrating practical competence related to a particular job. In many cases, after obtaining certification the recipient must keep up with the latest job requirements by participating in continuing education, often offered through workshops or sessions at professional conferences.

Whether certification is required depends on the specific campus recreation job. For example, most positions in aquatics require certification as a water safety instructor, lifeguard, or pool operator. Many intramural sport positions require professional staff to be certified as sport officials through their local state high school association. Fitness professionals typically must obtain various certifications, including those relating to personal training or group fitness instruction. Outdoor recreation staff typically need to be certified in wilderness first aid and in specific outdoor activities, such as belaying or white-water kayaking.

For more than 20 years, NIRSA offered the Certified Recreational Sports Specialist (CRSS) exam, which was a general certification for campus recreation professionals. However, in 2005, the CRSS was suspended, and in 2007 the NIRSA board of directors approved the establishment of the Registry of Collegiate Recreational Sports Professionals (RCRSP). The registry was designed to encourage and recognize ongoing professional development in areas critical to campus recreational sport professionals, including philosophy and theory, programming, management, business procedures, facility management, planning and design, research and evaluation, legal liability and risk management, and personal and professional qualities (NIRSA, 2014).

CONCLUSION

Campus recreational sport has a long, rich history, from the earliest days of contests staged in the old intramural buildings at the University of Michigan and Ohio State to the full-service, multimillion-dollar recreational sport and student life buildings being constructed on campuses today. Much about campus recreation has changed over time, including the diversification of program offerings, the close integration with student development and learning, and the professionalization of staff. However, the core of campus recreational sport remains the same—a commitment to providing all students (and in many cases faculty and staff) with access to recreational sport opportunities to enhance their college experience.

RESEARCH TO REALITY

Sweeney, T.P., & Barcelona, R.J. (2012). An integrative review of published research in the *Recreational Sports Journal*, 1998-2010. *Recreational Sports Journal*, *36*, 91-103.

The authors of this study examined the published research related to recreational sport in the *Recreational Sports Journal* since the late 1990s. Findings suggested that published research primarily focused on topics related to campus recreation, including participation and constraints; recreational sport administration; benefits and outcomes; research and program evaluation; health and wellness; facilities, equipment, and technology; marketing; risk behavior; and sociodemographic differences. The authors also found that most of what is published on campus recreation is nonempirical (i.e., not research based) and lacks grounding in sound social science theory.

This study provides a direction for researchers in campus recreation to improve research efforts in the field. Campus recreation professionals can use the results of the study to identify published research in areas that they are interested in, particularly to improve agency practice. In addition, the study provides opportunities for professionals and researchers to partner together on studies that can bridge theory and professional practice. If one or more of these research areas interests you, perhaps you can do some research to see how campus recreation departments can better meet the needs of students, faculty, staff, and the university community.

REFLECTION QUESTIONS

1. What are the major historical periods that shaped the development of campus recreation, and what are some of the key trends that helped define them?
2. How does campus recreation contribute to student learning and development?
3. Provide an example from your school of a specific activity that is offered under each of the major campus recreation programming areas.
4. What is a signature campus recreation facility?
5. What are the key academic knowledge areas and professional competencies for a campus recreation professional?

LEARNING ACTIVITIES

1. Interview one of the full-time campus recreation staff members at your college or university. Find out how he became interested in the field, what his academic background was, what kind of experiences he had as an undergraduate and graduate student that helped him prepare for his career, and where he sees his career going in the next 5 or 10 years. Map out a career plan in campus recreation for yourself based on this information.
2. Develop a campus recreation program that is guided by one or more of the student development theories discussed in this chapter.
3. Take a tour of the campus recreation facilities at your school. Look at how the facilities were designed and how they are managed. If you could redesign the activity spaces or change the way the facility is managed, what would you do?

chapter

14

INTERNATIONAL INFLUENCE ON RECREATIONAL SPORT

LEARNING OUTCOMES

By the end of the chapter, readers will be able to

- identify sport models in other countries,
- develop a plan for using international sport models as examples to implement within their own organization, and
- describe the organizational structure of international sport and its ties to national and local federations and associations.

Case Study

PROGRAMMING LOCALLY FOR THE OLYMPICS

Ottawa has just been awarded the 2020 Olympic Games and the organizing committee is beginning to put plans into place for the venues, city infrastructure, and transportation improvements that will need to be made. It is also beginning to amass the workforce that will be needed to pull the Games off in a successful and economically responsible way. As a new graduate of a recreational sport management program, Brooklyn is looking for a job within the field and has always enjoyed watching the Olympics on television and cheering her fellow Canadians to the finish line. When she hears that her local park and recreation agency is hiring an Olympic partner programmer to specialize in designing and implementing programs that the Canadian Olympic Committee will have for the communities in the area, she applies and is offered the position. As a new graduate, she recognizes that this will be a challenge, but this job has the potential to combine her love of sport and the Olympics with the benefits that she knows quality programming can bring to a community.

The Canadian Olympic Committee has chosen to focus on two main areas of the Olympic movement within the city—the torch run and an energizing volunteer program. Brooklyn decides that starting a short-distance running program (1K-5K maximum) would be a neat way to not only bring the running community together but also to get people out and moving who normally might not be runners because the short distance is much more appropriate for new runners. This type of event could then be parlayed into applications in the Olympic Torch Relay that takes place up to a year in advance of the Games coming to the city.

Brooklyn also wants to address the energizing volunteer programs, so she partners with the local professional sport venue to commit five volunteers from her facility to every event that takes place over the course of the season. Brooklyn realizes that a program like this can provide a sense of community involvement for her volunteers coupled with a sense of accomplishment in making the community a better place, and it allows the volunteers to see a side of the professional sport field that few ever get to see. In addition, the venue she is partnering with is hosting one of the Olympic events in 2020. She has worked out a deal with the volunteer coordinators for the Canadian Olympic Committee in Ottawa to allow each volunteer who works at least 10 shifts for the professional team to then be highly considered for a competitive volunteer position with the Olympics when they arrive in the city as a reward for making a commitment to the venue and Brooklyn's program.

As sport continues to evolve across the United States with better training facilities, higher-quality coaching, advances in equipment, and improved training regiments, the rest of the world certainly continues to keep pace. In some sports, such as soccer, track and field, and rugby, the United States is feeling the pressure to improve performance as other countries are advancing at a faster rate. Similarly, many of the benefits and opportunities that sport can provide in the United States are equally as beneficial to participants all across the globe.

In addition to the personal benefits that sport can provide, the global benefits have a profound effect on nations and their political unity. Events such as the Olympics, World Cup of soccer, and Cricket World Cup provide opportunities for not only national pride and bragging rights for sport supremacy but also respect, understanding and promotion of peaceful competition, increased sport participation at the local and regional levels, and increased funding and support of athletes and facilities. According to USA Swimming, participation rates in 2009, the year following Michael Phelps' success in the 2008 Beijing Olympics, increased 11.3 percent, and this trend has been consistent for the years following Summer Olympics several times (usaswimming.org). Clearly, professional and international sport performance, visibility, and success have a profound impact on recreational sport within the individual countries that are successful. Kids want to grow up playing the sports that they see their fellow countrymen and women succeeding at. For this reason, it is important to understand some of the unique aspects of international sport, as well as how other countries organize their sport programs from youth through the professional ranks.

SPORT AS A UNIFYING BODY

In many areas of the world, sport has been seen as a unifying body where countries with differing views and political ideals can come together and compete in a common cause. Certainly the Olympics and the World Cups of soccer, cricket, and rugby are a testament to this, as are world championship events in sports such as hockey and track and field. Athletes from all around the world compete for their country to achieve the highest levels. Spectators embrace the competition as national pride is on the line, and viewership of many world sporting events continues to grow (Billings, 2008). Rarely are the differences of one country not set aside in the interest of a peaceful sporting event, and even when a political incident does arise, such as in the Munich Games of 1972 or the 1980 and 1984 boycotts of the Olympics, the events continue with relatively few interruptions. After the bombings in the United States on September 11, 2001, the media picked up on sporting events resuming as the message that the country was moving forward. Now veterans are honored at sporting events, and heroes are paraded in front of the crowd so people can pay their respects to the firefighters, police officers, rescue workers, and everyday heroes who risk their lives for a cause. In more recent events, such as the Boston marathon bombing, the Red Sox baseball team was again the beacon that people could look to as a sign of unity and progress. Obviously the running of the marathon the next year was also indicative of progress and resilience.

Sport has this ability that not many other social constructs have, and countries witness this and seek ways to capitalize on it. Sport is more than a ball or a bat in the hand of an athlete. It has become a symbol of prosperity, a tool for development, and an avenue for education. Most notably, sport has the ability to address vast social issues and bridge economic gaps.

Social Issues

Many countries have looked to the power of well-organized sport as the way out of societal difficulties such as poverty or drug abuse. Jamaica, for example, is looking at sport as a means to encourage sociopolitical change in addition to providing a positive spin on the country in an effort to boost tourism and foster a greater sense of national identity (Hume, 2012). In this case, Jamaica is looking to its performance on the world stage in track and field to heighten its brand as a sport country in hopes of attracting major sporting events to boost the economy, provide jobs, and encourage youth to follow in the steps of their national heroes.

The difficulty with such an effort is that its success lies in the success of just one person or a few people within the country. If the athletes are not successful for a few years or performance is poor at the Olympic Games, it would take another four years to have the opportunity to reestablish dominance, and the country may be in limbo and struggle for an identity during that time.

What countries like Jamaica need to do, then, is develop sport as a way into the community, not as a way out of it. When sport is simply seen as an avenue to perform at the highest levels in order to get a professional contract and then get out of the community or even the country, only a small number of people can actually accomplish this. Change within the community does not happen unless the successful person then puts millions of dollars back into the community.

When sport is seen as a way into the community, it truly becomes the agent for social change that the community seeks (Lawson, 2005). The community rallies around the sporting events, and children grow up in the sporting community, gaining the valuable skills and benefits mentioned in many of the previous chapters. Local sponsors tend to get involved, and families come to not only watch the game but more importantly to be involved in the community event. In a sense, the sport within the community is the cool thing to do and therefore is regarded as important to the community, not as a way out of the community. If a few elite athletes emerge from these events and go on to greatness, it's an unanticipated bonus. The real benefit of the sporting event when sport is seen as a way into the community is that the community becomes stronger and no one has to leave the community in order to support it. The difference is subtle but important, and this is why it is necessary to understand the international nature of sport and the impact it has on a local community.

In many countries, the sport participation of women is also influenced by international sport. In some cultures, women are still placed in the traditional role of taking care of the home and raising children and are not involved in physical activity. This obviously translates to elite competition in that if young females are not being involved in sport, a country has a difficult time producing elite female athletes. For example, Sarah Attar, the first female track and field athlete from Saudi Arabia to compete for her country, did more than simply run a race. She demonstrated to her country and to the world that it is okay for women to be physically active in sport. Perhaps more importantly, it led to a discussion of permitting girls in private schools to participate in sport, a monumental step in Saudi Arabia. However, funding for physical education and sport for women is still virtually nonexistent and there is no official curriculum for it in government schools, so clearly the country has a way to go for women to be valued within its sport system (HRW, 2012).

Economic Issues

There is little doubt that sport is a multibillion-dollar industry around the world. The National Football League (NFL) alone has an annual operating budget of billions of dollars, so clearly sport has the ability to influence the economies of entire countries. The 2002 FIFA World Cup of soccer in South Korea provided an estimated $1.35 billion U.S. dollars in economic impact in South Korea alone (Lee & Taylor, 2005). The FIFA World Cup is such an international event that it would be virtually impossible to determine its global economic impact in each country. However, what is important for a recreational sport professional to understand is that when a country does well in a world sporting event, such as swimming at the Olympics or soccer at the World Cup, youth participation rates almost always spike the following year, and recreational sport agencies need to parlay this new interest in the sport from a potentially untapped population into better programs and opportunities for the community. For example, when the U.S. women won the World Cup in 1999, youth soccer for girls saw an obvious jump in participation rates compared with soccer for boys. Leagues grew, programs started, and interest has continued to grow, generating revenue for communities hosting tournaments and leagues. Other countries have developed their women's soccer programs with the recognition that soccer exposure is good business, and more and more international soccer players are getting scholarships at U.S. institutions as coaches see programs producing solid players. Sport simply has an ability to generate revenue if done well.

After the World Cup in 1999, youth soccer for girls had a jump in participation rates.

INTERNATIONAL SPORT ORGANIZATIONS

Most sport at the international level falls under the auspices of **International Olympic Committee (IOC)**. The IOC is a nongovernmental agency that oversees the Summer and Winter Olympics as well as the Youth Olympic Games. The IOC also is charged with promoting sport ethics and good governance, ensuring the regular celebration of the Olympic Games, and encouraging the development of sport for all (www.olympic.org).

In partnership with the IOC, most sports throughout the world have **International Sports Federations (IFs)** that help govern a particular sport; an example is World Rugby, the governing body of rugby union. Some federations govern multiple sports, such as the International Skating Union, which oversees both short- and long-track speed skating, figure skating, ice dancing, and synchronized skating. Many of these federations function independently by hosting their own world championships, but they also work in cooperation with the IOC in many respects.

In addition, many countries have their own National Olympic Committees (NOCs). For example, the United States has the United States Olympic Committee (USOC). The mission of USOC is *"to support U.S. Olympic and Paralympic athletes in achieving sustained competitive excellence and to preserve the Olympic Ideals, thereby inspiring all Americans"* (www.teamusa.org). Much like the mission of the IOC is to promote sport globally and support the various NOCs and IFs, the USOC is designed to assist the national governing bodies in the United States.

A second example is provided in figure 14.1, which illustrates the structure of billiards in the Philippines and its international governance. It begins with the IOC, and the Philippine Olympic Committee (POC) and the World Confederation of Billiards Sports (WCBS), which is the IF, are both connected to it. The third level of organizations contains a number of federations listed under WCBS that act almost as regional federations, such as the International Billiards and Snooker Federation (IBSF), or subregional federations, such as the Asian Confederation of Billiard Sports (ACBS). Finally, at the country level the Billiards and Snooker Congress of the Philippines (BSCP) acts as the in-country, sport-specific governing body that provides guidance to the local clubs and organizations that have multiple coaches and athletes. This is a common structure for many sports around the world, from track and field to swimming.

It is important to understand the hierarchy of sport organizations and international federations because decisions at the highest levels have influence at the local level, even down to the local recreation facility. Rule changes or safety and equipment modifications at the international level eventually trickle down to the local hockey league or swimming pool. In addition, much as there is an international level of sport administration, there are national, regional, and local levels of sport administration that govern how leagues are run and many of the rules that a sport must abide by. Without governing organizations, it would be difficult to standardize rules, there would be few groups willing to organize competitions, and the future direction of the sport would be left up to individual communities. In addition, individual sports within the same country that are not functioning within the same framework tend to seek differing goals or try to reinvent the wheel instead of using a system that already has been successful in another sport. As a result, sport groups operate in isolation, and a community swimming program and tennis program end up with different goals for the community rather than one unified goal for the betterment of all the members involved.

INTERNATIONAL SPORT MODELS

Around the world, countries have their own visions for how recreation and sport should be implemented. Some countries are fragmented in that most sport organizations function independent of one another and design their own sport models within the sport. The entrepreneurial spirit of the United States, for example, has led to various groups starting their own leagues or tournament events with little to no oversight from any governing authority. As sport continues to grow, bringing large revenues for organizers, countries such as Canada have recognized the potential difficulty in individual sport entities having a multitude of goals and objectives. So, Sport Canada decided to implement a unified front on sport organization and training to bring all the sport entities in the country onto the same page within a framework of guidelines. Other

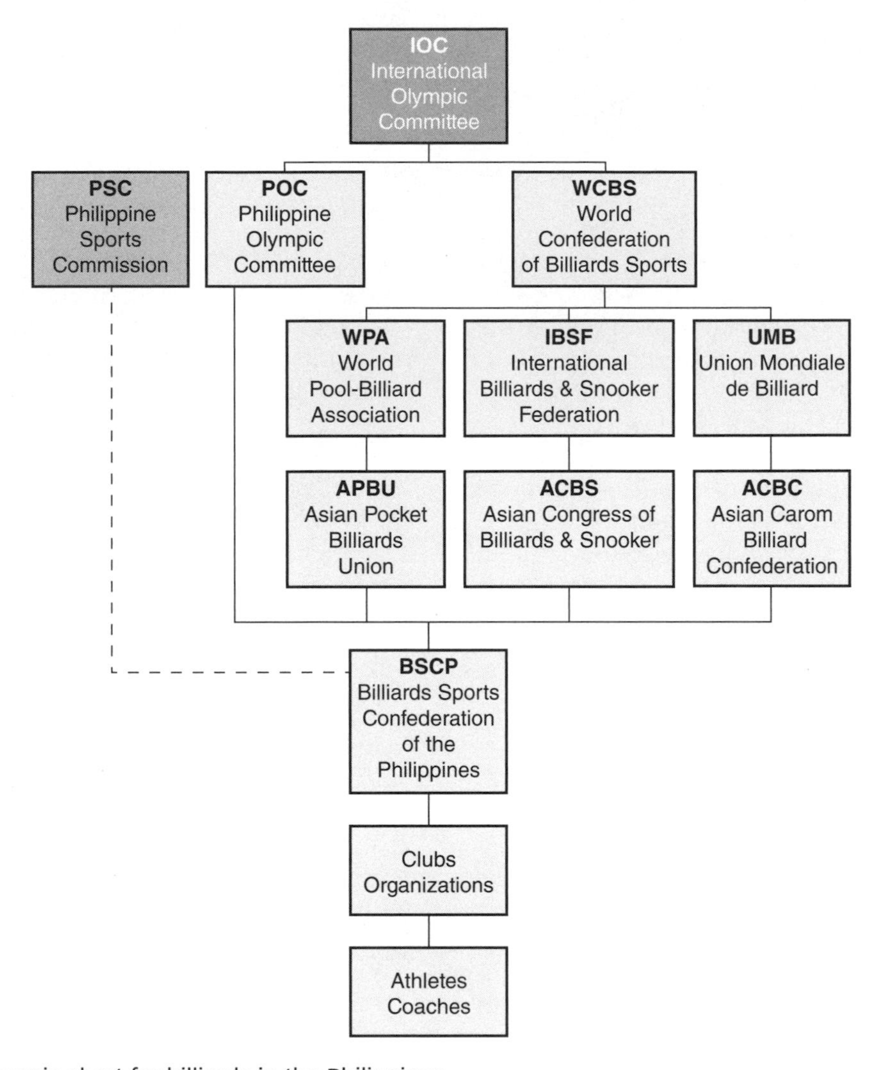

Figure 14.1 Olympic chart for billiards in the Philippines.

Reprinted, by permission, from Billiards Sports Confederation of the Philippines.

countries, such as the United Kingdom, have entire clubs with teams ranging from recreational all the way up to professional within one sport, but there is little cohesion across sports.

British System

As a result of London hosting the 2012 Summer Olympics, sport and club organizations within the United Kingdom have made an effort to bridge the gap between school sport and community sport by providing funds to clubs in order to encourage sport participation within the same club even beyond the school years. Children who begin sport activities in their school may also play for a local community club that is likely linked to a professional program at the highest level. Participants either continue to play and train in that program at the local level or progress to the more competitive levels while still remaining within the club structure. Upon completion of their schooling, regardless of their level of play, participants have the opportunity to continue playing for their local clubs. This encourages a sport-for-life model within the sport organization in partnership with the schools.

People at the highest levels of sport in Britain recognized two things. First, many programs were competing for the same athletes, which was creating fragmentation and difficulty within communities rather than providing benefits for children by keeping a systematic developmental progression in place. Second, not every child will perform at the highest levels. In the older, more fragmented system, once children got too good, they often had to move out of their community to play for a more competitive team. In the more modern program, they begin in an existing club or a school program with a club link, and they can remain within that club system all the way through their skill progression. This limits the jumping around and the athlete poaching, and it ultimately creates a more positive and progressive experience for children within the community or region all the way to their adult years. However, although this model is progressive in thought, it is still usually only for one sport.

Canadian Model

The Canadian sport system has devised a more complete, unified model that is now being implemented across multiple sports in similar ways. Following is a discussion of the model with basic modifications to generalize the content. Sport Canada, in cooperation with many of its sport organizations, developed a sport-for-life philosophy that takes youth participants from an active start to training at an international level and back to active-for-life activities. According to Sport Canada, the **Long-Term Athlete Development (LTAD) model** is "a movement to improve the quality of sport and physical activity in Canada. Canadian Sport for Life (CS4L) links sport, education, recreation, and health and aligns community, provincial, and national programming" (www.ltad.ca).

The LTAD model is designed to inform athletes and coaches as well as parents, educators, and recreation professionals (see figure 14.2). Seven stages make up the developmental spectrum, each designed to build on one another while also acting independently. Participants can enter the Active for Life stage, for example, at any age as they transition out of increasing levels of sport competition and back to less intense, more lifelong sport activities.

Within the seven stages, sport can be classified as either early- or late-stage specialization. Sports such as gymnastics and diving tend to be performed at the international level at much younger ages, whereas most other sports (e.g., soccer, rugby) fall within the late-stage specialization of skills. The seven stages tend to be directed toward late-specialization activities.

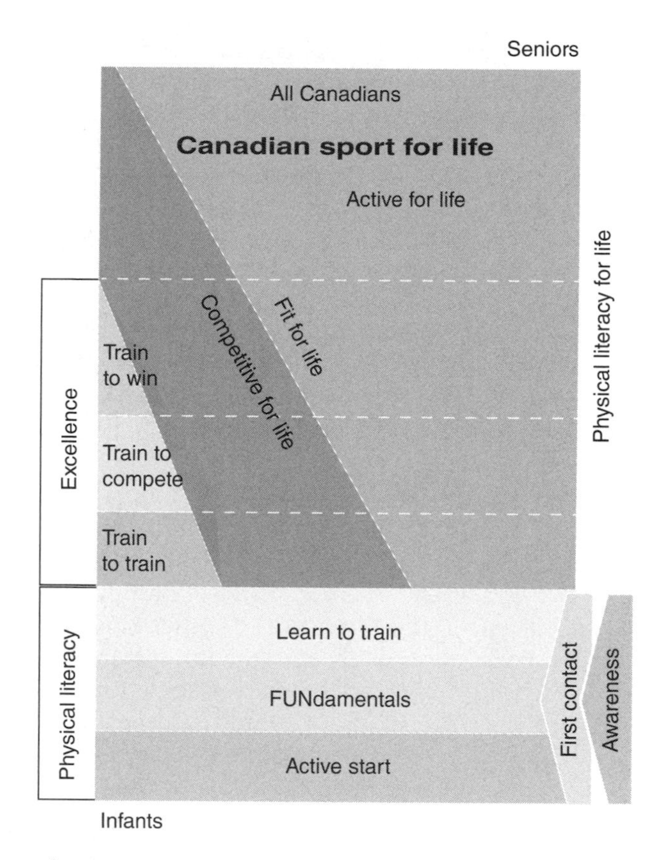

Figure 14.2 LTAD model for Canada.

Reprinted, by permission, from Canadian Sport for Life, 2014, *Canadian Sport for Life: Long term athletic development, 2.0* (Victoria, British Columbia: Canadian Sport Institute), 11. Available: http://canadiansportforlife.ca/sites/default/files/user_files/files/CS4L%202_0%20EN_April16_webpdf.pdf

Stage 1: Active Start

Active Start is geared toward youth aged 0 to 6. It is designed for overall fitness and movement skills that any child would need for normal skill development. Activities such as running, throwing, jumping, and kicking are examples that children at this age should be working on for healthy development. Active Start emphasizes that children within this age range should not be sedentary for longer than 60 minutes except when sleeping or resting. Some organized physical activity can be included, but creative play and movements are equally important and effective in most cases. This stage follows the philosophy of letting kids be kids rather than placing unnecessary pressures on them to perform and develop sport-specific skills too early. Parents, coaches, and sport programmers need to focus on providing safe, creative environments for the children so that exploration and risk taking can progress. Suggested activities might be open floor space, structured gymnastics with equipment exploration, and swimming programs with a lot of play activities. The Active Start stage is from ages 0 to 6, but ages vary slightly in the later stages because males and females tend to develop at slightly different rates and even within the same gender children develop differently, allowing for overlap in stages.

Stage 2: FUNdamental

The second stage is FUNdamental, which fits well for boys aged 6 to 9 and girls aged 6 to 8. In this stage, activities become more gamelike, although it is still important to participate in games that emphasize skill development and fun. Activities should focus on the ABCs of physical activity—agility, balance, and coordination—to prepare the young athlete for more advanced game skills and to encourage mastery of fundamental movement skills, leading to a more positive sense of self and activity efficacy. Play should still be fairly unstructured, and a variety of sports and activities should still dominate this stage rather than sport-specific skills or specialization. This stage is typically where early-specializing activities such as gymnastics tend to move toward more activity-specific skills, while late-specializing activities such as hockey remain oriented toward skill development in a safe yet challenging environment with a variety of activities.

This is typically the stage when children begin to read the activities around them, making adjustments for space, speed, and timing. This allows a coach or teacher to introduce basic rules and sport ethics into practice and play sessions so both participants and parents can see the bigger picture. Physical education in school can also play a role in the movement toward general skill mastery as well as in sport-specific skill exploration and development.

Stage 3: Learning to Train

In this stage, girls should be between 8 and 11 years old and males between 8 and 12. The concept of mental training is introduced, and athletes can progress toward an overall physical, mental, and cognitive training regiment. Participants should be making the transition from general activity movements to more sport-specific skills that will lead them to desired sport games and activities. It is suggested that participants pick perhaps three sports to focus on so they can develop sport-specific skills. However, mirroring sport skills, such as in tennis and swimming, are less advised because similar body movements are performed; rather, soccer and baseball would be a nice complement, for example, because soccer is largely a lower-body activity with a cardiorespiratory base and baseball is mostly upper-body movements with less cardiorespiratory demand. Nevertheless, sport-specific activities should only be performed three times a week while other sport and physical activities are performed the other three or four days a week to continue to encourage general skill mastery and to avoid overtraining and overuse injuries. Physical training should be limited to activities such as body-weight exercises, medicine ball activities, and band resistance training to encourage healthy training regiments. This stage is too early to introduce true weightlifting because growth plates are still undeveloped and proper form and technique are difficult to maintain.

Stage 4: Training to Train

In the Training to Train stage, girls are typically 11 to 15 whereas males are 12 to 16. Participants can begin to build an endurance base because their bodies are now capable of moderate cardiorespiratory development. In addition, proper speed and strength training with free weights in the latter part of the stage can lead to performance benefits that are sustained in later stages. Participants should continue to develop not only their physical but also their mental, emotional, and cognitive athletic capacities as knowledge of the sport, tactics, training programs, and ethics continue to be reinforced. It is helpful for athletes to continue to participate in general skill activities that complement the sport-specific skills that are being performed six to nine times per week. In addition, because this is an important growth stage, musculoskeletal evaluations should be performed frequently to ensure that the sport training is not interfering with overall development. Perhaps most importantly, many athletes will experience a divide in this stage as specialization in one sport becomes more evident, so there must be constant reminders and encouragement to see the Active for Life stage (stage 7) as the end point regardless of skill level or sport involvement. Some athletes will feel the need to continue to progress to stages 5 and 6, while others remain in this stage for a longer period of time and then transition directly to stage 7.

Stage 5: Training to Compete

In the Training to Compete stage, ages range from 15 to 21 for females and from 16 to 23 for males; however, these ranges are sport specific. For instance, a swimmer might experience this stage of participation from 15 to 17, whereas a hockey player might transition to this phase at closer to 20 to 23 years of age to remain competitive in the sport. This stage seeks to optimize fitness and position-specific skills necessary to compete at regional, national, and international levels of competition. Tactical, technical, and positional training are important in this stage as the athlete continues to specialize and develop the sport knowledge necessary to compete at more advanced levels. Advanced mental and physical preparation is encouraged and training often occurs 9 to 12 times per week in various sport-specific and complementary ways. Again, not all athletes will even seek to reach this stage but would rather remain at the recreational level of activity with continued skill development, moving straight to the Active for Life stage.

Stage 6: Training to Win

In Training to Win, ages typically range from 18 and up, depending on the sport standards and requirements, because this stage focuses on high levels of performance and achievement. Continued emphasis is placed on technical, tactical, and playing skill development as well as maintenance of the high levels of physical development and training that have been achieved to this point. At this stage, training regiments can be extremely intense, so frequent bouts of rest and break periods are important to allow for recovery and prevent injury. The athletes in this stage are generally looking to achieve national and international levels of competition leading to professionalism.

Stage 7: Active for Life

In the Active for Life stage, athletes should experience a smooth transition from their competitive career to an active lifestyle that involves frequent participation in physical activity of any kind and not necessarily sport-specific involvement. This is the end goal of all the previous stages, so athletes can use their physical literacy skills learned in the other stages to assist with positive aging and sport participation. In addition, athletes may transition into sport careers, volunteering in the sport of interest or coaching to remain active in the sport. The emphasis is on 60 minutes of moderate daily physical activity or shorter periods of intense activity. As mentioned, athletes could skip over stages 5 and 6; they never reach the Train to Compete or Train to Win stage and simply wish to use their skills in a more lifelong activity.

Although this model is a good guide for how sport could develop from infancy to older adulthood, not every athlete will go through every step. It obviously depends on the participant's level of skill, commitment, and desire to participate. However, the key end point is the active-for-life view of recreational sport. Perhaps more importantly, this model can be seen as a best practices tool that local and recreational sport programs can be modeled on. As in the case of Sport Canada, it can expand beyond the local level to the provincial or national level. It is based in sound literature and certainly involves aspects of healthy lifestyle development, positive youth development, and physical, emotional, psychological, and mental training, all of which can be used as tools across the life span.

The UK club sport model and the Sport Canada model are two examples of how countries can work to implement a unified front in a single sport or in a multisport model. Regardless of the model, ideally a program even at the community level can see a developmental progression that builds upon each stage in the child development process as well as the athlete development process. Unfortunately, many programs, particularly in the United States, simply focus on achieving maximum skill mastery in the hopes of earning professional paychecks in the sport of choice. These programs tend to focus on the elite level, even to the point of suggesting that the recreational programs help financially support and supplement the elite teams and athletes.

Within the United States, less than 2 percent of high school athletes get a college scholarship, and most of those are partial scholarships such as a book stipend or splitting a scholarship with three other athletes for 25 percent, leaving the athletes to pay the remaining 75 percent on their own. This leaves the remaining 98 percent of high school athletes to resume recreational sport participation, if programs are even available to them. In the state of South Carolina for example, the ratio of academic scholarships to athletic scholarships is approximately 10:1 in terms of dollar amounts and may be as high as 30:1, all in favor of a greater amount of academic dollars to athletic dollars (www.ncaa.org). Although the elite 2 percent of athletes are certainly important, the job of recreational sport professionals should be to accommodate the other 98 percent of athletes who will not get a college scholarship for athletics and should focus on sport-for-life models of participation. It has been suggested that if parents actually took all the money they spent on the elite training programs and paid for tutors while enrolling their children in local recreational leagues that cost far less, the children's likelihood of a college scholarship, albeit academic, would dramatically increase and they would be on the path to a more healthy sport-for-life philosophy.

Unfortunately, in many programs around the United States, the sport-for-life model is not being considered. Overtraining, specializing in sport too early, and neglecting positive youth development components of sport in particular are leading to unpleasant sport experiences, too much pressure to perform, and overtraining injuries, ultimately leading youth to drop out of sport altogether.

Organizations have become so fragmented that each league has different goals and objectives that are driven by the parent's or coach's agenda for the week rather than a unified front of program philosophy and mission-driven programs that lead to positive life lessons and sport for life. Parents who do not like what is being done in one organization or want their child's team to become even more elite and competitive are permitted to go off and design their own league, with little to no formal training in coaching, youth development, or sport programming. They can then recruit children to play in the league, and if they meet some basic standards, they are able to get sanctioned and compete. Local sport agencies then feel the pressure to rent facilities to these individual programs because they need to generate enough revenue to remain sustainable, and the incentive for sport programs that focus on positive youth development and are run by trained recreational sport professionals is disappearing. This is not to suggest that other countries do not have some of the same issues but rather to highlight how a unified sport model with similar goals and objectives that lead to the end goal of sport for life can provide guidance for changing sport and youth development through sport.

SPORT AND THE OLYMPICS

The Summer Olympics are by far the most watched sporting event in the world. As many as 3.5 billion people watch Olympic events to cheer on their country's athletes, watch a favorite sport, or see the latest trends in international competition. From the beginning of the modern Olympics, though, the Games have also been a symbol of the host country and a branding agent for countries to identify what they represent.

The economic and social impacts on the host countries have been displayed in the media on numerous occasions, both good news and not so good. There is significant debate from many sides about the effects on a country that hosts the Olympics, but the evidence is clear. Hosting the Olympic Games puts that nation in the global spotlight for longer than simply the length of the athletic events. The bidding process to simply host the Games takes place some seven to nine years away from the actual Games date. Olympic cities are determined approximately six to seven years out from the Games and a significant planning process then ensues. The most recent Olympic hosts have invested billions of dollars in construction of not just sport venues and housing but also roads, subways, train systems, airports, and restaurants. Jobs are created to support the construction and job seekers come from all around the world to be involved in an event at such a grand international scale.

Economic Impact

All this comes with a cost, of course. That money has to come from somewhere, and typically local, regional, and national governments have to put forth funds to support all of the building and infrastructure, which means taxpayers pay at least part of the bill. Construction means inconveniences for local travelers and residents well in advance of any athlete stepping foot in a venue to compete. New buildings mean old ones often come down, displacing people from their homes and businesses. The belief is that all the inconvenience will be rewarded with a positive image when the world sees the Games and with the benefits of the improved infrastructure, but long-term gains are often difficult to see in the short term.

Hosting the Olympic Games has some significant economic and social impacts. It is estimated that the 2000 Olympics in Sydney have generated an additional $6.5 billion in increased economic activity, and the tourism and visitor effects continue to be felt (Haynes, 2001). However, in recent Olympics the economic expenses are beginning to outweigh the benefits. Most recently, the 2014 Sochi Olympics cost some $51 billion, far more

Jose Gil/fotolia.com

Sport facilities that are built for the Olympic Games are often used even after the Games are over and they can contribute to the economic engine of a community.

than any other Olympics to date and likely a deficit that will take Russia many years to come out of. However, the long-term economic impact of the Sochi Olympics will take many years to be realized because the tourism impact cannot be immediately measured.

Social Impact

The social benefits of hosting the Olympics are perhaps even more pronounced than the economic benefits, and certainly for recreation sport professionals this is where the impact of the Games really matters. A host country assumes that sport and participation in leisure activities will increase both before and after the Olympics have taken place, and in Australia, this was certainly true. Pre-Olympic events such as world test events and educational and community Olympic programs that are designed to get the country excited about the Games coming to town increase participation rates in not only sport but also volunteerism and community involvement. After the Olympics, as in the case of Sydney and within the United States, there tends to be an immediate influx of participation in events that the country performed well in at the Olympics. However, this influx tends to be short lived (six months to a year), and participation numbers tend to decline again more than one year after the Olympics. It is important to understand how to capture this initial interest and parlay it into more sustained community sport involvement (Hayes, 2001).

The Beijing Olympic Games resulted in some unique social benefits. The world put significant pressure on the Chinese government to acknowledge the human rights problems the country was experiencing, and world media certainly put additional attention on the difficulties. China promoted the entire Olympic process as the people's Olympics, providing at least the perception that the citizens of the country mattered and their involvement was valued. It was also likely hoping to quell any pushback it might get from the international community about human rights (Ong, 2004).

JOBS AND CAREER OPPORTUNITIES

Having a better understanding now of the scope of international sport and how it affects local recreational sport, it is important for new professionals to see that the skills they have learned by being in recreational sport can also be valuable tools in a global sport economy. Ultimately, employees want to progress in their jobs. Some see progression as moving up within the same organization, but others might see progression as moving from a local community sport program to a more regional program and then to a national or international organization.

Local Opportunities

As discussed, the time immediately following the Olympics tends to bring new participants to community recreation centers and sport leagues. For instance, when Michael Phelps was so successful in his bid for Olympic gold in swimming, swim programs all around the United States reported increased numbers. This meant more jobs for local coaches, more resources directed toward the pool such as lifeguards and pool staff, and more programming for public swim and maintenance. Soccer programs saw similar effects when the

U.S. women's team won World Cup gold. It will be interesting to see what happens in the coming years as new sports are reintroduced to the Olympic Games. It is entirely possible that a sport such as rugby, introduced back into the Olympics for the 2016 Rio Games, will help increase participation numbers in countries all around the world.

There are also local organizations that support the various NOCs around the country, such as club and state representatives of the governing bodies. Often these positions are voluntary or in partnership with a job or agency that is working with the sport at the local level and is sanctioned by the NOC. For example, various soccer clubs are affiliated with U.S. Soccer, and there are job opportunities at the local level to support their programs and initiatives, from referees to coaches to administrators to field and facility maintenance providers.

National Opportunities

Much like local job opportunities, there is job potential at the national level of the sport agencies that support or contribute to international sport. For example, as USA Rugby continues to prepare for the Olympic Games, it has jobs in administration, coaching, media communications, marketing, and logistics. There are also internships in many of these areas to expose students and young professionals to the game and to national and international sport. USA Rugby also assists with youth and high school leagues, has community outreach jobs, and has jobs that seek to grow the sport of rugby in the United States through ticket sales, event planning, marketing, advertising, and sponsorship acquisition.

In addition, USOC has hundreds of jobs nationwide to support its organization (www.teamusa.org). Jobs range from research and donor stewardship to program coordination to various internships all around the country as well as at several sport-specific training sites. It is important to recognize that sport jobs with national and international organizations can be local and can offer partnership opportunities with small community clubs or groups.

International Opportunities

The organizations mentioned in the beginning of the chapter all offer sport opportunities at the highest levels. For example, the International Ice Hockey Federation (IIHF) has jobs, although most are not based in the United States and many require several years of experience in hockey-related administration. Because many tournaments are run by host nations, IIHF suggests that job seekers contact the organizing bodies of the host nation for job openings. Sport jobs at the international level are difficult to obtain because they receive applications from all around the world. Similarly, although there are a number of jobs with the IOC, they would require you to move to Switzerland, where the IOC headquarters are.

In addition, national and international events such as the Olympics and various world championships have job opportunities that tend to be temporary, around one to three years in duration, but do provide great experiences. Also, many large sport events all around the world require volunteers, and this is a great way to at least get exposed to the organization and potentially gain employment in the future.

CONCLUSION

Although this book focuses on recreational sport management, it is important to understand the role that international sport plays at the local level. The various international and national sport agencies can have a large impact on local policy and rules and subsequently influence sport at the individual and community levels. In addition, success for athletes at the international level can have a profoundly positive impact on local and community sport programs as participants flock to pools, gyms, and fields to swim like their idol or run as fast as their favorite star athlete. This can provide additional revenue, interest, and opportunity for recreational sport programs to increase their participation numbers.

It is also important to recognize what other countries are doing with their sport programs in order to keep pace from a competitive standpoint and to potentially mimic a program that might be successful in other parts of the world. The LTAD model in Canada is one such concept that would help in providing a unified sport front for an agency or ultimately an entire country to work toward keeping in mind the positive aspects of recreation, sport, youth development, and lifelong fitness.

RESEARCH TO REALITY

Billings, S.B., & Holladay, J.S. (2011). Should cities go for the gold? The long-term impact of hosting the Olympics. *Economic Inquiry*, *50*(3), 754-772.

The Olympics are the most widely televised events in the world and bring much publicity and notoriety. Billings and Holladay discuss both the benefits (e.g., an estimated $10 billion in visitor spending for the event alone) and the negatives (e.g., additional spending on highway improvements and infrastructure often passed on to taxpayers of the host city). Yet, what is often lost in the mix of the Olympic bid and anger over the spending of taxpayer dollars on the games are the number of jobs brought to the area, the worldwide attention paid to the host city and country, and the long-term benefits of the infrastructure improvements, which are used by the local community well after the event has ended.

Billings and Holladay sought to compare the impact of the Olympics on the host nation with similar nations that did not get awarded the Olympics in the same year. They determined that although there are some benefits, many of the potential long-term benefits may be bid away as a means to actually win the bid for the Games, thus decreasing the potential economic impact. The authors also suggested that although direct impacts such as tourism might not be as large as estimated, indirect impacts such as improved work productivity as a result of improved roads might benefit the host city in the long run. Certainly as bids continue to increase and expectations for host nations grow, potential host cities will need to do a detailed cost–benefit analysis.

REFLECTION QUESTIONS

1. What opportunities are available for people to participate at all levels of sport in your community?
2. What aspects of the Olympics are most important for a community, a region, and a country?
3. If you were asked to identify how your local recreational sport program contributed to social and economic development much as the Olympics or a mega event can, what components would you focus on?

LEARNING ACTIVITIES

1. Using the LTAD model that Canada has implemented, organize a similar model for your community leagues and programs.
2. If the big city in your area were to host a mega event such as the Olympics, what programs would you create to capitalize on the energy and excitement of the event coming to the area?

chapter 15

CAREERS IN RECREATIONAL SPORT

LEARNING OUTCOMES

By the end of this chapter, readers will be able to

- describe the key career settings and job functions in recreational sport,
- assess and apply the key competency areas for recreational sport professionals,
- conduct a career self-assessment on the 10 core competency areas related to recreational sport, and
- list the steps involved in preparing oneself for a job in the field of recreational sport.

Case Study

CAN I REALLY MAKE A LIVING DOING THIS?

Kate Malken was in a quandary as she sat in her dorm room contemplating her future. Kate was a second-semester sophomore and an undeclared major at Edgewood State University, and she had just gotten a letter from the campus registrar telling her that the deadline was approaching for her to declare a major. Of course, Kate knew that this deadline was on the horizon, but like many of her friends, she just couldn't find a major that corresponded to a career that she was interested in. In her time at Edgewood State, Kate took classes in psychology, business, marketing, and even education. All of them interested her to one degree or another, but none was close to what she wanted to do for a career.

Kate thought about all of this as she dressed in her campus recreation uniform for her part-time job as an intramural sport supervisor, and she continued to mull it over as she walked across campus to work her shift. She arrived at the rec center early and stopped in to see her boss, Bob Manzel, the associate director for intramural sport and sport clubs. Kate had a good relationship with Bob, and she confided in him.

"I need to pick a major, but I have no idea what I want to study. I'm not sure what I even want to do for a career. I thought I wanted to teach and coach, but I realized after taking some education classes that isn't for me," Kate said. "I really liked my psychology classes—I'm a people person. But I also like to organize, plan, and manage things. I think I'm a pretty good leader—after all, I've become a supervisor here after just 2 years—and I like solving problems. I'm pretty creative, I'm a half-decent public speaker, and I like technology—and not just Facebook. I'm pretty sure I don't want to work in some generic desk job. I'm 20 years old, but I don't know what I want to do for the rest of my life."

Bob listened thoughtfully, but had a pretty good idea of how to respond. He asked, "Kate, do you have a résumé?"

"No, not an official one," Kate replied.

Bob continued, "Well, think about the things that you've done in your life—part-time jobs, volunteer experiences, extracurricular activities. What do those look like?"

Kate answered, "Well, I played just about every sport in high school. I was the captain of my soccer team my senior year, and I competed in the state games for lacrosse. I worked as a summer camp counselor between my freshman and sophomore year. I work for intramurals here on campus, and I coach and officiate for the local park and recreation department. I also volunteered to work at the Hoop It Up tournament on campus last month."

"Have you ever thought about majoring in recreation or sport management?" Bob asked. "Edgewood has a pretty good program, you know."

Kate thought for a moment. She had seen some of the courses offered by the department of recreation and sport management but had never given them much thought. She asked, "Is that a real major? I mean, can I actually make a living doing this?"

Bob laughed. "Look at me," he replied. "I work full time managing the university's intramural sport and sport clubs program. Look at your supervisor at Edgewood Parks and Recreation—she works full time managing all of the city's sport and athletics programs. The tournament manager for Hoop It Up? He manages a full-time staff of sport and recreation managers planning and running three-on-three basketball tournaments up and down the coast. And the state games? They have a whole host of full-time staff who design, market, and deliver events; sell sponsorships; work with media; and do a lot of other things that make the state games go. So yes, you can make a living doing this. Lots of people do!"

Kate thought about it. Maybe this was it: a career that combined her love of sport with her love of working with people, planning, leading, and managing. It was a career that allowed her to get paid for what she loved to do—a career that involved doing work that might not feel like work. "Recreation and sport management," Kate said. "Looks like I found my major!"

Does Kate's experience sound familiar to you? Whether or not your school requires you to choose a major before your freshman year or after your sophomore year, at some point you will undoubtedly need to think about what you want to study and what you want to do for your career. It would be nice if every graduating high school senior knew about the opportunities to work in the field of recreational sport, but most students discover this career path sometime during their college years. For many students, it takes a mentor who is working in the field to give career direction and advice. For others, it might be a college adviser or faculty member. For still others, it might be an introductory recreation or sport management class. For most students, it is a combination of interests, experiences, and information that leads them to a career path in recreational sport.

If you can relate to Kate in some way—knowing what you love and what you are good at but not knowing exactly what you want to do with the rest of your life, then chapter 15 will be useful to you as you begin to explore a future career in recreational sport. Or, if you have always known that this is something that you want to do for a living but you don't know exactly what the field offers or how to land your first job, read on. There are many opportunities for careers in recreational sport, including jobs that will require you to develop and run sport programs; manage sport facilities and venues; plan large-scale sport events; train and manage coaches, officials, and other recreational sport personnel; schedule leagues and tournaments; help develop athletes at every age level; solicit corporate sponsorships; and work with the media. This chapter highlights some of the careers in recreational sport and will help you understand the competencies and knowledge areas that you will be responsible for if you want to be in the best position to find a good job in the field.

THE RECREATIONAL SPORT FIELD

The recreational sport field can be seen as a subset of both the recreation and leisure and the sport management industries; that is, recreational sport professionals work in jobs that provide sport opportunities for the widest range of participants. Recall our discussion of the foundations of recreational sport back in chapter 1. The philosophy that underlies recreational sport is that of sport for all—a philosophy that speaks to the provision of active, participatory sport experiences. The competencies and skills that underlie the recreational sport field support this philosophy and are common to the various job settings and functions in the field. **Job settings** are the places where recreational sport professionals work, including the management sector and the type of agency or organization where the job takes place. **Job functions** are the specific kinds of jobs that recreational sport professionals perform.

As you consider potential jobs in the recreational sport field, remember that there is a tremendous amount of diversity in the various recreational sport settings and job functions. A recreational sport professional could find herself working in educational, community, or business settings doing any number of jobs, such as programming sport tournaments and leagues, managing sport venues and facilities, leading instructional activities, supervising sport staff, planning and marketing sport events, or doing some combination of all these things. The diversity of the recreational sport field is one of the attractive things about it; there is a tremendous amount of choice for job seekers looking to match their skills and interests in sport to particular jobs. However, it can also be challenging because there are so many job avenues to pursue. As you read through the following sections, think about the job settings that are most attractive to you. Also, think about the kinds of jobs that you would be most interested in doing in those settings. Thinking about this now can help you better plan how to frame your academic and practical experiences in the field, thus helping you better position yourself for the recreational sport career that is most attractive to you.

Diverse Job Settings

Recreational sport professionals work in diverse organizations and settings. They are needed in any organization where sport programs are offered to meet the needs of active participants (primarily enjoyment) and enhance a wide range of individual and societal outcomes. As mentioned previously, recreational sport agencies and organizations operate in the public, not-for-profit, and commercial sectors of the economy, and the philosophies and missions of these organizations often differ depending on which sector they operate in. The terms *agencies* and *organizations* are often used interchangeably, including in this book. However, **agencies** typically are public-sector recreational sport entities, and **organizations** are typically recreational sport providers in the nonprofit or commercial sectors.

Career settings, the places and contexts where jobs in recreational sport take place, can include the following:

- Municipal and county recreation departments, including adult and youth sport
- Military MWR organizations
- School (PK-12) and college intramural and recreational sport
- Resort sports, such as ski and golf
- Sport facilities and venues, such as arenas, stadiums, and recreation complexes
- Sport and fitness clubs, such as martial arts studios and fitness centers
- Sport councils and sport tourism
- National governing bodies and sport federations
- Community nonprofit agencies, such as the YMCA and Boys and Girls Clubs
- Sport for people with disabilities

Recreational sport programs are offered through a variety of organized types, like this private health and fitness club.

It might be tempting to think that there is a typical recreational sport organization, but think again. The organizations that provide recreational sport opportunities are varied and diverse. Recreational sport activities and programs are offered by municipal park and recreation departments; nonprofit organizations, such as the YMCA; resorts; cruise ships; and colleges and universities through programs such as intramural sport, sport clubs, and campus fitness. Even professional sport leagues and teams offer community-based programs to a wide range of participants. These programs are often used to grow the sport in nontraditional communities. Examples of these initiatives include programs such as the National Hockey League's Hockey is for Everyone initiative or Major League Baseball's Reviving Baseball in Inner Cities (RBI) program.

Some recreational sport programs are designed specifically to leverage positive developmental outcomes for adult participants. For example, there are Senior Games all over the United States, Canada, and Europe. The Senior Games use sport and physical activity to focus on a number of strategic outcomes, including helping seniors to lead healthy lifestyles that result in healthy aging, enhanced wellness, and increased quality of life (National Senior Games Association, 2012). At the other end of the age spectrum are organizations that use recreational sport to promote positive youth development. These programs use sport as a tool to engage young people, and they are intentionally planned to promote healthy development and to help youth thrive. Girls on the Run (running) and The First Tee (golf) are examples of recreational sport programs that focus on youth development (Barcelona, Hurd, & Bruggeman, 2011).

Other organizations offer recreational sport opportunities for specific groups of athletes. Northeast Passage, a sport-based recreation program for athletes with disabilities at the University of New Hampshire, provides recreational sport opportunities to clients of all ages and at all levels of the sport development pyramid. For example, an athlete with a disability may start participating in a foundational sled hockey program designed to introduce the game; progress through recreational-focused sled hockey programs designed to foster participation; compete in local, regional, and sled hockey national tournaments; and have the opportunity to train and compete at the highest levels, such as the Paralympic Games.

These are just a few examples of the diverse job settings where recreational sport activities take place. As you investigate more, you may find yourself attracted to a specific job setting, or you may be interested in a number of job settings. If you have an idea about what kind of setting you want to work in, the next step is to think about the kind of job you want to do within that setting.

Diverse Job Functions

Recreational sport professionals are attracted to their jobs because they have the opportunity to be involved in the direct provision of sport opportunities by working closely with participants, volunteers, and paid staff. Job duties tend to be varied and can include programming sport events, designing and maintaining facilities, developing policies, monitoring program budgets, training staff and volunteers, scheduling tournaments, managing risk, and engaging in marketing and promotional strategies. In other areas of the sport industry, such as professional sport management or college athletics administration, sport managers may be focused on a specific task, such as selling tickets or advertising. However, in recreational sport, there are typically multiple opportunities to engage in a wide range of job-related duties.

Recreational sport professionals often need to wear many hats in their jobs. A supervisor of youth athletics in a municipal park and recreation department might need to schedule teams and leagues; develop and monitor a program budget; develop a marketing strategy; hire, train, and schedule staff; handle the media; and engage in program evaluation efforts. Although the scope of job duties will depend on the organization and the specific job, staff working in larger organizations tend to have more specialized job duties, whereas staff in smaller organizations need to demonstrate a wider range of skills.

PROFESSIONAL AND CAREER DEVELOPMENT IN RECREATIONAL SPORT

Careers in this field start with a love of sport. This is an important start, because there is wisdom in the saying that if you choose a job that you love, you will never have to work a day in your life. A love of sport and a passion for working with people are good foundations for a career in recreational sport; however, they are not enough. As a recreational sport professional, you will need to possess many professional competencies that have little to do with sport per se. For example, you will need to understand and apply theoretical frameworks, financial accounting and budgeting procedures, personnel management practices, marketing tactics, tournament scheduling formats, risk management principles, policy formulation, technology applications, communication skills, and research and evaluation strategies (Barcelona & Ross, 2005). In addition to these core competencies, specific jobs may require you to have specialized skills, such as officiating, coaching, and aquatic or fitness certifications.

In addition to understanding the key competencies of recreational sport professionals and having a good sense of what skills you need to strengthen, professional development involves academic preparation, practical experience, professional involvement, and the job search process. Most professional positions—even those at the entry level—will require you to have experience working in recreational sport settings. In the opening case study, Kate Malken was well on her way to becoming a recreational sport professional because she had already put together an impressive list of practical experiences in the field. As she starts to complete classes in her major, she will begin to develop the theoretical, philosophical, and practical knowledge related to recreation and sport management that will build a sound professional foundation for her full-time job. Professional development in recreational sport is not just about getting the right degree or having the right amount of practical experience and professional involvement. Ideally, it is a combination of both academic knowledge and real-world experiences that enables graduates to get the jobs that they want the most.

Recreational Sport Competencies

Professional competencies are those traits, skills, knowledge areas, or attributes that are required for successful job performance (Barcelona et al., 2011). They refer not only to what people can do but also to what they are willing to do. Ten main competency areas are required of recreational sport professionals—business procedures, communications and public relations, technology and computing skills, facilities and equipment management, governance, legality and risk management, management techniques, theory and philosophy, programming techniques and event management, and research and program evaluation (Barcelona & Ross, 2005). These competency areas mirror the eight core competencies developed by NIRSA and found in the Registry of Collegiate Recreational Sports Professionals (NIRSA, 2013). In addition, recreational sport competencies are also reflected in the learning outcomes associated with the foundational curriculum in accredited park and recreation management programs (NRPA, 2013). These competencies should be familiar to you, particularly because they have been covered in the previous chapters of this textbook!

All of these critical competency areas are described next. As you read, ask yourself how well prepared you are in each competency area. Specifically, consider asking yourself the following questions.

- **Do you need more knowledge about the competency or the subjects that make up the competency?** If so, this knowledge may be covered in specific classes in your major, such as foundations of recreation, program design, management, or research and evaluation. You could also seek classes outside your major for specialized expertise, such as technology and computing applications, human growth and development, or finance and budgeting. Additionally, you might consider going to professional conferences through your state park and recreation association and attending sessions and workshops covering the areas that you need more information about. The last section of this chapter discusses how you can get involved with state or national professional associations in the field.
- **Do you need more practical experience to better demonstrate and apply the competency?** For example, you might have taken classes on tournament scheduling and program design, but you need to get more practical experience doing these things. Learning by doing is important for a few reasons. First, real-world experiences help you to put into practice what you have been learning in the classroom. Second, these experiences translate into bullet points on a résumé—bullet points that are critical in helping you get a paying

Volunteering with local recreational sport programs is a valuable learning experience and helps build one's professional resume.

job in the future! Last, professional experiences often puts you in contact with recreational sport professionals who can help mentor and guide you. These mentors can become part of your professional network—a network that can be very useful in your job search. Practical experiences will be discussed in more detail later. Service learning classes, internships, part-time work, and volunteering are all excellent ways to practice the knowledge that you've gained in the classroom.

After critically examining where you are with respect to each of these competencies, you will be better able to engage each step of the job search process.

Business Procedures

Business procedures comprise those competencies that lead to effective organizational and program administration and leadership. They include leadership skills such as problem solving, decision making, and creative thinking. This area also includes competencies related to financial management; accounting; budgeting; revenue generation, including securing sponsorships, donations, and other forms of giving; strategic and master planning; and partnership formation and maintenance. Knowledge of ethical principles in the field and commitment to upholding ethical standards are also important components of business procedures. These competencies are not only important at the administrative level of an organization but at the entry or program level as well.

Communications and Public Relations

Communications and public relations are those competencies that help ensure successful internal and external communication. **External communication** focuses on the organization's customers or potential customers and key constituents. **Internal communication** focuses on messaging within the organization as well as the interpersonal communication skills needed between coworkers. Communications and public relations competencies include skills such as marketing programs and events, using positioning and repositioning strategies, developing effective media campaigns, and working with print, broadcast, and digital media. Competencies in this area also include interpersonal communication skills, an ability to empathize, and effective listening. Finally, strong writing and public speaking are critical to the success of recreational sport professionals.

Technology and Computing Skills

As discussed earlier in the text, proficiency with technology platforms is an important competency for recreational sport professionals. This competency area includes proficiency with basic personal and desktop computing functions, including word processing, spreadsheets, presentation software, and the Internet. It may also include Web publishing and social media use. Also required is familiarity with field-specific software applications, such as tournament or facility management software, accounting programs, contact management software, and point-of-sale programs. It is true that different organizations will use different technology platforms, hardware, and software programs, and some organizations will prefer job candidates who are proficient in using specific technology applications. However, most will want to see that you are familiar with technology and that you can quickly learn the specifics of particular technology platforms.

Facilities and Equipment Management

This competency area refers to those skill sets associated with effective facility management, planning, and design as well as effective management of recreational sport equipment. Specific competencies include developing policies and procedures related to facility operations, scheduling the facility, creating a plan for routine and ongoing maintenance, planning future facility enhancements or additions, engaging in new facility planning and design, identifying and working with facility contractors and maintenance staff, and managing events held at or within the facility. In addition to facilities, this competency area comprises familiarity with recreational sport equipment, including repairing and replacing equipment, using inventory systems, identifying and working with equipment vendors, and purchasing.

Governance

As recreational sport has grown in scope and complexity, the need for adequate governance systems, effective oversight, and sound policy has become even greater to ensure participant safety, program integrity, and fair play. Governance competencies are related to the development of sound policies and procedures that guide oversight of recreational sport. They include knowledge of key sport policy areas, such as eligibility, sportsmanship, coaching, the role of competition, participant health, uniforms and equipment, protests, player and coach conduct, and performance-enhancing drugs. Knowledge of sport governing bodies and sanctioning organizations, such as USA Hockey, Little League Baseball, or the American Youth Soccer Organization (AYSO), is also important, particularly for those recreational sport organizations that provide opportunities for sanctioned sport participation. In addition, governance competencies include establishing a judiciary process for dealing with program concerns and possessing the ability to work with and supervise governing or appeals boards.

Legality and Risk Management

Working to ensure participant safety is a critical concern for recreational sport professionals. Competencies related to legality and risk management include having a working knowledge of basic legal terminology, such as *negligence* and *liability*; developing a risk management plan for sport programs and events; training staff on legal and safety issues; understanding laws and legislation pertaining to sport and recreation, including laws related to access and equity (e.g., ADA, Title IX) and legal liability or immunity; and implementing and monitoring waivers of liability and informed-consent documents for recreational sport programs. In addition, recreational sport professionals must be able to ensure proper and safe conduct of recreational sport activities, including conducting routine inspections of equipment, facilities, and playing areas; monitoring weather conditions and making weather-related decisions about game play; and training staff to control games and enforce program policies, procedures, and rules.

Management Techniques

Management techniques are used in the day-to-day operations of recreational sport programs and services, including managing staff and interacting with customers. Specific competencies include developing job descriptions; hiring, training, scheduling, evaluating, and recognizing staff and volunteers; maintaining payroll information and records; developing personnel policies and procedures; creating a positive work environment; consulting staff and volunteers in program and event planning and facility operations; and empowering and motivating staff and volunteers. Management techniques also encompass interactions with customers, including providing sound customer service, recruiting participants for programs, and developing relationships with key customers.

Theory and Philosophy

The theoretical and philosophical aspects of recreational sport provide the foundation for professional practice. Theory and philosophy help to explain why recreational sport professionals do what they do. Theory helps to explain and predict

As a recreational sport professional you could be working in a stadium or managing a sport complex.

participant behavior, and philosophy helps to answer big questions about the field—questions that are fundamental to understanding access and equity, participation eligibility, competition level, and a host of other practical questions that need to be answered every day. It is true that specific areas of the recreational sport field require specific theoretical knowledge that might not be applicable to other areas of the recreational sport profession. For example, a key campus recreational sport competency is having a working knowledge of student development theory, and fitness and physical activity professionals need to be knowledgeable about human anatomy and physiology. However, core competencies related to theory and philosophy that are applicable to most recreational sport professionals include knowing the history of recreational sport; understanding the relationships between categories of sport (e.g., educational, recreational, athletic, professional) and the philosophies that differentiate each; knowing psychological and sociological theories that help explain recreational sport motivation, satisfaction, and participation (including constraints to participation); applying knowledge of human growth and development in the design of recreational sport activities; and understanding the connection between recreational sport and health.

Programming Techniques and Event Management

The ability to conceptualize, design, schedule, run, and evaluate programs and events is the core of what most recreational sport professionals do. Core programming and event planning competencies include understanding the broad spectrum of recreational sport opportunities; knowing the organizational and operational aspects of various programs, leagues, meets, and special events; implementing planning strategies for programs and events, including the development of program logic models; scheduling tournaments, leagues, and meets; and managing programs and special events. Programming and event management requires the integration of many of the competency areas outlined in this chapter. For example, effective programming requires knowledge of business procedures, legality and risk management, management techniques, communication and public relations, and research and program evaluation. We will discuss competency integration briefly after we finish discussing the individual competency areas.

Research and Program Evaluation

Research and program evaluation competencies relate to the ability to gather, analyze, and synthesize information related to recreational sport and use the information gathered to improve programs, facilities, and operations. Research and program evaluation competencies include using research databases and information portals to access outside information and data pertaining to recreational sport; knowing the trends affecting the recreational sport field; developing surveys and other data collection tools; conducting needs assessments to determine priorities for new programs or facilities; collecting data to assess key outputs related to program operations, including participation numbers and program satisfaction; and collecting and analyzing data to demonstrate program effectiveness, including assessing program outcomes. Research and evaluation competencies also involve having a good understanding of quantitative and qualitative research strategies, including knowledge of basic descriptive and inferential statistics and interviewing and focus-group techniques.

Although these competencies are listed as distinct areas, they are interrelated. The example that was used regarding programming underscores this point, and the same can be said about any number of these competency areas. That is why these 10 areas are so important for recreational sport professionals. If you are weak in communication, it will be tough to be an effective manager. If you are weak in research and evaluation, it will be almost impossible to be an effective organizational leader and employ effective business procedures. As you critically assess your own skills in these 10 areas, think about how you might put yourself in situations that allow you to practice competency integration. Competency integration refers to the process of becoming proficient in multiple competency areas to increase overall job effectiveness. For example, seek classroom experiences and assignments that can help you gain writing, research, and public speaking skills, or seek volunteer or part-time job experiences that provide opportunities to lead programs, interact with customers, and perhaps even manage staff or volunteers. These are all excellent arenas for learning and bringing together the core knowledge areas in the field.

Academic Preparation

Almost all full-time professional positions require successful candidates to have at least a bachelor's degree, typically in recreation, leisure studies, sport management, or a related field. Although a degree in a discipline closely associated with recreation or sport management is not absolutely necessary for every position, good undergraduate programs provide exposure to the competencies noted previously and require field-based work opportunities, such as practicums and internships. Most academic programs for recreation and leisure studies provide coursework focused on the core competencies in recreational sport, particularly programs that are accredited through the Council on Accreditation of Parks, Recreation, Tourism and Related Professions (COAPRT). Presently there are 81 undergraduate degree programs accredited by COAPRT (NRPA, 2013). Undergraduate programs in sport management also often provide students with exposure to recreational sport careers (Masteralexis, Barr, & Hums, 2005).

Students can supplement their academic preparation by completing a minor or an academic emphasis in a related field. For example, a minor in physical education, business administration, or youth development can add depth to academic studies. Graduate degrees are rarely required for entry-level positions in recreational sport, with the exception of university campus recreation jobs (e.g., intramural sport, sport clubs, campus fitness). However, graduate degrees in recreation or sport management can be useful for professional advancement or to obtain upper-level administration positions after gaining sufficient practical experience in the field.

Practical Experience

Your academic degree and curriculum preparation in recreation and sport management will help to open doors for you in your job search. However, real-world experience in the field of recreational sport will allow you to walk through the door. Recreational sport is an applied field that is grounded in a body of knowledge and a defined set of professional competencies. Think of the body of knowledge that underlies recreational sport as the foundation of your professional preparation. It is the base of information that allows you to frame and ground the work that you do. However, academic preparation by itself

© Bob Barcelona

A good way to build a recreational sport résumé is to seek out experiences leading and facilitating recreation activities for others.

is not enough, and it would be unwise to expect that an academic degree is enough to guarantee a job. Most employers expect serious candidates for recreational sport jobs to have an academic degree, but they will look closely at the candidates' relevant practical experiences in relation to the position.

There are many ways to gain practical experience in the field of recreational sport. If you look at your current work career, you probably already have the start of a pretty good résumé. If you are a volunteer youth sport coach, work as a camp counselor, are certified as a lifeguard or swim instructor, teach group fitness classes, work the front desk at your university's recreational sport center, or officiate high school or college intramural sport, then you are on your way to building a recreational sport résumé.

If you have some of these experiences already, seek out others. Try to demonstrate a well-rounded view of the field with relevant work experience in a variety of program areas, such as sport, fitness, or aquatics, or better yet, try to show progressive areas of responsibility. For example, you might start out as a lifeguard and then move to a position as a head lifeguard or shift supervisor. Even more impressive is the student who comes out of college with significant management or administrative experience. This could be experience scheduling or training other staff, designing programs and events, handling budgets, or engaging in customer service. Most reputable academic programs require an extensive internship as part of the academic experience. Be sure to make the most of this, and challenge yourself to do something new. The majority of graduating students say that the internship is the most important factor in the job search.

Professional Involvement

Involvement in the profession is the third leg of the stool for career preparation in recreational sport. Students can demonstrate professional involvement by joining membership associations, attending conferences and workshops, and obtaining relevant certifications. There are a number of professional associations that represent various areas of the recreational sport field. Most of these organizations offer student memberships at discounted rates. Professional associations provide resources and information related to jobs; offer conferences, trainings, and workshops; provide access to a network of like-minded professionals; and often provide access to job opportunities and information about recreational sport careers.

You should consider the area of the recreational sport field that you would like to work in and then investigate the relevant professional associations that represent it. If you are interested in campus recreational sport, you should consider joining NIRSA. Likewise, if you are interested in working in a municipal recreation organization, you should consider joining NRPA or one of the many state-level park and recreation associations. For example, the South Carolina Recreation and Parks Association (SCRPA) offers student memberships for a small fee. Other professional associations that might be of interest to recreational sport professionals include the Resort and Commercial Recreation Association (RCRA); the International Health, Racquet and Sportsclub Association (IHRSA), and the Society of Health and Physical Educators (SHAPE America), formerly the American Alliance for Health, Physical Education, Recreation and Dance (AAHPERD).

Employment Outlook

The good news for those interested in recreational sport careers is that jobs in the recreation industry as a whole are expected to grow faster than average in the United States over the next decade. This is attributed to the increasing demand for recreation services for both youth and seniors, the increasing concern about health and fitness, and the need to replace staff who leave the field due to retirement (Bureau of Labor Statistics, 2012). The field also offers many opportunities for part-time and seasonal work, which bodes well for those who are starting out in their careers and looking to gain practical experience. Although job prospects in recreational sport are more favorable than in other segments of the sport industry (Masteralexis et al., 2005), full-time administrative positions are competitive. Applicants who have college degrees, have practical experience, and demonstrate professional commitment have the best opportunities for obtaining full-time positions in the field.

CONCLUSION

Students who have a passion for sport and an interest in management can find numerous job opportunities in the recreational sport field. Jobs in the field are diverse and are found in many settings and management sectors, including public, nonprofit, and commercial agencies and organizations. There is an established set of core competencies that underlie the recreational sport field, and these competencies can be used to create a plan for professional and career development. Recreational sport professionals need to be able to understand and apply sport and leisure theory, financial accounting and budgeting procedures, personnel management practices, communication and marketing tactics, programming and event management, tournament scheduling, legality and risk management principles, governance and policy formulation, technology and computer applications, and research and evaluation strategies.

Students interested in careers in recreational sport can best prepare for their future careers by taking classes in accredited recreation or sport management programs, engaging in practical real-world experiences, and getting involved in professional organizations. The job market and demand for recreational sport professionals are promising. However, the best jobs will go to those who have demonstrated a strong mix of academic preparation, practical experience, and professional involvement.

RESEARCH TO REALITY

Hurd, A. (2007, Nov/Dec). Becoming competency driven: Reaching agency efficiency and effectiveness. *Illinois Parks and Recreation.* Retrieved from www.lib.niu.edu/2007/ip0712tc.html.

In this paper, Hurd discusses what job competencies are and what they do for recreation agencies. The author argues that the purpose of encouraging competency development among individual employees is to increase organizational efficiency and effectiveness. The idea is that as individual performance increases, organizational performance also increases. Individual competencies relate to what an employee is willing and able to do on the job. The paper also goes on to describe how to use competencies to create a competency-based hiring and employee evaluation process. Hurd makes the case that staff must be involved in determining the competencies that are necessary for various job positions and in describing what the specific competencies look like. Interview questions and performance appraisal systems can then be built around these specific job competencies.

As you examine your own preparedness to meet the competencies of an effective recreational sport professional, ask yourself not only "Can I do this?" but "Am I willing to do this?" Just because an employee can do something does not mean that he will do it once he is hired. Part of career preparation is being honest with yourself and trying to uncover your passion. Likewise, if you are in a position to hire volunteers and staff, think about how you might phrase an interview question to try to uncover a candidate's ability and willingness to perform critical job functions. A competency-based approach to career preparation, hiring, and performance appraisal can be a useful tool to improve organizational efficiency and effectiveness.

REFLECTION QUESTIONS

1. Name five of the major job settings or contexts where recreational sport takes place. Which of these settings most interests you?
2. Look at the 10 core competencies for recreational sport professionals. Which of the competencies do you feel most comfortable performing? Which do you feel least comfortable performing?
3. What are some examples of professional associations that you could get involved with to learn more about careers in recreational sport?

LEARNING ACTIVITIES

1. To get more in-depth information on a particular recreational sport organization, conduct a short case study of an actual organization. Collect information from websites, professional or trade associations, research journals, statistical information, personal interviews, and other relevant sources. Use diverse sources! Research and analyze the following information:

    - Introduction of the agency or organization, including a discussion of its management sector (public, nonprofit, commercial) and funding structure (taxes, fees, grants, fund-raising, sponsorships)

- Organizational mission and goals
- Description of the types of services, programs, and facilities offered
- Description of the users of the service—whom does the agency target or try to attract to its programs?
- Description of employee positions, types of jobs, qualifications, and so on, including full-time, part-time, and volunteer positions (if applicable)
- Several issues or trends affecting the agency or organization or the wider recreational sport context in which it operates (e.g., public sector, nonprofit sector, commercial sector)
- Additional information related to the industry segment, including information taken from personal interviews, key statistics or indicators, or other sources that will enable you to better understand this recreational sport organization or career setting

2. Go online and identify some recreational sport jobs that interest you. There are many online sites for finding recreational sport jobs. A couple of good places to look are www.bluefishjobs.com (campus recreational sport) and www.nrpa.org/careers (municipal recreation jobs). See if you can find other job listings from other sites as well. Analyze the job listings and answer the following questions:
    - What is the job title?
    - What are the requirements for the position (e.g., education, skills)?
    - What are the key competencies that a successful candidate would need for this position?
    - What are the job responsibilities?
    - What is the salary range?
    - What do you need to do to apply for the position?
    - Is this a job you would be interested in? Why or why not?

GLOSSARY

agencies—Recreational sport providers in the public sector.

alternative sport—Refers to sports that are seen as nontraditional because they are outside the realm of what has previously been offered in organized sport programs (e.g., skateboarding, parkour).

animation—Taking an ordinary activity or event and bringing it to life with props, design, energy, music, history, characters, intensity, or visuals.

apps—Software applications designed to run on a variety of electronic devices, such as computers, tablets, and smartphones.

attractive nuisance—A human-made, dangerous condition that may entice children to visit the property, putting their safety at risk.

background check—Process in which criminal records are reviewed to determine the appropriateness of a person as a potential employee or volunteer.

biometric recognition—Identification of people by their anatomical traits, such as fingerprints, palms, face, or eyes.

blended program—Program that presents a variety of offerings.

blogs—Websites that provide an ongoing series of information in the form of text, images, video, and user-generated comments.

boards—Governing bodies within agencies that are composed of external stakeholders who are either elected or appointed.

breach—A violation of duty.

bye—When an odd number of teams are in a league or bracket, one or more teams does not play in a given round.

campus recreation—All of the recreation and leisure programs and facilities offered on college or university campuses.

career settings—The places and contexts where jobs in recreational sport take place.

cause—Something that leads to a particular effect.

cause in fact—The direct result of an action.

certifications—Credentials given by a governing body or professional association that acknowledge a recipients' qualifications to perform a specific job.

challenge tournaments—Creative, participant-centered tournament formats that allow entries to challenge one another to play matches over an extended period of time.

charrette—An intense planning session where stakeholders collaborate with designers to share information and provide feedback during the design process.

civil law—Wrongs committed by individuals against individuals that can result in compensated losses.

cloud computing—System of shared computing resources, such as networks, servers, storage, applications, and services, that can be easily accessed by users.

cognitive development—Growth of a person's ability to acquire intelligence and increasingly advanced thought and problem-solving ability across the life span.

cognitive theories—Theories that focus on how students perceive, organize, and reason through the experiences they have while attending college.

college impact models—Models that focus on the interaction between college students and their environments and examine what students do while they are in college in order to understand student development.

commercial sector—Recreational sport organizations that exist to make a profit for their owners or shareholders.

community—A group whose members share a general location, government, culture, or heritage.

conceptual skills—The ability to analyze situations, determine causes and effects, come up with solutions to organizational challenges, and see the big picture.

constraints—Limitations placed on a person's frequency, intensity, duration, or quality of participation; factors that limit the formation of leisure preferences or inhibit or prohibit participation and enjoyment in leisure.

contingent staff—Personnel who are hired for short-term job assignments or on an as-needed basis.

continuing education units (CEUs)—Points that certified or licensed staff earn through completing continuing education.

criminal law—Wrongs committed by individuals against the state, typically prosecuted by the government, that can result in imprisonment and fines.

crossover scheduling—Method of scheduling double-elimination tournaments to avoid having entries play one another in close succession.

cross-training—Preparing staff to perform tasks associated with multiple jobs within the organization.

customer service—The relationships or interactions between employees or representatives and the people they serve.

deferred maintenance—The practice of postponing maintenance due to budget constraints.

desktop computer—Personal computer that is generally fixed to a single location.

direct competition—When two individuals or teams compare their skills against one another, yielding a winner and a loser.

direct costs—Expenses that relate specifically to the production of a particular service or product.

discretionary time—Time that is free from obligation.

discrimination—When someone unjustly acts on prejudice.

diversity—Diversity simply refers to the many ways that people are different. This often includes things like race, religion, age, culture, gender, sex, disability, socioeconomic status, education, marital status and appearance in addition more abstract concepts like the value system and ideas that an individual might have.

double-elimination tournaments—Tournaments that are similar to single-elimination formats, but teams can lose one game and continue to play until they lose again. When they lose two games, they are out.

duty—A responsibility to provide care or service to another.

empirical—Physical and factual evidence about things that can be measured.

explicit bye bracket—Elimination bracket that depicts the first-round bye games.

external communication—Communication that focuses on the organization's customers or potential customers as well as its key constituents.

extramural sport—Competitive and cooperative recreational sport opportunities that take place between students from different colleges and universities.

extrinsic motivation—Motivational state where the focus is on doing activities that are oriented toward some desired individual or societal end.

facilitate—To provide assistance in making something easier or less difficult.

foreseeability—The ability to see that something is likely to happen.

general obligation bond—A financing instrument issued by state and local government agencies that is backed by the full faith and credit of the issuing agency and guaranteed by tax revenues.

GI Bill—Legislation that provides U.S. servicepeople with financial assistance to attend colleges and universities.

hardware—Physical components of a computing system or operating device.

Healthy Campus 2020—A planning framework for improving the overall health on college campuses in the United States.

human capital—Value that is created from an employee's knowledge, talents, skills, abilities, and creativity.

human relations skills—The ability to work with, lead, and understand other people, including both individuals and groups.

identity development—Growth in how a person begins to describe who she is as an individual across the life span.

implied bye bracket—Elimination bracket where bye games are indicated by a blank space.

indirect competition—When individuals or groups compare their skills against their own past performance, focusing on skill improvement or mastery.

indirect costs—Expenses that must be covered in order to run a service or create a product but that do not relate specifically to the immediate production of that service or product.

informal recreation—Pickup or drop-in recreational sport or fitness opportunities that are available to students in a format that allows them to participate in their own time and their own way.

injury—The violation of another's legal right, for which the law provides a remedy.

in-kind gifts—Donations provided through services, goods, or commodities rather than direct financial support.

innovation—Development and implementation of new ideas, structures, processes, products, systems, or services that increase efficiency and productivity (Jaskyte, 2010).

instant scheduling—Tournament registration where individuals or teams schedule themselves in the tournament divisions that are most appealing to them in advance of the tournament start date.

instructional sport—Activities that introduce participants to a particular sport or recreation activity or help participants develop the skills needed in that activity.

intentional tort—Tort committed by a person who intends to do so.

internal communication—Communication that focuses on messaging within the organization and the interpersonal communication skills needed between coworkers.

International Olympic Committee (IOC)—Nongovernmental agency that oversees the Summer and Winter Olympics as well as the Youth Olympic Games.

International Sport Federations (IFs)—Nongovernmental agencies responsible for overseeing the most important functions of a sport, such as administration, rules, development, player welfare, promotion, and organization of international tournaments.

Internet—Worldwide network of computers that store and share information.

intramural sport—Competitive and cooperative recreational sport opportunities available to students, faculty, and staff enrolled at a particular school.

intranet—Private, password-protected Web available only to authorized units, such as employees in an organization.

intrinsic motivation—Motivational state where the focus is on doing activities primarily for their own sake.

job announcements—Written statements that provide information for job seekers about open positions.

job functions—The specific kinds of jobs that recreational sport professionals perform.

job settings—The places where recreational sport professionals work, including the management sector and the type of agency or organization where the job takes place.

laptop computer—Portable computers that typically weigh between 2 and 10 pounds (1-5 kg).

LEED (Leadership in Energy and Environmental Design)—Program developed by the U.S. Green Building Council that rates green buildings.

leisure—A broad area of human development focused on nonwork activities that are freely chosen and done primarily for intrinsic reasons; usually classified as free time, recreational activity, or a psychological state of mind.

liability—A relationship in which a legal obligation exists to another individual, to an entity, or to society.

Long-Term Athlete Development (LTAD) model—Model that uses a series of stages to systematically develop an athlete from a youth to an adult participant. The model is used at community, state, and national levels to unify sport development across the ages.

magic number—The number of teams in a single-elimination round plus 1. This will also be the sum of the seeds in each bracket in the round.

management by objectives—Evaluation of job performance based on the employee's ability to meet job-related goals.

master plan—Outlines how organizations can use their existing facilities and resources and think about the types and locations of new facilities and resources to be developed to support the achievement of goals. Typically focuses on large- to small-scale planning related to the development of entire communities or from large areas down to what specific sites within a community might be used for.

mastery orientation—Motivational state where the focus is on building competence in sport by improving or mastering sport-related skills.

modalities—Methods or facilitating agents that help to produce critical student development outcomes.

moderate physical activity—Physical activity requiring a medium amount of effort to engage in; typically accelerates the heart rate a noticeable amount.

Moore's law—Law stating that technology capabilities such as speed, memory, storage capacity, and power double every 18 months.

Morale, Welfare, and Recreation (MWR) programs—U.S. military program designed to enhance the community lives of soldiers and their families.

municipal recreation—Recreation programs supported by a local community governmental structure such as a city or county.

negligence—Failing to do what the average person would do to prevent harm.

NIRSA (National Intramural-Recreational Sports Association)—The largest professional association representing campus recreation programs and professionals.

nonroutine maintenance—Tasks done on a periodic, preventive, or emergency basis.

not-for-profit sector—Sport and recreation organizations that operate in the public interest but do so outside the direct control of the government. These organizations are not designed to yield a profit; instead, all revenue must be returned to the program.

operating system—Software that drives a computer.

organizations—Recreational sport providers in the nonprofit or commercial sectors.

outsourcing—Contracting out the management of campus recreation programs, services, and facilities to an external private vendor.

participation styles—The various ways in which people prefer to participate in recreational sport activities.

performance appraisal—Method for providing feedback to employees based on their job performance.

performance bond—Insurance policy guaranteeing that the contractor will perform the work in accordance with the construction documents. If the work is not completed in a satisfactory manner or the contractor goes bankrupt, the project will be completed by the insurance company.

person–job fit—Tight alignment between the personal and professional goals of the employee and the overall organization.

personnel—Paid and volunteer staff who work directly for or on behalf of recreational sport organizations in the design and delivery of programs.

philosophy—A system of knowledge and beliefs about the truth of things—their characteristics, value, relative goodness, and beauty.

physically active recreational sport—Recreational sport activities that engage a person in either moderate or vigorous physical activity.

physiological development—Changes in a person's physical abilities and growth across the life span.

planned obsolescence—Business strategy in which the usability of a product is planned to diminish or disappear over time.

professional competencies—Traits, skills, knowledge areas, or attributes that are required for successful job performance.

progressive discipline—System for correcting employee behavior or addressing poor performance through implementing a series of steps based on severity of consequences.

proximate cause—An act of omission that leads to a particular effect.

psychological development—Growth in a person's status in terms of emotional, moral, social, and other abilities across the life span.

psychosocial theories—Theories that focus on the way people change and grow across the life span as a function of both intra- and interpersonal processes.

public sector—Government-sponsored sport and recreation services.

recreation—Freely chosen, organized, nonwork activity pursued for the attainment of personal and social benefits.

recreational sport—Participant-focused sport activities engaged in by the widest possible audience primarily for intrinsic reasons.

recreational sport facilities—Any indoor, outdoor, natural, or human-made structures, areas, or spaces that are designed, managed, or used for recreation, sport, and leisure activities. Recreational sport facilities can be public or private, active or passive, and formal or informal in nature.

recreational sport profession—Designing and managing sport programs for the primary purpose of encouraging active participation in sport.

revenue bond—A financing instrument issued by state and local government agencies that is paid back using fees generated by the project being developed.

risk—The possibility of harm occurring.

risk management—The procedure of systems used to minimize accidental losses.

round—Completed set of games where every team in a league is scheduled to play (or has a bye) in one game.

round-robin—Popular tournament design where every entry plays all other entries in the assigned league at least once.

round-robin divisions—Participation categories that a tournament administrator might offer to help manage competition or enhance the participation experience, such as skill level, age, or gender.

round-robin leagues—The smallest grouping to which entries are assigned; sometimes referred to as *pools* or *groups*.

round-robin tournament—The overall round-robin tournament event encompassing all of the participating teams.

routine maintenance—Tasks done on a daily basis to keep a facility running; includes activities such as cleaning, garbage removal, and field lining.

seeding—Ranking teams based on their ability and scheduling to provide the highest chance of the best teams facing off in later stages of the tournament.

self-concept—The idea or mental image one has of oneself.

self-confidence—Realistic belief in one's own abilities.

signature facility—Showcase campus recreation facility that stands out in terms of architectural form and usable functionality.

single-elimination tournaments—Popular tournament design where teams continue to play games until they lose; when they lose, they are out.

SMART objectives—Specific, measurable, achievable, relevant, and timed objectives.

smartphones—Cellular telephones that include digital voice services as well as a variety of built-in applications and Internet access.

social capital—A network of social connections between people with shared values and behavioral norms; often leads to social cooperation that benefits the community as a whole.

social networking—Networking that takes place in online virtual communities that allow people to share up-to-the-minute information with others within their network.

software—What powers the physical components of a computer or electronic device; the tools that make computers useful for everyday work.

specifications—The written portion of the construction documents, which includes three parts: bidding and contract requirements, general requirements, and construction specifications.

sport—Competitive and cooperative physical activities that require skill and that are institutionalized, are organized, and have a gamelike structure and form.

sport clubs—Student-organized and led programs that provide opportunities to participate in a specific recreational sport in a deeper and more engaging way.

sport for all—The belief that sport is a human right and should be available to everyone regardless of age, race, sex, economic status, disability, or any other potential barrier.

sport management—The professional career of planning, organizing, leading, and controlling sport events, programs, personnel, and facilities.

sportsmanship—Attitudes and behaviors exhibited in a sport setting that demonstrate support and respect for rules, officials, opponents, the game itself, and other social conventions within the game.

state of mind—An attitude, a psychological construction, or a state of being related to personal experiences.

stereotype—Simplified characteristics or images that are associated with certain groups of people and are often circulated within various societal circles.

strategic planning—Process where organizations take a step back and assess, evaluate, develop, change, or refine their vision, mission, and goals.

support staff—Those who help to facilitate the work of others in the organization, such as secretarial support, maintenance, transportation, and food services.

tablet computers—Personal computers that use a single panel and a touch screen for navigation.

targeted program—Program where an organization focuses on a limited type or number of programs.

target market—A group of customers to which a business or organization aims its marketing materials in the hopes of attracting customers.

technical skills—Job-specific knowledge and techniques that enable an employee to do a job.

technology tools—A combination of skills, knowledge, abilities, techniques, materials, computers, and other equipment (Jones, 2004).

technostructure—Those who manage processes critical for organizational information and accountability, including accountants, purchasing agents, marketing specialists, and technology support.

tiered program—Program where participants can join a variety of activities at multiple levels of participation.

tort—A civil wrong, other than breach of contract, for which a remedy may be obtained, usually in the form of damages.

transferable skills—Skills that students obtain through their jobs, volunteer work, and participation in out-of-class activities that are transferable to a variety of employment settings and that can assist in career development.

typological theories—Theories that examine the individual characteristics or group of characteristics that affect certain areas of development.

waiver—The voluntary relinquishment of a legal right; also refers to the forms collected by an organization in order to prove a person has relinquished that right.

warranty—Guarantee that the contractor provides with the building that usually covers the period from occupancy to 12 months. Warranties cover defects such as pooling water in parking lots, leaky roofs, and major system failures.

wellness—State of optimal well-being oriented toward maximizing an individual's potential (Patton, 2009).

working drawings—Blueprints that include the information to build and complete a project.

vigorous physical activity—Physical activity requiring greater effort than moderate physical activity, leading to a substantial increase in heart rate.

virtual reality—Computer-generated simulated world.

volunteers—People who work for an organization for no pay except for expenses.

wikis—Shared Web spaces that allow multiple users to author unique content and edit the work of others.

World Wide Web—Subset of the Internet that consists of electronic pages accessed by their unique address using a Web browser.

REFERENCES

Chapter 1

Barcelona, R.J. (2010). Sport management. In C. Stevens, J. Murphy, E. Sheffield, & L. Allen (Eds.), *Introduction to recreation, parks, and tourism careers.* Urbana, IL: Sagamore.

Barcelona, R.J. (2004). Examining the importance of recreational sport management competencies based on management level, agency type, and organizational size. *Recreational Sports Journal, 28*(1), 45-63.

Barcelona, R.J., & Young, S.J. (2010). The role of municipal park and recreation agencies in enacting coach and parent training in a loosely coupled youth sports system. *Managing Leisure, 15*(3), 181-197.Coakley, J. (2004). *Sports in society: Issues and controversies.* New York: McGraw-Hill.

Crone, J.A. (1999). Toward a theory of sport. *Journal of Sport Behavior, 22,* 321-340.

Daniels, A.M. (2007). Cooperation vs. competition: Is there really such an issue? *New Directions for Youth Development, 115,* 43-56.

Doty, J. (2006). Sports build character?! *Journal of College and Character, 7*(3), 1-9.

Forsyth, C.J. (2005). Discerning the symbiotic relationship between sport, leisure, and recreation: A note on the sportization of pastimes. *Sociological Spectrum, 25,* 127-131.

Grecic, D., & Collins, D. (2013). The epistemological chain: Practical applications in sports. *Quest, 65*(2), 151-168.

Henderson, K. (2010). Importance of leisure to individuals and society. In G. Kassing (Ed.), *Dimensions of leisure for life: Individuals and society.* Champaign, IL: Human Kinetics.

International Olympic Committee (IOC). (2012). Sport for All Commission. Retrieved from www.olympic.org/sport-for-all-commission.

Jackson, E.L. (2000). Will research on leisure constraints still be relevant in the twenty-first century? *Journal of Leisure Research, 32,* 62-68.

Kelly, J.R., & Freysinger, V.J. (2000). 21st Century Leisure: Current Issues. Needham Heights MA: Allyn & Bacon.

Lumpkin, A., & Cuneen, J. (2001). Developing a personal philosophy of sport. *Journal of Physical Education, Recreation, & Dance, 72*(8), 40-43.

Nixon, H.L. (2008). *Sport in a changing world.* Brookline, MA: Paradigm.

Russell, R. (2005). *Pastimes: The context of contemporary leisure.* Urbana, IL: Sagamore.

United Nations Interagency Task Force on Sport for Development and Peace (2003). Sport for development and peace: Towards achieving millennium development goals. Retrieved from http://www.un.org/wcm/webdav/site/sport/shared/sport/pdfs/Reports/2003_interagency_report_ENGLISH.pdf.

U.S. Bureau of Labor Statistics. (2012a). Charts from the American Time Use Survey. Retrieved from www.bls.gov/tus/charts/.

U.S. Bureau of Labor Statistics (2012b). *Occupational outlook handbook, 2010-11 edition.* Retrieved from http://www.bls.gov/ooh/.

Young, S.J., Ross, C.M., & Barcelona, R.J. (2003). Perceived constraints by college students to participation in campus recreational sports programs. *Recreational Sports Journal, 27*(1), 47-62.

Chapter 2

Bailey, R. (2006). Physical education and sport in schools: A review of benefits and outcomes. *Journal of School Health, 76*(8), 397-401.

Baker, J., Fraser-Thomas, J., Dionigi, R.A., & Horton, S. (2010). Sport participation and positive development in older persons. *European Review of Aging and Physical Activity, 7,* 3-12.

Bergeron, M.F. (2007). Improving health through youth sports: Is participation enough? *New Directions for Youth Development, 115,* 27-41.

Berk, M. (2007). Should we be targeting exercise as a routine mental health intervention? *Acta Neuropsychiatrica, 19,* 217-218.

Biddle, S.J.H., Wang, C.K.J., Chatzisarantis, N.L.D., & Spray, C.M. (2003). Motivation for physical activity in young people: Entity and incremental beliefs about athletic ability. *Journal of Sports Sciences, 21,* 973-989.

Blair, S.N. (2009). Physical inactivity: The biggest public health problem of the 21st century. *British Journal of Sports Medicine, 43,* 1-2.

Bocarro, J., Kanters, M., & Casper, J. (2006). Research update: Leisure for life. *Parks and Recreation,* June, 22-27.

Brockman, R., Jago, R., & Fox, K.R. (2011). Children's active play: Self-reported motivators, barriers and facilitators. *BMC Public Health, 11,* 461-467.

Butt, J., Weinberg, R.S., Breckon, J.D., & Claytor, R.P. (2011). Adolescent physical activity participation and motivational determinants across gender, age, and race. *Journal of Physical Activity and Health, 8,* 1074-1083.

Casper, J.M., Bocarro, J.N., Kanters, M.A., & Floyd, M.F. (2011). "Just let me play!"—Understanding constraints that limit adolescent sport participation. *Journal of Physical Activity and Health, 8*(Suppl. 1), S32-S39.

Castelli, D.M., & Erwin, H.E. (2007). Chapter 4: A comparison of personal attributes and experiences among physically active and inactive children. *Journal of Teaching in Physical Education, 26,* 375-389.

Cohen, D.A., Ashwood, S., Scott, M., Overton, A., Evenson, K.R., Voorhees, C.C., Bedimo-Rung, A., & McKenzie, T.L. (2006). Proximity to school and physical activity among middle school girls: The trial of activity for adolescent girls study. *Journal of Physical Activity and Health*, *3S*, S129-S138.

Da Silva, M.A., Singh-Monoux, A., Brunner, E.J., Kaffashian, S., Shipley, M.J., Kivimaki, M., & Nabi, H. (2012). Bidirectional association between physical activity and symptoms of anxiety and depression: The Whitehall II study. *European Journal of Epidemiology*, *27*(7), 537-546.

Davey, J., Fitzpatrick, M., Garland, R., & Kilgour, M. (2009). Adult participation motives: Empirical evidence from a workplace exercise programme. *European Sport Management Quarterly*, *9*(2), 141-162.

DeBate, R.D., Gabriel, K.P., Zwald, M., Huberty, J., & Zhang, Y. (2009). Changes in psychosocial factors and physical activity frequency among third- to eighth-grade girls who participated in a developmentally focused youth sport program: A preliminary study. *Journal of School Health*, *79*, 474-484.

deMontes, L.G., Arruza, J.A., Arribas, S., Irazusta, S., & Telletxea, S. (2011). The role of organized sports participation during adolescence in adult physical activity patterns. *Sport Science Review*, *20*(5-6), 25-56.

Dodge, T., & Lambert, S.F. (2008). Positive self-beliefs as a mediator of the relationship between adolescents' sports participation and health in young adulthood. *Journal of Youth and Adolescence*, *38*, 813-825.

Donaghy, M.E. (2007). Exercise can seriously improve your mental health: Fact or fiction? *Advances in Physiotherapy*, *9*, 76-88.

Dunton, G.F., Schneider, M., & Cooper, D.M. (2007). An investigation of psychosocial factors related to changes in physical activity and fitness among female adolescents. *Psychology and Health*, *22*(8), 929-944.

Edwards, M.B., Kanters, M.A., & Bocarro, J.N. (2011). Opportunities for extracurricular physical activity in North Carolina middle schools. *Journal of Physical Activity and Health*, *8*, 597-605.

Edwardson, C.L., & Gorely, T. (2010). Parental influences on different types and intensities of physical activity in youth: A systematic review. *Psychology of Sport and Exercise*, *11*(6), 522-535.

Engberg, E., Alen, M., Kukkonen-Harjula, K., Peltonen, J.E., Tikkanen, H.O, & Pekkarinen, H. (2012). Life events and change in leisure time physical activity: A systematic review. *Sports Medicine*, *42*(5), 433-447.

Fairclough, S.J., Ridgers, N.D., & Welk, G. (2012). Correlates of children's moderate and vigorous physical activity during weekdays and weekends. *Journal of Physical Activity and Health*, *9*, 129-137.

Fedewa, A.L., & Ahn, S. (2011). The effects of physical activity and physical fitness on children's achievement and cognitive outcomes: A meta-analysis. *Research Quarterly for Exercise and Sport*, *82*(3), 521-535.

Hallal, P., Victora, C.G., Azevedo, M.R., & Wells, J.C.K. (2006). Adolescent physical activity and health: A systematic review. *Sports Medicine*, *36*(12), 1019-1030.

Hamilton, K., Cox, S., & White, K.M. (2012). Testing a model of physical activity among mothers and fathers of young children: Integrating self-determined motivation, planning, and the theory of planned behavior. *Journal of Sport and Exercise Psychology*, *34*, 124-145.

Hammond, R.A., & Levine, R. (2010). The economic impact of obesity in the United States. *Diabetes Metabolic Syndrome and Obesity: Targets and Therapy*, *3*, 285-295.

Hills, A.P., King, N.A., & Armstrong, T.P. (2007). The contribution of physical activity and sedentary behaviours to the growth and development of children and adolescents: Implications for overweight and obesity. *Sports Medicine*, *37*(6), 533-545.

Hirvensalo, M., & Lintunen, T. (2011). Life-course perspective for physical activity and sports participation. *European Review of Aging and Physical Activity*, *8*, 13-22.

Ketteridge, A., & Boshoff, K. (2008). Exploring the reasons why adolescents participate in physical activity and identifying strategies that facilitate their involvement in such activity. *Australian Occupational Therapy Journal*, *55*, 273-282.

Kilpatrick, M., Hebert, E., & Bartholomew, J. (2005). College students' motivation for physical activity: Differentiating men's and women's motives for sport participation and exercise. *Journal of American College Health*, *54*(2), 87-94.

Kjonniksen, L., Anderssen, N., & Wold, B. (2009). Organized youth sport as a predictor of physical activity in adulthood. *Scandinavian Journal of Medicine and Science in Sports*, *19*, 646-654.

Lata, P. (2010). Physical inactivity as a global risk factor for chronic diseases in women. *British Journal of Sports Medicine*, *44*(Suppl. I), i64.

Miles, L. (2007). *Physical activity and health*. London: British Nutrition Foundation.

Mountjoy, M. (2011). Health and fitness of young people: What is the role of sport? *British Journal of Sports Medicine*, *45*(11), 837-838.

Mutrie, N., & Parnell, S. (2011). Physical inactivity—What's the answer? *Sport and Exercise Scientist*, *28*, 20-21.

Myers, J. (2008). The health benefits and economics of physical activity. *Current Sports Medicine Reports*, *7*(6), 314-316.

Nowak, M.A. (2010). Relationships between the perception of the influence of physical activity on health and women's engagement in exercise or their physical passivity. *Polish Journal of Sport and Tourism*, *17*, 179-190.

Pano, G., & Markola, L. (2012). 14-18-year-old children attitudes, perception, and motivation towards extra curricular physical activity and sport. *Journal of Human Sport and Exercise*, *7*, s51-s66.

Pate, R.R., Mitchell, J.A., Byun, W., & Dowda, M. (2011). Sedentary behavior in youth. *British Journal of Sports Medicine*, *45*, 906-913.

Ratey, J.J., & Hagerman, E. (2008). *Spark: The revolutionary new science of exercise and the brain*. New York: Little, Brown.

Reed, C.E., & Cox, R.H. (2007). Motives and regulatory style underlying senior athletes' participation in sport. *Journal of Sport Behavior*, *30*(3), 307-329.

Riddoch, C., & O'Donovan, G. (2006). Moderate intensity physical activity versus vigorous activity: Today's best buy in public health. *Sport and Exercise Scientist*, *10*, 16-17.

Sagiv, M. (2011). Aerobic exercise effect on the elderly functional capacity. *Archives of Exercise in Health and Disease*, *2*(1), 63-64.

Sanz-Arazuri, E., Ponce-de-Leon-Elizondo, A., & Valdemoros-San-Emeterio, M.A. (2012). Parental predictors of physical inactivity in Spanish adolescents. *Journal of Sports Science and Medicine*, *11*, 95-101.

Saxena, S., Van Ommeren, M., Tang, K.C., & Armstrong, T.P. (2005). Mental health benefits of physical activity. *Journal of Physical Activity*, *14*(5), 445-451.

Seefeldt, V., Malina, R.M., & Clark, M.A. (2002). Factors affecting levels of physical activity in adults. *Sports Medicine*, *32*(3), 143-168.

Smith, A.L. (1999). Perceptions of peer relationships and physical activity participation in early adolescence. *Journal of Sport and Exercise Psychology*, *21*, 329-350.

Smith, J.C., Nielson, K.A., Woodard, J.L., Seidenberg, M., & Rao, S.M. (2013). Physical activity and brain function in older adults at increased risk for Alzheimer's disease. *Brain Sciences*, *3*, 54-83.

Taliaferro, L.A., Rienzo, B.A., & Donovan, K.A. (2010). Relationships between youth sport participation and selected health risk factors from 1999 to 2007. *Journal of School Health*, *80*(8), 399-410.

Taylor, A.H., Cable, N.T., Faulkner, G., Hillsdon, M., Narici, M., & Van Der Bij, A.K. (2004). Physical activity and older adults: A review of health benefits and the effectiveness of interventions. *Journal of Sports Sciences*, *22*, 703-725.

Telama, R., Laakso, L., Nupponen, H., Rimpela, A., & Pere, L. (2009). Secular trends in youth physical activity and parents' socioeconomic status from 1977 to 2005. *Pediatric Exercise Science*, *21*, 462-474.

Troiano, R. P., Berrigan, D., Dodd, K.W., Masse, L.C., Tilert, T., & McDowell, M. (2008). Physical activity in the United States measured by accelerometer. Medicine and Science in Sports and Exercise, 40, 181-188.

Warburton, D.E.R., Nicol, C.W., & Bredin, S.S.D. (2006). Health benefits of physical activity: The evidence. *Canadian Medical Association Journal*, *174*(6), 801-809.

White, J.L., Randsdell, L.B., Vener, J., & Flohr, J.A. (2005). Factors related to physical activity adherence in women: Review and suggestions for future research. *Women and Health*, *41*(4), 123-148.

Wickel, E.E., & Eisenmann, J.C. (2007). Contribution of youth sport to total daily physical activity among 6- to 12-year-old boys. *Medicine and Science in Sports and Exercise*, *39*(9), 1493-1500.

Woods, A.M., Graber, K., & Daum, D. (2012). Children's recess physical activity: Movement patterns and preferences. *Journal of Teaching in Physical Education*, *31*, 146-162.

World Health Organization (WHO). (2010). *Global recommendations on physical activity and health.* Geneva: Author.

Yan, J.H., & McCullagh, P. (2004). Cultural influence on youth's motivation of participation in physical activity. *Journal of Sport Behavior*, *27*(4), 378-390.

Yang, X., Telama, R., & Laakso, L. (2006). Parents' physical activity, socioeconomic status and education as predictors of physical activity and sport among children and youths—A 12-year follow-up study. *International Review for the Sociology of Sport*, *31*(3), 273-294.

Yungblut, H.E., Schinke, R.J., & McGannon, K.R. (2012). Views of adolescent female youth on physical activity during early adolescence. *Journal of Sports Science and Medicine*, *11*, 39-50.

Zick, C.D., Smith, K.R., Brown, B.B., Fan, J.X., & Kowaleski-Jones, L. (2007). Physical activity during the transition from adolescence to adulthood. *Journal of Physical Activity and Health*, *4*, 125-137.

Chapter 3

Allen, J.T., Drane, D.D., Byon, K.K., & Mohn, R.S. (2010). Sport as a vehicle for socialization and maintenance of cultural identity: International students attending American universities. *Sports Management Review*, *13*, 421-434.

Americans With Disability Act (n.d.). www.ada.gov.

Arthur-Banning, S.G., & Wells, M.S. (2010). For pay or for play: Minimizing professionalization in youth sport. *NRPA 2010 General Educational Session*. Minneapolis.

Blodgett, A.T., Schinke, R.J., Fisher, L.A., George, C.W., Peltier, D., Ritchie, S., & Pickard, P. (2008). From practice to praxis: Community-based strategies for aboriginal youth sport. *Journal of **Sport** & Social Issues*, *32*(4), 393-414.

Centers for Disease Control and Prevention (CDC). (2014). Healthy living. Retrieved from www.cdc.gov/ncbddd/disabilityandhealth/healthyliving.html.

Center for Parent Information and Resrouces (.nd.). http://www.parentcenterhub.org/topics/disability/

Ellis, G. & Rademacher, C. (1986) .*A literature review of the presidents commission on American outdoors,motivation.* Washington DC .Us .Government printing office.

Erikson, E.H. (1968). *Identity: Youth and crisis.* New York: Norton.

FIFA. (2013, June 14). FIFA statement on head covers. Retrieved from www.fifa.com/aboutfifa/organisation/ifab/news/newsid=2109325/.

Harder, A.F. (2002). The developmental stages of Erik Erikson. Retrieved from www.support4change.com/index.php?option=com_content&view=article&id=47&Itemid=108.

Hasbrook, C.A. (1986). The sport participation–social class relationship: Some recent youth sport participation data. *Sociology of Sport Journal*, *3*, 154-159.

Nathan, S., Kemp, L., Bunde-Birouste, A., MacKenzie, J., Evers, C., & Tun, A.S. (2013). "We wouldn't of made friends if we didn't come to Football United": The impacts of a football program on young people's peer, prosocial and cross-cultural relationships. BMC Public Health, *13*(1), 1-16.

Ohtake, Y. (2004). Meaningful inclusion of all students in team sports. Teaching Exceptional Children, *37*(2), 22-27.

Report reveals that disabled children take part in less sport than their able-bodied counterparts (n.d.). Retrieved from www.collegesportsscholarships.com/disabled-children-sports.htm.

Smith, A., & Waddington, I. (2004). Using 'sport in the community schemes' to tackle crime and drug use among young people: Some policy issues and problems. European Physical Education Review, *10*(3), 279-298.

United Nations (UN). (2004). World population to 2300. Retrieved from www.un.org/esa/population/publications/longrange2/WorldPop2300final.pdf. Author: New York.

Women's Sports Foundation. (2008). Go out and play. Retrieved from www.womenssportsfoundation.org/home/research/articles-and-reports/mental-and-physical-health/go-out-and-play.

Chapter 4

Creating objectives (n.d.). The Community Tool Box. Retrieved from http://ctb.ku.edu/en/tablecontents/sub_section_main_1087.aspx.

Fraser-Thomas, J.L., Cote, J., & Deakin, J. (2005). Youth sport programs: An avenue to foster positive youth development. *Physical Education and Sport Pedagogy, 10*(1), 19-40.

Mull, R.F., Bayless, K.G., & Jamieson, L.M. (2005). *Recreational sport management.* Champaign, IL: Human Kinetics.

Chapter 5

Associated Press (AP). (2012). Sabbath could end Orthodox Jewish school Beren Academy from basketball playoff game. Retrieved from http://abclocal.go.com/ktrk/story?section=news/sports&id=8561368.

Barcelona, R.J. (2008). Administration of intramural and extramural sport. In NIRSA (Ed.), *Campus recreation: Essentials for the professional.* Champaign, IL: Human Kinetics.

Byl, J. (2006). *Organizing successful tournaments* (3rd ed.). Champaign, IL: Human Kinetics.

National Federation of State High School Associations (NFHS). (2012). Basketball rules. Retrieved from www.nfhs.org/basketball.

Pilon, M. (2012). Jewish school loses in final of Texas basketball tournament. Retrieved from www.nytimes.com/2012/03/04/sports/beren-academy-loses-in-final-of-texas-basketball-tournament.html?_r=0.

Popke, M. (2000, May). Tournament Time! *Athletic Business*, 69-73.

TAPPS (Texas Association of Private and Parochial Schools). (2012). Retrieved from www.tapps.net.

Chapter 6

Dalvit, D. (2010). Construction cost per square foot of community centers in major U.S. cities. Retrieved from http://evstudio.com/construction-cost-per-square-foot-of-community-centers-in-major-us-cities/

Daly, J. (2000). *Recreation and sport planning and design* (2nd ed.). Champaign, IL: Human Kinetics.

Getting the best value for our construction dollars: A primer on construction delivery methods (n.d.). Retrieved from *www.maricopa.edu/facilitiesplanning/docs/delivery_methods.pdf.*

Lee, K.Y., Macfarlane, D., & Cerin, E. (2013, Winter). Objective evaluation of recreation facilities: Development and reliability of the Recreation Facility Audit Tool. *Journal of Park and Recreation Administration, 31*(4), 92-109.

National Intramural-Recreational Sports Association (NIRSA). (2009). *Space planning guidelines for campus recreational sport facilities.* Champaign, IL: Human Kinetics.

Peterson, J.A., & Tharrett, S.J. (2012). *ACSM's health/fitness facility standards and guidelines* (4th ed.). Champaign, IL: Human Kinetics.

United States Department of Energy (2015). Buildings. Retrieved from http://energy.gov/eere/efficiency/buildings.

Chapter 7

Akyildiz, M., Argan, M.T., Argan, M., & Sevil, T. (2013). Thematic events as an experiential marketing tool: Kite festival on the experience stage. *International Journal of Sport Management, Recreation, and Tourism, 12*, 17-28.

Dees, W. (2011). New media and technology use in corporate sport sponsorship: Performing activational leverage from an exchange perspective. *International Journal of Sport Management and Marketing, 10*(3/4), 272-285.

DeGraaf, D.G., Jordan, D.J., & DeGraaf, K.H. (2010). *Programming for parks, recreation, and leisure services: A servant leader approach* (3rd ed.). State College, PA: Venture.

Evans, D. (2012). *Social media marketing: An hour a day* (2nd ed.). Indianapolis: Wiley.

Howat, G., Murray, D., & Crilley, G. (1999). The relationships between service problems and perceptions of service quality, satisfaction, and behavioral intentions of Australian public sports and leisure customers. *Journal of Park and Recreation Administration, 17*, 42-64.

Lee, H., Lee, Y., & Yoo, D. (2000). Determinants of perceived service quality and its relation with satisfaction. *Journal of Service Marketing, 14*, 217-219.

Mullin, B.J., Hardy, S., & Sutton, W.A. (2007). *Sport marketing.* Champaign, IL: Human Kinetics.

Nike Foundation. (n.d.). Our work. Retrieved from http://nikeinc.com/pages/our-work.

Osman, R.W., Cole, S.T., & Vessell, C.R. (2006). Examining the role of perceived service quality in predicting user satisfaction and behavioral intentions in a campus recreation setting. *Recreation Sports Journal, 30*, 20-29.

Robert Wood Johnson Foundation. (n.d.). Program areas. Retrieved from http://www.rwjf.org/en/our-topics/topics/childhood-obesity.html.

Rossman, J.R., & Schlatter, B.E. (2008). *Recreation programming: Designing leisure experiences* (5th ed.). Champaign, IL: Sagamore.

Sterne, J. (2010). *Social media metrics: How to measure and optimize your marketing investment.* Hoboken, NJ: Wiley.

Sureschchandar, G.S., Rajendran, C., & Anantharaman, R.N. (2002). The relationship between service quality and customer satisfaction. *Journal of Service Marketing, 16*, 363-373.

Tian-Cole, S., Crompton, J.L., & Wilson, V. (2002). An empirical investigation of the relationships between service quality, satisfaction and behavioral intentions among visitors to a wildlife refuge. *Journal of Leisure Research, 34*, 1-24.

van der Smissen, B., Moiseichik, M., & Hartenburg, V.J. (2005). *Management of parks and recreation agencies.* Ashburn, VA: National Recreation and Park Association.

Yoshida, M., & James, J.D. (2010). Customer satisfaction with game and service experiences: Antecedents and consequences. *Journal of Sport Management, 24*, 338-361.

Chapter 8

Carpenter, L.J. (2008). *Legal concepts in sport: A primer* (3rd ed.). Champaign, IL: Sagamore.

Dombrowski v. City of Omer, 502 N.W.2d 707 (1993).

Dougherty, N., Goldberger, A.S., & Carpenter, L.J. (2007). *Sport, physical activity and the law.* Champaign, IL: Sagamore.

Garner, B.A. (Ed.). (2009). *Black's law dictionary.* St. Paul: West.

Johnson v. Rapid City Softball Association, 514 N. W. 693 (1994).

Lowe v. California League of Professional Baseball, 56 Cal. App. 4th 112 (1997).

Scott v. Pacific West Mountain Resort, 834 P.2d 6 (1992).

Spengler, J.O., & Hronke, B.B. (2011). *Legal liability in recreation, sports, and tourism* (4th ed.). Urbana, IL: Sagamore.

Chapter 9

Barcelona, R.J., & Ross, C.M. (2004). An analysis of the perceived competencies of recreational sport administrators. *Journal of Park and Recreation Administration, 22*(4), 25-42.

Barcelona, R.J., & Young, S.J. (2010). The role of municipal park and recreation agencies in enacting coach and parent training in a loosely coupled youth sports system. *Managing Leisure, 15*(3), 181-197.

Bolman, L.G., & Deal, T.E. (2008). *Reframing organizations: Artistry, choice, and leadership.* San Francisco: Jossey-Bass.

Bureau of Labor Statistics. (2011). Volunteering in the United States. Retrieved from www.bls.gov/news.release/volun.nr0.htm.

Bureau of Labor Statistics. (2012). Job openings and labor turnover survey. Retrieved from www.bls.gov/news.release/jolts.htm.

Collins, J. (2001). *Good to great.* New York: Harper Collins.

Corporation for National and Community Service. (2012). Volunteering in America. Retrieved from www.nationalservice.gov/about/volunteering/index.asp.

Drucker, P.F. (2001). *The essential Drucker.* New York: Harper Business.

Eisner, D., Grimm, R.T., Maynard, S., & Washburn, S. (2009). The new volunteer workforce. Retrieved from www.ssireview.org/articles/entry/the_new_volunteer_workforce.

Hardy, S., Barcelona, R., Hickox, R., & Lazaro, C. (2006, May). Image isn't everything: While community-relations programs primarily benefit teams and leagues, a focus on community building can achieve even broader goals. Retrieved from http://www.athleticbusiness.com/image-isn-t-everything.html.

Herzberg, F. (1966). *Work and the nature of man.* Oxford, UK: World.

Hurd, A.R., Barcelona, R.J., & Meldrum, J.T. (2008). *Leisure services management.* Champaign, IL: Human Kinetics.

Imagine Canada. (2010). 2010 Canada survey of giving, volunteering and participating. Retrieved from www.statcan.gc.ca/daily-quotidien/120321/dq120321a-eng.htm.

International Association for Continuing Education and Training (IACET). (2012). About the CEU. Retrieved from www.iacet.org/ceus/about-the-ceu.

Kouzes, J.M., & Posner, B.Z. (2008). *The leadership challenge.* San Francisco: Jossey-Bass.

McGlone, C.A., & Rey, S. (2012). Managing, leading, and supervising student employees and staff. In G.S. McClellan, C. King, & D. Rockey (Eds.)., *The handbook of college athletics and recreation administration.* San Francisco: Jossey-Bass.

Mintzberg, H. (1979). *The structuring of organizations.* Upper Saddle River, NJ: Prentice Hall.

Mulvaney, M.A., McKinney, W.R., & Grodsky, R. (2008). The development of a pay for performance appraisal system for public park and recreation agencies: A case study. *Journal of Park and Recreation Administration, 26*(4), 126-156.

Murphy, M. (2012). *Hiring for attitude: A revolutionary approach to recruiting star performers with both tremendous skills and superb attitude.* New York: McGraw-Hill.

National Alliance for Youth Sports (NAYS). (2012). Background screening in youth sports, 2012 edition.

Retrieved from www.nays.org/cmscontent/File/Screening_UPDATE_2012.pdf.

Watson, M.R., & Abzug, R. (2010). In D.O. Renz (Ed.), The Jossey-Bass handbook of nonprofit leadership and management (3rded., pp. 669-708). San Francisco, CA: Jossey-Bass.

Chapter 10

Active Network. (2012). League management. Retrieved from www.activecommunities.com/technology-solutions/league-management.htm.

Barcelona, R.J., & Rockey, D.L. (2010). Using collaborative learning technologies to facilitate effective group work. *Journal of Physical Education, Recreation & Dance*, *81*(4), 12-14.

Blunt, G.H., & King, K. (2011). Developing a fitness center-based, self-guided instructional program using MP4 player technology. *Recreational Sports Journal*, *35*(1), 61-69.

Brenner, J. (2012). Pew Internet: Social networking. Retrieved from http://pewinternet.org/Commentary/2012/March/Pew-Internet-Social-Networking-full-detail.aspx.

Gross, D. (2012). Mac vs. PC gap is the narrowest since '90s. Retrieved from www.cnn.com/2012/07/05/tech/gaming-gadgets/mac-vs-pc-graph/index.html?hpt=hp_t2.

Hayden, T. (2012). How Americans use their smartphones: What's happening? Retrieved from www.edelmandigital.com/2012/06/21/how-americans-use-their-smartphones/.

Hindle, T. (2008). *Guide to management ideas and gurus.* London, UK: Profile Books.

Jaskyte, K. (2010). Innovation in human services organizations. In Y. Hasenfeld (Ed.), *Human services as complex organizations*, 2nd ed. Thousand Oaks, CA: Sage

Jones, G.R. (2004). Organizational theory, design, and change (4th ed.). Upper Saddle River, NJ: Prentice Hall.

Moore, M.G. (2007). Web 2.0: Does it really matter? *American Journal of Distance Education*, *21*(4), 177-183.

National Institute of Standards. (2011). Final version of NIST cloud computing definition published. Retrieved from www.nist.gov/itl/csd/cloud-102511.cfm.

O'Reilly, T. (2005). What is Web 2.0: Design patterns and business models for the next generation of software. Retrieved from http://oreilly.com/web2/archive/what-is-web-20.html.

Parker, R. (2012). The end of e-mail. Retrieved from http://savannahnow.com/column/2012-08-06/parker-end-email#.ULpWHYZ3ZsI.

PCMag.com. (2012). Encyclopedia of over 20,000 IT terms. Retrieved from www.pcmag.com/encyclopedia/.

Popke, M. (2011). Survey: Social networking impacts sports participation. Retrieved from http://www.athleticbusiness.com/survey-social-networking-impacts-sports-participation.html.

Saint Louis, C. (2011). Cellphones test strength of gym rules. Retrieved from www.nytimes.com/2011/12/08/fashion/struggle-to-ban-smartphone-usage-in-gyms.html.

Snider, M. (2012). Survey: Smartphone, tablet usage still on rise. Retrieved from http://content.usatoday.com/communities/technologylive/post/2012/07/survey-smartphone-and-tablet-usage-continues-to-rise/1#.ULo-eYZ3ZsI.

U.S. Census Bureau. (2012). Adult computer and adult Internet users by selected characteristics. Retrieved from www.census.gov/compendia/statab/2012/tables/12s1158.pdf.

U.S. Department of Commerce. (2011). Exploring the digital nation: Computer and Internet home use. Retrieved from www.esa.doc.gov/Reports/exploring-digital-nation-computer-and-internet-use-home.

Vermont Systems. (2012). Products. Retrieved from www.vermontsystems.com.

Chapter 11

Autry, C.E., & Anderson, S.C. (2007). Recreation and the Glenview neighborhood: Implications for youth and community development. *Leisure Sciences*, *29*, 267-285.

Becker, C., Cooper, N., Atkins, K., & Martin, S. (2009). What helps students thrive? An investigation of student engagement and performance. *Recreational Sports Journal, 33,* 139-149.

Belch, H. A., Gebel, M., & Maas, G. M. (2001). Relationship between student recreation complex use, academic performance, and persistence of first-time freshmen. *NASPA Journal, 38*(2), 254-268.

Bergman, R.J., Bassett, D.R., & Klein, D.A. (2008). Validity of 2 devices for measuring steps taken by older adults in assisted-living facilities. *Journal of Physical Activity and Health*, *5*(S1), S166-S175.

Burnett, C. (2006). Building social capital through an 'active community club.' *International Review for the Sociology of Sport*, *41*(3-4), 283-294.

Cela, A., Kowalski, C., & Lankford, S. (2006). Spectators' characteristics and economic impact of local sports events: A case study of Cedar Valley Moonlight Classic soccer tournament. *World Leisure Journal*, *48*(3), 45-53.

Coaffe, J. (2008). Sport, culture and the modern state: Emerging themes in stimulating urban regeneration in the UK. *International Journal of Cultural Policy*, *14*(4), 377-397.

Coakley, J. (2004). *Sports in society: Issues and controversies* (8th ed.). New York: McGraw-Hill.

Cooper, N., Schuett, P.A., & Phillips, H.M. (2012). Examining intrinsic motivations in campus intramural sports. *Recreational Sports Journal*, *36*, 25-36.

Cortis, N. (2009). Social inclusion and sport: Culturally diverse women's perspectives. *Australian Journal of Social Issues*, *44*(1), 91-106.

Dixon, A., Hegreness, R., Arthur-Banning, S.G., & Wells, M.S. (2007). Economic potential of youth sport tournaments. *Youth First*, *2*(2), 24-28.

Draper, C.E., Kolbe-Alexander, T.L., & Lambert, E.V. (2009). A retrospective evaluation of a community-based physical activity health promotion program. *Journal of Physical Activity and Health, 6*, 578-588.

Forrester, S., Arterberry, C., & Barcelona, B. (2006). Student attitudes toward sports and fitness activities after graduation. *Recreational Sports Journal, 30*, 87-99.

Glover, T.G. (2004). The 'community' center and the social construction of citizenship. *Leisure Sciences, 26*, 63-83.

Hall, S. (2010). Impact of facility maintenance on campus recreational sports departments at public universities in the United States. *Recreational Sports Journal, 34*, 103-111.

Henchy, A. (2011). The influence of campus recreation beyond the gym. *Recreational Sports Journal, 35*, 174-181.

Kellett, P., Hede, A., & Chalip, L. (2008). Social policy for sport events: Leveraging (relationships with) teams from other nations for community benefit. *European Sport Management Quarterly, 8*(2), 101-121.

Lyle, D., Hobba, J., Lloyd, K., Bennett, D., George, T., Giddings, N., Griffin, N., Chew, P.C.L., Harris, M., & Heading, G. (2008). Mobilising a rural community to lose weight: Impact evaluation of the WellingTonne challenge. *Australian Journal of Rural Health, 16*, 80-85.

Miller, I. (2003). Navy looking for afloat fitness and recreation specialists to serve sailors at sea. *Parks and Recreation*, 107.

Miller, J. (2011). Impact of a university recreation center on social belonging and student retention. *Recreational Sports Journal, 35*, 117-129.

O'Brien, D. (2007). Points of leverage: Maximizing host community benefit from a regional surfing festival. *European Sport Management Quarterly*, 7(2), 141-165.

Piatt, J.A., & Wells, M.S. (2012). *Beyond the event: Developing a sport identity.* Paper presented at the Paralympic Leadership Conference, Colorado Springs, CO.

Skinner, J., Zakus, D.H., & Cowell, J. (2008). Development through sport: Building social capital in disadvantaged communities. *Sport Management Review, 11*, 253-275.

Thorpe, H. (2009). Understanding 'alternative' sport experiences: A contextual approach for sport psychology. *International Journal of Exercise Psychology*, 7, 359-379.

U.S. Army. (2010). *Military Morale, Welfare, and Recreation programs and nonappropriated fund instrumentalities.* Washington, DC: Author.

Wilson, R. (2006). The economic impact of local sport events: Significant, limited or otherwise? A case study of four swimming events. *Managing Leisure, 11*, 57-70.

Chapter 12

Arthur-Banning, S.G., Paisley, K.P., & Wells, M.S. (2007). Promoting sportsmanship in youth basketball players: The effect of referees' prosocial behavior techniques. *Journal of Park and Recreation Administration, 25*(1), 96-114.

Barber, B.L., Eccles, J.S., & Stone, M.R. (2001). Whatever happened to the Jock, the Brain, and the Princess? Young adult pathways linked to adolescent activity involvement and social identity. *Journal of Adolescent Research, 16*(5), 429-455.

Brooks, S. (2010). *Score big: Youth sport education program for coaches and parents* (Unpublished master's project). University of Utah, Salt Lake City, UT.

Butcher, J., Lindner, K.J., & Johns, D.P. (2002). Withdrawal from competitive youth sport: A retrospective ten-year study. *Journal of Sport Behavior, 25*(2), 145-163.

Coakley, J. (2004). *Sports in society: Issues and controversies* (8th ed.). New York: McGraw-Hill.

Coatsworth, J.D., & Conroy, D.E. (2009). The effects of autonomy-supportive coaching, need satisfaction, and self-perceptions on initiative and identity in youth swimmers. *Developmental Psychology, 45*(2), 320-328.

Crain, W. (2000). *Theories of development: Concepts and applications* (4th ed.). Upper Saddle River, NJ: Prentice Hall.

Eccles, J.S., Barber, B.L., Stone, M., & Hunt, J. (2003). Extracurricular activities and adolescent development. *Journal of Social Issues, 59*(4), 865-879.

Eitzen, D.S. (2003). *Fair and foul: Beyond the myths and paradoxes of sport* (2nd ed.). Lanham, MD: Rowman and Littlefield.

Ellis, G.D., Henderson, H.L., Paisley, K.P., Silverberg, K.E., & Wells, M.S. (2004). Bringing sportsmanship back to your youth sport leagues. *Parks and Recreation*, June, 47-51.

Engh, F. (2002). *Why Johnny hates sports: Why organized youth sports are failing our children and what we can do about it.* Garden City Park, NY: Square One.

Hedstrom, R., & Gould, D. (2004). *Research in youth sports: Critical issues status.* East Lansing, MI: Institute for the Study of Youth Sports.

Keating, D.P. (2004). Cognitive and brain development. In R.M. Lerner & L. Steinberg (Eds.), *Handbook of adolescent psychology* (pp. 45-84). Hoboken, NJ: Wiley.

Mandigo, J.L, & Couture, R.T. (1996). An overview of the components of fun in physical education, organized sport and physical activity programs. *Avante, 2*(3), 56-72.

Martens, R. (1993). Psychological perspectives. In B.R. Cahill & A.J. Pearl (Eds.), *Intensive participation in children's sports* (pp. 9-18). Champaign, IL: Human Kinetics.

National Council of Youth Sports. (2008). *Report on trends and participation in organized youth sports.* Retrieved from www.ncys.org/pdfs/2008/2008-ncys-market-research-report.pdf.

Rodriguez, D., Wigfield, A., & Eccles, J.S. (2003). Changing competence perceptions, changing values: Implications for youth sport. *Journal of Applied Sport Psychology, 15*, 67-81.

Scanlan, T.K., Russell, D.G., Beals, K.P., & Scanlan, L.A. (2003). Project on elite athlete commitment (PEAK): II. A direct test and expansion of the sport commitment model with elite amateur sportsmen. *Journal of Sport and Exercise Psychology*, *25*, 377-401.

Seefeldt, V.D., & Ewing, M.E. (1996). Youth sports in America: An overview. *PCPFS Research Digest*, *2*(11). Retrieved from http://fitness.gov/youthsports.pdf.

Stevenson, B. (2007). Title IX and the evolution of high school sports. *Contemporary Economic Policy*, *25*(4), 486-505.

Storm, H., & Jenkins, M. (2002). *Go girl: Raising healthy, confident, and successful girls through sports.* Naperville, IL: Sourcebooks.

Stricker, P.R. (2006). *Sports success R_x: Your child's prescription for the best experience: How to maximize potential and minimize pressure.* Elk Grove Village, IL: American Academy of Pediatrics.

Tye, L. (2001). Kids and sports: Injured at an early age. In D.S. Eitzen (Ed.), *Sport in contemporary society: An anthology* (6th ed.; pp. 136-141). New York: Worth.

Weiss, M., & Smith, A.L. (2002). Friendship quality in youth sport: Relationship to age, gender, and motivational variables. *Journal of Sport and Exercise Psychology*, *24*, 420-437.

Wells, M.S., Arthur-Banning, S.G., Paisley, K.P, Ellis, G.D., Roark, M.F., & Fisher, K. (2008). Good (youth) sports: Using benefits-based programming to increase sportsmanship. *Journal of Park and Recreation Administration*, *26*(1), 1-21.

Wells, M.S., Ellis, G.D., Arthur-Banning, S.G., & Roark, M. (2006). Effect of staged practices and motivational climate on goal orientation and sportsmanship in community youth sport experiences. *Journal of Park and Recreation Administration*, *24*(4), 64-85.

Wells, M.S., Paisley, K.P., Ellis, G.D., & Arthur-Banning, S.G. (2005). Development and evaluation of a program to promote sportsmanship in youth sports. *Journal of Park and Recreation Administration*, *23*(1), 1-17.

Chapter 13

American College Health Association (ACHA). (2012). American College Health Association— National College Health Assessment II: Reference group executive summary fall 2011. Hanover, MD: Author.

Astin, A.W. (1984). Student involvement: A developmental theory for higher education. *Journal of College Student Personnel*, *25*, 297-308.

Barcelona, R.J. (2004). Examining the importance of recreational sport management competencies based on management level, agency type, and organizational size. *Recreational Sports Journal*, *28*(1), 45-63.

Barcelona, R.J., & Ross, C.M. (2002). Participation patterns in campus recreational sports: An examination of quality of student effort from 1983 to 1998. *Recreational Sports Journal*, *26*(1), 41-53.Blumenthal, K. (2009). Campus recreational sports: Pivotal players in student success. *Planning for Higher Education*, *37*(2), 52-62.

Bryant, J., Anderson, B., & Dunn, J.M. (1994). *Rationale for independent administration of collegiate recreational sports programs: A position paper.* Corvallis, OR: NIRSA.

Byl, J. (2002). *Intramural recreation: A step-by-step guide to creating an effective program.* Champaign, IL: Human Kinetics.

Cassel, J. (2011). The history of aerobics. Retrieved from www.livestrong.com/article/324355-the-history-of-aerobics.

Centers for Disease Control and Prevention (CDC). (2012). Physical activity. Retrieved from www.cdc.gov/physicalactivity/.

Chickering, A., & Reisser, L. (1993). *Education and identity* (2nd ed.). San Francisco: Jossey-Bass.

Erickson, E. (1993). *Childhood and society.* New York: Norton.

Ferrara, C., St. Laurent, C., & Wilson, T. (2008). The benefits of a weight loss contest in overweight and obese college students. *Recreational Sports Journal*, *32*(1), 45-51.

Forrester, S., Arterberry, C., & Barcelona, R.J. (2006). Student attitudes toward sports and fitness activities after graduation. *Recreational Sports Journal*, *30*(2), 83-94.

Forrester, S., Ross, C., Hall, S., & Geary, C. (2007). Using past campus recreational sports participation to explain current physical activity levels of alumni. *Recreational Sports Journal*, *32*(2), 83-94.

Haines, D.J. (2007). *National Intramural-Recreational Sports Association Member Survey Results.* Columbus, OH: National Research Institute for College Recreational Sports & Wellness, The Ohio State University.

Hatch, K., Blumenthal, K., Accetta, A., Su, P., & Ling, B. (2011). *Campus recreation: Bold partners in sustainability.* Retrieved from http://heasc.aashe.org/sites/heasc1.drupalgardens.com/files/Campus_Recreation_Partners_in_Sustainability.pdf.

Huesman, R.L., Jr., Brown, A.K., Lee, G., Kellogg, J.P., & Radcliffe, P.M. (2009). Gym bags and mortarboards: Is use of campus recreation facilities related to student success? *NASPA*, *46*(1), 50-71.

Hums, M.A., & MacLean, J.C. (2008). *Governance and policy in sport organizations* (2nd ed.). Phoenix: Holcomb-Hathaway.

Jackson, D.L., Walling, L., & Thompson, A. (2007). Recreational sports participation as a mediating factor for college student alcohol use. *Recreational Sports Journal*, *31*(2), 119-130.

Kanters, M. (2000). Recreational sport participation as a moderator of college stress. *Recreational Sports Journal*, *24*(2), 10-23.

Keeling, R.P. (2004). *Learning reconsidered: A campus-wide focus on the student experience.* Washington, DC: National Association of Student Personnel Administrators.

Keeling, R.P. (2006). *Learning reconsidered 2: A practical guide to implementing a campus-wide focus on the student experience.* Champaign, IL: Human Kinetics.

Kolb, D.A. (1984). *Experiential learning.* Englewood Cliffs, NJ.: Prentice Hall.

Komives, S.R., & Schoper, S. (2006). In R.P. Keeling (Ed.). *Learning reconsidered 2: Implementing a campus-wide focus on the student experience.* Champaign, IL: Human Kinetics.

Kuh, G.D. (1993). In their own words: What students learn outside the classroom. *American Educational Research Journal, 30*(2), 277-304.

Lewis, J.B., Jones, T.R., Lamke, G., & Dunn, J.M. (1998). Recreational sport: Making the grade on college campuses. *Parks & Recreation, 33*(12), 72-77.

National Intramural-Recreational Sports Association (NIRSA). (2008). *Campus recreation: Essentials for the professional.* Champaign, IL: Human Kinetics.

National Intramural-Recreational Sports Association (NIRSA) (2012a). NIRSA History. Retrieved from http://nirsa.net/nirsa/about/history/

National Intramural-Recreational Sports Association (NIRSA). (2012b). NIRSA's strategic values. Retrieved from http://nirsa.net/nirsa/about/strategic-plan/

National Intramural-Recreational Sports Association (NIRSA). (2014). Core competencies underpin NIRSA's professional development opportunities. Retrieved from http://nirsa.net/nirsa/registry/core-competencies/.

Pascarella, E.T., & Terenzini, P.T. (2005). *How college affects students: A third decade of research* (Vol. 2). San Francisco: Jossey-Bass.

Patton, J. (2009). Student health, student rec compatible under one campus-wellness roof. Retrieved from http://www.athleticbusiness.com/rec-center/student-health-student-rec-compatible-under-one-campus-wellness-roof.html.

Rockey, D.L., & Barcelona, R.J. (2012). An overview of fitness and recreation in collegiate settings. In G. McClellan, C. King, and D. Rockey (Eds.)., *Handbook of college athletics and recreation administration.* San Francisco, CA: Jossey-Bass.

Solomon, B. (1986). *In the company of educated women.* New Haven, CT: Yale University Press.

Sweeney, T.P., & Barcelona, R.J. (2012). An integrative review of published research in the *Recreational Sports Journal*, 1998-2010. *Recreational Sports Journal, 36*, 91-103.

Tinto, V. (1975). Dropout from higher education: A theoretical synthesis of recent research. *Review of Educational Research, 45*, 89-125.

Tinto, V. (1987). *Leaving college.* Chicago: University of Chicago Press.

Toperzer, L., Anderson, D., & Barcelona, R. (2011). Best practices in student development for campus recreation professionals. *Recreational Sports Journal, 35*(2), 145-156.

U.S. Department of Veterans Affairs (USDVA). (2012). GI Bill. Retrieved from www.gibill.va.gov.

Chapter 14

Billings, A.C. (2008). *Olympic media: Inside the biggest show on TV.* New York: Routledge.

Billings, S.B., & Holladay, J.S. (2011). Should cities go for the gold? The long-term impact of hosting the Olympics. *Economic Inquiry, 50*(3), 754-772.

Haynes, J. (2001). *Socio-economic impact of the Sydney 2000 Olympic Games.* Barcelona: Centre d'Estudis Olimpics. Retrieved from http://olympicstudies.uab.es/pdf/wp094_eng.pdf.

Human Rights Watch. (2012). Olympics: For Saudi women, only a starting line. Retrieved from www.hrw.org/news/2012/07/26/olympics-saudi-women-only-starting-line.

Hume, J. (2012). *Branding Jamaica through sport: The prospects for socio-political transformation in Jamaica.* 1st Global Conference on Sport: Probing the Boundaries proceedings.

Lawson, H.A. (2005). Empowering people, facilitating community development, and contributing to sustainable development: The social work of sport, exercise and physical education programs. *Sport, Education and Society, 10*(1), 135-160.

Lee, C.K., & Taylor, T. (2005). Critical reflections on the economic impact assessment of a mega-event: The case of the 2002 FIFA World Cup. *Tourism Management, 26*(4), 595-603.

Chapter 15

Barcelona, R., Hurd, A., & Bruggeman, J. (2011). A competency-based approach for preparing staff as recreation and youth development specialists. *New Directions for Youth Development, 130*, 121-139.

Barcelona, R.J., & Ross, C.M. (2005). An analysis of the perceived competencies of recreational sport administrators. *Journal of Park and Recreation Administration, 22*(4), 25-42.

Bureau of Labor Statistics. (2012). *Occupational outlook handbook, 2010-11 edition.* Retrieved from www.bls.gov/oco/pdf/ocos058.pdf.

Hurd, A. (2007, Nov/Dec). Becoming competency driven: Reaching agency efficiency and effectiveness. *Illinois Parks and Recreation.* Retrieved from www.lib.niu.edu/2007/ip0712tc.html.

Masteralexis, L.P., Barr, C.A., & Hums, M.A. (2005). *Principles and practice of sport management* (2nd ed.). Sudbury, MA: Jones & Bartlett.

National Intramural-Recreational Sports Association (NIRSA). (2013). Core competencies underpin NIRSA's professional development opportunities. Retrieved from http://nirsa.net/nirsa/registry/core-competencies/.

National Recreation and Park Association (NRPA). (2013). Council on Accreditation of Parks, Recreation, Tourism, and Related Professions. Retrieved from www.nrpa.org/coa/.

National Senior Games Association. (2012). Who we are. http://nsga.com/.

INDEX

Note: Page references followed by an italicized *f* or *t* indicate information contained in figures or tables, respectively.

A

ACSM (American College of Sport Medicine) 102, 103
Active Network 182
activity analysis 60-61
ADA. *See* Americans with Disabilities Act of 1990
adaptive sports 39
adolescence 35*f*, 37
adults, physical activity recommendations 19*t*, 20
aerobic capacity 208
aerobic dance 220
Aerobics (Cooper) 220
Aerobics and Fitness Association of America (AFAA) 233
affirmative action checklist 163
agencies 254, 265
alternative sport 265
alternative sport programming 193-194
American College of Sports Medicine (ACSM) 102, 103, 233
American College Personnel Association—College Student Educators International (ACPA) 233
American Council on Exercise (ACE) 233
American Recovery and Reinvestment Act of 2009 107
Americans with Disabilities Act of 1990 33, 38-39, 137, 198
animation 46, 61-63, 265
apps 177, 265
Association of Outdoor Recreation and Education (AORE) 233
attitudinal constraints 42
attractive nuisance 136, 265

B

background checks 139, 156, 164-165, 265
balance 207
Beijing Olympics 247
binge drinking 224
biometric recognition 172, 173, 265
blended program 54, 265
blogs 181, 265
boards 154, 265
bonds 107-108
breach 134, 265
British sport models 242-243
broadcast media 121-122
byc 83, 265

C

campus recreational sport
- about 195-196, 217
- administrative structure 221
- case study 216-217
- defined 265
- early years of 218-219
- extramural programming 229-230
- facilities 226-227
- family and youth programming 231
- fitness and wellness 230
- foundations of 217-226, 222*f*, 223*f*, 224*f*
- growth and diversification of 219-220
- health and wellness effects 224-225
- history of 218-221
- informal recreation 231
- instructional sport 231
- intramural programming 228-229
- intramural sport movement 219
- outdoor recreation 231
- philosophical orientation of 221-224, 222*f*, 223*f*, 224*f*
- physical skills and competence 225
- professional development in 231-234
- professionalization of 220
- program areas 227-231
- significance of 224-226
- sport clubs 230
- student development focus 221-223, 222*f*
- student leadership 226
- student learning imperative model 223-224, 224*f*
- student recruitment and retention 225-226

Canadian sport models 243-246, 243*f*
cardiovascular system 21
careers in recreational sport. *See also* professional development, campus recreation
- about 253-255
- academic preparation 261
- business procedures 257
- campus recreational sport 231-234
- career settings 254, 265
- case study 252-253
- communication and public relations 257
- employment outlook 262
- event management 260

careers in recreational sport. *(continued)*
- facilities and equipment management 258
- governance 258
- job functions 255
- job settings 254-255
- legality and risk management 258
- love of sport 255-256
- management techniques 258
- practical experience 261-262
- professional competencies 256-260
- professional involvement 262
- programming techniques 260
- research and program evaluation 260
- technology and computing skills 257-258
- theory and philosophy 258-260

case studies
- campus recreation 216-217
- careers 252-253
- community programs 190
- competition *versus* compassion 150-151
- customer service 116
- international sport 238
- liability 130
- physical activity 18
- programming challenges 52-53
- recreation and sport participation 4, 5, 6, 10
- religious diversity and 32
- technology use 172
- tournaments 72
- youth sport programs 202

cause 134, 265
cause in fact 134, 265
Center for Parent Information and Resources 34
certifications 163, 166, 233-234, 265
Certified Recreational Sport Specialist (CRSS) credential 220, 234
challenge tournaments 89-92, 265
charrette 104, 265
checklists 67, 68*f*
children, physical activity recommendations 19-20
chronic health issues 21
civil law 135, 265
cloud computing 181, 265
club sports 8*f*
coaches 212
cognitive benefits of physical activity 22
cognitive development 208-209, 265
cognitive theories 222, 265
college impact models 222-223, 265
colleges and universities. *See* campus recreational sport
commercial sector 9, 9*t*, 265
communication analysis 61
communication constraints 42
community 265
community recreational sport programming
- about 190
- alternative sport 193-194
- benefits 190-191
- campus recreation 195-196
- military MWR programs 195
- municipal recreation 192
- in nontypical communities 195-198
- not-for-profit 193
- for people with disabilities 198-199
- resort and commercial 192-193
- senior communities 196-198
- tournaments, matches, and meets 193
- types of programs 191-194

comparative needs approach 57
competency integration 260
competition 11-12, 75
competitive bid process 104
conceptual skills 265
constraints on participation 42-43, 265
construction manager at risk 105
consultants 102
consumptive constraints 42
contingent staff 154-155, 265
continuing education units 166, 265
Cooper, Kenneth 220
corporate sponsorships 119
Council on Accreditation of Parks, Recreation, Tourism and Related Professions (COAPRT) 261
criminal law 135, 265
crossover scheduling 89, 265
cross-training 160, 265
customer service 116, 124-126, 265

D

deferred maintenance 112, 265
design-bid-build process 104
design-build process 104
desktop computer 176, 265
development, Erikson's stages of 35-38, 35*f*
diabetes 21
direct competition 11, 266
direct costs 117, 266
disabilities, persons with 38-39, 135, 137, 198-199
discretionary time 6, 266
discrimination 33, 136-137, 163, 266
display and print media 122
diversity
- about 32, 266
- age 35-38, 35*f*, 39*f*

animation and 46
case study 32
coaching 44
constraints on participation 42-43
demographics 38-42, 41*f*
disability 38-39
environmental modifications 45
equipment modifications 46
intentionality and 45
legislation regarding 33-34
marketing 44
mentors and role models 44
population 43-44
programming considerations 43-46
race 39-40
religion 40-41, 41*f*
rules modifications 45-46
sex 41
social class 41-42
social environment 44
sport for all 33
time modifications 46
double-elimination tournaments 86, 266
Dropbox 181
drop-in sports 8*f*
duty 134, 266

E

early childhood 35*f*, 36
economic constraints 42
electronic media 122-123
elimination tournaments 85-89, 88*f*, 90*f*
emergency medical preparedness 138
empirical 14, 266
employees. *See also* human resources
recruitment 160-162
retention 165-168
selection 162-165, 165*t*
environmental constraints 43
environment analysis 60
equipment
adaptations to youth 211
equipment animation 62
in facilities planning and design 109-110
financing 117-118
technology and 182-183
tournaments 78
E-QYP (Equipping Youth and Professionals) 178, 179
Erikson's stages of development 35-38, 35*f*
evaluation, of programming 65-69, 67*f*, 68*f*
experience constraints 43
explicit bye bracket 88, 266
extended tournaments 89-92
external communication 257, 266
extramural sport 229-230, 266
extrinsic motivation 8, 266

F

Facebook 122-123, 180
facilitate 73, 266
facilities, recreational sport. *See also* facilities planning and design
about 98, 268
case study 96-97
scheduling software 181-182
tournaments at 78
facilities planning and design
about 98-99
benchmarking and space standards 102-103
campus recreational sport 226-227
construction process 104-105, 106-107
design process 104-106
equipment 109-110
financing 107-108, 117
maintenance 110-112
master planning process 98, 100-102, 103*f*
program statements 103-104
risk management and safety 109
senior programming 198
strategic planning process 98, 99-102, 99*f*
sustainability and LEED 108-109
technology 112, 182-183
facility animation 62
FIFA World Cup 240
financial analysis 61
financial risk 132
financing
corporate sponsorships 119
direct and indirect costs 116-117
equipment 117-118
expenditures 116-118
facilities 107-108, 117
grants 120-121
insurance 118
marketing budget 118
partnerships 120
private donations and gifts 119-120
program fees and charges 118-119
public funding 118
revenue sources 118-121
senior community programming 197-198
staffing budget 118
supplies 118
technology 184

financing *(continued)*
fine motor skills 206*t*, 208
flexibility 208
focus groups 69, 101
foreseeability 134, 266
formative evaluations 66
freedom 10

G

Gantt charts 63-64, 63*f*
general obligation bond 107, 266
GI Bill 219, 266
goals and objectives, programming 58-60, 59*f*
grants 120-121
gross motor skills 206

H

hardware 176, 266
health, physical activity and 21-22
health constraints 42-43
Health/Fitness Facility Standards and Guidelines (ASCM) 103
Healthy Campus 2020 230, 266
hearing impairments 39
heat tolerance 208
hiring processes 160-162
historically black colleges 219
honesty 124
human capital 165, 266
human relations skills 266
human resources. *See also* staff
  about 151
  employee recruitment 160-162
  employee retention 165-168
  employee selection 162-165, 165*t*
  interviews, hiring 163-164, 165*t*
  job announcements 160-161, 266
  organizational chart 153*f*
  orientation and training 166-167
  performance appraisal 167
  personnel 151-156, 152*f*, 153*f*
  personnel planning 159-160
  processes 156-168
  professional standards and competencies 157-159, 158*f*
  progressive discipline 168
  scheduling software 181-182
  volunteers 155-156
  work motivation 167-168

I

IDEIA. *See* Individuals with Disabilities Education Improvement Act of 2004
identity development 205, 266
implied bye bracket 89, 266
indirect competition 11, 266
indirect costs 117, 266
Individuals with Disabilities Education Improvement Act of 2004 34
infancy 35*f*, 36
informal recreation 231, 266
injury 134, 266
in-kind gifts 119, 266
innovation 175, 266
instant scheduling 75, 266
instructional sport 8*f*, 225, 231, 266
insurance 118, 141-142
intentional tort 135-136, 266
internal communication 257, 266
International Health, Racquet and Sportsclub Association (IHRSA) 262
International Ice Hockey Federation (IIHF) 248
International Olympic Committee (IOC) 241, 266
International Sport Federations (IFs) 241, 266
international sport influences
  about 238-239
  British sport models 242-243
  Canadian sport models 243-246, 243*f*
  economic issues 240
  international opportunities 248
  international organizations 241, 242*f*
  international sport models 241-246, 243*f*
  local opportunities 247-248
  national opportunities 248
  Olympic Games 246-247
  social issues 239-240
  sport as unifying body 239-240
Internet 178-181, 266
Internet marketing 122-123
interpersonal skills 205
interviews, feedback 69
interviews, hiring 163-164, 164*t*
intramural sport 228-229, 266
intranet 178, 266
intrinsic motivation 5, 8, 10, 266

J

Jamaica 239
job announcements 160-161, 266
job applications 162
job functions 253, 266
job settings 253, 267

L

ladder tournaments 90, 91*f*
laptop computer 176-177, 267
late adulthood 35*f*, 38

league sports 8*f*
learning disabilities 39
LEED (Leadership in Energy and Environmental Design) 108-109, 267
leisure 6-9, 10, 267
leisure value and skills constraints 43
Let's Move campaign 26
liability 130-131, 267
listening 124
Long-Term Athlete Development (LTAD) model 243-246, 243*f*, 267

M

magic number 88, 267
maintenance, facility 110-112
management by objectives 167, 267
management software 181-182
market churn 183
marketing
  about 121
  broadcast media 121-122
  budget 118
  considerations 123-124
  customer service 124-126
  display and print media 122
  electronic media 122-123
  research 124
master plan 98, 100-102, 103*f*, 267
mastery orientation 11, 267
membership management software 181-182
middle adulthood 35*f*, 37-38
military MWR programs 195
mind maps 67
modalities 226, 267
moderate physical activity 19, 267
Moore's law 183, 267
Morale, Welfare, and Recreation (MWR) programs 195, 267
motivation, work 167-168
municipal recreation and sport management 191, 192, 267
musculoskeletal system 21-22

N

National Alliance for Youth Sports (NAYS) 165, 213
National Association of Student Personnel Administrators (NASPA) 233
National Intramural Association (NIA) 219
National Intramural-Recreational Sports Association (NIRSA) 102, 103, 157-159, 158*f*, 219, 220, 233, 262, 267
National Olympic Committees 241
National Recreation and Park Association (NRPA) 102-103, 262
National Research Institute for Collegiate Recreational Sports and Wellness 220
National Strength and Conditioning Association (NSCA) 233
National Youth Sports Coaches Association (NYSCA) 166
needs assessments 56-58, 101
negligence 133-135, 267
NFL Play 60 26
NIRSA (National Intramural-Recreational Sports Association). *See* National Intramural-Recreational Sports Association (NIRSA)
NIRSA Journal 220
NMTC program 107
nonroutine maintenance 111, 267
not-for-profit recreational sport programming 8-9, 9*t*, 193, 267
NRPA (National Recreation and Park Association). *See* National Recreation and Park Association (NRPA)

O

observations 67
Occupational Safety and Health Administration (OSHA) 131
older adults, physical activity recommendations 19*t*, 20
Olympic Games 239, 246-247
operating system 176, 267
opportunity analysis 99
organizations 254, 267
outsourcing 218, 267

P

parents 212-213
participant needs approach 58
participants. *See also* diversity
  constraints on participation 42-43
  needs assessments 56-58
  negligence concerns and 134-135
  participant-centered programming 58-59
  participation styles 7-8, 267
  risk transfer to 142-145
  technology and relationship management 174-175
  tournament 73-75, 76-78
  waivers 142-145, 142*f*-143*f*
partnerships 120
performance appraisal 167, 267
performance bond 107, 267
person-job fit 157, 267
personnel. *See also* human resources
  about 151-156
  defined 267
  personnel planning 159-160
  tournaments 78
personnel analysis 60

PERT charts 64, 64*f*
philosophy 13-15, 267
physical activity/inactivity
case study 18
classifications of 19
cognitive benefits of 22
how to create physically active recreational sport programs 25-28
motivation for activity 25
physical benefits of 21-22
promoting 22-28
psychosocial benefits of 22
reasons for inactivity 22-25
recommendations and rates 19-20, 19*t*
physical impairments 39
physically active recreational sport
accessibility issues 24
defined 18, 267
education and training 26-27
enjoyment of 23-24
facilities 27
focus on lifetime health 27-28
how to create 25-28
life stage issues 24-25
rule adaptations 27
support issues 24
physical risk 131-132
physiological development 206-208, 267
planned obsolescence 184, 267
political risk 132-133
polling systems 102
Positive Coaching Alliance (PCA) 213
preschool 35*f*, 36
print media 122
privacy 136, 184
private donations and gifts 119-120
private sector financing 108
problem solving 125-126
professional competencies 157-159, 158*f*, 256-260, 267. *See also* careers in recreational sport
professional development, campus recreation. *See also* careers in recreational sport
about 231-232
certifications 233-234
graduate preparation 233
professional organizations 233
undergraduate preparation 232
professional needs approach 57-58
program data evaluation 67-69
programming, recreational sport
about 53
activity analysis 60-61
case study 52-53
evaluation 65-69, 67*f*, 68*f*
form and structure of 6-7
goals and objectives determination 58-60, 59*f*
implementation 63-64, 63*f*, 64*f*
modifications for diversity 43-46
needs assessments 56-58
philosophy development 53-55
program animation 61-63
program design 54-55
troubleshooting 64-65
programming modifications, for diversity 43-46
progressive discipline 168, 267
props 63
PRORAGIS system (NRPA) 102-103
proximate cause 134, 267
psychological development 209, 267
psychological risk 132
psychosocial benefits 22, 205
psychosocial theories 222, 267
public funding 118
public sector 8, 9*t*, 267
pyramid tournaments 92, 92*f*

Q

questioning 124-125
questionnaires 66-67, 67*f*

R

race, and participation 39-40
recreation 6, 268
recreational sport. *See also* physically active recreational sport
benefits 8
defined 268
and discretionary time 6
form and structure 6-7
as leisure 5, 13
participation styles 7-8
philosophy of 13-15
sectors and organizations for 8-9, 9*t*
spheres of participation 8*f*
and state of mind 10
recreational sport profession 4-5, 13-15, 22-28, 268
Recreational Sports Journal 220
referees and officials 212
Registry of Collegiate Recreational Sports Professionals (RCRSP) credential 220, 234
religion, and participation 40-41, 41*f*
religious diversity 32
Resort and Commercial Recreation Association (RCRA) 262
revenue bond 107-108, 268

risk 131-133, 268
risk management and safety
about 130
background checks 139
case study 130
constitutional rights 136-137
defined 268
emergency medical preparedness 138
financial risk 132
hazards 137-139
intentional torts 135-136
liability concerns 133-139
natural features 138
negligence 133-135
perceived risk 133
physical risk 131-132
plan development 109, 139-145, 140*f*, 142*f*-143*f*
political risk 132-133
psychological risk 132
risk checklist 147*f*
risk evaluation 140*f*, 141
risk identification 140, 140*f*
risk treatment 140*f*, 141-145
risk types 131-133
technology and 183
transportation 139
waivers 142-145, 142*f*-143*f*
weather and natural disasters 138-139
round 268
round-robin 80, 268
round-robin divisions 81, 268
round-robin leagues 81, 268
round-robin tournaments 80-85, 81*f*, 83*t*, 84*t*
routine maintenance 111, 268

S

safety 109
scheduling software 181-182
school age 35*f*, 36-37
seeding 75, 268
self-concept 209, 268
self-confidence 209, 268
sex, and participation 41
sexual abuse 132, 156
signature facility 227, 268
single-elimination tournaments 85-86, 268
situational analysis 99
SMART objectives 59-60, 59*f*, 268
smartphones 177-178, 179, 268
Sochi Olympics 246-247
social and cultural constraints 43
social capital 191, 268
social class, and participation 41-42
social constructs 239
social interaction 210
social networking 122-123, 180-181, 268
Society of Health and Physical Educators (SHAPE America) 262
software 176, 268
Sorenson, Jacki 220
Space Planning Guidelines for Campus Recreational Sport Facilities (NIRSA) 103
specifications 105, 268
speech and language impairments 39
sport 10-13, 268
sport clubs 230, 268
sport development pyramid 13, 13*f*
sport-for-all movement 14, 33, 268
sport management 13, 268
sportsmanship 205, 268
staff. *See also* human resources
business and support operations 155
contingent staff 154
financing 118
middle management 154
program staff 154
upper-level administration 152-154
state of mind 10, 268
stereotype 41, 268
strategic planning 98, 99-102, 99*f*, 268
strength 208
stress management 209, 224
summative evaluations 66
supplies and equipment analysis 60-61
financing 117-118
support staff 155, 268
surveys 101
sustainability, facilities' 108-109
Sydney Olympics 246

T

tablet computers 177, 268
targeted program 54, 268
target market 123, 268
technical skills 156, 159, 160, 268
technology
about 173
advances in 182-183
blogs 181
case study 172
challenges in use of 183-184
cloud computing 181
computers 176-178
customer relationship management 174-175

techology *(continued)*
desktop computers 176
efficiency of 174
in facility planning and operation 112
innovation in 175
Internet 178-181
laptop computers 176-177
management software 181-182
reasons for using 173-175
smartphones 177-178, 179
social networking 180-181
tablet computers 177
technology tools 173, 269
wikis 181
technostructure 155, 269
temporal constraints 42
tiered program 54, 269
Title IX (Education Amendments of 1972) 33-34, 203, 219-220
Title VI (Civil Rights Act of 1964) 33
tort 135, 269
tournament design
about 72-73
case study 72
challenge or extended format 89-92
considerations for 75-79
elimination format 85-89, 88*f*, 90*f*
facility and equipment limitations 78
goals 73-75
ladder format 90, 91*f*
participant characteristics 76-77
participant concerns 77-78
participant demand/limits 78-79
personnel limitations 78
philosophy and objectives 76
pyramid format 92, 92*f*
round-robin format 80-85, 81*f*, 83*t*, 84*t*
scheduling software 181-182
sport-specific rules and regulations 79
tournament sports 8*f*
transferable skills 226, 269
transportation safety 139
traumatic brain injuries 39
travel sports 8*f*
Twitter 180
typological theories 222, 269

U

United States Olympic Committee (USOC) 248

V

vigorous physical activity 19, 269
virtual reality 175, 269
vision 99, 102
visual impairments 39
visual skills 207
volunteers 155-156, 160, 166, 269

W

waivers 142-145, 142*f*-143*f*, 269
warranty 269
Wasson, William 219
weather and natural disasters 138-139
wellness 230, 269
wikis 181, 269
working drawings 105, 269
World Wide Web 178-180, 269

Y

young adulthood 35*f*, 37
youth sport programs
about 202
adaptations for improving 210-211
benefits of 204-205
case study 202
changing current culture of 211-213
cognitive benefits of 204-205
cognitive development 208-209
developmental concerns 206*t*
moral benefits of 205
needs of young athletes 205-211
participation 203
physical benefits of 204
physiological development 206-208
psychological development 209
psychosocial benefits of 205
youth-adult differences 205-206

ABOUT THE AUTHORS

Robert Barcelona, PhD, is an associate professor in the University of New Hampshire's department of recreation management and policy. He teaches courses in recreational sport management, youth development, and organizational administration and leadership for both undergraduate and graduate students.

Since 1999 Barcelona has worked with numerous recreation and sport organizations in both programming and research efforts. His teaching interests focus on recreational sport management and youth development leadership in school and community-based settings. Barcelona's research examines recreation and sport as developmental contexts for youth and focuses on the ways that recreation and sport organizations build healthy and sustainable programs and communities. His research has been published in numerous national and international publications, and he has authored several book chapters on recreation and sport management. He is one of the authors for *Leisure Services Management.*

Barcelona has won teaching excellence awards at both Indiana University and the University of New Hampshire. He is active with youth sport coach training through his involvement with CoachSmartNH, and he is engaged in recreation planning, consulting, and program evaluation projects with community recreation and youth development organizations throughout the United States.

Mary Sara Wells, PhD, is an associate professor in the University of Utah's department of parks, recreation, and tourism. She teaches courses in youth development, community recreation, and sport management.

Since 2004 Wells has researched sportsmanship issues in youth sport. She has published her research in numerous journals, presented at several national and international conferences, and conducted trainings and evaluations for multiple municipal youth sport agencies across the country.

Skye Arthur-Banning, PhD, is an associate professor at Clemson University in the department of parks, recreation and tourism management. He teaches graduate and undergraduate classes in sport management and sport for development as well as in the core curriculum, and he advises graduate students in amateur sport for community and youth development.

Arthur-Banning's research focus is in amateur sport and specifically on sport for development, ethical behavior in sport, and sportsmanship as it relates to coaches, players, parents, and referees. He has published in numerous journals and has done work with or presented for various organizations, including the Canadian Coaches Association, United States Soccer Federation, United States Navy Child and Youth Program, and various city, county, and state or provincial recreation agencies across North America and East Africa.

Arthur-Banning certified by the NCAA and US Soccer Federation as a national referee emeritus, national assessor, and national instructor. He draws on those amateur and semiprofessional sport experiences. Finally, he has worked with several international sport organizations to organize programs, make connections, and take students on various study-abroad trips using sport as a tool for youth and community development.